Guerrilla Marketing

Books by Jay Conrad Levinson

Earning Money Without a Job

555 Ways to Earn Extra Money

Get What You Deserve: How to Guerrilla Market Yourself (with Seth Godin)

Guerrilla Advertising

Guerrilla Creativity

The Guerrilla Entrepreneur

Guerrilla Financing (with Bruce Jan Blechman)

Guerrilla Marketing

Guerrilla Marketing Attack

Guerrilla Marketing CD-ROM

Guerrilla Marketing During Tough Times

Guerrilla Marketing Excellence

Guerrilla Marketing for Attorneys (with R. W. Lynch)

Guerrilla Marketing for Consultants (with Michael McLaughlin)

Guerrilla Marketing for Financial Advisors (with Grant Hicks)

Guerrilla Marketing for Franchisees (with Todd Woods)

Guerrilla Marketing for Free

Guerrilla Marketing for Job Hunters (with David Perry)

Guerrilla Marketing for the Home-Based Business (with Seth Godin)

Guerrilla Marketing for the Nineties

Guerrilla Marketing for Writers (with Michael Larsen and Rick Frishman)

Guerrilla Marketing Handbook (with Seth Godin)

Guerrilla Marketing in the New Millennium

Guerrilla Marketing in 30 Days (with Al Lautenslager)

Guerrilla Marketing in 30 Days Workbook (with Al Lautenslager)

Guerrilla Marketing Meets Teleseminars (with Jay Aaron)

Guerrilla Marketing 101 Lab Workbook

Guerrilla Marketing 101 Lecture CD/DVD

GUERRILLA MARKETING

FOURTH EDITION

*Easy and Inexpensive Strategies
for Making Big Profits
from Your Small Business*

Jay Conrad Levinson

with Jeannie Levinson
and Amy Levinson

Houghton Mifflin Company
Boston New York

For information about permission to reproduce selections from
this book, write to Permissions, Houghton Mifflin Company,
215 Park Avenue South, New York, New York 10003.

Visit our Web site: www.houghtonmifflinbooks.com.

Library of Congress Cataloging-in-Publication Data
Levinson, Jay Conrad.
    Guerrilla marketing : easy and inexpensive strategies for making
big profits from your small business / Jay Conrad Levinson with
Jeannie Levinson and Amy Levinson. — 4th rev. ed.
        p.   cm.
    Includes index.
    ISBN-13: 978-0-618-78591-9
    ISBN-10: 0-618-78591-4
    1. Marketing.   2. Small business — Management.   3. Advertising.
    I. Levinson, Jeannie.   II. Levinson, Amy.   III. Title.
    HF5415.L477 2007
    658.8 — dc22   2006033833

Printed in the United States of America

DOC 10 9 8 7 6

I DEDICATE THIS BOOK TO

Mike Lavin
Thane Croston
Alexis Makar
Wally Bregman
Taylor Middleton
Charles Kessler
Norm Goldring
Elaine Petrocelli
Mark Steisel
David Garfinkel
Bill Quateman
Steve Savage
Les McGhee
Tom Pollgreen
Chet Holmes
David Hancock
Mark S. A. Smith
Grant Hicks
George Reskin
Don Cooper
Jason Crain
Dan Solomon
Mike Stemnock

Loral Langemeier
Allan Caplan
Jill Lublin
Rick Frishman
David Perry
Charles Rubin
Bob Kaden
Al Lautenslager
Theo Brandt-Sarif
Jeff McNeal
Liz Hymans
Jay Abraham
Alex Mandossian
Roy Williams
Mike McLaughlin
Al Ries
Jack Trout
Tony Buzan
Joel Christopher
Mark Drevno
Terri Lonier
Joe Sugarman
Seth Godin

T. Harv Eker
Steve Nease
Declann Dunn
Jonathon Mizel
Armand Morin
Joe Vitale
Jeremy Huffman
Mark Joyner
Scott Holman
Marty/Laura Higgins
Tony Robbins
Joshua Huffman
Mark Victor Hansen
Bob Allen
Bill Gallagher
Frank Adkins
Sharon Ro
Monroe Mann
Bill Gallagher Jr.
Howard Gossage
Leo Burnett

. . . GUERRILLAS EACH AND EVERY ONE

Contents

Part IV. New-Media Marketing

Part V. The Nature of the Guerrilla

Introduction

I remember the shock I felt at age fifty when I learned that the average college graduate is better informed than the average fifty-year-old. But unless that fifty-year-old studied all the important new books and all the magazines, newspapers, TV documentaries, Web sites, and webcasts, he or she would know less than that college guy or gal, whose daily curriculum diet included the cream of the new information.

This fourth edition of *Guerrilla Marketing*, a scion of the first edition, which I wrote as a service to my college students at the University of California, Berkeley Extension Division, is like that college grad. It's got all the new and good stuff about marketing — some timeless, some brand new — all insights that can give you the upper hand in the marketing battles.

Marketing continues to evolve and mature, just like that former student. This edition is a chip off the old guerrilla block. It's not going to abandon its principles, as humans have not abandoned their natures. But it is going to give you a clue or two about the multitude of ways that marketing has changed since I wrote the first edition and each edition after that. *C'est la guerre.*

Take heart that every change can represent money in your life *if* you learn about it and do something about it. There is no way that you can capitalize on all the changes, so you'll have to pick and choose. If you're as bright as you look, you'll pick some of the tried and true marketing weapons and tactics and more than a smattering of the new ways to leave your competitors standing on scorched ground.

I'm intentionally going out on a limb by cautioning you that failure to upgrade your marketing effort is a symptom of corporate demise. Success-found companies are either growing and changing or dying. Failure to adapt is the leading cause of death.

This new edition is all about the adaptations you can make to power up your marketing. It's also about the attitudes and attributes that are mandatory in the current and coming business environment. A key to prospering with guerrilla marketing is the art of *paying attention*. You've got to be constantly attuned to the media, the competition, the customers, the current events, the whole scene. If you're not paying close attention, you'll nibble on your popcorn at the movie while the on-screen hero reaches for a box of your competitor's snack treats. That's the kind of attention I mean. That's the kind of marketing I mean. That's the kind of buzz you want. That's the kind of change I mean.

You'll read some of the guerrilla marketing advice in this book and say to yourself, "I knew that." You'll read other revelations and say, "We could do that!"

I don't blame you for being excited. I've been excited since I first thought of bringing guerrilla marketing into the b-age, the age when entrepreneurs think of billions rather than millions. Marketing experts see today as two separate ages. One requires the age-old principles of patience and commitment for the eventual profit. The other requires a can't-refuse offer, a large and responsive mailing list, and online dexterity for the quick profit. The guerrilla marketer of today operates comfortably in both ages.

Guerrilla marketers are delighted that marketing is undergoing so many changes. These marketeers are aware that most of their competitors are looking the other way when it comes to modernizing their marketing and getting it to bloom in the sunshine rather than simply look pretty.

But to get it to bloom, you've got to be the sun. You've got to be the energy that keeps your marketing alive. Lean closer and become intimate with the reality of the next two sentences.

1. *Guerrilla marketing is about theory and action.* I supply the theory. What kind of action are you supposed to take? The first is gaining an understanding of what marketing really is and why guerrilla marketing is putting so much money into so many bank accounts around the world.
2. *Become aware of your options as a guerrilla marketer.* With so many new options now available to guerrillas, it's almost too easy to succeed. But I know that's your job, and it's my job to help. So let's get going.

PART I

The Guerrilla Approach

What Is Guerrilla Marketing Today?

Marketing *is every bit of contact your company has with anyone in the outside world.* Every bit of contact. That means a lot of marketing opportunities. It does not mean investing a lot of money.

The meaning is clear: Marketing includes the name of your business; the determination of whether you will be selling a product or a service; the method of manufacture or servicing; the color, size, and shape of your product; the packaging; the location of your business; the advertising, public relations, Web site, branding, e-mail signature, voicemail message on your machine, and sales presentation; the telephone inquiries; the sales training; the problem solving; the growth plan and the referral plan; and the people who represent you, you, and your follow-up. Marketing includes your idea for your brand, your service, your attitude, and the passion you bring to your business. If you gather from this that marketing is a complex process, you're right.

Marketing is the art of getting people to change their minds — or to maintain their mindsets if they're already inclined to do business with you. People must either switch brands or purchase a type of product or service that has never existed before. That's asking a lot of them. Every little thing you do and show and say — not only your advertising or your Web site — is going to affect people's perceptions of you.

That's probably not going to happen in a flash. Or a month. Or even a year. And that's why it's crucial for you to know that marketing is a process, not an event. Marketing may be a series of events, but if you're a guerrilla marketer, marketing has a beginning and a middle but not an ending.

By the way, when I write the word *marketing*, I'm thinking of your prospects and your current customers. Nothing personal, but when you read the word *marketing*, you're probably thinking of prospects only. Don't make that mistake. More than half your marketing time should be devoted to your existing customers. A cornerstone of guerrilla marketing is customer follow-up. Without it, all that you've invested into getting those customers is like dust in the wind.

Marketing is also the truth made fascinating.

When you view marketing from the vantage point of the guerrilla, you realize that it's your opportunity to help your prospects and customers succeed. They want to succeed at earning more money, building their company, losing weight, attracting a mate, becoming more fit, or quitting smoking. You can help them. You can show them how to achieve their goal. Marketing is not about you. It's about them. I hope you never forget that.

Marketing, if you go about things in the right way, is also a circle. The circle begins with your idea for bringing revenue into your life. Marketing becomes a circle when you have the blessed patronage of repeat and referral customers. The better able you are to view marketing as a circle, the more you'll concentrate on those repeat and referral people. A pleasant side effect of that perspective is that you'll invest less money in marketing, but your profits will consistently climb.

Marketing is more of a science every day as we learn new ways to measure and predict behavior, influence people, and test and quantify marketing. It's more of a science as psychologists tell us more and more about human behavior.

Marketing is also unquestionably an art form because writing is an art, drawing is an art, photography is an art, dancing is an art, music is an art, editing is an art, and acting is an art. Put them all together, and they spell marketing — probably the most eclectic art form the world has ever known.

But for now, brush aside those notions that marketing is a science and an art form. *Drill into your mind the idea that at its core, marketing is a business. And the purpose of a business is to earn profits.* If science and art help a business earn those profits, they're probably being masterminded by a guerrilla marketer — the kind of business owner who seeks conventional goals, such as profits and joy, but achieves them using unconventional means.

A bookstore owner had the misfortune of being located between two enormous bookselling competitors. One day, this bookstore owner came to work to see that the competitor on his right had unfurled a huge banner: "Monster Anniversary Sale! Prices slashed 50%!" The banner was larger than his entire storefront. Worse yet, the competitor to the left of his store had unveiled an even larger banner: "Gigantic Clearance Sale! Prices reduced by 60%!" Again, the banner dwarfed his storefront. What was the owner of the little bookstore in the middle to do? Being a guerrilla marketer, he created his own banner and hung it out front, simply saying "Main Entrance."

Guerrilla marketers do not rely on the brute force of an outsized marketing budget. Instead, they rely on the brute force of a vivid imagination. Today, they are different from traditional marketers in twenty ways. I used to compare guerrilla marketing with textbook marketing, but now that this book is a textbook in so many universities, I must compare it with traditional marketing.

If you were to analyze the ways that marketing has changed in the twenty-first century, you'd discover that it has changed in the same twenty ways that guerrilla marketing differs from the old-fashioned brand of marketing.

1. Traditional marketing has always maintained that to market properly, you must invest money. Guerrilla marketing maintains that if you want to invest money, you can — *but you don't have to if you are willing to invest time, energy, imagination, and information.*
2. Traditional marketing is so enshrouded by mystique that it intimidates many business owners, who aren't sure whether marketing includes sales or a Web site or PR. Because they are so intimidated and worried about making mistakes, they simply don't do it. *Guerrilla marketing completely removes the mystique and exposes marketing for exactly what it really is — a process that you control — rather than the other way around.*
3. Traditional marketing is geared toward big business. Before I wrote the original *Guerrilla Marketing* in 1984, I couldn't find any books on marketing for companies that invested less than $300,000 monthly. Although it is now true that many Fortune 500 companies buy *Guerrilla Marketing* by the caseload to distribute to their sales and marketing people, *the essence of guerrilla marketing — the soul and the spirit of guerrilla marketing — is small business*: companies with big dreams but tiny budgets.
4. Traditional marketing measures its performance by sales or responses to an offer, hits on a Web site, or store traffic. Those are the wrong numbers to focus on. *Guerrilla marketing reminds you that the main number that merits your attention is the size of your profits.* I've seen many companies break their sales records while losing money in the

process. Profits are the only numbers that tell you the truth you should be seeking and striving for. If it doesn't earn a profit for you, it's probably not guerrilla marketing.

5. Traditional marketing is based on experience and judgment, which is a fancy way of saying "guesswork." But guerrilla marketers cannot afford wrong guesses, so *it is based as much as possible on psychology* — laws of human behavior. For example, 90 percent of all purchase decisions are made in the unconscious mind, that inner deeper part of your brain. We now know a slam-dunk manner of accessing that unconscious mind: repetition. Think it over a moment, and you'll begin to have an inkling of how the process of guerrilla marketing works. Repetition is paramount.

6. Traditional marketing suggests that you grow your business and then diversify. That kind of thinking gets many companies into hot water because it leads them away from their core competency. Guerrilla marketing suggests that you grow your business, if growth is what you want, *but be sure to maintain your focus* — for it's that focus that got you to where you are in the first place.

7. Traditional marketing says that you should grow your business linearly by adding new customers one at a time. But that's a slow and expensive way to grow. So guerrilla marketing says that *the way to grow a business is geometrically* — by enlarging the size of each transaction, engaging in more transactions per sales cycle with each customer, tapping the enormous referral power of each customer, and growing the old-fashioned way at the same time. If you're growing your business in four different directions at once, it's tough not to show a tidy profit.

8. Traditional marketing puts all its effort on making the sale, under the false notion that marketing ends once that sale is made. Guerrilla marketing reminds you that 68 percent of all business lost is lost owing to apathy after the sale — ignoring customers after they've made the purchase. For this reason, *guerrilla marketing preaches fervent follow-up* — continually staying in touch with customers — and listening to them. Guerrillas never lose customers because of inattention to them.

9. Traditional marketing advises you to scan the horizon to determine which competitors you ought to obliterate. Guerrilla marketing advises you to scan that same horizon to determine which businesses have the same kind of prospects and standards as you do — *so that you can cooperate with them in joint marketing efforts*. By doing so, you're expanding your marketing reach, but you're reducing the cost of your marketing because you're sharing it with others. The term that guerrillas use for this outlook is *fusion marketing.* "Fuse it or lose it" is their motto. You're watching TV and see a commercial for McDonald's. Midway through, you realize that it's really a commercial for Coke, and by the time it's over, you see that all along, it was for the latest Disney movie. That's fusion marketing. And that's just some of the big guys who do it — like FedEx and Kinko's, too — but most of the fusion marketing in the world, as led by Japan, happens on the level of small business.

10. Traditional marketing urges you to have a logo that represents your company — a visual means of identifying yourself. Points made to the eye are 78 percent more memorable than points made to the ear. Guerrilla marketing cautions you that a logo is passé these days — because all it does is remind people of the name of your company. Instead, *guerrilla marketers have a meme that represents their company* — a visual or verbal symbol that communicates an entire idea, such as international traffic signs. In these days of record-breaking clutter, a meme says the most in the least time. It is a godsend on the Internet, where people may spend no more than a few seconds at your Web site. We'll talk a bit more about memes up ahead. It's a new word that was coined in 1976. And it's a guerrilla idea that can revolutionize your profit-and-loss statement.

11. Traditional marketing has always been "me" marketing. Visit almost any Web site, and you'll see "About our company." "About our history." "About our product." "About our management." But people don't care about you. Me marketing makes them sleepy. *That's why guerrillas always practice "you" marketing,* in which every word and every idea is about the customer, the visitor to a Web site. Don't take this personally, but people simply do not care about your company. What they care about is themselves. And if you can talk to them about themselves, you'll have their full attention.

12. Traditional marketing has always thought about what it could take from a customer. Guerrillas have a full understanding of the lifetime value of a customer, but they also concern themselves with *what they can give a customer.* They're always thinking of things they might give away for free, and now that we're smack dab in the middle of the information age, they try to give away free and valuable information — such as booklets, informative Web sites, brochures, TV infomercials — wherever they can. Don't forget what I said about marketing as your opportunity to help your prospects and customers succeed at attaining their goals. It's also your golden chance to help them solve their problems. Can you do it for free? If you can, you're a guerrilla.

13. Traditional marketing would have you believe that advertising works, that having a Web site works, that direct mail and e-mail work. To those antiquated notions, guerrilla marketing says *nonsense, nonsense,* and *nonsense.* Advertising doesn't work. Not anymore it doesn't. Web sites? Get serious. People learn daily that they are paths to financial oblivion and shattered dreams. Direct mail and e-mail used to work. But not anymore. So what does work? Guerrillas know that *marketing combinations work.* If you run a series of ads, have a Web site, and then do a direct mailing or an e-mailing, they'll all work, and they'll each help the others work. The days of single-weapon marketing have been relegated to the past. We're living in an era when marketing combinations open the doors to marketing success. I know a small retailer who runs small ads and short radio spots — all directing people to his Web site. That Web site motivates people to visit his showroom, where he sells his $3,000 beds briskly, effortlessly, and profitably. The ads and spots, combined with his Web site, are the marketing combination that brings home the bacon for him.

14. Traditional marketers, at the end of the month, count money. *Guerrillas count new relationships.* Knowing that people actually do want relationships, guerrillas do everything they can to establish and nurture a bond between themselves and each individual customer. They certainly do not disdain money, as indicated by their penchant for profits, but they know deep down that long-term relationships are the keys to the vault.

15. Traditional marketing has rarely emphasized technology, primarily because the technology of yesterday was too expensive, limited, and complicated. But that has changed completely, as today's technology gives small businesses an unfair advantage. It enables them to do what the big spenders do without the necessity to spend big. *Guerrilla marketing requires that you be very technocozy;* if you're not, your technophobia is holding back your small business. If you suffer from that affliction, make an appointment with your technoshrink immediately. Technophobia is fatal these days.

16. Traditional marketing has always aimed its message at groups: the larger the group, the better. *Guerrilla marketing aims its message at individuals or, if it must be a group, the smaller the group, the better.* Traditional marketing broadcasts; guerrilla marketing narrowcasts,

microcasts, and nanocasts. Let's say that you market a product for erectile dysfunction. If you run a TV spot on network television, that's broadcasting. If you run it on a cable channel devoted to men, that's narrowcasting. If you run it on a cable channel program focused on men's health, that's microcasting. If you run it on a cable channel program centered on men's sexual issues, that's nanocasting. The smaller the group, the bigger the bull's-eye.

17. Traditional marketing is, for the most part, unintentional. Although it embraces the big guns of marketing — radio, TV, newspapers, magazines, and Web sites — it tends to ignore the little details, such as how your phone is answered, the décor of your office, the attire worn by your employees. *Guerrilla marketing is always intentional.* It pays close attention to all the details of contact with the outside world, ignoring nothing and realizing the stunning importance of those tiny but supercharged details.

18. Traditional marketing believes that you can make the sale with marketing. That may have been so a long, long time ago, but that doesn't often happen anymore. That's why *guerrilla marketing alerts you to the reality that marketing today can hope only to gain people's consent to receive more marketing materials from you.* Most people will withhold their consent, and you've got to love them for doing that, because they're telling you to save your money and not waste it on them. But some will want to learn more, giving rise to one of the newer terms in the dictionary: *opt in.* A woman operating a summer camp in the Northeast runs ads in the camping directories in the back of several magazines. She does not attempt to sell the camping experience, only to get people to request her free DVD. She has a booth at local camping shows and gives away the same DVD. People view her DVD and see happy campers, trained counselors, beautiful surroundings, and superb equipment. Does the DVD attempt to sell the camping experience? No. It simply attempts to motivate people to call for an in-home consultation, at which more than 80 percent of parents sign their kids up for camp. And not just one kid: sometimes, a brother or sister as well. And don't forget the cousins and classmates who might come along for the summer. And we're not talking just one summer. Summer camp can be for four or five summers or more. And all because the camp director didn't go for the sale. She merely went for consent, and then she broadened that consent. The whole idea is wonderfully described by Seth Godin in his landmark book, *Permission Marketing.*

19. Traditional marketing is a monologue. One person does all the talking or writing. Everyone else listens or reads. Hardly the basis of a relationship. *Guerrilla marketing is a dialogue.* One person talks or writes. Someone else responds. Interactivity begins. The customer is involved with the marketing. That's one of the joys of the Internet. Relationships grow from dialogues. You've got to invite dialogue by asking people to register for something, sign up for your newsletter, send for a freebie, enter a contest, vote in an online poll. And you've got to respond to them. Small businesses can do this. Big corporations aren't usually quite as fast and flexible on their feet.

20. Traditional marketing identifies the heavy weapons of marketing: radio, TV, newspapers, magazines, direct mail, and the Internet. *Guerrilla marketing identifies two hundred weapons of marketing,* and many of them are free.

The heart of guerrilla marketing is the proper utilization of those weapons you choose to use. A basic precept of guerrilla marketing calls for you to be aware of all two hundred weapons, to utilize and test many of them, and then to eliminate those that failed to hit it out of the park for you. The idea is for you to end up with an arsenal of lethal and proven weapons.

2

The Need for Guerrilla Marketing

If you're an entrepreneur, you need guerrilla marketing more than ever because the competition is smarter, more sophisticated, and even more aggressive than it was in the past. That is not a problem for guerrillas.

Assume that you have a fine business background and are well versed in the fundamentals of marketing as practiced by the giant corporations. Admirable. Now forget as much as you can. Your marketing agenda as an entrepreneur is vastly different from that of an esteemed member of the Fortune 500. Some of the principles may be the same, but the *details* are different. A good analogy is that of Adam and Eve. In principle, they were very much the same, but they varied in crucial ways — and thank heaven for that.

You're about to become a master of guerrilla marketing, the type of all-out marketing necessary for entrepreneurial success. Guerrilla marketing used to be virtually unknown to the large corporations, though some of them are catching on. Be grateful that guerrilla marketing tactics are rarely practiced by the titans, for the large corporations have the benefit of big bucks, and you don't.

You must rely on something just as effective but less costly. I'm happy to report that your size is an ally when it comes to marketing. If you're a small company, a new venture, or a single individual, you can use the tactics of guerrilla marketing to their fullest. You have the ability to be fast on your feet, to use a vast array of marketing tools, and to gain access to the biggest marketing brains and get them at bargain-basement prices. You may not need to use every weapon in your potential marketing arsenal, but you will need some of them. Therefore, you should know how to use them all. And the Internet must become one of your favorite comfort zones.

Your business may not need to advertise. But it will need a marketing plan. Word of mouth may be so favorable and spread so rapidly that your venture can reap a fortune simply from it. If this is the case, the word of mouth was most likely motivated by an effective marketing strategy. In fact, a strong word-of-mouth campaign is part of marketing. And so are business cards, stationery, hours of operation, and the clothes you wear. Location is also important in marketing, though it is becoming more and more apparent that the best location is online.

Marketing is the painfully slow process by which you move people from their place in the sun to their place on your customer list, gently taking a grasp of the inside of their minds and never letting go. Each component that helps you sell your product or service is part of the marketing process. No detail is too insignificant. In fact, the smaller the detail, the more important it is to a customer. The more you realize that, the better your marketing will be. And the better your marketing is, the more money you will make. I'm not talking about sales; I'm talking about profits: the bottom line.

That's the good news. The bad news is that one day, you'll no longer be an entrepreneur. If you successfully put the principles of guerrilla marketing into practice, you'll become rich and famous and may no longer have the lean, hungry mentality of the entrepreneur.

Once you've reached that stage, you may resort to the textbook forms of marketing, for you may feel too encumbered with employees, traditions, paperwork, management levels, and bureaucracy to be flexible enough for guerrilla marketing. However, you probably won't mind that state of affairs too much. After all, Coca-Cola, Microsoft, Procter & Gamble, and Ford were all started by entrepreneurs. You can be certain that they practiced guerrilla marketing techniques as much as possible in their day. You can also be sure that they do their marketing by the numbers these days. And I doubt that they complain about it.

In time, large companies may be surpassed in size by companies that are today being founded and nurtured by entrepreneurs such as you. This will happen owing to the result of a combination of factors. Marketing genius will be one of them. Count on it.

I am assuming that you understand that to be successful, you must offer a quality product or service. Even the best marketing in the world won't motivate a customer to purchase a poor product or service more than once. In fact, guerrilla marketing can speed the demise of an inferior offering, because people will learn of the shoddiness that much sooner. Do everything in your power to ensure the quality of your product or service. If you're selling quality, you are ready to practice guerrilla marketing.

It is also mandatory that you have adequate capitalization — that is, money. Note that I didn't say that you need a lot of money. Sufficient capitalization to engage in guerrilla marketing will be enough. This means that you'll need enough cash or cash reserves to promote your business aggressively for at least three months and ideally for a full year. It might take $300; it might take $30,000 or even $300,000. It depends on your goals.

There are thousands of small businesses in the United States. Many of them offer superb products and highly desirable services. But fewer than one-tenth of 1 percent of those businesses will make it to the point of phenomenal financial success. The elusive variable that makes the difference between merely being listed in the yellow pages and being listed on the New York Stock Exchange is the *marketing* of the product or service.

You now hold in your hand the key to becoming part of that tiny percentage of entrepreneurs who go all the way. By realizing that many facets of your business can fall into the category of marketing, you have a head start on competitors who don't see the difference between *advertising* and *marketing.*

The more aware of marketing you are, the more attention you will pay to it. And the increased attention will result in better marketing of your offerings. I'd venture a bold guess that fewer than 10 percent of the new- and small-business owners in America have explored as many as a dozen of the marketing tools available to them. Among these methods are a Web site, canvassing, personal letters, telephone marketing, circulars and brochures, signs on bulletin boards, classified ads, outdoor signs, direct mail, samples, seminars, demonstrations, sponsoring of events, exhibitions at trade shows, T-shirt ads, public relations, using searchlights, such advertising specialties as imprinted ballpoint pens, and advertising in the yellow pages, newspapers, and magazines and on radio, television, and billboards. Guerrilla marketing *demands* that you scrutinize *each* of these marketing methods, and a lot more, and then *use the combination* that is best suited to your business.

Once you've launched your guerrilla marketing plan, keep track of which weapons are hitting your target and which are missing. Merely knowing can *double* the effectiveness of your marketing budget.

No advertising agencies specialize in guerrilla marketing. When I worked as a senior executive at some of the world's largest (and smallest) advertising agencies, I found that the agencies didn't have a clue as to what advertising or marketing tactics make an entrepreneur successful. They could help the big guys but were helpless without the bulging muscles of big bucks. So where can you turn to for help? The first place is *Guerrilla Marketing*. Next, take advantage of your own ingenuity and energy. And finally, you will probably have to seek the advice of a marketing or advertising professional in the areas where guerrilla marketing overlaps traditional marketing. But don't expect the pros to be as tough in the trenches as you are. Most likely, they operate best from high in a posh skyscraper.

Guerrilla marketing requires you to comprehend every facet of marketing, experiment with many of them, winnow out the losers, double up on the winners, and then use the marketing tactics that prove themselves to you in the battleground of real life.

Guerrilla marketing involves recognizing the myriad opportunities out there and *exploiting every one of them*. In the marketing of any product, problems are certain to arise. Solve these problems, and continue to look for new problems to solve — problems of prospects and customers. Businesses that solve problems have a greater chance of success than those that don't. Today, with time becoming recognized as even more important than money, businesses that save time for people will flourish. Why? Lack of time is a problem, and growing numbers of people in industrialized societies see it as such. The time-saving industry will become an important one in our society.

You must seize the important opportunities, yet you cannot neglect the smaller opportunities or overlook the minor problems. You've got to go all out. This is one of the foundations of successful guerrilla marketing.

Energy alone is not enough, however. Energy must be directed by intelligence. Intelligent marketing is marketing that is first and foremost focused on a core idea. All your marketing must be an extension of this idea: the advertising, the stationery, the direct mailings, the telephone marketing, the yellow pages advertising, the package, the Internet presence, the whole thing. It isn't enough to have a better idea; you need to have a focused strategy. Today, many large and supposedly sophisticated companies go to one expert for a trademark, another expert for an advertising program, yet another expert for direct-mail planning, and possibly one more professional for location selection. This is nonsense. Nine times out of ten, each of these experts will pull the company in a different direction.

What must be done is to have all the marketing pros pull in a common direction — a preagreed, long-term, carefully selected direction. When this is done, a synergistic effect is automatically created, and five types of marketing tactics do the work of ten. The preagreed direction will always be clear if you encapsulate your thoughts in a core concept that can be expressed in a *maximum* of, first, seven sentences and then seven words. That's right: a *maximum* of seven. Think it can't be done? Try it for your own business.

Here's an example. An entrepreneur wanted to offer courses in computer education but knew that most people suffer from "technophobia" — fear of things technical. His advertisements for proposed courses in word processing, accounting by computer, and the electronic spreadsheet produced little response, so he decided to restate the basic premise of his offering. At first, he stated it thus: "I wish to alleviate the fears that people have regarding computers so that they will recognize the enormous value and competitive advantages of working with computers." He then reduced this thought to a seven-word core concept: "I will teach people to operate computers." This brief statement clarified his task — clarified it for himself, his sales staff, and his prospective students. Later, he developed a name for his company, one that reduced his core concept to three words: *Computers for Beginners.* This bypassed the problem of technophobia, stated his premise, and attracted hordes of beginners. Originally, his concept was six pages long. By condensing his ideas, he was finally able to achieve the succinctness necessary to ensure clarity. And clarity led to success. It usually does.

The concept of focusing your marketing on a core idea is a simple one. When you begin to market your offering this way, you are a member of an enlightened minority, and you're well on your way to marketing success — a prerequisite for financial success.

Guerrilla Marketing simplifies the complexities and explains how entrepreneurs can use marketing to generate maximum profits from minimum investments. Put another way, this book can help make a small business big. This book can help an individual entrepreneur make a lot of money as painlessly as possible. Often, the only factor that determines success or failure is the way in which a product or service is marketed. The information in these pages will arm you for success and alert you to the shortcomings that lead to failure.

Stop for a moment and ask yourself whether you're marketing properly right now. You can be pretty certain that the answer is a resounding no! if any of these seven danger signals is present.

1. My sales are driven mostly by price.
2. Customers cannot distinguish my products or services from those of my competitors.
3. I use disconnected sales gimmicks.
4. I do not have a unified plan for imparting my message to my customers and to the trade.

5. Most sales leads come from my sales staff.
6. Longtime customers say, "I didn't know you offered that."
7. I do not have a customer or prospect database.

If you're guilty of generating any one of those signals, let's change all that. Even with the changes in marketing, markets, and the media, the guerrilla approach remains the sensible one for all marketers. For entrepreneurs, for small businesspeople, and for all businesspeople, the guerrilla approach is crucial. The successful small-business owners who have prospered in the face of a limited budget and a torrent of competitors will tell you that it is crucial that you make the guerrilla attitude and smarts part of your permanent mindset.

Here is what guerrilla marketing is not: expensive, easy, common, wasteful, taught in marketing classes, found in standard marketing textbooks, practiced by advertising agencies, or known to the majority of your competitors. Be grateful that it is not these things. If it were, all business owners would be guerrillas, and your path to success would be a paved one rather than a secret route to the end of a rainbow with a bigger pot of gold than you ever imagined.

In an article in the *Harvard Business Review*, John A. Welsh and Jerry F. White remind us that "a small business is not a little big business." An entrepreneur is not a multinational conglomerate but a profit-seeking individual. To survive, that individual must have a different outlook and must apply different principles to his or her endeavors than does the president of a large or even medium-size corporation.

Another difference between small and big businesses is that small businesses suffer from what the *Harvard Business Review* article calls "resource poverty." This is an opportunity that requires an entirely different approach to marketing. Where large ad budgets are not necessary or feasible, where expensive ad production squanders limited capital, where every marketing dollar must do the work of two dollars, if not five dollars or even ten, where a person's company, capital, and material well-being are all on the line: That is where guerrilla marketing can save the day and secure the bottom line.

A large company can invest in a full-scale advertising campaign run by an ad agency, and that company has the resources to switch to a different campaign if the first is not successful. And if the company ad manager is smart, he or she will hire a different agency the second time around. This luxury is not available to entrepreneurs, who must get it right the first time. Entrepreneurs who are guerrillas get it right because they know the secrets — and so will you.

This is not to say that I hold the techniques used by the big corporations in contempt; quite the contrary. While creating advertising for Alberto-Culver, Quaker Oats, United Airlines, Citicorp, Visa, Sears, and Pillsbury, I frequently used big-company marketing techniques. I was acting properly. But to suggest that the individual entrepreneurs I advise use the same techniques would be irresponsible, not to mention financially wasteful. Instead, I resort to the techniques of guerrilla marketing, techniques that might get me laughed out of a Procter & Gamble or IBM conference room.

Many of the approaches and some of the techniques overlap. Entrepreneurs need to govern tactical operations by marketing strategy and to weigh their marketing efforts against that strategy. They also need to examine all the marketing avenues available to them. The critical difference is the bottom line: Entrepreneurs must keep a far keener eye on the bottom line than do the giant firms. If a guerrilla had a tattoo, it would be of a bottom line.

Entrepreneurs have to spend far less money testing their marketing tactics; their marketing must produce results at a fraction of the price paid by the biggies. The entrepreneur's use of marketing will be more personalized and realistic.

Large companies think nothing of producing five television commercials for testing purposes only. Small companies wouldn't dare do this. Large companies employ many levels of management to analyze the effectiveness of their advertising. Small companies entrust the judging to one individual. Large companies look first to television — along with the Internet, the most far-reaching of all the marketing media. Small companies usually look first to small newspaper ads in local papers. Big companies hire expensive consultants to maximize their presence on the Internet. Small companies do this themselves. Both are interested in sales that generate profits but will achieve that goal in dramatically different ways.

Large companies often aim to lead an industry or to dominate a market or large market segment, and they use marketing ploys designed to attain those lofty ambitions. *However, small companies or individual entrepreneurs can flourish merely by gaining a tiny slice of an industry, a fraction of a market.* Different wars require different tactics.

Large companies must advertise from the outset and continue to advertise with virtually no interruption, but smaller enterprises may advertise only during the start-up phase and then rely solely on guerrilla weapons and word-of-mouth advertising. Can you imagine what would happen if Budweiser depended on word-of-mouth advertising? Miller would sell many more six-packs.

An individual entrepreneur may be able to get enough business simply by dealing with one gigantic company. An acquaintance of mine was able to survive financially (and in gracious style, I might add) merely by conducting small seminars for one large banking firm. No large company could exist off the income he was generating, but my friend was able to target that one firm until he was given his first assignment. Then there were others, and still others. Now, he is conducting his seminars for a large chemical company. Working with companies of that size, he needs very few customers. Needless to say, his marketing was tailored to this reality.

A descriptive brochure sent to a single large corporation may result in enough business to keep an energetic telephone marketing trainer in the chips for a long time. Try to find a New York Stock Exchange–listed company that could do the same. Impossible!

Many entrepreneurs get all the business they need by posting signs on bulletin boards. A large company would never consider such a possibility. If it did, it would be known as Shrinking, Inc., in short order. The point is obvious: Sauce for the small goose is not necessarily sauce for the large goose. And vice-versa.

For example, an executive at a large company may carry business cards that are plain and straightforward. The executive's name, company name, address, and phone number are suitable. Perhaps a title is necessary. For a smart practitioner of an individual enterprise, however, the business card should contain more information. For example, a word processor I know has a business card with the preceding information, along with the message "Legal, theses, statistical, manuscript, resume, and business word processing." Her card does double duty, and it needs to. That is what guerrilla marketing is all about.

A business card can double as a brochure, a circular, a wallet-size advertisement, and a listing of your services or products. It can open up to become a minibrochure. Customers appreciate such minibrochures: Their time and space are at a premium, and your card saves them time while taking up little space. The cost to produce such a card is not much more than that for a standard card. A business card can be more than a mere listing of one's name, address, and phone number; it can be a marketing weapon.

A huge corporation can run radio or television commercials and at the end of each message tell the audience to get the address of the nearest dealer by consulting the yellow pages.

But the individual entrepreneur dare not direct listeners or viewers to the yellow pages. That would only alert prospective customers to the competition or to the dominance of certain competitors. Instead, the astute entrepreneur directs prospects to the white pages, where there will be no competitive ads, where the organization's small size will not appear as a detriment, and where recognizable promotion themes and symbols will not woo a customer away.

Perhaps the biggest difference between an individual businessperson and a large corporation is the degree of flexibility each possesses. Here the balance tips in favor of the small business. Because it hasn't indoctrinated numerous levels of management and a gigantic sales organization in the tactics and strategies of its marketing plan, the small business can make changes on the spot. It can be fast on its feet and can react to market changes, competitive ploys, undeveloped service niches, economic realities, new media, newsworthy events, and last-minute offers.

I recall how a major advertiser once was offered an unbelievably good media buy for a fraction of its normal price. Because the offer did not fit into the company's engraved-in-bronze plan, and because the person to whom the offer was made had to check with so many bosses, the company turned down the offer. A tiny business then accepted it: a thirty-second commercial just before the Super Bowl, for the incredible price of $500. The cost of this commercial slot (in the San Francisco Bay area) normally sold for ten times that amount at that time. Owing to a lack of flexibility, the giant corporation was unable to take advantage of the bargain. Speed and flexibility are the essence of guerrilla marketing.

Business in each decade is fueled by a single burning concept. In the 1980s, that concept was *quality*. Quality was so important that it became the ticket to admission to doing business in the 1990s. The concept of the 1990s became *flexibility*. The more you can offer, the better service you can provide and the more customers you can satisfy. Word-of-mouth marketing will flourish from the spring of flexibility. During the first decade of the twenty-first century, the key concept has been *innovation*. However, guerrilla marketers should first develop a reputation for quality and flexibility and live up to their praises consistently. Then they can focus on innovation.

A success-bound entrepreneur must learn to think about marketing and advertising on a different wavelength than does a corporate advertising executive. Although you must think about the primary marketing tools much as the executive does, you must also develop a sixth sense for the other opportunities available to entrepreneurs. It may be that a personal letter or visit is in order. A corporate manager might never consider such mundane tactics. Perhaps a telephone marketing campaign is in order. Can you picture Coca-Cola getting involved in telephone marketing to customers? Can you imagine Shell Oil going one on one with its prospects?

The one-on-one capabilities of the small business represent an extraordinary opportunity to business owners who recognize a good thing when it stares them in the face. Small businesses can win and keep business; they build and grow the business by focusing on seemingly tiny details. The small business can get up close and *personal* with its customers.

There's a certain warmth associated with being a mom-and-pop business. And even though you may run yours with the acumen of the multinational conglomerates — most of which are not run with much acumen, or they'd focus more acutely on their prime talents — you can benefit from the close personal connection associated with small business simply by injecting an extra dollop of warmth into your modus operandi.

You have the flexibility, the speed, and the disregard of image that enable you to use radio commercials and to hire high school students to distribute printed circulars on street corners. You don't have a body of rules to follow, a committee to answer to, a set structure to follow. You're a guerrilla. You *are* the organization. You answer to yourself. You make the rules and you break the rules. That means you get to be amazing, outrageous, surprising, unpredictable, brilliant, and quick.

You also may be able to enjoy the rare luxury of relying on consistent word-of-mouth advertising. If you're really good at your work and know how to generate word-of-mouth marketing and referral business, it might be enough to keep your coffers brimming. I know of no Fortune 500 companies that can enjoy that amenity.

Incidentally, please understand that what appears to be word-of-mouth advertising is often a combination of newspaper, magazine, radio, direct-mail, and word-of-mouth advertising. It's the mouth that gets the credit, not the media. Don't delude yourself: You cannot succeed without media advertising. Succeeding with this strategy would be like winning the lottery with your first ticket. It can happen, but don't bet your boots or your business on it.

The point to remember is that no large corporation can succeed by means of word-of-mouth advertising alone, and some entrepreneurs can. Do yourself a favor and don't leave everything up to the recommendations of your happy customers. They probably have more important things to talk about. Even for a guerrilla, consistent marketing is crucial to success.

An overall marketing plan for a person engaged in individual enterprise might consist of a listing in the yellow pages, a Web site, an e-mail campaign, a mailing of circulars and business cards, a posting of signs, and a follow-up telephone call to prospects to whom the promotional material was sent. That six-pronged effort (yellow pages, Web site, e-mailing, mailing, sign posting, and telephoning) might be all it takes to get a business off and running. You can be certain that no big company has a marketing plan so short, simple, and inexpensive.

Imagine that a staple gun and a handful of circulars were the only marketing tools necessary to conduct a business. IBM would boot me out of its corporate offices for suggesting such a thing. However, many a successful word processing service uses only these devices. The word processing woman I mentioned earlier started out by typing her circulars, thereby lending credibility to her typing ability. She posted them with her staple gun on bulletin boards on local college campuses. Today, she no longer posts circulars, and her staple gun gathers dust. Word of mouth has taken over, and she gets all the business she needs through referrals.

Entrepreneurs can enjoy month after month of profitable business merely by advertising in the classified pages and in the many classified sections now online. I'm sure you've seen rafts of ads by independent contractors while perusing the classified ads. You do look through them, don't you? The classified ads are recommended reading for entrepreneurs. They give you ideas. They alert you to the competition. They clue you in as to current prices. You'll read more about them up ahead. The point I'm making here is that classified ads are an important tool for independent businesspeople. They are not a tool for large companies. I doubt whether the most professional advertising agencies in the world are well versed in proper use of the classified pages, but the classifieds may be invaluable to freelance earners.

The use of classified ads is hardly a secret to anyone. But there are significant marketing secrets that must be known by all businesses, large and small. Sixteen secrets in all. Even the tiniest of entrepreneurs must be aware of them. Your awareness will begin when you begin reading the next chapter.

3

The Sixteen Monumental Secrets
of Guerrilla Marketing

If you're a guerrilla, these sixteen secrets are not secrets to you at all. I'm hoping that they are tattooed on your body, engraved on brass plaques in the offices of all who market or plan marketing for you, and pinned up — ideally in neon — inside your brain. These proven gems of marketing wisdom have somehow escaped the ken of large and small marketers alike. I keep wanting to say that there are no secrets at all, but there really are sixteen. I sincerely believe that it is next to impossible to market a product or service successfully unless these secrets are known and put into practice. I also believe that merely by learning these secrets and then living by them, you're 80 percent of the way toward success with your marketing. Nope, make that 90 percent.

If you have a small business and want it to become a large business, forget it — until you put these sixteen secrets into practice. If you allow these concepts to become part of your mental marketing framework, you've got a giant head start on those who do not.

So as not to keep you in suspense any longer, I'll reveal the secrets right here and now. They can be summarized in sixteen words, each ending with a handy memory crutch for you — the letters *ent*: commitment, investment, consistent, confident, patient, assortment, subsequent, convenient, amazement, measurement, involvement, dependent, armament, consent, content, and augment.

1. You must have *commitment* to your marketing program.
2. Think of that program as an *investment*.

3. See to it that your program is *consistent.*
4. Make your prospects *confident* in your firm.
5. You must be *patient* in order to keep a commitment.
6. You must see that marketing is an *assortment* of weapons.
7. You must know that profits come *subsequent* to the sale.
8. You must aim to run your firm in a way that makes it *convenient* for your customers.
9. Put an element of *amazement* in your marketing.
10. Use *measurement* to judge the effectiveness of your weapons.
11. Prove your *involvement* with customers and prospects by your regular follow-up with them.
12. Learn to become *dependent* on other businesses and they on you.
13. You must be skilled with the *armament* of guerrillas, which means technology.
14. Use marketing to gain *consent* from prospects, and then broaden that consent so that it leads to the sale.
15. Sell the *content* of your offering rather than the style; sell the steak *and* the sizzle, because people are too sophisticated to merely buy that sizzle.
16. After you have a full-fledged marketing program, work to *augment* it rather than rest on your laurels.

To make you an even happier guerrilla, keep in mind that these sixteen words come with a guarantee. If you memorize all sixteen and run your business by the concepts they represent, you will exceed your most optimistic projections. Memorize only fifteen, and don't blame me if things go awry on your trip to the promised land.

Let me illustrate this for you with a story. I was employed by an advertising agency in Chicago, and we were called in to a New York cigarette company, which was dismayed by its ranking — thirty-first largest-selling brand in America — and its perception as a feminine brand. It was true in the early 1960s, more women smoked than men. But men smoked more cigarettes. So the client asked whether we were up to the job of improving that dismal ranking of the brand while changing the perception of it to something more masculine.

"Can you do that?" they asked. "We can try," we countered, so we flew back to Chicago and to the ad agency. Immediately, we dispatched two photographers and one art director to a ranch owned by a friend of the art director. The ranch was in west Texas and ran a giant herd of cattle. We told the photographers to spend two weeks shooting cowboys working on the ranch.

"Unposed pictures," we told them. "Show cowboys, horses, and beautiful scenery. No cows, no women, no poses."

While they were gone, we invented a new place. "Marlboro Country," we called it. And we came up with a theme line: "Come to where the flavor is. Come to Marlboro Country." When the photographers returned, we developed their pictures, blew them up, and pasted our words across them. We thought we had accomplished our task and were psyched about making our presentation to the Marlboro brand group. We flew from O'Hare to JFK, hopped a taxi to the Park Avenue headquarters of Philip Morris, the parent company of Marlboro, and began to talk excitedly about the presentation we were about to make. The taxi driver caught wind of our conversation, turned his head and asked, "You guys in the ad game?"

"Uh, yes, we're in the ad game," we responded. "Do you really believe that stuff works?" asked the taxi driver.

"We believe it works," was our answer.

The cabbie's reply: "It sure doesn't work on me. I've never bought anything as a result of marketing or advertising. I never have and I never will." One of our guys asked him, "What kind of toothpaste do you use?" The cabbie answered, "Oh, I brush with Gleam, but it's got nothing to do with the advertising. It's because I drive a cab and I can't brush after every meal."

At that time, Gleam's theme line was, "For people who can't brush after every meal." But the real punch line to this story was still to come. We presented the Marlboro cowboy to the brand group — Marlboro Country, the theme line, TV storyboards (we had rented the music to *The Magnificent Seven* for $50,000 a year because it was legal in those days to hawk carcinogens on radio and TV), billboards, and layouts for newspaper and magazine ads.

They loved it. In fact, they agreed to invest $18 million in the campaign the first year. The Marlboro Man was on radio, TV, newspapers, magazines, signs, billboards, all over the place. He had, in less than one year, become a cultural icon. At that time, there had been no correlation between cigarette smoking and lung cancer. We were oblivious to it, too. The Secretary of the Navy got on our case for using tattoos on our Marlboro Men, fearing infections to sailors at less-than-sanitary tattoo parlors, but the Surgeon-General remained silent.

After a year had passed, we flew back to New York to get our high fives, our pats on the back, and our well-deserved congratulations. After one year, Marlboro cigarettes, which had been the thirty-first-largest selling brand in

America, was still thirty-first. Focus-group interviews in five cities revealed that this brand, once considered a feminine brand, was still perceived of as a feminine brand! We had shown real cowboys doing what real cowboys do on a real ranch. Every graphic we used was macho to the core. But still, people considered Marlboros to be a ladies' brand.

Now, switch to today. We see that Marlboro is the number-one-selling brand in America. It's number one to men. It's number one to women. In fact, it's the most popular cigarette brand in the world. One out of five cigarettes sold on Earth is a Marlboro. But here's the real punch line: Nothing had changed in the marketing or advertising. It's still the Marlboro Man. It's still Marlboro Country. No more radio and no more TV in the United States, but the campaign has remained totally unchanged since it first made its debut.

It is now known as the best-marketed brand in history. The real hero of the campaign was Joseph Cullman IV, the chairman of Philip Morris. When we learned from him that the brand was still mired in thirty-first place, we were at a loss for words. But the good Mr. Cullman reminded us, "Hey, you guys said this would take time. Well, I can hang in there with the best of them."

Commitment

That brings us to the first *ent* word: commitment. I hate admitting this in print, but mediocre marketing with commitment works better than brilliant marketing without commitment. What makes marketing work? If you were looking for a one-word answer to that question, that word is *commitment*. What makes a marriage work? What makes a business work? How do you finish running a marathon? Commitment is the answer, and all the winners know it.

If you're not committed to a marketing or advertising program, it's probably not going to work for you. I tell my clients that the single most important word for them to remember while they are engaged in marketing is *commitment*. It means that they are taking the marketing job seriously. They're not playing around, not expecting miracles. They have scant funds to test their marketing — they must act. Without commitment, marketing becomes practically impotent.

You evolve a marketing plan, revise and rerevise it until it is *a powerful plan for your purposes*. You put it to work and you stay with it, no matter what (in most cases). You watch it slowly take effect, rise and falter, take a bit more effect, slide back a bit, start taking hold even more, stumble, then finally grab on and soar, taking you with it. Your plan is working; your cash register is ringing; your bank balance is swelling. And this is because you were *committed* to your *marketing program*.

Let's examine that last paragraph. What if you weren't patient enough during the time your plan "slowly" took effect? You might have changed the plan. Many entrepreneurs do. What if you dropped the plan the moment it faltered? You would have lost out. Many marketers do. What if you lost your cool when your sales slid backward? You might have scrubbed the plan. Suppose that you dropped it when it stumbled, as virtually all marketing plans do, at least temporarily. Disaster would have ensued. However, because you stayed with the plan — because you were committed to it — it took hold. Your success was very much due to your understanding of the concept of commitment. If you hadn't been in touch with the essence of the concept, you probably would have killed the plan — and killed your chances along with it. If you understand the meaning of *commitment*, it will pay off for you.

A new sleep shop was opening in Boulder, Colorado. The owner of the business had heard about me, so he flew out to northern California to talk. We hit it off. We discussed the idea of commitment to a marketing program. He admitted that he knew zilch about marketing and turned the whole thing over to me. I developed a marketing plan, secured his approval, and then reiterated the importance of his commitment to the program. Mind you, I'm talking about a guy with one small store.

The marketing strategy was implemented. Six weeks later, my new client called me to tell me that although he was still committed to the program, he hadn't seen much proof that it was for him. He said that he was completely relaxed about the whole thing because he felt he understood about commitment. After twelve weeks, he called to tell me he was beginning to see hints that the program was taking effect. After six months, he opened his second store. After nine months, he opened his third, and at the end of the year, he had five stores. He remained committed to the marketing program and within six years had forty-two stores in Colorado, Iowa, Kansas, Wyoming, and Missouri.

I doubt that my client would have progressed to the point where he could have justified a second store if he hadn't stayed with the plan. He could have wavered and veered from the plan. But it was a well-conceived plan, a plan that was tailored to his needs.

At the outset, you won't have any way of knowing whether your plan is good or bad, except for low-cost testing, your own intuition, and the counsel of others in whom you believe. But once you believe in your plan, you've got to back your belief with *patience*. Patience is commitment.

My client's plan called for weekly newspaper advertising, daily radio advertising, strong in-store signs, weekly sales training, consistent customer follow-up, and free gifts for customers during promotions. That was in the 1970s. In the 1980s, it was augmented by daily TV advertising three weeks out of every four. And for the 1990s, though the business was sold for an obscene sum, it was supported even more by a video brochure and a Web site connected to other local and global businesses. But the framework remained the same — because the mindset of the owner would remain that of a guerrilla.

Create a sensible plan, and then stick with it until it proves itself to you. How long might that take? Three months, if you're lucky. Probably six months. Possibly as long as a year. It took even longer than that for Marlboro. But you will never, ever, know within the first sixty days whether the plan is working. Commitment is directly related to time. The longer you live by a plan, the deeper your sense of commitment. If your boat sinks in the ocean and you start swimming to shore, you shouldn't give up if you don't hit the beach within one hour — or even five hours. To survive, you've got to be *committed* to swimming to that beach.

Think of this, and think of Marlboro when you consider altering your marketing plans after a short time. Lest you misunderstand, think about the following list each time you run an ad and get a response that doesn't meet your expectations.

1. The first time a man looks at an ad, he doesn't see it.
2. The second time, he doesn't notice it.
3. The third time, he is conscious of its existence.
4. The fourth time, he faintly remembers having seen it.
5. The fifth time, he reads the ad.
6. The sixth time, he turns up his nose at it.
7. The seventh time, he reads it through and says, "Oh, brother!"
8. The eighth time, he says, "Here's that confounded thing again!"
9. The ninth time, he wonders whether it amounts to anything.
10. The tenth time, he will ask his neighbor if he has tried it.
11. The eleventh time, he wonders how the advertiser makes it pay.
12. The twelfth time, he thinks it must be a good thing.
13. The thirteenth time, he thinks it might be worth something.

14. The fourteenth time, he remembers that he wanted such a thing for a long time.
15. The fifteenth time, he is tantalized because he cannot afford to buy it.
16. The sixteenth time, he thinks he will buy it someday.
17. The seventeenth time, he makes a memorandum of it.
18. The eighteenth time, he swears at his poverty.
19. The nineteenth time, he counts his money carefully.
20. The twentieth time he sees the ad, he buys the article or instructs his wife to do so.

The preceding was written by one Thomas Smith in London in 1885. So much for commitment. Now let's talk about another *ent* word — *investment* — the second of the sixteen most important secrets of all.

Investment

Marketing and advertising should be considered conservative *investments*. They are not miracle workers. They are not magic formulas. They are not instant gratifiers. If you don't recognize that marketing is a conservative investment, you'll have difficulty committing yourself to a marketing program.

Suppose that you buy a blue-chip stock. If it drops after a few weeks, you don't sell it. You hold on to it in hopes that its value will increase. And in all likelihood, it will. Such is the nature of a conservative investment. Look at marketing in the same way. If it doesn't produce instant results, it's because most marketing doesn't. If it does produce instant results, excellent — but don't expect this to happen every time.

Marketing will contribute to slow but steady increases for you. At the end of a year, you'll be able to say that you've invested X dollars in marketing and received X plus Y in sales. Don't expect marketing to suddenly double your sales. Although that has happened, it is unusual. Recognizing this, you'll feel good about making a conservative investment in marketing the next year and the year after that. If you expect more from marketing, chances are that you'll be disappointed. If you expect only that, chances are that you'll be gratified. And successful.

Here is an example of a nearsighted business decision: I worked with a client who had never engaged in newspaper advertising. We developed a marketing plan for his four eyeglass stores, a creative strategy, and a media plan. We discussed commitment. Then we ran the ads. After four weeks, my client called to tell me that he was dropping the entire advertising program.

When I asked why, he told me that he had expected his sales to at least double by this time. He admitted that I had explained that advertising does not work this way. But he said that he didn't want to spend money on an expense that didn't produce instant sales. I told him that although it might feel like an expense in the pit of his tummy, it's really an investment.

I wish I had informed him even more emphatically that his advertising expenditure was a really conservative investment. Perhaps he would have better understood its powers — and limitations. But instead, he dropped the plan and lost his money. He didn't understand the investment concept. He was expecting miracles, instant results, dramatic changes. Marketing does not work that way. Don't expect it to. Don't lose money because of it. Whenever you spend one dime for any type of marketing, use the term *investing* to describe your expenditure. By *investing* your money in marketing, you'll earn more money than by *spending* your money in marketing. See the difference?

Consistent

The third major marketing secret is to make your marketing *consistent*. Don't change media. Don't change messages. Don't vary your graphic format. Change your offers and headlines and even your prices, if you wish, but do not change your identity. Don't drop out of the public eye for long periods. When you are ready to market your product or service, be prepared to put the word out *consistently*. Consistently means regularly — and for a goodly period of time. It means that instead of running a couple of large newspaper ads once every few months, you'll run smaller newspaper ads and run them frequently. Instead of airing fifty-five radio commercials in one week every few months, run twelve radio commercials per week every week. You can even drop out of sight one week out of four. As long as you are a consistent marketer, you can pull out of the media for brief periods.

Consistency breeds familiarity, familiarity breeds confidence, and confidence breeds sales. If your products or services are of sufficient quality, your confidence in your offering, more than any other attribute, will attract buyers.

Confident

Actually, the fourth secret is to make prospects *confident* in your offering. Confidence is extremely important to you — more important than quality, than selection, than price, than service. Confidence will be your ally. And commitment, as proven by consistent marketing, will breed confidence.

I have a retail furniture client who has been with me more than forty years. When she first began to market her product, she spent a fortune advertising on television. Could she afford it? Of course not. But she believed that television was her key to success. With the number of dollars she had to invest, television was her key to doom because she could afford to run only two commercials per week, even though they were on the highest-rated show at the time. Ratings are virtually meaningless with only two spots a week. It doesn't take a guerrilla to know that one can't expect TV to produce profits with so few commercials. Today, my client runs lots of commercials on local cable TV, investing only a tiny portion of her marketing budget and enjoying exceptionally gratifying profits as a result. We'll discuss TV in greater detail later, but for now, suffice it to say that unless you can use a medium *effectively*, you shouldn't use it at all.

My client was able to salvage her business from her disastrous TV experience. When she met with me, we talked about commitment, investment, and consistency. We talked about the other guerrilla secrets as well. Since that day, she has run a tiny ad in the newspaper every Sunday, and her sales have continued to rise. She dramatically increased her sales without increasing her marketing investment as a percentage of her gross revenue. It happened over a period of several years. Her store has quadrupled in size, and her profits have followed suit. As I mentioned, she's also back on television — running ten commercials per day, two weeks out of every four. The key to her glittering success was consistent advertising. She calls her Sunday newspaper ad, now not so tiny, her "meal ticket." And she's right. She tells me that most people who come into her store say that they've seen the original ad. You'd find that difficult to believe if you saw the small size of the original ad, but you'd find it easy to believe if you knew that she's been running that and similar ads in the same newspaper in the same section on the same day for years. People are *familiar* with her operation. They're *confident* in her offerings. And they buy from her.

Patient

She is committed. She sees her marketing as an investment. She is consistent and patient. And she has since added a multitude of weapons to her marketing arsenal.

Assortment

This *assortment* of weapons generates many new, higher-than-projected profits for her. The wider the assortment of weapons in your marketing arsenal, the wider the grin on your face when you review your financial statements.

Does my client send follow-up mailings to all her customers? Of course she does. She has learned that marketing doesn't end with the sale.

Subsequent

It's the marketing done *subsequent* to the sale that leads to the juicy profits. It costs six times more to sell a product or a service to a new customer than it does to an existing customer. My client always mails to existing customers, and she benefits from the repeat sales, which are the inevitable payoff.

Convenient

Her store is known as a very *convenient* place for buying. It's open seven days a week. Hours are extended for the convenience of her customers — not for her own convenience. She has a fascinating Web site. She accepts every credit card under the sun. She takes checks, arranges partial-payment plans, delivers, installs, and is accessible twenty-four hours a day via voicemail, e-mail, and fax. And parking is convenient.

Amazement

Although she takes much of her business for granted, she knows that her marketing must *amaze* people. So her marketing mentions that her custom-designed furniture is available at factory-direct prices because she has her own factory. The prices are amazing, and so is the homemade touch. It enables her to custom-design furniture and offer it at an off-the-floor price. This element of *amazement* attracts attention to her ads.

Measurement

Most amazing of all, she has doubled the effectiveness of all her marketing! How did she do such a wondrous thing? The answer is *measurement*, as if you didn't know. She measured the effectiveness of all her marketing, asking people where they first heard of her. In this way, she was able to eliminate the weapons and newspapers that weren't pulling their weight, and she doubled those that gave her the biggest bang for her bucks. The result: a doubling of her profits. The reason: measurement (also called *sourcing* by those in the know).

Involvement

One of the most delightful daily aspects of her showroom is the return of satisfied customers, who are always treated warmly and helpfully. There is a powerful feeling of *involvement*, the eleventh secret, between these people and the business. The business proves that it's involved with customers by means of its continual follow-up: sending mailers, inviting customers to private sales, offering a selection tailored to their needs, providing a helpful Web site for them, and being especially nice to them, almost always remembering their names. The customers prove that they're involved by coming back several times during the year to see what's available for their homes and usually finding something to buy. They prove it by referring the store to their friends and frequently bringing friends in tow when they're making a shopping foray. They show their involvement by providing testimonials and by completing questionnaires.

Dependent

My client does not see herself as a free-standing, self-contained, independent business owner. She instead views herself as quite *dependent* on her manufacturing business, her suppliers, on nearby furniture showrooms carrying noncompeting lines, on the media that alert her to special opportunities and open their minds to bartering time and space for a comfy sofa or two, and on competitors from distant places, with whom she trades war stories and chronicles successes during trade shows. These people are, in turn, dependent on her for information, business, and referrals. Everybody is learning that the more dependent they are, the higher their profits will be. Dependency is another guerrilla secret. Many small-business owners view themselves as independent souls, but guerrillas know that power comes from teamwork more than from rugged individualism.

When the first edition of this book was published, my client knew as much about computers as I know about what you ate for dinner last night. But today, her computer is an integral part of her business, enabling her to boost her profits while cutting down on her marketing expenses.

Armament

Dictionaries describe the equipment necessary to wage and win battles as *armament*. The armament of the guerrilla is technology. Armament is your computer, your online presence, your cellphone, your pager, your electronic connections within your business and within the entire world, voicemail, fax machines, and wireless connections to delivery vans. Within your factory, it also means equipment that allows you to produce more and better for less and with less. You can now create all these marketing weapons with an inexpensive desktop publishing system. The list is long and imaginative, lethal to those who deign to compete, regardless of their size and bankroll.

Consent

At this point, I want to call your attention again to that relatively new phrase in the dictionary. That term is *opt in*, and it means voluntarily open to receiving new information about a topic or a company. These days, it is almost impossible to make a sale with an ad. So the best ads and the best marketing simply attempt to gain people's *consent* to hear from you. Your job is to broaden that consent and then to make the sale. Remember the woman from Chapter 1 who successfully markets her summer camp by going after consent with her video, then broadening that consent until it leads to an in-home consultation. Web sites around the globe are aiming to gain consent, to widen that consent until it paves the way to a completed sale. The more you realize that, the less frustrated you will be with marketing, and the better it will work for you.

Content

The fifteenth secret — *content* — reminds you that consumers are savvier than ever and less prone to be won over by special effects and razzle-dazzle. They know the difference between style and substance. Although they may be attracted by style, they pull out their credit cards and write their checks for substance. The content of your offer — the real meat and potatoes that you offer — will win their hearts and their business. Like Clara Peller, the elderly woman in the old Wendy's TV spots, the real money comes into your life when you can answer her famous question, "Where's the beef?" You can pile on the lettuce and tomatoes and special sauce, but people are looking for the beef, the content that you offer. If it's not there, people will look elsewhere, just as you would.

Augment

And finally, the sixteenth secret nudges you in the ribs with its elbow when you're sitting back thinking that your job is all over. Keep in mind that your competitors are getting smarter every single day. So your real job is to *augment* your marketing attack. Strengthen your plan. Beef up your Web site. Add a few more weapons to your arsenal. Add more fusion-marketing partners. Try to earn more profits from your marketing investment. Marketing is changing daily. What new tactics and techniques might you use to get a louder bang for a smaller buck?

These sixteen secrets — as embodied by sixteen words — are the most valuable secrets you'll learn in this book. They are also extremely difficult rules to follow.

Your friends, employees, coworkers, partners, family, and suppliers may advise you to change your marketing plan when they don't see instant results. These same well-meaning people will question a marketing program that does not produce a dramatic increase in sales over a short period of time. And they'll be the first to tire of your marketing, to become bored with your ads or commercials. But your customers won't feel this way. They'll go through the process of developing confidence in your offering, and you should do everything in your power not to undermine that process.

The moral: When you do develop your marketing plan, don't give it your stamp of approval until you are ready to commit yourself to it. Don't approve it until you are ready to invest in it with a realistic expectation of return. And don't implement it until you are prepared to stick with it consistently. This isn't to say that you can't make changes. Of course you can. But make changes while remaining consistent.

- Your task: to make prospects *confident* in you
- Your secret weapon: *commitment* to your plan
- Your personality: *patient*
- Your marketing: an *assortment* of at least twenty weapons
- Your format: the spirit of *consistency*
- Your finances: some wise *investment* in marketing
- Your energy: apparent prior to and *subsequent* to the sale
- Your operation: *convenient* for customers
- Your creative message: one that leaves readers in *amazement*
- Your unglamorous but extremely profitable chore: *measurement* of who your customers are and where the heck they heard of you
- Your relationship with customers: one of *involvement* with them

- Your relationship with other businesses: *dependent* on one another for mutual profitability
- Your arsenal for marketing: brimming with the *armament* of guerrillas — easy-to-use technology
- The goal of your marketing: to gain *consent* from prospects and customers to receive more marketing materials from you
- The reason people continue to visit your Web site or shop at your store: lush *content*, loaded with good ideas that fire their imagination
- Your constant and never-ending task: to *augment* your marketing arsenal, understanding, and prowess, leaving your competitors shuddering at the very mention of your name

There. Now you can never say that you weren't made fully aware of the sixteen most important marketing secrets. By knowing them and by making them a cornerstone of your business, you have a head start on your competition. Now let's increase that head start. Let's examine what it takes to develop a successful plan in the first place. But, first, here's a seventeenth secret. *Implement* these secrets. Putting them into action is your main mission as a guerrilla.

4

Developing a Guerrilla Marketing Plan

You know the secrets. Does that mean you're ready to launch a full-scale marketing attack? Not even close. Before you launch, you need a *core story*: a real-life story about a problem involving the people to whom you're telling the story and how your solution to that problem can make life better for them.

Right here and right now, let me tell you the two most important things you should know if you're to succeed with guerrilla marketing: (1) *Start with a plan* and (2) *commit to that plan*. If you do those two things, you're off to the right start, and you're primed for success.

But how do you develop the kind of plan to which you ought to commit? You engage in research, attend to all details, and give the matter quite a bit of deep thought. You develop a core story. Rest assured, the difference between many a success and failure is market planning and nothing else. It's having or not having a core story. Whether you're a one-person band or you work from a home office, you must operate according to a strategy, just like the big corporations. As a guerrilla, your core story can be more powerful than that of the big guys because it can be more personalized.

A word that you should now start to use and understand is *positioning*: determining the specific niche that your offering is intended to fill. What will you stand for in the minds of your prospects and customers? You and I both know of JetBlue — an airline that commenced operations during a time when most airline business was drastically down. By establishing a solid marketing plan, the new airline took off with astounding speed. It positioned itself as a one-class, high-frills airline that could boast of spacious and comfortable leather seats, with generous legroom, private TV, a wide choice of movies at each seat, and surprisingly low fares. Success came rather easily. This marketing idea was a result of intelligent market planning and brilliant positioning.

One of the best-known names in American advertising circles is David Ogilvy. After spending several billion dollars on advertising, Mr. O. listed thirty-two things his advertising agency had learned. He said that of the thirty-two, the single most important decision involved *positioning the product*. He claimed that marketing results depended less on how advertising was written than on how the product or service was positioned.

The guerrilla marketing plan or strategy should serve as the springboard for marketing that sells. When doing your own market planning, review your offering with regard to your objectives, the strengths and weaknesses of your offering, your perceived competition, your target market, the needs of that market, and the trends apparent in the economy. This should be instrumental in your establishing a proper position. Ask yourself these basic questions: What business am I in? What is my goal? What benefits do I offer? What are my competitive advantages? What do I fear?

When you fully understand the true nature of your business, your goal, your strengths and weaknesses, your competitors' strengths and weaknesses, and the needs of your target market, your positioning will be that much easier to determine and your strategy that much easier to plan.

Small businesses have an advantage over large businesses in that they can occupy smaller niches and prosper by dominating them. A small business's specialty might be palm trees rather than a full-scale plant and tree nursery. Not a huge niche, but perfect for the small company that operates such a firm very successfully in my neck of the galaxy.

Ask yourself: Who is my target market? The answers you had when you started in business may be different today. Many enormous new markets are being identified in the United States, and many guerrilla marketers are enjoying record-breaking profits by aiming at these markets. Guerrilla fact: The more markets you target, the more profits you receive.

Be careful that you don't limit your marketing to only one target market. The largest copying company in the San Francisco Bay Area, marketing to business in general, allocated a portion of its marketing funds to target the legal industry, because that's where the most copies are generated. This effort led to a 31 percent increase in profits in one year without investing an extra cent in marketing costs. You must identify *all* your target markets. Then take careful aim at each.

The Big Four

Four relatively new markets have emerged as viable target audiences. They are now bombarded with marketing — an effort that is certain to continue. The markets are *older people; women; ethnic groups, especially Asian Americans and Hispanics; and small businesses*, especially home-based businesses.

The University of Michigan informs us that older people rely on mass-media marketing even more than on friends and family when it comes to consumer information. Surveys from several sources show that seniors rank health first, financial security second, a closer relationship with God third, and a closer relationship with family fourth. In the past, people died when they got old. Today, they control the purse strings of a $1.5 trillion pocketbook.

When communicating with older people, guerrillas use the term *older* rather than *elderly* or *senior citizen*. And instead of saying "fifty-five and older," say "fifty-five and better." When using graphics, show older people as *actively old* and living life to its fullest. Avoid anything trendy. Older people respond well to products and services that appeal to their autonomy and independence. These people now have taken responsibility for their own health care. But their eyesight is faltering, so use large type in your printed material. Do you know which magazine has the largest circulation in the United States? It used to be *Reader's Digest*; then it was *TV Guide*; now it's *AARP*.

Today, more than half of the new businesses in the United States are started by women, and these businesses have higher success rates than those started by men. The kinder, gentler, entrepreneurial woman of the twenty-first century is very different from the woman of the twentieth. Today, one in six businesses in this country is owned by a woman. Research shows that 57 percent of women have nurtured the dream of running their own firm, with 48 percent saying that being their own boss is the reason why.

Women own 10.6 million firms, which is nearly half of all privately held small businesses. Women employ more than 19 million people and are growing their businesses at twice the national rate. Women generate $2.5 trillion — with a *tr* — in annual sales.

The woman of today has more interests and can be reached through more marketing vehicles than ever before. Women have power. Examples: although 79 percent of bed-purchase decisions are made by women, a man pays for the bed 77 percent of the time. Similar percentages can be found regarding other expensive items, including houses and cars, which are typically the most expensive purchases people will make in their lifetime.

Guerrillas not only include women as a target audience in their general marketing but they also direct much of their marketing directly to women and only to women. Women's purchasing power is on the rise, as is their stature in business. It's important to know the powers and the myths about women.

Let's talk about the powers of women. They control more than 60 percent of all wealth and influence in the United States. They also handle 75 percent of family finances. The majority of single adults in the United States are women. In 1970, 1 percent of business travelers were women; in 2005, 45 percent. The Internet supersource Jupiter tells us that women now account for 50 percent of Internet use.

Seven myths about women come to us courtesy of futurist Faith Popcorn:

- Myth 1: *You can market to women on product differentiation alone.* This isn't true, because women want a relationship. They'd rather buy dishwashing liquid from a company that sponsors after-school programs. Relationship innovation is more important to women than product innovation is.
- Myth 2: *Products are finite and self-contained.* Another myth. Marketers need to create a dialogue. Each communication needs to become two-way.
- Myth 3: *Women like to shop.* A report by the *Wall Street Journal* reveals that 60 percent of women feel that shopping is a negative experience.
- Myth 4: *Single-exposure advertising research is a useful guide to women's preferences.* Faith Popcorn says that it isn't possible to gauge an ad's ability to build a long-term relationship with only one isolated viewing.
- Myth 5: *Corporation policies are unimportant.* A company's values are inseparable from its marketing activities.
- Myth 6: *Service is the preserve of the service department.* Service is the ultimate marketing function. It is everybody's preserve — or else.
- Myth 7: *Women aren't entrepreneurial.* Women start companies at twice the rate of men and employ more people than the Fortune 500 combined.

Unfortunately, work brings stress. *Working Woman* magazine asked its readers to name the best cures for stress. The response indicated that in 61 percent of the cases, more money would do the trick; 56 percent, more time.

Ethnic groups are a potential lode of purchasing power. Asian Americans today number 10 million, many of whom are affluent, educated, and, happily for the guerrilla, have no brand loyalties — yet.

The Hispanic and Asian markets have a combined purchasing power of $216 billion, and they don't assimilate as they used to. They know that they don't have to if they don't want to. Changes in communication technology allow new arrivals to retain their cultural and linguistic identities and allow guerrillas to target these markets with extreme accuracy.

As a guerrilla, you ought to be aware of the buying power of the various races in the United States. In 2004, the white segment was the leader, with $8,600 billion. Next came blacks, with $7,077 billion; Asians, with $363 billion; multiracial, with $258 billion; and American Indian, with $47 billion. By 2008, the combined buying power of African Americans, Asian Americans, and Native Americans will exceed $1.5 trillion. Get to know them. Get them to know you. That's why I'm telling this to you.

Members of the nation's population born in foreign countries now account for more than 10 percent, a total of nearly 30 million people. This is a larger segment than at any time in the past five decades.

Although the Asian market segment is the smallest of the major ethnic groups, it is growing rapidly. Statistics prove that this segment's median household income is above average in the United States.

Guerrillas emphasize the values deemed traditionally important to Asians: *independence, leisure, and family unity as a means to achieve financial success and social status.* Guerrillas emphasize their product's or business's *stability.* Asian Americans are attracted to businesses that have credibility and experience. The Asian American market segments include the Chinese, Koreans, Japanese, Vietnamese, and Laotians.

To reach ethnic communities, consider placing ads in their newspapers, running spots on their cable TV channels, interacting with their online forums, becoming a presence in their online chat groups and conferences, experimenting with direct mail, sponsoring events aligned with the groups that are your target audiences, and linking to their Web sites if you can add value to them. Many ethnic groups rely on native-language media for their consumer information.

Some marketing honchos are terrified of ethnic markets, foreign cultures, and unfamiliar languages. Guerrillas accept that challenge, working with ethnic ad agencies. Specialized advertising agencies can help you gain access to and communicate with virtually any ethnic market. More firms with this type of specialization are springing up. Several advertising agencies specialize in serving the huge African American market. You can find more information about them through contacts, in your favorite search engines, and in publications such as *Adweek*.

Another bright and astonishingly fast-growing market is small business. Small business represents more than 90 percent of all business in America, and 24 percent of Americans consider themselves to be telecommuters. More than 40 million Americans work from home, according to IDC/Link, a marketing research firm. And the number of home-based businesses is growing by about 20 percent each year. In 1993, there were 12.4 million home-based companies. In 2005, that number exceeded 20 million.

The average worker from home is 40.2 years old, has a household income of $59,200, is white collar, and lives in or around a major metro area. An impressive 48 percent of home workers are college graduates, and 65 percent are married. What kind of work do they do at home? The most common careers of home workers are management consultant, financial adviser, technology consultant, graphic artist, sales rep, writer, wholesaler or retailer, marketing consultant, and Internet counselor.

Sound like a reasonable target market to you? It should, because technology is making it easier to succeed as a small business, to work at home, and to prosper as never before.

Clarifying Your Position

When you have clearly focused on your market or markets, you can clarify your market position. Then you should measure the position against four criteria: (1) Does it offer a benefit that my target audience really wants? (2) Is it an honest-to-goodness benefit? (3) Does it truly separate me from my competition? (4) Is it unique and/or difficult to copy?

Unless you are completely satisfied with your answers, continue searching for a proper position. When you've answered the questions to your own satisfaction, you'll have a sensible position — and that should lead you to your goal. An accurate market position requires clear, constructive goals and effort. Positioning is the key to marketing. No guerrilla would think of doing a speck of marketing without a proper marketing plan that includes a positioning statement.

Before writing your marketing plan, practice thinking big. At this time, your imagination is not a limiting factor, so open your mind to all the possibilities for your venture.

You may write your finished plan in ten pages. At first, though, try to state it in one paragraph — keeping in mind that it can be stated in seven words, as you've seen. But let's focus on the gold standard: the seven-sentence guerrilla marketing strategy.

The Seven-Sentence Guerrilla Marketing Strategy

Don't leave home without this. Leave home? Don't even go into business without this. Go into battle with neither offensive weapons nor armor, but don't go into business without a simple marketing plan. Guerrillas create strategies with seven simple sentences:

1. The purpose of the marketing — the physical action you want your prospect to take, such as clicking to a Web site, visiting your store, clipping a coupon, calling a toll-free number, looking for your product when shopping, taking a test drive, asking the doctor about your product.
2. How you'll achieve this purpose — your competitive advantage and benefits.
3. Your target market — or markets.
4. The marketing weapons you'll use.
5. Your niche and your position and what you stand for.
6. The identity of your business.
7. Your budget, which should be expressed as a percentage of your projected gross revenues. In 2006, the average U.S. business invested 4 percent of gross revenues in marketing.

How Did Freedom Press Do It?

Suppose that you call your business Freedom Press and intend to sell books about freelancing. Let your strategy start with the words:

> The purpose of Freedom Press marketing is to motivate people to order the book online or by mail so as to sell the maximum number of books at the lowest possible selling cost per book. This will be accomplished by positioning the books as being so valuable to freelancers that they are guaranteed to be worth more to the reader than their selling price. The target market will be people who are or plan to be engaged in freelance earning activities.

Next, the paragraph might say:

> The marketing tools we plan to use include classified advertising in maga-
> zines, newspapers, and online; direct mail; sales at seminars; publicity
> in newspapers and on radio and television; direct sales calls to book-
> stores; mail-order display ads in magazines; weekly postings on online bul-
> letin boards oriented to freelancers; e-mailings to known freelancers and a
> Web site linked to many others that serve freelancers. The niche that Free-
> dom Press occupies is a business that provides valuable information for
> freelancers. Our identity will be one of expertise, readability, and quick re-
> sponse to customer requests. Thirty percent of sales will be allocated to
> marketing.

That's a long paragraph. And it's a simplistic paragraph. But it does the
job. It's for a product rather than a service, for an earning venture that entails hardly any contact with the public. This mail-order venture requires
very little in the way of marketing, considering all the options. It works
beautifully in real life; it has worked for me since 1974.

The plan starts with the purpose of the marketing — that is, it starts with
the bottom line. Then it connects with the benefits that will beautify that
bottom line and with those who will contribute to that line — the target audience. The marketing tools are then listed. Next comes the positioning
statement, which explains what the product and company stand for — why
the offering has value and why it should be purchased. The identity (not the
image, which is phony compared with the honesty of an identity) comes
next. The cost of the marketing wraps it up.

Take a moment to understand clearly the crucial difference between an
image and an *identity*. *Image* implies something artificial, something that is
not genuine. *Identity* defines what your business is really about, your personality. You have one, you know. Let's just hope it's what you want it to be.
If you put it in writing, it's more likely to be what you want it to be.

A business owner gets together with his staff, and they develop an image,
which is defined by many dictionaries as "a façade." Their marketing plan
reflects the image they choose. However, if customers find that the business
isn't exactly what they expected, they will feel distrustful of the company.

Another business owner gets together with her staff, and they identify
their identity — they base it on truth. Their marketing reflects this identity.
People come in and see that the business is exactly what they expected.
They feel relaxed. They know they can trust this company.

Which of these two business owners is the guerrilla? What's better for
your company: a phony image or an honest identity? We both know the
right answers.

This is the marketing strategy of the company Tech-Know Academy:

> The goal of Tech-Know Academy marketing is to have members of our target market register online at our Web site, with a goal of filling 100 percent of the company's available time for computer education. This will be done by establishing the credentials of the educators, the location of the operation, and the equipment. The target market will be local businesspeople who can benefit from learning how to operate a computer. The marketing tools that will be used include a combination of e-mail, a Web site, personal letters, circulars, brochures, signs on off-line and online bulletin boards, a blog, classified ads in local newspapers, yellow page advertising, direct mail, advertising specialties, free seminars, sampling, and publicity in local newspapers, on radio, and on television. The company will be positioned as the prime source of one-on-one, guaranteed instruction in the operation of computers; positioning will be intensified by an online presence in the local community, office decor, employee attire, telephone manners, and location selection. Our company's identity will be a blend of professionalism, personal attention, and warm human regard for our students. Ten percent of sales will be allocated to marketing.

Most marketing plans, especially if they are reduced to one paragraph, seem deceptively simple. A complete business plan, which can run as short as five paragraphs — the marketing plan, the creative plan, the media plan, the financial plan, and the management plan — or as long as ten or even one hundred ten pages (not recommended), should serve as a *guide*. It need not spell out all the details.

The chairman and chief executive officer of the Coca-Cola Company recognized this need for simplicity when he said, "If I had to state our business plan in one sentence, it would be this: 'We are going to build on our marketing strength in order to achieve profitable growth in the decade ahead.'"

Naturally, the marketing plan identifies the market. It provides the framework for creating the advertising — as will be seen in the next chapter. The marketing plan specifies the media to be utilized, along with costs, as will be seen in Chapter 6. And that's all it really has to do. Of course, it can do more, such as specifying the color of the car driven by the chief executive. But it need not go that far.

A guerrilla marketing strategy is short because then, you will be forced to focus when you create the plan — and when you show it to your employees, fusion-marketing partners, suppliers, and other allies, it will not put them to sleep.

A business plan may require support documents, such as results of research, the overall competitive situation, financial projections, and other details. However, you shouldn't include these details in the marketing plan itself. Guerrilla marketing plans are brief. A good road map lists the name or number of the highway wherever appropriate, not wherever possible.

The marketing plan should be the essence of simplicity. When your employees read the plan, they should understand your goals immediately, because your strategy is clear and direct. The briefer your plan, the easier it will be to follow. Bolster it with as many support documents as you wish. But don't include support information in the plan itself. Leave the details for other documents.

Once you've given your plan the proper focus, you can expand it in those areas pertinent to your business. As you do so, remember that your main purpose is to obtain maximum profits. Profits are very different from sales. Anyone can achieve sales, but it takes a guerrilla to consistently turn honest profits. You'll turn profits if you clearly list all your goals — including timing, budgets for *all* business-related plans, and projections. Without projections, you won't have a measuring stick. Your expanded plan should first address your long-term vision, then your vision for the near future. A goal is a dream with a deadline.

Many expanded marketing plans include a situational analysis. This includes information about your key customers, your expected competition, and the possibilities, probabilities, and reality of the marketplace at the moment. As you analyze your situation, always keep your eye on your bottom line. Don't let business get in the way of the *purpose* of business. Be sure that your own efforts include working on your own business rather than simply the business it attracts. The means should not interfere with the end.

Computers now enable us to project results based on hypothetical instances. An expanded marketing plan or business plan may examine these what-if situations. It should have the framework for incorporating alternative courses of action based on contingencies. An expanded marketing plan can embrace lists of objectives, priorities, monitoring methods, problems, opportunities, and responsibilities. However, it is more of a luxury than a necessity. Many entrepreneurs get bogged down and datalogged with details to the point that the flame of their initial thrust grows dim. Huge corporations also get carried away with technology, and then they are distracted from their original dreams.

Whether it is brief or expanded, you should reexamine your marketing plan yearly. Your goal should be to maintain it. The conservative philosophy should apply: If it is not necessary to change, it is necessary not to change.

But whatever bells and whistles you have attached to your basic plan, whatever MBA documentation you have affixed to it, you must still know who you are, where you are going, and how you will get there. You must start with a bare-bones marketing plan, short and simple. The plans I include in this chapter will enable you to start and succeed. The first example is for a real company; the second is for a fictional company. These plans can be implemented by entrepreneurs who have a bent toward mail-order book marketing (you can write or buy the books) or computer education (you can do or delegate the teaching). Both follow a simple formula that can serve as the basis for virtually any venture. Best of all, both plans can be easily adapted to fit your business.

Such plans allow for some flexibility, but not a great deal. For example, Tech-Know Academy may run one magazine ad only once in one regional edition and run radio commercials every day of the year. The marketing plan would still be fulfilled.

A good marketing plan should not allow for too much flexibility. After all, the plan is created to be followed. If you want changes, make them *before* you write the plan. And never forget — especially when you first show the plan to your people — you must *commit* yourself to the plan. If you do, you're a leader. If you don't, you're a charlatan posing as a leader.

When you've positioned your business with a marketing plan, what do you do next? You develop a creative plan that explains what your marketing will say — what the message is. Finally, you should create a media plan that provides exact media details: costs, names of newspapers, TV stations or radio stations, dates and sizes of ads, frequency of advertising, advertising specialties to be used, contacts for obtaining free publicity, online marketing strategy, and the identity of your business.

You've established a marketing plan that describes how you'll promote your earning endeavor. You have a creative plan that dictates your message and your identity. You have a media plan that explains exactly where you'll spend your money. Now, if you put the rest of your earning act in order — the financial side, management, legal issues, accounting, the ability to offer a lot of quality in either your products or your services, the appropriate technology, and the right mental attitude — you can start earning money.

Guerrillas begin at this point, but they sometimes get cold feet when they see the early results and then halt the marketing campaign so they can think things over. *This is not a good idea.* If after starting a business and launching a marketing program — which entails investing serious cash in promoting the business (serious being between $100 per month and $1,000,000 per month) — you decide to halt your marketing plan, immediately read the following list of reasons why you *should* continue to market.

1. *The market is continually changing.* New families, new prospects, and new lifestyles change the marketplace. One in five Americans moves each year. One-third of all Americans in their twenties move each year. The average American moves eleven times in a lifetime. Nearly 6 million Americans get married each year. If you stop marketing, you miss evolving opportunities, and you are no longer part of the process — you aren't even in the game.

2. *People forget quickly.* Each and every day, Americans are bombarded with approximately 4,700 advertisements and marketing messages, though I read one study that put the number closer to 30,000. In one study, a specific commercial was shown on TV once a week for thirteen weeks. After the thirteen weeks, 63 percent of the people surveyed remembered the spot. One month later, 32 percent recalled it. Two weeks after that, 21 percent remembered it. This means that 79 percent forgot the commercial after six weeks.

3. *Your competition won't quit.* People spend money to make purchases; if you don't make people aware that you are selling something, they'll spend their money elsewhere.

4. *Marketing strengthens your identity.* If you halt your marketing program, you shortchange your reputation and reliability, and your customers will lose confidence in you. When economic conditions turn sour, smart companies continue to market. The bond of communication is too precious to break capriciously.

5. *Marketing is essential to survival and growth.* With very few exceptions, people won't know that your business exists unless you get the word out. And when you cease marketing, you're on the path to non-existence. Just as you can't start a business without marketing, you can't maintain one without it.

6. *Marketing enables you to keep your customers.* Many enterprises survive on repeat and referral business. Loyal customers are the key to both. When your customers cease to hear from you or about you, they tend to forget you.

7. *Marketing maintains morale.* Your morale improves when you see your marketing at work, and your employees' morale is similarly uplifted. Also, some customers who actively follow your advertising may see your lack of marketing as a signal of failure.

8. *Your marketing program gives you an advantage over competitors who have ceased to market.* A troubled economy can offer a superb advantage to a marketing-minded entrepreneur. If your competitors stop

marketing, you can pull ahead of them and attract some of their customers. In ugly economic situations, there are always winners and losers.

9. *Marketing allows your business to continue operating.* You still have some overhead: telephone bills, yellow page ads, Internet access, rent and/or equipment cost, and possibly a payroll. Marketing creates the air that overhead breathes.

10. *You stand to lose out on the money, time, and effort you've invested.* If you halt your marketing, you lose all the money you invested for ads, commercials, and advertising time and space. Also, you lose consumer awareness. Sure, you can buy it again, but you'll have to start from scratch. Unless you're planning to go out of business, it is rarely a good idea to cease marketing completely.

Consider this: If you put an end to your marketing program, will you save money? You will in the way that stopping your wristwatch saves time. In other words, don't kid yourself.

I'll tell you this one more time because so many confused marketers continue to forget it: Keep your commitment to your marketing program. That's like reminding you to love your spouse. Consider your marketing investment mandatory and automatic, like rent or paying the mortgage. A marketing plan is necessary — in fact, crucial — for a company or an entrepreneur. However, the plan is like a fancy, comfortable, powerful, great-looking car without gas. The fuel that powers your vehicle is the marketing itself: what it says and how it looks. The creative process comes into play in marketing, and it must be used with style and power. There are ways to make the creative juices flow. I'll let you in on the secrets in the following pages.

5

Developing Truly Creative Marketing

Guerrillas have only one definition of creativity in marketing: something that generates profits for their business. Big profits? Very creative. No profits? Not creative. Creativity in marketing has everything to do with profitability and nothing to do with awards and compliments.

It's true that the most enjoyable aspect of the marketing process is usually the creativity that's involved. And if you want to make your small business big, you should realize that creativity applies to every aspect of the process. But let's begin by looking into how you can make your marketing itself creative. Then we'll explore how you can be creative in media selection, marketing planning, and public relations.

Almost any marketing person worth his or her salt will tell you that *marketing is not creative unless it sells the offering*. You can be fairly certain that you will have creative marketing if you first devise a *creative strategy*. Such a strategy is similar to a marketing plan but is limited to marketing materials only — and directed solely at their content.

If you think that there's a simple formula for establishing such a strategy, you're absolutely right. Here, in the simplest terms possible, is a typical three-sentence guerrilla creative strategy covering the purpose of the creative message, the benefits to be stressed to accomplish the purpose, and the personality of the brand.

> The purpose of Kid-a-Licious breakfast cereal marketing will be to convince our target audience — mothers of children twelve years of age and younger — that Kid-a-Licious breakfast cereal is the most nutritious and

healthful boxed cereal on the market. This will be accomplished by listing the vitamins and minerals in each serving of the cereal. The mood and tone of the advertising will be upbeat, natural, honest, and warm.

See if you can determine which product this creative strategy may be for.

The purpose of _____ battery advertising will be to convince our target audience — primarily males eighteen to fifty-four — that _____ batteries last an inordinately long time. This will be accomplished by creating a bunny that marches on and on through the years, powered by an _____ battery. The mood and tone of the advertising will be humorous and single-minded, to embed the idea of the battery's durability, while making the TV commercials fun to watch.

When you create your marketing program, your first step is to write a simple creative strategy, such as Eveready's Energizer may have done to focus on durability. Practice first by writing creative strategies for current advertisers. Pick a newspaper advertiser, a television advertiser, a Web site, and a direct-mail advertiser; then compose three-sentence creative strategies that apply to each of them. Do the same for your competitors. This will guide you in establishing your own positioning and prevent you from imitating other marketing campaigns.

After you've devised your strategy — one to which you've devoted much time and thought — you can embark on a seven-step program to assure yourself of successful marketing. Let's check all seven steps.

1. *Find the inherent drama within your offering.* After all, you plan to make money by selling a product or a service or both. The reasons people will want to buy from you should give you a clue as to the inherent drama in your product or service. Something about your offering must be inherently interesting; otherwise, you won't sell it. In Kid-a-Licious breakfast cereal, it's the high concentration of vitamins and minerals.

2. *Translate that inherent drama into a meaningful benefit.* Always remember that people buy benefits, not features. People do not buy shampoo; people buy great-looking or clean or manageable hair. People do not buy cars; people buy speed, status, style, economy, performance, and power. Mothers of young kids do not buy cereal; they buy nutrition, though many will buy anything that they can get their kids to *eat*. Find the major benefit of your offering and write it down. It should come directly from the inherently dramatic feature. And even

though you have four or five benefits, stick with one or two — three at most.

3. *State your benefits in as believable a way as possible.* There is a world of difference between honesty and believability. You can be 100 percent honest (as you should be), and people still might not believe you. You must break the barrier that advertising has erected by its tendency toward exaggeration and state your benefit in such a way that it will be accepted beyond doubt. The company producing Kid-a-Licious breakfast cereal might say, "A bowl of Kid-a-Licious breakfast cereal provides your child with almost as many vitamins as a multivitamin pill." This statement begins with the inherent drama and turns it into a benefit. The word *almost* lends believability.

4. *Get people's attention.* People do not pay attention to advertising; they pay attention only to things that interest them. Sometimes, people find those things in advertising. Therefore, you must grab the attention of potential customers and spark their interest. Be sure you interest them in your product or service, not just your advertising. I'm sure you're familiar with advertising that you remember for a product you do not remember. Many advertisers are guilty of creating advertising that's more interesting than whatever it is they are advertising. You can prevent yourself from falling into that trap by memorizing this: *Forget the ad. Is the product or service interesting?* The Kid-a-Licious company might create an interesting image by showing a picture of two hands breaking open a multivitamin capsule from which pour flakes that fall into an appetizing-looking bowl of cereal. In the background, a kid licks his lips in anticipation.

5. *Motivate your audience to get involved.* Tell your audience to visit the store, make a phone call, fill in a coupon, write for more information, ask for your product by name, visit your Web site, or come in for a free demonstration. Don't stop short. To make guerrilla marketing work, you must tell people exactly what you want them to do.

6. *Be sure you are communicating clearly.* You know what you're talking about, but do your readers or listeners? Recognize that people aren't thinking about your business and that they'll give only about half their attention to your ad — even when they are paying attention. Knock yourself out when putting your message across. The Kid-a-Licious company might show its ad to ten people and ask them what the main point is. If one person misunderstands, 10 percent of the audience will misunderstand. And if the ad goes out to 500,000 people, 50,000 will miss the main point. That's unacceptable. You want 100 percent of the audience to understand the main point. The company might accomplish this by stating in a headline or subhead, "Giving your kids Kid-a-Licious breakfast cereal is like giving your kids vitamins — only tastier." Zero ambiguity is your goal.

7. *Measure your finished advertisement, commercial, letter, Web site, and/or brochure against your creative strategy.* The strategy is your blueprint. If your marketing fails to fulfill the strategy, it's a lousy ad, no matter how much you love it. Scrap it and start again. Always use your creative strategy to guide you, to give you hints as to the content of your ad. If your ad is in line with your strategy, you may then judge its other elements.

The key to creative marketing is a smart creative strategy. The test of creative marketing is profits. If what you want to sell doesn't generate profits for your business, you are not truly being creative. Your creative challenge is not over. Creativity doesn't end with the creation of your marketing.

Once you've established your marketing weapons — in the form of your Web site, the wording of your e-mail, ads, commercials, blog, signs, circulars, and/or store decor — you must be creative in the way you use them. I know of a deodorant company that introduced its product via TV advertising during the winter. Why advertise in the winter, when people aren't buying as much deodorant? Because this company lacked the funds to go head to head with the big guys. Instead of vying for public attention during the summer, when its competition would be fierce, the company advertised its product and attracted attention when it had the stage to itself, during the winter.

There are other ways to be creative. Have your personal letters hand delivered, or send them via Express Mail, Federal Express, or via an out-of-the-ordinary delivery service. Canvass creatively by wearing a unique outfit and handing a small gift to each prospect. Put your signs in unusual places, such as in the hands of paid picketers (this is a unique but real marketing vehicle). In the yellow pages, you can be creative with the size of your ad and its message, color, and graphic treatment. Be creative in the use of newspaper advertising by running six small ads in one issue rather than one large one. Be creative in your e-mail and on your Web site. If your advertisements generate profits for your company, you're succeeding at being creative. If not, you've got more work to do.

As you can see, there are limitless ways to exercise creativity in all facets of marketing. In one of my earlier books, *Earning Money Without a Job*, I wrote about a couple who got married in their boutique after they informed the local newspapers and TV station about the wedding. Naturally, they received a lot of free coverage.

A former boss and idol of mine, the late Leo Burnett, used to remind his staff that a person can be creative by coming downstairs with socks in his or her mouth — but what's the point? There must be a reason for your creativity, and your creativity should never detract from your message. The Budweiser Clydesdales ad campaign is both creative and directed squarely at the target audience. Such well-directed creativity is difficult to find, to develop, and to compete against. That's why guerrillas place great emphasis on *creativity with a point to it.*

When practicing guerrilla marketing, you must be more creative than your competition in every aspect of marketing. Be sure that you create your marketing plan properly, intelligently, clearly, creatively, and consistently. Then you can assure yourself that you are successfully marketing your product or service. You don't have to know how to write or draw to be creative. All you have to do is supply the creative idea. That's the ticket right there: *the idea.* You can always hire someone to write or draw for you, but it's not easy to hire someone to be creative about your business for you. That task should fall to you. And you should revel in it. Let's look at a few examples of creativity in action.

- A CPA wanted to create more business, so he wrote a tax newsletter and sent it every three months, free of charge, to a long list of prospects. By doing so, he established himself as an authority and dramatically improved his business. This isn't an earthshaking act of creativity, but it was an extremely successful plan.
- A waterbed retail store wanted to cast off its counterculture identity, so it relocated to an elegant shopping center, required its staff to dress impeccably, and hired a man with a strong, intelligent voice to serve as the announcer on its radio commercials. The results were excellent.
- A jeweler wanted to attract attention to his business during the holiday season, so he invented outlandishly expensive gift ideas, such as a Frisbee with a diamond in the center. Price: $5,000. Another was a miniature hourglass that used real diamonds instead of sand. Price: $10,000. Another was a jewel-encrusted backgammon set with a price tag of $50,000. The jeweler rarely sold such items, but he attracted national publicity, and his holiday sales soared.
- An attorney wanted to establish warm relationships with his clients, so he made it a point to walk with them from his office to the elevator, take the elevator twenty-three stories down to the lobby with them,

then walk with his clients to their car or the public transportation that would take them to their next destination.

Note that in none of these examples did I talk about the creativity one usually associates with ads themselves. That's the obvious place to be creative. But these examples describe how to be creative in your prospecting, store decor, employee attire, and methods of gaining free publicity. Train yourself to think that the opposite of creativity is mediocrity, and you'll force yourself to use marketing tools in the most creative manner possible. In Chapter 11, on e-media, you'll read of a promising and provocative new technology called RSS — Real Simple Syndication. Is it a creative technology? Only if you make it so. It's all up to you. RSS doesn't care. Neither does a Ferrari.

Where does creativity come from? I was once invited to Geneva, Switzerland, by Nestlé if I could tell the company where creativity comes from. I asked all my creative friends and contacts that same question. Each had the same answer. It comes from knowledge. I realized, then spoke about, and tell you now: *Creativity comes from knowledge.* You must have knowledge of your own product or service, your competition, your target audience, your marketing area, the economy, current events, and the trends of the time. With this knowledge, you'll have what it takes to develop a creative marketing program, *and* you'll produce creative marketing materials.

I gain knowledge by keeping abreast of world events in the usual manner. I read one daily news site online, and I receive breaking-news dispatches all day from two sources, one weekly newsmagazine, two industry-specific e-zines, and ten monthly special-interest magazines. I watch a headline news show each morning on the tube and often watch the late TV news. And a handful of talk shows. And another handful of top-twenty TV series. I read one daily newspaper. I read five newsletters weekly. I also surf the Net for about an hour a month. And I'm always just starting, in the middle of, or finishing reading a book — fiction and nonfiction. I also get off on fare from the Game Show Channel and Court TV. Okay, okay, *Survivor* and *American Idol*, too. And every White Sox game I can catch. But my TV education and guilty pleasures aren't enough for an aggressive business owner.

Guerrillas should be attuned to world happenings, the world situation, the local situation, and up-to-the-minute trends. It's important to take a look at competitors' marketing campaigns. If you're not keeping up, you're falling behind. Guerrillas can't afford to fall behind.

Armed with this knowledge, you can do what many people define as the essence of creativity: You can combine two or more elements that haven't ever been combined. For instance, when it wanted to boost its sales up there with Coca-Cola and Pepsi Cola, 7UP referred to itself as "the Uncola." This put it in the category of the colas yet proudly proclaimed that it was different. By combining the prefix *un*, which means *not*, with the word *cola*, 7UP exercised great creativity. The advertising person who dreamed up the concept used his knowledge of popular art and chose psychedelic art for print and television advertisements. By using its knowledge of its product, competition, target audience, current users, and the trends of the day, 7UP produced an exceptionally creative advertising campaign. The proof of that creativity was in the increased sales and profits enjoyed by 7UP. And the seed was basic knowledge.

The Marlboro cigarette company exercised creativity when it combined the ideas of a cowboy and a cigarette. The AT&T telephone company used creativity when it combined the ideas of an emotionally charged situation and a telephone ("Reach out and touch someone"). Avis Rent-a-Car showed creativity when it capitalized on being the second-largest, rather than the largest, car rental company, and flatly stated, "We try harder." In truth, Avis was the third-largest, trailing Hertz and National, but "second-largest" sounded more appealing. Microsoft showed creativity in TV commercials that demonstrated many of the business and personal capabilities of owning a computer and its effect on people, starting when they were kids. Nike, in aiming to be a global leader, established its name not with words but with a simple line it calls a "swoosh," creatively crossing all language barriers. In all these cases, creativity started with plain and simple knowledge.

It's not only in mass-media marketing that you can exert creativity. When customers of Crystal Fresh Bottled Water request to have the water delivered, they receive a thank-you note signed by Jeanette, Lee, Joyce, Diane, Jered, Nancy, Chet, Tim, Walt, Raye, Shelly, and Dan. Customers probably mention this to several of their friends and neighbors. The guerrilla style of creativity takes time, energy, imagination, and information. But you can see that it doesn't have to take much money.

As a guerrilla, you are obligated to become knowledgeable about a broad range of topics. Guerrillas are generalists, not specialists. Guerrillas know that to remove the mystique from the creative process, they must *think backward*. They start by picturing the mind of their customer *at the moment that customer makes a decision to purchase*. What led to that decision? What were the thought processes? What made them take place? What were the customer's buttons, and what did you do to push them? Thinking backward takes you to the needs and desires that are crucial to motivation.

But if you're to be creative and successful, it also makes sense to *think forward.* Get the prospects to visualize life after they have made the purchase you want them to make. Convince them to sense the feeling they'll have once they have made that investment. The ability to do that separates the guerrillas from the monkeys.

Let's take a moment to examine marketing in the light of psychology. *Skinnerian marketing* dictates that the customer modifies his or her behavior — this kind of marketing says, shows, or does something that causes a customer to change his or her behavior (so as to act in the way you want that customer to act). You gently nudge the customer to buy, click to a site, call, visit, compare, clip a coupon, follow your command by a certain date, usually right around the corner.

Freudian marketing is addressed to the subconscious — the most powerful part of a person's mind. *Skinnerian marketing* is addressed to the conscious — less powerful but more easily activated.

Guerrilla marketing is addressed to the conscious *and* the subconscious. It changes attitudes while modifying behavior. It comes at the customer from all directions. It persuades, coerces, tempts, compels, romances, and orders the customer to do your bidding. It leaves little to chance. Although people associate creativity with a free and unbridled spirit, it is the essence of precise planning.

As technology evens the playing fields in all the marketing arenas, guerrilla marketers understand their role in the community and are creative in filling it. I quote from a very successful ice cream company's brochure: "At Ben and Jerry's, we're as concerned about our responsibility to the community, both local and global, as we are about making great ice cream." Then they prove their devotion to humanity by sponsoring altruistic causes, such as the Children's Defense Fund, voter registration, peace on Earth, saving rain forests, less military spending, and more recycling. Ben and Jerry sponsor concerts to spread the word — not about their ice cream as much as about their desire to save the planet. Ben and Jerry say, "Business has the responsibility to give back to the community." This is their creative platform. It sells sanity. It sells honesty. It sells nobility. It sells ice cream.

In the 1950s, this creative platform would have been considered crazy. In the first decade of the twenty-first century, it's considered brilliant marketing as well as humanitarian.

Ben and Jerry's is famous for its good deeds. But what about Sears? Sears is pushing for recycling these days. And so are Safeway, Bank of America, Coca-Cola, American Airlines, 3M, Anheuser-Busch, DuPont, UPS, and guerrilla marketers across the nation whose businesses are not yet famous. A valid creative strategy today is to back a noble cause.

Apparel maker Liz Claiborne ran ads aimed at helping victims of domestic violence. Patagonia, the outdoor clothing company, promotes environmental awareness. Esprit, the clothing maker, urges people to vote. Well over a billion dollars yearly are spent on cause-related marketing. This includes such causes as AIDS, breast cancer, multiple sclerosis, domestic violence, healthy eating, and helping the homeless. Corporate philanthropy dawned years ago — in the mid 1980s, American Express promoted restoration of the Statue of Liberty.

Are creative strategies based on noble causes successful? In one survey, 83 percent of shoppers said that based solely on environmental concerns, they had changed brands, and 80 percent of shoppers said that a company's environmental reputation is important. Consumers even said that they'd pay a premium for "green" products.

Along with this public and corporate conscientiousness, we see a strong move toward products stamped "Made in the USA," primarily among women and older consumers on the East Coast and in the Midwest. Consumers aged eighteen to thirty-five are not as influenced by it, having grown up with foreign-made products in their homes.

Retailers report that "Made in America" promotions of apparel made domestically increase sales from 25 percent to 50 percent. These are numbers to be taken seriously. And so should cause-related marketing.

A word of caution: Be wary about basing your creative strategy on rapid societal changes that are more anecdotal than factual. The guerrilla is alert but knows the difference between a real change and a media-perceived change.

"What should I talk about?" That's probably the most intelligent question a guerrilla can ask. Pay close attention as I reveal the answer: *Talk about the feelings that the prospect will experience after owning what you are selling.*

Can marketing really be that simple? It can if you don't make it complicated. Guerrillas adapt their marketing, creative message, and entire philosophy to the realities of the times. Instead of fighting change, they adapt to it. And their profitability attests to the wisdom of this attitude.

The goal of their creative message is not marketing that causes people to say, "That was incredibly creative!" but marketing that causes people to say, "I want that product!"

6

Selecting the Most Lethal
Marketing Methods

If you are conscientious, you can create a brilliant creative strategy and promote a noble cause. However, there are many ways you can go wrong; one is to run the right advertising in the wrong media. How do you tell the right from the wrong? Every method of marketing has its own particular strength. Radio, along with telephone marketing and the Internet, is one of most *intimate* of the media, allowing you to spend chunks of time in one-on-one situations with your audience. Sometimes, the listeners will be in crowded restaurants. But other times, they'll be in their cars or in their homes — alone. Ranking just as high or higher in the intimacy department is the Internet because of its built-in interactivity, chances for feedback, immediacy, and cozy chat sessions.

The newspaper is a prime medium for disseminating the *news*. And that strength can become your strength. Advertising in the newspaper, other than in the classified section, should be newsy, interruptive, and to the point.

Magazines are a medium with which readers become involved; this medium bestows on you the greatest credibility. Whether they buy individual newsstand copies or subscribe, readers take a good, long time to read them. In your magazine ad, you can attempt to capture the editorial "mood" of the magazine. You can put forth more information because readers will be willing to take more time reading a magazine ad than a newspaper ad. The credibility of the magazine becomes partly linked to you.

Television is the most comprehensive medium: It enables you to convince your prospects by means of *demonstrations*. Demonstrations — powerful selling devices — are not possible by any other means except seminars, fairs, stores, digital brochures, flash video on Web sites, and live contact with audiences. Television allows you to combine words with pictures and music and to get into the minds of your potential customers. It is a *visual* medium. In fact, because so many viewers mute the commercials with their remote controls, advertisers must tell the story visually; otherwise, they're not telling their story at all and therefore not selling their products. Television advertising can also be very costly, so it must be done properly. This is not a medium in which to dabble.

Cable and satellite TV have put the medium within the reach of all advertisers. To a guerrilla, this is glorious news. A prime-time TV spot for under $20? It wasn't possible in the twentieth century. Today, it is. And many a small business is becoming a big business as a result. Think of advertising on cable and satellite TV as an invitation to give serious consideration to what some describe as "the undisputed heavyweight champion of marketing."

Direct mail, which includes e-mail, allows you to take *the most careful aim* at your target audience. Created skillfully, direct-mail advertising enables you to go through the entire selling process — from securing your prospects' attention to obtaining sales by means of coupons the prospects can complete and toll-free phone numbers they can call. Like TV, direct mail can be very costly when misused, especially as postage rates continue to rise and the number of mailed pieces increases. To a guerrilla, postage rates aren't as important as response rates. If it costs twice as much postage to get three times the response, only a nitwit would save on postage rates. Also, guerrillas know that they should follow their direct-mail campaign with follow-up mailings, ultraselective targeting, telemarketing, and unique mailing packages. Don't ever forget what I said about direct mail providing you with that precision aim.

Although canvassing takes more time than any other marketing method, it is highly effective. There are few limitations, and it provides *personal contact*. It will often be difficult to manage canvassing on your own, so you may want to delegate the job to a professional salesperson or a college or high school student, depending on the complexity of your sales presentation. Canvassing should be backed by mass-marketing methods.

Outdoor signs and billboards, superb at *reminding* people of your existence and your reason for being, aren't successful as a sole means of marketing except in rare instances. However, they work well in combination with other marketing methods. Indoor signs are a different matter altogether because they generate impulse reactions exactly where they ought to — at the place of purchase, where 77 percent of purchase decisions are made. Worded and designed successfully, indoor signs *capitalize on the momentum generated by your other means of marketing.* Leo Burnett, founder of one of the best ad agencies in the world, always reminded us to "plan the sale when you plan the ad." He loved the immense power of indoor signs. They should be designed to pick up where your other ads leave off. An indoor sign might be a video message, a hologram, or a moving sign. Don't limit your advertising areas to your own inside premises; the inside of many other premises will work very well. If your prospects are there, you too should try to be there. Consider airports, hotel lobbies, club bulletin boards, and stores owned by people with whom you've established tie-in arrangements.

Online marketing presents guerrillas with the marketing medium of their dreams — where the golden opportunity is *interactivity* blended with action, connectivity, targetability, community, and economy — if they go about things in the proper manner. Online guerrilla marketing, which is the true 40-trillion-pound gorilla if you learn how to tame it, encompasses e-mail, postings on bulletin boards of special-interest groups, audio postcards, video postcards, chat rooms, forum boards, blogs, and Web sites. The great strengths of the online medium are the interactivity I mentioned, as well as involvement and the ability to provide as many details as your prospect wants. Do not think of your site as a *thing*, as you'd think of a TV spot, but instead as a *session*, because people visit you and stay as long as they wish. And then they leave. Will they ever return? That depends on the nature of your content and how quickly you reciprocate. For successful online marketing, you must equally emphasize eight elements: planning, content, design, involvement, production, follow-up, promotion, and maintenance. Regardless of the techno bells and whistles that Silicon Valley and its brethren dream up, the keys to online success are·the list to which you send e-mail, the content of your site, the speed of your response, the freshness of your data, and the personalization of your message. Brevity is paramount if you're to lead people to your Web site, where brevity is a bad idea. As soon as you go online, promote your site off line. In cyberspace, people come to you and then leave their names. Guerrillas use those names!

Remember this: In golf, the name of the game is putting. In baseball, it's pitching. In basketball, it's defense. And in Internet marketing, it's the quality and quantity of your mailing list.

Yellow pages marketing and classified advertisements hit the *very hottest* of prospects. People who use these sources are searching for the kind of information you're offering, so you don't have to expend much energy to get their attention or to sell the general benefits of your product or service. Your headline can gain or lose profits for you. Create yours with a lot of careful thought. This advertising also places you in direct confrontation with your competition, which should inspire you to be more precise with your message.

Brochures offer the greatest opportunity to go into detail about your product or service. People expect a lot of information from a brochure, and you should feel encouraged to provide it — you can be very informative. With the right software, it's easier and less expensive to design and produce a compelling brochure. If you have a brochure, you should have a Web site on which to provide and display your brochure.

Telephone marketing provides opportunities to be more intimate than you can be in radio advertising and also offers you *great flexibility*. But keep abreast of the law! Don't call people who have signed up to be on the Do Not Call list, or you'll be in serious trouble. Since its inception in 2003, more than 60 million people have added their names to that list.

Your telephone marketing campaign can be supplemented by direct mail or any other marketing method, or it can stand alone. You might even consider a postcard mailing asking people to opt in to a phone call from you, letting you know the best day and time to call. A telephone campaign can change a person who is apathetic about your product or service into someone who is prepared to purchase.

And you can take orders if your prospects have credit cards. As a guerrilla, take credit cards — all of them. If folks have reached their limit on Visa and MasterCard, take American Express, Discover, Carte Blanche, and Diners Club. Make it as easy as possible for customers to pay by accepting PayPal, an online wire transfer used by eBay and many other wise e-merchants. This may seem mercenary, but you are offering *convenience* to your prospects, and they will appreciate the fact that you make it easy for them to buy from you. It's always a good idea to offer autopayment and autorenewal plans if people might buy your product or service on a repetitive basis. Their credit cards are automatically charged each month, simplifying life for both of you. You might offer a discount to people who sign up for this service.

Tiny signs on bulletin boards serve to make you part of *the community*, and they heighten people's confidence in you. They are also extremely inexpensive, and if your product or service meets unfulfilled needs, these signs often prove to be the most fruitful of marketing methods. As do yellow page and classified ads, signs on bulletin boards tend to attract serious browsers. This is not the case with, for example, television advertising.

Advertising specialties, such as T-shirts, pens, calendars, mousepads, and baseball caps, work like billboards and signs to *remind* people of your existence. They won't perform the entire selling job, but they can pave the way to acceptance of your offering when used in conjunction with other marketing vehicles. The same goes for the sponsorship of teams and events.

Marketing at trade shows and exhibits gives many businesses a terrific shot in the sales curve. They find the opportunity there to *make contacts with purchase-minded people* who are thinking about the primary topic of the show or exhibit. It is highly advantageous to reach people who have this mindset. Fewer barriers prevent completed sales. Some companies and entrepreneurs get all the business they need by this one method of marketing. If you fall into this category, your life will be simpler.

Public relations, which encompasses community relations, publicity, and memberships in clubs and organizations, is a marketing method that should be seriously considered for the credibility it gives you. Many people take ads with a grain of salt but take PR as gospel. Public relations works well with virtually all other methods, and it is often the key to success. Publicity adds a great deal to your *credibility* and, at worst, puts your name in the public eye. Guerrillas, however, do not buy into the saying, "Even bad publicity is good publicity as long as they spell your name right." Bad publicity is harmful to your company and your goals. Avoid it at all costs.

By becoming involved in community relations — service to your community — you make powerful contacts, especially if you work your tail off for the community (and not merely to serve your business needs). You can better prove your conscientiousness with your *deeds* than you can with your words. When potential customers learn that you're working for the community on an unpaid basis, they'll assume that you work twice as hard for your business. This, naturally, attracts them to you. If you join clubs and organizations, you'll be in contact with people who can help you. It seems somewhat self-serving to join with this purpose in mind, but many do. And it serves their purposes well. A subtle point: *Guerrillas are aggressive in their marketing, but they are never crass.*

With limitless marketing weapons available to you, and one hundred of the finest examined in juicy detail in this book, which weapons do you, as a guerrilla, choose? *Choose as many as you can do well. The process of guerrilla marketing begins by (1) being aware of all the marketing weapons available; (2) launching many of them, keeping careful track of which are failing and which are working wonders; and then (3) eliminating those that miss the target and doubling those that hit the bull's-eye.*

Once you've selected the marketing vehicles that can propel you to your goal, be sure you use them in an orderly, logical manner. This can best be accomplished by using a *marketing calendar* to help make all the elements in your program mesh. It enables you to plan your budget and to avoid unforeseen expenditures. It prevents you from engaging in hit-or-miss marketing, protects you from marketing lapses, precludes surprises, and aids enormously in planning, buying, and staffing. Clients who operate from one report that it is their most precious business asset. They tell me it's akin to getting into heaven without the inconvenience of dying.

Guerrilla marketing calendars address themselves to the weeks of the year, the marketing vehicles that you'll use during those weeks, the specific online promotions or off-line events in which you will be engaged, the length of each promotion, fusion-marketing promotions, and, when applicable, any co-op funds that will be available from manufacturers to help pay the tab for all your activity or even some of it. In addition, some calendars include the cost of the marketing for each promotion.

Armed with a marketing calendar, as all guerrillas should be, you can see into the future. The marketing process will come into clearer focus for you. And you will find it considerably simpler to be committed to your marketing program, to see it as the investment it is, and to appreciate its consistency.

A guerrilla makes use of as many marketing vehicles as he or she can implement effectively. A marketing calendar indicates whether you can use these methods properly, because it forces you to come to terms with the costs and realities of the media you select.

Let's examine the marketing calendar on page 64. Note that this calendar runs fifty-two weeks. By looking at the calendar, the owner of this small retail store can infer which ads are best to run, which products should be in inventory, what costs to project, and what sales to plan.

The calendar projects the use of the *Chronicle* every single week but staggers the monthly use of the *Sun*, the *News*, the *Independent-Journal*, and the *Gazette*. It also allows for a testing of the *Times* and the *Reporter*. This seems like a lot of newspapers, but it is clear that the *Chronicle* will be the marketing flagship.

The lengths of the marketing activities vary from one to five weeks, with a healthy balance of long, short, and medium-length events; this prevents the marketing from being too predictable. Radio is used but not every week. With such a calendar, Electronic Alley is following a well-conceived plan. Promotions and sales are balanced.

Do not use a marketing vehicle unless you are going to use it like a pro. You must put time, energy, money, talent, and the results of your uncanny knowledge into it. This means that you should select marketing tools that are compatible with your business. All the compatible marketing methods that you can possibly use with skill, and on a regular basis, should be put to work for you. In Chapter 4, we saw that the entrepreneur named Tech-Know Academy committed to using fifteen methods of marketing — and that didn't include decor, attire, and location. Tech-Know Academy has the option of being a single individual or a multiemployee company, yet its marketing plan calls for the use of personal letters, circulars, brochures, webinars, teleseminars, a content-laden Web site with unique and congruent information, signs on bulletin boards, classified ads in local newspapers, display ads in local newspapers, magazine advertising, radio advertising, direct-mail advertising, advertising specialties, free seminars, sampling, online classified ads, and publicity in newspapers, on radio, and on television. Sounds like this is going to cost Tech-Know Academy a huge sum of money. It won't. You don't have to spend a bundle to market like a guerrilla — in fact, you may be doing it wrong if you do spend too much money. Mind you, you won't get all that marketing for free. You'll have to invest. However, it's possible to engage in a large number of marketing methods and save money with each.

Begin the process of selecting marketing methods by identifying your target audience. Just as it's better to know something about your spouse than everything about marriage, the better you understand your prospects, the easier it will be to attain accuracy with your marketing plans.

ELECTRONIC ALLEY MARKETING CALENDAR

Weeks of	Marketing Thrust	Number of Weeks	Co-opable	Radio	Newspapers	Cost per Promotion
9/13	Giant Screen TV	1	Yes	Yes	Chron/Sun	$726
9/20–10/4	New Plasma TV	3	Yes	Yes-2	Chron/News	$1,860
10/11–10/18	Video Experience	2	No	No	Chron/IJ	$998
10/25–11/15	Names to Drop	4	Yes	Yes-2	Chron/Gaz	$2,697
11/22	Thanksgiving Sale	1	Yes	Yes	Chron/Sun	$708
11/29	DVR Promotion	1	Yes	No	Chron/News	$750
12/6–12/20	Xmas Promotion	3	Yes	Yes	Chron/IJ	$2,309
12/27	Last Week to Save	1	Yes	Yes	Chron/Gaz	$744
1/3–1/17	TV Rut	3	No	No	Chron/Sun	$1,494
1/24–2/7	Trade-in Time	2	No	No	Chron/News	$1,200
2/14–2/21	iPOD & MP3 Gear	2	Yes	Yes	Chron/IJ	$2,484
2/28–3/28	Solve TV Problems	5	No	Yes-2	Chron/Gaz	$3,555
4/4–4/18	High Definition TV	3	Yes	Yes-2	Chron/Times	$2,444
4/25–5/2	Surround Sound	2	No	No	Chron/News	$1,200

Weeks of	Marketing Thrust	Number of Weeks	Co-opable	Radio	Newspapers	Cost per Promotion
5/9–5/16	Home Theatres	2	Yes	No	Chron/IJ	$1,184
5/23	Memorial Day Sale	1	Yes	Yes	Chron/Gaz	$831
5/30–6/13	Credit Is Easy	3	No	Yes-1	Chron/Sun	$2,025
6/20–6/27	DVRs Promotion	2	Yes	No	Chron/Rep	$1,276
7/4–7/11	Video Experience	2	No	No	Chron/IJ	$1,284
7/18–7/25	Gaming Chairs	2	No	Yes	Chron/Gaz	$1,522
8/1–8/8	Free Home Demo	2	No	No	Chron/Sun	$630
8/15–8/29	Giant Screen TV	3	Yes	Yes-2	Chron/News	$2,550
9/5	Satellite TV	1	No	No	Chron/IJ	$592
9/12	Game Machines	1	No	No	Chron/Gaz	$951

Kids don't read newspapers. Teenage girls rarely read business magazines but do listen to certain radio stations. Adult males rarely subscribe to *True Romance*. Those are the realities of the marketplace, and you have to tailor your selection of marketing methods to them.

Select as many methods as you can, but select only the ones that will be read, seen, or heard by your target audience. Many business owners select methods that appeal to them, but unless your prospects and customers are just like you, you're selecting for the wrong audience — and that's a very expensive mistake.

Although marketing budgets are as unique as snowflakes, you might get a better bead on your target if you study the budgets of three fictitious companies. One is a small, year-old contracting company, Handyman Hero, located in a town of 40,000 but within a marketing area of 150,000. The second, Computer Smarts, is a three-year-old two-person computer education organization located outside a city of 500,000 in a market area of 600,000 people. The third, Music Mart, is a retail stereo store that has been in business five years smack-dab in a city of 1 million people.

Suppose that Handyman Hero grosses $4,000 monthly in sales. The owner is willing to spend 7.5 percent of sales dollars for marketing — a total of $300 per month, or $3,600 per year. Computer Smarts takes in $20,000 in monthly sales and invests 10 percent of that in marketing: $2,000 monthly, or $24,000 per year. Music Mart grosses an average of $54,000 in monthly sales. An aggressive 12.5 percent is put back into marketing, permitting $6,750 for marketing each month, or $81,000 per year.

Because these companies are not brand new, they needn't invest heavily in advertising to get public attention. They already have a logotype, two have memes, and all three have business cards, stationery, and invoice forms. They even invested from $500 (Handyman Hero) to $5,000 (Music Mart) for professional marketing consultation before they got started in marketing. So they each have a marketing plan, a creative strategy, and a media strategy. Their investment with the consultants has also netted them advertising themes, clear identities, and a visual format. Handyman Hero obtained such a large amount of consultation for such a low price by building a sun deck for the marketing consultant in a barter arrangement. Computer Smarts and Music Mart worked a similar agreement, if I know my guerrillas. Look at the tables on this page and page 67 to see how these guerrillas would apportion their funds.

Handyman Hero's owner has selected many marketing methods. The primary marketing medium is newspapers, yet quite a bit of business comes through signs posted on bulletin boards and the owner's free seminars. The online classified ads are beginning to net new business, as more people discover the ease and convenience of selecting service providers online. Handyman Hero's signs, seminars, and online postings didn't cost any extra money, and all three are successful, according to Handyman Hero, because of the newspaper advertising. Handyman Hero installed a skylight for a graphic artist, who in return provided nearly $1,000 in artwork — layouts, illustrations, type, and a finished mechanical — all ready for the printer. The Handyman Hero owner set up a trade-show booth at the Home Improvement Show, distributing circulars freely and establishing a mailing list. Handyman Hero's $300 monthly investment in marketing runs 7.5 percent of sales this year. The owner projects that $300 will represent only 5 percent of sales next year, indicating an expected sales increase as a result of the consistent marketing program. (The prices quoted here are remarkably similar to those when I first wrote this book. Competition from the online world keeps them reasonable. It's tough to compete against free e-mail and free classified ads.)

HANDYMAN HERO ($300 MONTHLY)

Marketing Method	Monthly Cost	Comments
Canvassing	$0	Main investment is time
Personal letters	$0	Main investment is time
Circulars	$20	Cost of $240 yearly, amortized
Brochures	$50	Cost of $600 yearly, amortized
Signs on bulletin boards	$0	Posts own circulars
Classified ads	$40	Runs ads in two newspapers, once weekly

Marketing Method	Monthly Cost	Comments
Yellow pages	$20	Small listing, one directory
Newspaper display ads	$100	Runs ads in one newspaper, once weekly
Direct mail	$10	Postage only
Free seminars	$0	Distributes brochures at seminars
Trade-show booth	$10	Built booth, one-time cost amortized
Public relations	$20	Cost of materials only, handles own publicity
Production	$30	Amortized over one year, traded for a painting
Online classified ad	$0	Listed in four separate areas

COMPUTER SMARTS ($2,000 MONTHLY)

Marketing Method	Monthly Cost	Comments
Personal letters	$0	Uses these to gain corporate jobs
Circulars	$30	Cost of $360 yearly, amortized
Brochures	$80	Cost of $960 yearly, amortized
Signs on bulletin boards	$30	Monthly fee to have company's flier posted
Classified ads	$40	Uses one newspaper twice a week
Web site	$150	Monthly cost to pay Internet service provider and Webmaster
Yellow pages	$30	Medium listing, one directory
Newspaper display ads	$940	One ad weekly, two newspapers
Magazine ad (one time)	$100	One full-page ad in *Time*, amortized over one year
Radio spots	$400	Spends $100 weekly; on one FM station
Advertising specialties	$30	Cost of computer-oriented calendars
Free seminars	$0	Distributes brochures at these
Sampling	$0	Offered to corporations
Public relations	$20	Amortized for one publicity push yearly
Production	$200	Amortized over one year — all production of circulars, brochures, ads, commercials
Online classified ads	$0	Placed in four categories

Computer Smarts receives a lot of referral business. The brochures spur word-of-mouth recommendations, and the newspaper ads sell prospective customers completely, inspiring them to phone Computer Smarts, which gives a sales pitch and encourages them to send for a free brochure. The radio spots direct people to make a phone call. Although it spends little for telephone marketing, Computer Smarts engages in a good deal of it as a result of responses to the newspaper and radio advertising.

Computer Smarts would love to demonstrate its proficiency on TV but simply cannot afford it. Each year, its September publicity stunt of donating used and reconditioned computers to elementary schools results in free TV coverage, the main PR effort. The figure of 10 percent of sales invested in marketing will drop to 7.5 percent next year because of an increase in sales. Actual marketing outlays will remain the same.

THE MUSIC MART ($6,750 MONTHLY)

Marketing Method	Monthly Cost	Comments
Brochures	$200	General brochures with no prices
Point-of-purchase signs	$205	One-time cost, amortized over one year
Yellow pages	$200	One large listing in two directories
Newspaper display ads	$2,800	Two large ads weekly, two newspapers
Radio spots	$1,400	Consistently run on three FM stations
Television spots	$500	Two one-week TV splashes, amortized
Direct mail	$300	Three yearly mailings, amortized
Free seminars	$0	Held at store, sales made afterward
Searchlight	$20	For one yearly promotion, amortized
Production	$625	Amortized over one year
Web site	$500	For design, promotion, and maintenance

It's fascinating here to note that Music Mart, which has the largest of the three budgets, uses the fewest marketing methods. However, it uses two methods seriously: radio and newspaper advertising. The radio rates are very low, since spots are purchased through the company's internal ad agency at a very favorable one-year contractual rate. The newspaper ads are also available at one-year contract rates, at a substantial discount. Television advertising is used with force two times a year: The cost is $3,000 for each week. The Web site costs pay for an attractive and comprehensive multipage site that is updated weekly and provides price lists for many categories of products, not to mention color photos.

Like other guerrillas, Music Mart spends a large amount — 12.5 percent — on marketing. This tactic has eliminated several competitors that spent less boldly. (Although they enjoyed higher annual sales than Music Mart, their marketing did not reflect this.) Music Mart, like all smart guerrilla marketers, plans to spend the same amount on marketing next year but expects that it will represent only 10 percent of sales. The following year, that amount should represent 7.5 percent of sales. The plan is to spend no less than 7.5 percent on marketing, because the sound and electronics business is highly competitive.

Desktop publishing can cut some of the costs, especially if the costs include newsletters and a lot of direct mail. In the past, I've alerted small-business owners to the fact that marketing is not a do-it-yourself process and that desktop publishing is best left to savvy experts. I was wrong about the desktop publishing part. Listen to the music: Existing computer software makes desktop publishing so incredibly easy (read *The Desktop Publisher's Idea Book* by Chuck Green or *Web Design and Desktop Publishing for Dummies* by Roger Parker) that I consider desktop publishing to be the guerrilla's secret weapon. It's simple to use, and it creates materials that earn so much credibility that I sincerely believe that it gives small-business owners an unfair, yet welcome, advantage. The price of first-rate credibility has dropped considerably since guerrilla marketing was invented and codified. So run — don't walk — to new computer software if you want to save big money on the production and design of newsletters, fliers, brochures, circulars, signs, direct mail, Web sites, and more.

When advertisers discuss media, they talk of *reach* and *frequency*. *Reach* refers to the number of people who will be exposed to the message; *frequency*, to the number of times each person will be exposed. Although you'll strive for reach in certain endeavors, *frequency is best*. Remember, familiarity breeds confidence, and confidence serves as the springboard to sales. Frequency does a whole lot better for you than reach in the area of confidence.

Before you select a marketing method, remember that it is not necessary to say everything to everybody; nor is it possible. If you try to say everything to everybody, you'll end up saying everything to nobody or nothing to everybody. Instead, strive to say something to somebody. Your marketing message is the "something." Your target audience is the "somebody." Just as you take care in selecting what you will say, take equal care in selecting to whom it will be said. It is not acceptable to say the right thing to the wrong people. Although TV advertising does wonders for the ego, if your prospective customers don't watch much television, it is folly.

I want to underscore my belief in nanocasting and prove my commitment to podcasting. One of the most promising new guerrilla marketing weapons is Internet radio, consisting of podcasting and nanocasting. Because it is delivered over the Web, this form of radio is a very low cost way to reach a global audience, build credibility, build brand awareness, find new customers, and market your products and services. In 2005, Guerrilla Marketing International teamed up with Jackstreet Media to launch a Guerrilla Marketing radio pilot called "A Guerrilla Marketing Minute with Jay Conrad Levinson — On the Road." The program was created to promote the Guerrilla Marketing Association and has become a very popular feature on the Web site, with many visitors worldwide listening to multiple segments during a single visit. The daily audience continues to grow with the popularity of podcasting, nanocasting, and Internet radio, and more than a thousand GMA members have become Nanocasting Affiliates, airing the program on their sites and driving additional new members to the GMA. The "Tell-a-Friend" feature has been particularly effective, as visitors to the site routinely send the GMA Minutes to their peers, generating word of mouth and encouraging their friends to join the Guerrilla Marketing Association.

I suggest that you embrace the idea that you'll give a shot to absolutely every marketing method listed in this chapter. Then cut the list on the basis of who your audience is, whether you can use the method properly, and whether you can afford the method. With the methods that are left on your list, go for glory. Maximize your utilization and mastery of each. When you combine two surefire marketing methods with two other surefire marketing methods, the total is greater than four: A synergistic effect is created whereby two plus two equals five and six and seven. And when you combine five marketing methods with five others, your possibilities for success increase manyfold.

The more methods of marketing you use and the greater your skill at using and selecting them, the greater your bank balance. The idea is to combine the right marketing message with the right marketing media. That's the guerrilla truth.

7

Secrets of Saving Marketing Money

Guerrillas think first of saving marketing money by not wasting marketing money. Be sure you understand the distinction. Getting the lowest price on something isn't nearly as important as getting the most profitable results from something. Saving is nice, but it's secondary to profiting. Still, I must admit that saving money is important to almost everyone — consumers, large companies, and entrepreneurs — especially entrepreneurs. Entrepreneurs are, for the most part, suffering from resource poverty, and not a penny can be wasted. All money should pull more than its own weight. But is this possible? Bright entrepreneurs make it possible. This chapter suggests several ways to stretch your marketing dollars without decreasing their effectiveness one iota.

First of all, *don't feel that you must continually change your marketing campaigns.* Changing campaigns requires you to spend more production money and dilutes the overall effect of your marketing. Stick with one campaign until it loses its pulling power. This is difficult to do. In the beginning, most people will like your ad or Web site. Then you'll become bored with it. Next, your friends and family will get tired of it. Soon, your fellow workers and associates will be bored, and you'll want to change the ad. Don't do it! Let your accountant tell you when to change ads. That's right, your accountant — the person who takes long looks at your profit picture. You can be sure that your accountant won't get tired of an ad that continues to pull in business over the long term. The public's reaction to your ad is most important, and it takes a long, long time for the public to get tired of a marketing campaign — online and off line. If you always keep this in mind, you'll stretch your media money and save production dollars. I'll tell you several ways to save money in this chapter, but all of them pale in comparison with the way I've just mentioned. *The best way to save money marketing is to stick with your marketing program*. Abandoning your program too soon is the best way to waste money. Can I say it more clearly?

Another way to save impressive sums is to make use of the concept of *barter*. Your local radio station or newspaper may not want what you are selling but does want *something*. In all likelihood, you can trade with someone who has what the radio station or newspaper wants. If so, you'll get your media ads for a fraction of their usual cost, since you'll be paying with your own services or goods at their *full retail price*. You can learn of the exciting world of barter by visiting Google, typing in *barter* and becoming dazzled by the 18 million sites currently listed and hoping for a visit from you. It may be worth your time to check out this immense part of the world's economy.

Here's an example of bartering. A stereo dealer wanted to advertise on radio but couldn't afford the cost and so offered to trade recording equipment, but the station wasn't interested. The station was interested, however, in constructing a new lobby. The stereo dealer found a contractor who wanted new stereo equipment. Result: The contractor received $5,000 worth of stereo and television equipment; the radio station got its new lobby; the stereo dealer received $5,000 worth of radio time. Yet the dealer's cost was only $2,500 in equipment. In fact, the cost was less than that because the dealer traded discontinued merchandise that otherwise would have been discounted.

Many magazines trade ad space for whatever it is they need. Policies vary at publications, however, and trades must be individually negotiated. Remember that everyone needs something. By learning what your selected media need, you may be able to set up a money-saving trade. In the online world, barter abounds. If you're really and truly a guerrilla, you'll check this out.

When I discovered the world of barter, it was much like the first time I went scuba diving. An entire world existed within my own world, and I wasn't aware of it. To give you an inkling of the magnitude of barter in today's economy, consider that more than half of media is not purchased but obtained by barter.

You can also save money by gaining access to *cooperative advertising funds*. Many large advertisers pay cash fees to small advertisers who mention their name or show their logo in their ads. I know a woman who owns a small furniture store. When she mentions the name of a large mattress company in her ads, she receives a small sum of money from that company. Naturally, most of her ads mention the name of a large manufacturer that offers co-op ad funds. Look into co-op advertising: It not only helps save money for entrepreneurs but also lends credibility to their offerings by mentioning the name of a nationally known company. Some companies that offer co-op funds insist that they be the only company mentioned. Others don't care, just as long as you spell their names correctly. Still others demand that you include their theme lines or logos in your ad. A smart entrepreneur, interested in saving marketing money, will include the names of several co-op-oriented companies, thereby saving a large percentage of the ad cost — frequently more than 50 percent. This requires research and organization, but if you're interested in saving money, it's worth it.

Talk to your suppliers and simply ask them about their co-op program. If they don't have one, ask them to start one. One of my clients consistently has more than half of his marketing costs covered by co-op funds. His business is video rentals; the co-op funds come from movie studios. Very few advertising agencies will help you obtain co-op funds, so it's your job. Because it significantly reduces your investment in marketing, it's worth every minute you or your designated guerrilla devote to it. Who says you can't get something for nothing?

I also suggest that you set up a PI (per inquiry) or PO (per order) *arrangement with an advertising medium*. This is a fairly common method that entrepreneurs use to save and make money. As I write this, Google is brimming with more than 10 million entries under *per inquiry advertising*.

Here's an example of how it works. You contact a television station to ask whether it's interested in establishing a PI or PO arrangement with you (the station gives you television time, and in return, you give a prearranged sum of money per inquiry or per order). Suppose that you want to sell books for $10 by mail. You strike up a deal with a TV station: The station gives you commercial time, and you give the station, say, $3 per order. At this point, no money has changed hands. Now, the TV station provides you with the equipment to produce a commercial heralding your book. Normally, the station might charge $100 to run a one-minute commercial, but it gives you the time for free. Then the commercial runs, and fifty people order the book. The TV station receives $150 (at $3 per order), which is a good deal for the station. You also do well because you receive fifty orders ($500) and risk no marketing costs. Now, if you can make that same arrangement with one hundred other TV stations, you can clearly make very substantial profits without risking marketing outlay.

PI and PO arrangements are possible to establish with many magazines, radio stations, and television stations, and especially Web sites. I've never heard of such arrangements to be possible with newspapers, but I imagine that some farsighted publishers would welcome the idea. All it takes is a letter to your medium of choice, outlining the arrangement you're proposing. If the medium feels that it can make money on your offer, you're in business. In this way, you can engage in high-level marketing with virtually no up-front costs other than minimal production costs. The TV station might unfortunately put your commercial in a time slot after midnight — or a time slot that couldn't be sold to another advertiser — but you can bet that the TV station wants to make money on the arrangement. Therefore, it will go all out. And if it makes money, you make money.

Many an entrepreneur has made many a dollar with this little-known method of saving marketing dollars. A client of mine sold $3,000 worth of his newsletters through a PI arrangement with a magazine publisher. The publisher gave free ad space (a full-page ad typically would cost $900) in return for a $50 cut of a $100 subscription price. Thirty subscribers signed up. Result: $1,500 for the publisher and $1,500 for my client — the first year. Renewals will increase his profits.

The magazine wanted to repeat the ad — on the same PO basis. Naturally, my client nixed the offer and paid the magazine full price for the full-page ad.

People enjoy being asked about themselves; they enjoy talking about themselves. Take advantage of this human characteristic by *asking questions of your customers*. You'll get expensive research data for free. Prepare a survey that asks your customers all sorts of questions. Some will toss your questionnaire in the wastebasket. Others will answer it thoroughly and provide you with a wealth of information. If you were to get this research through standard research-company channels, it would cost you a fortune. But when obtained the way I've just described, this same information costs very little. More about this in the next chapter.

Perhaps the most fertile hunting ground for economy-minded guerrillas is the Internet. It teems with small businesses willing to barter with you, promote your products in return for your promoting their products, and pay you hefty commissions in return for your doing an e-mail to your mailing list promoting their product or their service. I recently ran across a man who said that he sells a $20 e-book but pays a $40 commission on each book sold by one of his online affiliates. He explained that he can afford to pay such a generous commission because of his *backend* — the products and courses and lavish learning systems he will sell to those who purchase his book. How much money does it cost him to create such a profitable venture? Zero money. His investments are the usual suspects: time, energy, imagination, and information — plus a gaggle of affiliates.

Once you're taking seriously the fortune that awaits you as a master of online marketing, be sure that you are getting the most for your money. If you're running a comprehensive marketing program with a solid combination of advertising media plus direct mail and e-mail, chances are that you've got leads and responses coming in from just about everywhere. How wonderful is that? But you must be able to tell which of your marketing tactics are stellar performers and which need to be replaced. Tracking your marketing responses is easier than you may think, and it's the smartest way to save marketing dollars by eliminating any nonperforming media and tactics.

The best way to track your advertising responses is to key each ad with a unique code so that every sale or lead can be identified according to its original source. Here are three ways to make every lead identifiable.

1. *Apply key codes.* Key codes are used in print advertising and direct mail. Suppose that you were running an ad campaign in a group of magazines. In order to track the responses from individual publications and issues, you would need to include a different key code in each of the response mechanisms. Your direct-response print ad in the January issue of *Ski* magazine could be coded *SK-1*, whereas another ad in the February issue of *Bodybuilder* magazine might be coded *BB-2*. These codes would appear in the *reply to* section of the ads, so when responses were generated, you could immediately determine the source of each lead.

   Key codes are often incorporated into the bounce-back mechanisms of direct mail. The next time you receive a direct-mail package, take a close look. Chances are, you'll see that the response envelope is imprinted with a code consisting of letters and/or numbers, and you'll also find that code on the order form or the response card.

2. *Provide a unique number or URL.* It's a good idea to acquire several toll-free numbers for use in different aspects of your marketing program. For example, you might track the results of a direct-response TV campaign by using a unique, memorable toll-free number and a different number to track the leads from a concurrent print or radio campaign. Another way to track responses from off-line campaigns is to provide unique URLs. By taking advantage of domain parking and pointing, you can have multiple versions of your domain name or dif-

ferent URLs that all point to a designated landing page on your Web site. For instance, respondents to an outdoor ad campaign might type in a simple URL that's easy to remember, such as MyBoat.com, and then be instantly forwarded to your primary site. Your Web logs would reveal the number of responses that came to each URL.

3. *Track online responses.* By now, I'm sure you know the importance of tracking. Whether you're monitoring the results of online ads or an e-mail campaign, be sure to have unique tracking codes for each. One way to measure responses to an individual ad or e-mail is to track hits to your Web pages by including a question mark after the URL, plus your code. For example, instead of using mydomain.com, your coded link might be mydomain.com?A. This will in no way alter the landing page and will show up in your log files. Another alternative is to create multiple copies of your landing page — each with a different file name — then link from your e-mail solicitations or online ads to specific landing pages.

Of course, the bottom line isn't merely to measure how many leads you generate but how many convert to sales. By tracking all responses according to their sources, you can test individual ad campaigns to see which marketing approaches and offers produce the most profitable results for your company.

Taking action on the topics I'm covering here, such as tracking responses, PI arrangements, and barter and corralling affiliates, doesn't and shouldn't happen overnight. But it is being practiced more and more by people who see the vision of financial independence and have the patience to turn that vision into reality. It's cool to build castles in the air — just as long as you have the patience to build foundations under them.

Impatience is a deterrent to both good marketing and inexpensive marketing. If you wish to gain the maximum effect from your marketing and to save money at the same time, avoid rushes like the plague. If you have a solid marketing calendar — a program that is planned ahead for a year — it will be quite easy to avoid them.

In order to save money in marketing, you must be aware of three variables — quality, economy, and speed. You get to select *any two* of them. Guerrillas opt for the first two. Their penchant for planning means that they are rarely in a rush, and they focus on quality and economy.

You can also save considerable sums of money if you realize that the cost of radio and TV time is nothing if not negotiable. Of course, prime time or drive time is difficult to buy and difficult to negotiate. However, if radio or

TV time is not sold, it is wasted forever. Therefore, stations will usually accept prices far below their normal rate-card prices. Deals abound.

To entice new advertisers — that is, entrepreneurs — TV stations will ordinarily offer attractive prices. Large advertisers know that rate cards are works of fiction, but small advertisers often believe what they read on rate cards. Don't you believe it. You can save media money by *making an offer you can afford*. You'll be surprised at how many radio and TV stations will accept your offer.

While we're on the subject of radio and television, keep in mind that a vast amount of research has proved that you can accomplish almost as much with a thirty-second commercial as you can with a sixty-second commercial. Save money by cutting the verbiage and saying your message in half a minute. If your message is concise and specific, it can be shorter than thirty seconds. In 2005, more than 80 percent of national TV commercials were less than thirty seconds long. The briefest messages are termed *electronic billboards* rather than TV commercials.

You'll save money by applying this truism to your print efforts. Unless you feel that it is absolutely necessary to run large, expensive newspaper or magazine ads, you can attract business just as successfully by running small, inexpensive newspaper or magazine ads — directing readers to your Web site.

You may not look as important as the purchasers of full-page ads, but you'll end up making more money. Don't forget: Consistency is one of the most important factors in marketing. You can achieve that consistency with small ads as well as large ones. The size of your ad does not produce the consumer confidence that consistency does — a truth that will save you impressive sums.

It is axiomatic that shoddy production gives you a shoddy image. Therefore, when running print ads, especially newspaper ads, it is usually silly to save money on production by having the newspaper or other medium design your ads. Instead, hire a professional to do this.

There are basically two types of professionals: high cost and low cost. To save the most money and achieve the greatest exposure, hire a high-cost designer to lay out your first ad and Web site and create a visual format for you. Then hire a low-cost designer to create all your follow-up materials, telling him or her to follow the format used in the original ad and clearly seen on the Web site. This will not infuriate the inexpensive designer, who will probably be thrilled with the business, and it won't anger the expensive designer, who received a fair sum for the talent expended. More and more graphic artists now charge by the usage of their creation and the places it will appear — so be buttoned up when you talk money. Following this model, you will always have sharp-looking ads, even though you paid through the nose only once. You have the best of two worlds: a classy look and format throughout the life of your marketing campaign and a low price for the production of all the graphics except the first. You shouldn't have to spend high production fees more than one time, but believe me, that one time is well worth it. Ask any entrepreneur who has used this tactic.

It's a good idea to tap the power of a pro for your magazine or newspaper ad, Web site, or TV spot. But you can save an extraordinary amount of money and reap generous profits if you create marketing materials with your own computer. Open your mind to posting fliers, offering brochures, providing catalogs, designing point-of-purchase and trade-show materials, making multimedia presentations, marketing with newsletters, and marketing aggressively on the Web. *You can create these guerrilla marketing weapons right at your desk.*

Half an hour. That's all it takes today to design a newsletter that would do any small-business owner proud. With easy-as-pie software, it's not a matter of creating new designs — you can choose from a generous selection of past designs. Select page designs, artwork, formats, mastheads, and typefaces by pointing and clicking. You'll be absolutely amazed at how creative you can be, how much money you can earn by creating a broad array of weapons, and how much money you can save by doing it on your own. Your kid can probably do it for you.

Save bundles by finding multiple uses for your marketing materials. That photo you used for your ad in the trade magazine? Use it in your brochure, at trade shows, in your catalog, in a PR story, on your Web site, on a calendar you distribute. The cost of the photo, which you may have thought to be high at first, becomes astonishingly low when amortized over time and multiple materials.

Save even more by writing timeless marketing materials. The Internet is a bastion of timeliness. You can make changes by the minute and the cost is barely noticeable. But the rules are different for materials that must be printed.

If yours is a business that needs printed materials, don't say in your brochure that your business is five years old, because then you'll have to update the information next year. Instead, say that your business was founded in 2003 — this will always be true. And don't show pictures of your employees, because one of them might be a competitor next year. Timelessness is the name of the economy game.

Another name is *experimentation*. Before you commit yourself to a campaign, experiment and test. Test your idea in a mailing, a chat room, a Web site survey, an inexpensive newspaper. Run the same ad in five local papers to see which paper evokes the greatest response; then run five different ads in that paper to see which is most successful. Pray that you don't get a five-way tie! Mail the same e-mail to five different lists and see which is most receptive to your offer. Then send five kinds of e-mail letters to your winning list to learn which one generates the greatest response for you. You must be willing to fail during the testing. Your goal during this phase is *solid information* rather than high profits. When you've got the right data, the bank deposits will follow.

Have you ever heard of remnant space? Probably not, unless you're in the marketing business. Many national magazines publish regional editions. When doing so, they sell advertising space to regional advertisers. Because of the way magazines are printed, publishers think in terms of four-page units, because it takes one large piece of paper folded in half to make four pages that fit comfortably into a magazine format. Often, a magazine will have sold only three of its four pages as publication date draws near. What does the publisher do with that extra page — that remnant space? Sells it at an astounding discount to a local advertiser. If you wish to be that local advertiser, contact the publication well in advance of the date you wish your ad to appear, or get in touch with Media Networks, Inc., a company devoted to selling remnant space to local advertisers. The company is national, and its toll-free number, from which you should request a free media kit, is 1-800-225-3457. Media Networks can put your ad in most national magazines, in the regional issues, at a far lower cost than you may think.

For example, a full-page, black-and-white ad in *Time* magazine costs approximately $85,000. Media Networks, Inc., can sell you a full-page black-and-white ad in *Time* magazine in Tucson, El Paso, Wilmington, Savannah, or many other cities for under $3,000 — an $82,000 savings. Some difference!

While we're on the subject of advertising space, we should look at one of the most efficient money-saving strategies in all of marketing — a house advertising agency. Advertising agencies earn their money by receiving a 15 percent discount from publications and broadcast stations where they place advertising. An ad or commercial time that costs an advertiser $1,000 costs an advertising agency only $850. This is known as an agency discount, and advertising agencies are entitled to every cent of it. The advertiser would have to spend $1,000 anyhow. By using an ad agency, the advertiser receives professional help at no extra cost, since the advertisement will cost $1,000 with or without an agency. And the ad agency picks up $150 for its efforts.

What do you do if your business is too small to require the service of an advertising agency? What if you don't *want* to use an advertising agency? *Establish your own in-house ad agency.* To create an in-house agency, you usually need only to tell the advertising medium that you are an in-house or internal agency for your business. In some cases, the medium may require that you have a checking account in your agency's name (ten dollars in an account will do nicely). And you may need agency stationery. Again, this is no problem. If your business is called Atlantic Manufacturing, just call your agency Atlantic Advertising, and print the name on stationery that you create yourself on your computer.

With a checking account and stationery, you are ready to establish your own in-house advertising agency. And you can save 15 percent on almost all the advertising you place for yourself. You can save on virtually everything but newspaper advertising, for which you pay only the retail rate, which is low to begin with. It's so easy to set up an internal agency that I'm surprised that more entrepreneurs don't do so. You can save a considerable sum of money — your $3,000 *Time* regional ad will cost you only $2,550.

If you ever use local television, start out with tight, well-written scripts. Record them onto a CD or tape. Plan a rehearsal session or two prior to the shooting date, then try to shoot three or four commercials in one session. In 2006, the average thirty-second TV commercial cost around $200,000 to produce — thanks to the soft drinks, beers, cars, fast-food chains, celebrity endorsements, and Steven Spielberg wannabes. But you can reduce the cost to less than $1,000 if you shoot several spots at once, work with thought-out scripts, shoot to an existing sound track, and avoid paying high talent fees to actors and actresses. Hmmm, $200,000 or $1,000 to produce a TV spot? Why do so many companies opt for the $200,000 tab? Corporate ego is the answer — and frequently is.

There are several reasons for the difference in these production costs: Full-scale TV productions usually involve large crews for lighting, props, makeup, hairstyling, and transportation of cameras, and this ordinarily involves union and inflated costs. Guerrillas work with skeleton crews and do not work with unions unless absolutely necessary. Guerrillas aren't anti-union; they're proefficiency.

The editing process is one of the most expensive aspects of TV production, especially if videotape is used. But digital TV production is ending the videotape nightmare. With well-planned scripts, your spot will require little editing.

Some advertisers feel that they must hire a celebrity to sell their wares. This adds from $5,000 to $500,000 to the tab. It's true that Nike committed X millions of dollars to Tiger Woods and Michelle Wie for their endorsements and may end up earning 10 times that in profits as a result. But guerrillas rely on the power of an idea and save the cash.

Production devices, such as complex scenery, special effects, and ornate sets, make commercials extremely expensive. Because many people are involved in the actual shooting, each scene may be shot four or five different ways to stroke four or five different egos. Guerrillas shoot each scene one way and get their ego kicks through sizable bank deposits.

In addition, TV professionals tend to shoot commercials to suit their own tastes and needs. They can spot flaws that most viewers would never see. So they reshoot and reshoot and reshoot. Guerrillas accept minor flaws and get on with the commercial.

All these strategies add up to a whale of a difference in money but not in quality. I have a reel of commercials, each costing under $500. TV pros who have seen them have estimated that the cost of each spot was $10,000 or more. In my opinion, unnecessary TV production costs are murdering many large-company production budgets. Amazingly, they are easy to avoid. So avoid them.

Guerrillas are also very careful to avoid vampire marketing, which sucks attention away from their primary message. Viewers remember the special effects but not the advertiser. It's the funny joke that people recall as they forget who paid to tell it. It's the clever presentation that bleeds dry the motivating offer by directing focus to itself and not the benefit to the prospect. The call to action is for viewers to laugh, when it should be to pick up the phone.

I've told you that the best way to save money is to commit to a marketing program and give it time to sprout wings and fly. Now I'll tell you the second-best way to save your valuable cash: Market primarily to *customers*, not to prospects. It costs one-sixth as much to sell something to a customer than to a prospect. Some experts now peg that fraction as one-tenth. Direct your marketing funds toward follow-up, surpassing customer expectations, gaining repeat business, earning referral business, and enlarging the size of your transactions. Your growth will pay off in profits even more impressive than the money you'll save by the inward, rather than outward, thrust in your marketing.

In the final analysis, there are two kinds of marketing: expensive and inexpensive. Expensive marketing is the kind that doesn't work. Inexpensive marketing is the kind that works — regardless of cost. You'll save the most if you always make sure to run inexpensive marketing — the kind that gives you the results you want. It has more to do with *results* than with cost. True economy for guerrillas is not in saving money but in not wasting money.

8

Research: The Starting Point
of a Guerrilla Marketing Campaign

There are two kinds of research: *free research*, which business owners do by themselves, as you'll see in the upcoming pages, and *paid research*, which costs money — but only in the way that an investment costs money. The payoff often is much larger than the investment. That's why many guerrillas use both kinds of research. When they're starting out, they use free research because they want the information. Later, when they're growing and humming, they use paid research because they need it.

Be clear on this: Research — although it can often serve as the spark for breakthrough thinking — is not intended to be a substitute for inspiration. The truth is that research is supposed to provide a connection with your customers or prospects that can get you where you want to go faster and more profitably.

At the heart of research is the keen belief that listening to the opinions of your consumers is important. When you ask the right questions, consumers will tell you what to do to make your business more profitable. Simply by listening to consumers, you will do the smart thing far more often than if you simply decide to go it alone.

Remember when Coca-Cola introduced New Coke and failed miserably? Here's what Sergio Zyman, who was Coke's chief marketing officer at the time, had to say about listening to the consumer:

> We orchestrated a huge launch [of New Coke], received abundant media coverage . . . were delighted with ourselves . . . until the sales figures started rolling in. Within weeks, we realized that we had blundered. Sales

tanked, and the media turned against us. Seventy-seven days after New Coke was born, we made the second-hardest decision in company history. We pulled the plug. What went wrong? The answer was embarrassingly simple. We did not know enough about our consumers. We did not even know what motivated them to buy Coke in the first place. We fell into the trap of imagining that innovation — abandoning our existing product for a new one — would cure our ills.

After the debacle, we reached out to consumers and found that they wanted more than taste when they made their purchase. Drinking Coke enabled them to tap into the Coca-Cola experience, to be part of Coke's history and to feel the continuity and stability of the brand. Instead of innovating, we should have renovated. Instead of making a product and hoping people would buy it, we should have asked customers what they wanted and given it to them. As soon as we started listening to them, consumers responded, increasing our sales from 9 billion to 15 billion cases a year.

In the case of New Coke, listening to the consumer might have prevented an expensive disaster. As with so many businesses large or small, too much entrepreneurial ego or downright stubbornness gets in the way of listening to the consumer. Sadly, one of the failings of many small businesses is their lack of consideration to the importance of research and listening to the consumer. And if it is even considered, it is likely to be written off as being unaffordable.

Know this: *Ignorance is more expensive than paid research.* The testing process often costs you money because you haven't yet determined a winner, though e-mail has drastically reduced the cost of ascertaining the truth. Small-business owners are continually confronted with the need to make decisions about media, copy, headlines, subject lines, prices, colors, sizes, frequency, and target audiences. At all times, they are given two options: wing it or test it.

A lot of marketing pros will tell you that the three most important things you need to do to market anything successfully are to test, test, and test. That is good advice. And the big secret is that you need not shell out any money to learn about your market. If you know what to look for and where to find it, you can obtain crucial information for nary a cent. Let's examine some of the things you might want to find out.

1. What should you market — your goods, your services, or both?
2. Should your marketing feature some sort of price advantage?
3. Should you emphasize yourself, your quality offerings, your selection, your convenience, your service, or only the existence of your business?

4. Should you take on your competition or ignore all competitors?
5. Exactly who are your competitors?
6. Who are your best prospects?
7. What income groups do they represent?
8. What motivates them to buy?
9. Where do they live?
10. What media do they read, watch, and listen to?
11. Do they have fax machines?
12. Are they online?
13. Do you have their e-mail addresses? The more answers you get, the more money you make.
14. Do they have children? If so, what are their ages?
15. What are their favorite sports teams?
16. What are their hobbies?
17. What do their spouses do for a living?
18. What activities most interest their kids at school?
19. Where did they attend high school and college?
20. What are their purchase plans for the coming year?
21. What do they most like about your company?
22. To make your company perfect, what do they suggest that you do?
23. Would they want a free subscription to your online newsletter?

Complete answers to these questions can prove invaluable to a marketing effort. A lack of answers can prove disastrous. Do what you must to get the answers.

In most cases, great advertising is preceded by great research. Four inexpensive research methods will provide you with the information that can make the difference between success and failure.

The first is to get to know your favorite search engines. Be on intimate terms with Google, Yahoo!, and Ask.com. I hope by now you have noticed that they have changed everything when it comes to research. I hope you noted the recent day when *google* was accepted in the dictionary — as a verb. Google that.

Don't want to fiddle with a computer? Go to your local library. The reference librarian, one of America's greatest untapped resources, can steer you to the right search engines, guide you through shortcuts, then direct you to books and other publications that contain a raft of moneymaking information for you. Today, reference librarians know the Internet more intimately than most other people do. After all, *reference* is part of their job title.

Some of the sources you will be directed to have market studies of your area, conducted by companies that paid impressive sums for the data. Others contain studies of products or services such as yours and indicate the level of their acceptance by the public. Still others include census reports, research reports, and industry studies. Whenever I used to write a book, I found myself in libraries, ferreting out information. When I write a book these days, I get my information from the Internet. I lean heavily on search engines, which are becoming easier to use and better at their job. Who is the true expert on those search engines? You've got it — your reference librarian.

The more customer information you have, the better equipped you'll be to serve those customers. This is where inquisitiveness pays off big.

An invaluable yet commonly overlooked way for you to get information is *to ask your own customers*. If you have a new business, I strongly suggest that you prepare a lengthy questionnaire for them. On it, ask them everything under the sun.

Large corporations that enclose brief questionnaires with their manufactured items, such as TV sets, electric razors, or blow dryers, report that fewer than half the questionnaires are returned. These questionnaires often consist of only five or six questions. On the other hand, I had a client who gave each of his customers a fifteen-question survey. Seventy-eight percent of the forms distributed were completed and returned. It seems that many people enjoy providing personal information, just as long as they can remain anonymous.

Suppose that you want to establish a company that provides auto mechanical services at people's homes rather than in a garage. You might prepare and distribute — by e-mail or surface mail and on your Web site — a survey that asks the following questions of your prospects, namely, motorists.

> *We are establishing an automotive service that makes "house calls." To help us serve you most effectively, please provide the following information:*
>
>   What type of car do you drive? _____
>   What year is it? _____ What model? _____
>   How long have you owned it? _____
>   Who usually performs mechanical services for your car? _____
>   Would you want these services to be performed where you live?
>   _____
>   List the three main reasons you would want "house calls" made to service your car. _____ _____ _____
>   Would you pay more to have "house calls" for your car? _____
>   What is your sex? _____ Your age? _____
>   Your household income? _____

What newspapers do you read? _____
What radio stations do you listen to? _____
What TV shows do you watch? _____
Which magazines do you read? _____
What type of work do you do? _____
Do you have a fax machine? _____ What is your fax number? _____
Are you online? _____ What is your e-mail address? _____
Do you have a Web site? _____ What is your Web address? _____
Would you purchase products as well as service from a traveling auto-
    motive service? _____
Who do you consider to be our competition? _____
Where would you expect us to advertise? _____
Do you have any other comments? _____

In this game of twenty questions, you always emerge the winner. By studying the *questions only*, you can easily see how much you'll learn. Think of how informed you'd be by studying the answers! This kind of questionnaire should be distributed for a number of months, and the answers should be studied each month so that trends can be spotted after the business is established. Note that the questionnaire doesn't ask the name or address of the customer. Anonymity is preserved, enabling you to ask many personal questions. Some questionnaires do ask for names and addresses, sacrificing the promise of anonymity in the quest for more detailed personal information. Guerrillas use both, knowing that the more personal data they have, the better they can target their marketing.

When you analyze the completed questionnaires, you'll learn specifics about your prospects, how best to reach them through the media, how to appeal to them, and what kinds of cars they drive. You can analyze the questionnaires by grouping the responses to each question. Perhaps you'll learn that the majority of people interested in patronizing your business drive foreign cars. This alerts you to the possibility of sending a mailing to foreign-car owners. Their names are available from mailing-list brokers. It might be that your customers are owners of older cars. Again, you can reach these people with a targeted mailing. The questionnaire will help you focus your advertising to the right people.

From the questionnaire, you can learn who your competition is by learning who usually performs mechanical services for your prospects. You can determine what it is you offer that is most enticing to your customers — again helping you choose the proper emphasis for your advertising. You'll discover the sex and age of your customers, and you'll learn exactly how and where to communicate with them once you ascertain the newspapers, radio stations, TV shows, and magazines that interest them. If your customers are primarily white-collar workers, the questionnaire will inform you of that fact, and you can tailor your media selection to that reality. You can learn which marketing vehicles will work most effectively for you, and you can get a report on your own service.

This analysis greatly helps you in determining your marketing thrust, yet it's extremely inexpensive. Use the information to update or revise your marketing plan. And just think, your only expense was for the duplication of the questionnaire — well under $100. This is free research at its best, and, frankly, you're nuts if you don't take advantage of it. Repeat it every few years to keep abreast of your market. Things change with lightning speed, including details about your customers.

The third way to take advantage of inexpensive research is to prepare a questionnaire similar to the preceding one and give it to people using the kinds of services you provide. By doing so, you research serious rather than potential prospects. You'll receive fewer returns than the 78 percent my client enjoyed, but you'll learn something — which is much more valuable than knowing nothing. Naturally, you won't hand your questionnaire to motorists if you're selling computer education. If that's your business, you'll want your questionnaires in the hands of people entering or departing computer stores. If you are a traveling hairstylist who makes house calls, hand your questionnaires to people leaving beauty salons or barbershops. Whatever your business, you can find prospective customers somewhere: with their kids at the playground, at the beach, in the park, downtown, at the hardware store, at the ballpark. Chances are, you've already got a line on where they are. All you have to do is go there and distribute your long list of questions.

How do you ensure that the prospective customers will return your questionnaires? You can furnish them with stamped envelopes. You can tempt them with offers of free but inexpensive gifts. You can offer them discounts, newsletter subscriptions, free reports — if they complete and return your questionnaire. And you can use pure honesty by explaining, at the beginning of the questionnaire, exactly why you are asking so many questions. Just be sure to include your address so that the questionnaires will be mailed (or brought) to the right place.

You should have an introductory paragraph atop your questionnaire, which could read:

> We're trying to learn as much as possible from motorists in the community so that we can offer them the best possible service. We apologize for asking you so many questions in this questionnaire, but we're doing it so that you

can benefit in the long run. We promise that your answers will remain anonymous (note that we are not asking for your name). And we also promise that we'll use the information to help you enjoy better automotive service.

An honest introduction such as this serves to disarm people who resent being asked so many questions, and it explains *exactly* why you are distributing the survey.

Once again, you end up with valuable information. And again, it costs you hardly a cent. A true guerrilla will use *all three methods* to get free research. Then he or she will put the information to work to create a first-rate marketing plan, using reliable data that can aid in selecting marketing methods, evaluating the competition, and framing the creative message.

The fourth method of free research is to tap the greatest information source ever developed: the Internet. It truly is, as Bill Gates said, the information superlibrary. And it is more conveniently located than your local library. If you can't find what you're looking for on the Internet, you're probably not looking in the right places. (However, I want to remind you that the most *crucial* information is not and probably never will be on the Internet — that is personal information about your customers. As much as I laud the Net, as much as I implore you to engage in a weekly surf to learn the intricacies and secrets of the Net, I realize that it can't tell me Thing One about my customers. Only my questionnaire can accomplish that.)

There are insights about Internet research known to all cyberguerrillas. These are the most important insights.

- If you're using the Internet to locate information about anything related to an industry, first locate the Web sites of businesses involved in that industry. You'll find them to be a treasury of information. When I wrote a chapter about computer networking for a recent book, I found more substantial and easy-to-understand information on the 3Com Web site than I did in technical journals. 3Com manufactured computer networking hardware, so it was in the company's best interest to present information clearly. Same for Cisco Systems.
- Use *several* search engines. Search engines undergo continual improvement and vie with one another to be easiest to use and most comprehensive. No one search engine is best for all purposes — each seems to have its own areas of specialization. Check a few if you want to get the most valuable and most recent information.
- Look beyond the Web when you're searching for information online. Millions of documents and files are available via Gopher, WAIS (wide

area information servers), and FTP (file transfer protocol), and you can use search utilities, such as TurboGopher, Win-Gopher, Archie, Anarchie, and Veronica, to find them. Gopher servers store university or government documents, such as trade statistics or opinion-poll results. WAIS store the full text of articles, reports, and speeches by famous people, among other facts. FTP servers store files containing lengthy reports, graphics, charts, demo programs, and video clips. Much of this data may never be available on the Web. Use these searching methods to avoid missing important information.

- Don't overlook the importance of chat rooms for quick responses to ideas, products, and marketing thoughts. Bright people are online chatting, and they are quick to render opinions. You can learn significant information by simply asking in a chat setting. Look for chat rooms where your questions might be appropriate, and then ask away.
- Use e-mail for customer surveys. It is so simple to respond to them that response rates for online surveys are appreciably higher than for mailed surveys. Don't worry about asking too many questions, but don't overdo a good thing. Offer to send responders the results of your survey, for they are probably inquisitive people if they're willing to answer your questions.

These are not the only methods of conducting inexpensive research; they are simply the most common and effective. There are free newsletters galore — good ones — on every topic you can imagine. Don't ask me where; ask your friendly search engine. You can also get information from your local or state chamber of commerce, any industry organizations to which you belong, and any industry publications of which you are aware. Make a field trip or two to poke around and talk to people in your business but who are not in your geographic area. Guerrillas abet their primary research with these additional sources of knowledge. Knowledge is the currency of the twenty-first century.

When questioning your target audience, it might help to list some of the basic needs people have. Ask them to make check marks by those that pushed their particular buttons. Most people will react to one or more of the following basic needs (known as "appeals" in advertising lingo):

Achievement
Ambition
Comfort
Convenience

Conformity (peer pressure)
Friendship
Health and well-being
Independence
Love
Power
Pride of ownership
Profit
Savings or economy
Saving time
Security
Self-improvement
Social approval (status)
Style

If you believe that people patronize you because you offer convenience and economy, you may be surprised to learn, via your questionnaires, that they give you their business because your work adds to their sense of security.

You can engage in more free research by conscientiously studying the other marketing that is going on in your community — not only that of your competitors but also that of *everyone*. Engage in frank conversations with your customers. Talk with your competitors. Talk with other businesspeople in your community. You'll find that they'll provide you with useful information and won't charge you for it. Research will help you save money and earn money, and free research will help you save and earn even more.

I'd be remiss if I didn't let Robert Kaden have a word about paid research. He's the author of *Guerrilla Marketing Research*, a valuable addition to any guerrilla library, and although he's all for free research, he doesn't want you to overlook paid research. Here, in his own wise words, is why:

> For small companies and entrepreneurs, research is one of the last things they think they can afford. Mostly, research is viewed as a highly discretionary expense. One that is difficult to justify because research costs aren't easily attributable to immediate paybacks.
>
> The owner of a small manufacturing company once said to me, "If I spend $50,000 on research, will I get $100,000 back"? I responded, "If you don't spend the money on research, how will you know that you won't ultimately waste $500,000 advertising your product using the wrong message?"
>
> Another said, "I could hire two salesmen for the cost of your research. If I do that, I know how much in sales and profit I can expect." My re-

sponse was, "Maybe you should hire one salesman and spend money you would have paid the second to learn about your customers and why they aren't buying more from you. In this way you can help the salesmen you now have be more effective. It just might be that if your salesmen were better informed, their selling efforts would increase dramatically."

Trusting the process is always in question the first time money is spent on research. The vague hope always exists that the results will lead to smarter decisions, which will increase sales and profits that would not have happened otherwise. This makes it all the more critical that great care be taken in planning the research and anticipating the kind of actions that will be taken when the research is completed.

It is also important to realize that research might suggest action not be taken. When considering a new venture or change of course, there are always costs associated with the risk. Often, research will indicate that an idea is not worth pursuing. Or that the money necessary to do the job effectively might be beyond company means.

In such cases, the payback from the research is the prevention of costly mistakes.

Just as one hallmark of the guerrilla marketer is ongoing learning, another is ongoing research. Researching your marketplace should never stop. And the Internet makes it so easy. With even a brief foray into the extraordinary world of search engines, you'll be bombarded by new research, facts, and information that will help you grow your business. You don't even have to try that hard.

You and your business will be better served if you do take a proactive approach. The Internet is an ever-expanding sea of information. Use it often. Ask it questions about your business. Go to the library. Talk to friends and relatives. Do everything that is free and that your time allows. As your business grows, you will reach a level of sophistication. When your continued growth will be dependent on the right answers to the right questions, only paid research can do the job you need.

Eventually, you may run out of questions to ask and feel that it is time to stop doing research. When that happens, these are Kaden's top ten questions for you. He suggests that if you answer yes to any of them, you should buy yourself a new car, yacht, RV, summer home, or whatever, because you obviously don't need the money for paid research.

1. Will your business grow profitability on pure momentum?
2. Will your business grow without improvements?
3. Do you know everything that your competitors can do to hinder your growth?

4. Are you convinced that you can't lose customers or gain new ones?
5. Are you convinced that there is nothing that can happen to cause your products to become obsolete?
6. Are you sure that your business isn't subject to changing trends?
7. Are you sure that you are the only one who can generate good ideas about how to run your business?
8. Are you clairvoyant?
9. Do you get tomorrow's stock market reports in today's newspaper?
10. Have you contracted for sale of your business that will make you millions?

There are two variables you must always consider in your quest for research. I've saved them for the end because I want them to remain in your mind whenever you engage in any kind of research — free or otherwise. The two variables are: (1) the quality of the information, and (2) the source of the information. You need both high-quality information and a reliable source for your research to be worth a hill of beans. If you have both, that research may be worth a mountain of money.

PART II

Minimedia Marketing

9

Truths About Minimedia Marketing

By necessity, guerrillas excel in minimedia marketing. Traditional marketers rarely resort to such marketing methods as canvassing, writing personal letters, sending postcards, marketing by telephone, distributing circulars, running ads in movie theaters, posting signs on bulletin boards, running classified ads, using signs other than billboards, putting the yellow pages to work, and making business cards do double duty. Fortunately, because the titans don't practice minimedia marketing, you'll come across very little competition in these arenas — except from fellow guerrillas. And be warned, there are more guerrillas *daily*, and your close attention to the media will alert you to their presence — as well as educate you by their examples. Be prepared to respond; giant companies aren't as fast on their feet as you. You can respond more quickly.

Your minimedia marketing must adhere to your marketing plan, be accomplished with talent and style, and still follow many of the fundamentals. But it can also break the rules. For instance, you can make letters highly personalized. You can post unique signs. You can take advantage of the smallness of your business when making telephone calls. Make them personal, friendly, and informal yet professional.

I urge you to use as many media as you can use correctly, and I urge you to use the minimedia to the max. Minimedia will rarely put a strain on your budget, as production costs are low. You'll have an opportunity to star in the minimedia more than in the maximedia, where you may be outspent even if you're not outthought. In the minimedia, your size is an advantage, not a disadvantage.

I hope you'll put all these marketing methods to work while you're still small. If you do, you'll know which to use as your business grows.

Your small size enables you to offer advantages in the area of customer service. If your market is your own locality, your geographic proximity — including the fact that you're a true-blue local — is a big weapon, possessed by few of the behemoths. You know folks on a first-name basis. You see them regularly. You can provide extremely individualized service, tailored to the realities of your customers' budgets. Few big companies can match you. By necessity, they're forced to run customer service by company policy, and that deprives them of flexibility.

As a guerrilla, you're the epitome of flexibility — and it can be translated into service that customers crave. A score for your team! The minimedia include maxiservice. Used properly, they can make you a juggernaut. The twenty-first century has brought to the minimedia a multitude of changes, all of which work to the advantage of the entrepreneur.

- E-mail facilitates the fastest of all communication and interactivity. Steer clear of "spamming" (junk e-mail), but don't worry about sending e-mail to your customers and prospects who say they want info from you.
- Faxes allow you to render speedier service than snail mail (but don't use faxes for marketing; people resent "junk faxes").
- Computer bulletin boards enable you to zero in on specific target audiences and communicate by posting notices or sending e-mail to members of the audience.
- You can run free online classified ads through a wide variety of venues and online services.
- Toll-free numbers (800, 888, 876, and 866) are less expensive than ever, so you can increase your response rates anywhere from 30 percent to 700 percent.
- Catalogs, newsletters, and brochures are simpler than ever to produce, thanks to desktop publishing.
- Desktop publishing is simpler, more inexpensive, and more attractive than ever for small businesses, which use computers to create eye-popping marketing materials without incurring the expense. Your creative genius can stop lurking within you and start working!
- A 900 number can be used as both a marketing weapon and a new profit center.
- More magazines today offer inexpensive regional editions, offering

you first-rate credibility at cut-rate prices. These magazines also offer classified sections.

- More newspapers today offer low-cost zone editions that reach prospects in targeted neighborhoods.
- Computer technology allows entrepreneurs to tap into computer networks, communicate with many people at once, and keep accurate databases.
- Because of the growth of cable, TV time has dropped in price to a point that almost any small business can (and should) consider it.
- Satellite TV transmission allows advertisers to home in on extremely specialized markets.
- Home shopping networks encourage viewers to buy instantly, providing advertisers and viewers with instant gratification.
- Cellphones, pagers, and satellite phones offer more sophisticated communication options, saving time and opening the door to more personalized service.
- VCR/DVD penetration has surpassed 90 percent, adding to the attractiveness of a video brochure.
- New breakthroughs in psychology are giving us a clearer view of human behavior, enabling us to create more effective marketing.
- New media are springing up all over the place: on airport luggage carousels, airplane movie screens, blimps in the sky, and even rockets in space; at grocery checkout counters; in restroom stalls, postcard decks, and lines at banks and post offices. New media are being integrated into major movies and TV shows and are appearing throughout cyberspace.
- People are being marketed to while on telephone hold, and many appreciate the data while they wait.
- Special-effects technology in television allows small advertisers to get a big-advertiser look without spending big bucks.

I'm just scratching the surface regarding the minimedia advances that have taken place since the original edition of this book. The maximedia, discussed in Chapter 10, were once the domain of the big spenders but are now your domain, too. As a guerrilla, your eyes must be open to the marketing options of the twenty-first century, as well as to those of days past. Potent marketing weapons, which are arriving in the marketing arena on a daily basis, are by-products of the age of the entrepreneur. Each represents an opportunity for you.

Whether you capitalize on the opportunity is up to you; whether you learn of the opportunities is up to me. And learn you will. Now's as good a time as any to start.

Canvassing

Where to begin? I know — at the beginning. With the not-very-glamorous but oh-so-effective tactic of *canvassing* — looking your prospects in the eye and asking for the order. That's probably the way it all began, anyhow.

The canvass existed before any other marketing methods. In fact, the very first sale in history probably occurred when one caveman asked another, "Want to trade me an animal skin for this fruit I picked?" Advertising wasn't necessary. Nor was a marketing plan. Life has become more complicated.

Canvassing can be the most inexpensive marketing method of all. In fact, it can be free, except for the time you devote to it. And if you're just starting out, time is something you have a great deal of in your inventory. After all, canvassing is merely asking prospective customers for business. If ever there was an interactive medium, canvassing is it. There's little question that it was the first of all interactive media, if not the first of all media. During a canvass, which the dictionary defines as "a soliciting of sales," you should engage in three steps.

The first step, called the *contact*, is when you first meet your prospect. That first impression counts like crazy. So make your contact friendly, upbeat, customer oriented, honest, and warm. Try to *establish a relationship*. Smile, look directly into the person's eyes, and if at all possible, *use the person's name*. You need not talk about business if you don't want to. And you really shouldn't. Some Fortune 500 companies require that their salespeople ask at least three nonbusiness questions before getting down to business. You can talk about personal matters, the weather, a current event, sports, or — ideally, your prospective customer. That's probably his or her favorite subject. It's best to avoid politics and religion, but everything else is fair game.

The second step of a canvass is called the *presentation*. It usually takes longer than the other steps, yet it need take no longer than one minute. During the presentation, you outline the features of your offering and the benefits to be gained from buying from you. Some pro canvassers say, "The more you tell, the more you sell." I'm not sure about that; it depends on what you're selling. If you're selling a home security system, your presentation might take fifteen minutes. If it's an offer to wash your prospect's car, the presentation might take a minute or less. Presentations to sell personal computers may take a few hours; presentations to sell home satellite systems, a day and a half; presentations to sell million-dollar computer switchers, up to a year and a half. The price of your product or service will dictate the time you should spend presenting it.

The third step of a canvass — the *close* — is the most important; it's the magical moment when you complete the sale. It's when your prospect says yes or signs on the dotted line or reaches for his or her wallet or merely nods affirmatively. If you are a poor closer, it doesn't really matter how good you are at the contact and the presentation. You've got to be a good closer to make canvassing work.

There are various ways to canvass. You can go from door to door. You can canvass in residential neighborhoods, in commercial neighborhoods, and at trade shows. Or you can presell your canvass by first calling or writing the people you intend to canvass. You have a choice of telling them you'll come by at some point, or you can set up an appointment. The latter is more like a sales presentation. Most guerrillas canvass with little or no advance warning to the customer. Sure, it helps if you advertise so that the prospective customers have heard of you when you come calling, but you don't have to advertise. If you make a good contact, a crisp presentation, and a dynamite close, and if you are offering a good value, canvassing may be the only marketing tool you ever need.

I mentioned that canvassing can be free, and I wasn't kidding. But it will help if you do invest a bit of money in it. For one thing, you want to look good so as to inspire confidence. That means you should look the part. If you are canvassing store owners with the idea of getting them to sign up for your window-washing business, you need not wear a coat and tie. But it helps if you're wearing spotless work clothes and even if you have a clean rag dangling from your rear pocket.

The investment increases a bit more if you offer a business card to the person you are canvassing. The card establishes that you are for real and enables a person to give you business later, if not now. It also helps your referral business — if you do a good job. Your investment will be even greater if you decide to canvass using a brochure or circular. If you do produce such materials, use them as sales aids while you are making your presentation, or give them away after you have closed the sale. Don't expect a person to read your literature and listen to your sales talk at the same time. Generally, I frown on presenting a circular during this contact, because it gives your prospect an opportunity to avoid buying by telling you that he or she will "study" your circular and get back to you.

If prospects don't buy now, figure that they won't buy later. Usually they won't. Another way to look at it is that someone will buy. Some entrepreneurs give free demonstrations or samples while they canvass. Although this adds to your investment, it is often a smart addition. Some companies say that it's akin to purchasing a customer.

Once you learn the best way to accomplish your canvassing, you'll be confronted with several choices. First, will you want to continue using this method of marketing? Second, are you doing it as well as it can be done? Third, should you be delegating the canvassing job to someone else? To several other people? To an organization of sales reps (called distributors)?

The advantages of canvassing are readily apparent. It doesn't cost much, if anything. It's a great way to get a brand-new business going. It strengthens your contacts, because looking a person directly in the eye is more personal by a long shot than writing a letter, making a phone call, or attracting attention with an ad. Canvassing is also a good way to learn the objections, if any, to your offering. It provides instant results and guarantees that your message is being heard. Like television advertising, it enables you to demonstrate. Like radio advertising, it enables you to be intimate. Like newspaper advertising, it allows you to be newsy. Like magazine advertising, it allows you to involve your prospect. And like direct-response marketing, it is geared to get you a direct response of the positive kind.

The success of canvassing depends on you and you alone. You can't blame the media if you mess up. And if you succeed, you deserve all the credit. Furthermore, canvassing is very accountable, meaning that you know darned well whether it's working. Results aren't as accountable when you use the more sophisticated media.

Let's say that you have a brand-spanking-new home security company. You sell and install burglar and smoke alarms. You've named your company Always Alert, and you've printed up business cards but nothing else. Your marketing plan calls for you to spend the first two months canvassing for business. The first month, you'll canvass commercial establishments. The second month, you'll canvass homes. Then you'll decide whether to concentrate on businesses or homes and whether to continue canvassing for new business. Let's assume that you're so short of cash that you cannot afford to run even one ad. I hope that is never the case, but, for now, let's stack the deck against you.

You're ready to make your detailed canvassing plans. What to wear? As a general rule, dress exactly as your prospects dress, whether it be Levi's or a three-piece suit. If you're calling on businesses, I suggest that, whether you are male or female, you wear a dark business suit. The dark colors — navy blue, black, deep gray, or charcoal — lend authority to what you say. The suit itself implies professionalism. Stay away from any accessories that detract from the professional look you wish to convey. Be sure that your hair is neat and your hands clean and that you have a handsome case to carry either samples or sales literature provided by the manufacturer. I'd feel so good that a smile would come easily. You can pick up a lot of details about presenting yourself in *Get What You Deserve: How to Guerrilla Market Yourself*, which I wrote with Seth Godin.

Once you're properly attired, you'll need to decide what to say during the contact, that first precious moment. It's usually best to make a comment first about the store you're visiting: "I like your window display. It seems just right for this location. My name is Tim Winston. My company is Always Alert. We offer security systems to businesses such as yours. What type of security system do you have now?"

During this contact, you complimented the prospect's window display, thereby indicating that you *noticed* it in the first place. I hope that you were smiling and making eye contact as you announced your name and the name of your company. Finally, you *qualified* your prospect with one single question. By "qualified," I mean that you determined your prospect's need for your product. If the prospect has a security system and tells you that it consists of both a burglar alarm and a smoke alarm, you can save time by making no presentation whatsoever and leaving after first thanking the person for the information imparted. You might inquire whether the person is happy with the current security system, and be sure to leave your card behind just in case he or she wishes to make a change later. You are best off keeping the time spent with nonprospects to a minimum. Once indicating that he or she already has what you're selling, don't waste your time or your prospect's.

Following a similar contact at the next store, the prospect may tell you that the business has no security system. That's your cue to make your presentation. While giving it, remember that whenever you mention a feature, *follow it with a benefit*. Hardly anyone buys features, but most of us buy benefits to ourselves. For instance, you could say, "Always Alert features security systems that run on solar power. They never need batteries. They use no expensive electrical power, and they are maintenance free." The feature is the solar power. The benefits are freedom from (1) purchasing batteries, (2) spending money for electrical power, and (3) maintaining the devices.

Continue your presentation, making it as long as it must be, yet as short as it can be. After all, both you and your prospect have other things to do. While presenting, always be on the lookout for closing signs. It may be that you've made the sale and that the prospect wants to buy. But if you don't look for signs that you've said enough, you could lose the sale. As the most successful salespeople say, "ABC — always be *closing*."

When you've finished your presentation, try to close with a question that requires more than a yes-or-no answer. Such a question might be, "Well, that about does it. Will it be better for me to install your alarm system Wednesday or Thursday?" Another could be, "Do you intend to pay for your alarm system at the time of installation, or should I bill you?"

Many excellent books on salesmanship carefully dissect the sale, examining the contact, the presentation, and the close. For reasons of enlarging your bank account rather than catering to my ego, I recommend that you read *Guerrilla Selling*, which I wrote with Bill Gallagher and Orvel Ray Wilson. If you're going to be a guerrilla, go all out; don't merely play at part of it.

Canvassing requires salesmanship. It requires a contact, a presentation, and a close. Furthermore, it requires *quality* in that salesmanship. And it requires far greater salesmanship in terms of quantity. A great car salesman may make ten contacts, presentations, and closes in one good day. You may make ten in one good hour. To succeed at canvassing, you must be enthusiastic about your product, honestly enjoy people, and have a load of determination.

If you're to succeed as an entrepreneur, however — if you're to build your small business into a large one — you must move beyond canvassing, even though it may remain as part of your marketing mix. The disadvantages of canvassing are that (1) it takes much of your time, (2) you can't reach enough prospects even in one high-energy day, and (3) it is limited in scope geographically. These disadvantages disappear when you delegate the canvassing to others. And if you succeed at canvassing, you'll soon become itchy to reach more people.

I want to make you the best canvasser possible, so let's examine the contact, the presentation, and the close in more detail. First, realize that *somebody* is going to close a sale with your customer. It might be a competitor of yours. It might be a friend of the customer. But it will be somebody. It can be someone else or you. While your customer is with you, you have a lot of control over who will close — the most control you will ever have. After you've left your customer, you have very little control, if any. So *the best time to close is while your customer is with you*. Remember that closing is the name of the canvassing game. And though you must make a contact and a presentation, you should be thinking *close, close, close* all along. By doing so, you are gradually closing the entire time you're with your customer. And that's good.

In spite of the importance of closing, it is crucial that you *make* your contact. If you don't, you may not have a chance to move on to the close. Do the contact well, and you may breeze through to the actual close. That's how important the initial contact is.

If your contact comes from a cold call and your prospect is a complete stranger, take steps to make that prospect a new acquaintance. If your contact comes from a lead — a recommendation from a friend, an answer to an ad you ran, or some other reason to make you believe that the prospect can be converted into a customer — refer to that relationship, that bond between you. It will help break the barriers that much more quickly. You are no longer a complete stranger. At the very least, you are now an acquaintance of an acquaintance. Here are some tactics that canvassing pros use.

- Greet your prospect warmly and sincerely, using eye contact.
- Allow your prospect some time to get acclimated to being with you, some time to talk. Don't come on too strong. But don't waste your prospect's time, either.
- Engage in casual conversation at first — especially about anything pertinent to your prospect. Make it friendly and not one-sided. Be a good listener, but also let the prospect know that your time is precious. You are there to sell, not to talk.
- Ask relevant questions. Listen carefully to the answers.
- Qualify the prospect. Determine whether he or she is the specific person to whom you should be talking: the person with the authority to give you the go-ahead, to buy. During the contact, try to learn what to emphasize in your presentation. Try to learn of your prospect's attitude toward your type of offering. Focus on his or her fears, expectations, and feelings so that you can tailor your presentation to them.
- Learn something about the person to whom your contact is directed so that he or she will feel like a person rather than a prospect. Make your prospect like you: People enjoy doing business with people they like. But don't be phony. The best possible thing you can do is to make your prospect *feel* unique, proving that you recognize his or her individuality and needs.
- Be brief, friendly, outgoing, and truly inquisitive. But be yourself.
- If you're in a retail environment, one of the best questions to initiate healthy contact is, "Mind if I ask what brings you into our store today?"

- Even though you are selling, don't think of yourself as a salesperson but as a partner to your prospect. This healthy mindset improves both your perspective and your chances of closing. Realize that you have an opportunity to *educate* your prospects to *succeed* at whatever they wish to succeed at. As soon as possible, learn what it is that your prospect wishes to succeed at; then show how what you are selling can make that success achievable.

Important elements of your contact are your smile, attire, posture, and willingness to listen and look directly into the prospect's eyes. Your nonverbal communication is as important as your verbal communication. The impression you make comes as much from what you don't say as from what you do say.

Often, the sale is clinched during the contact. This happens if your contact has truly opened up communications and you have convinced your prospect that you are honestly interested in helping him or her. During a successful contact, each party will have made a friend — and thereby paved the way to a sale, and, ideally, to continuing sales. The contact may be the shortest of the three phases of a canvass. But it does establish the basis for the presentation and the close.

When making your presentation, keep in mind that you are not talking by accident. You are there because of intent on your part. If your prospect is still with you and has not ended the canvass, there is intent on his or her part, too. And the intent is to buy. Either you will buy a story about why a sale cannot be made, or your prospect will buy what you're selling. It truly is up to you.

Don't forget that people do enjoy being sold to. They do like being persuaded by honest enthusiasm to buy. But they don't like being pressured. Here are some tips to make your presentations flow smoothly.

- List all the benefits, one by one, of doing business with you. The more benefits a prospect knows about, the more likely he or she will buy. When compiling your list of benefits, invite your employees and at least one customer. Don't take the benefits that you offer for granted — customers need to *hear* about them.
- Emphasize the *unique* advantages of buying from you. You should be able to rattle these off with ease. It is on these competitive advantages that you should base your marketing. Don't knock your competition, whatever you do, but don't hesitate to make comparisons between you and that unworthy lout — just as long as they're true.

- If your prospect has no experience with what you are selling, stress the advantages of your *type* of offering, then of your specific offering. If you're selling security devices, talk of the value of owning them, then of the value of owning yours.
- Tailor your presentation to information learned during your contact — and before. I hope you learned a lot before making any contact. Homework pays off tremendously to guerrillas.
- People do not like to be pioneers, because they know darned well that pioneers get arrows in their backs, so mention the acceptance of your products or services by others — especially people in their community. If you can mention names and be specific, by all means do so. The more specific you are, the more closes you'll make. But don't be tedious. You can't bore a prospect into buying.
- When you know enough about your prospect, you can present your product or service from his or her point of view. This ability will increase your number of closes dramatically. Emphasize what your product or service can do for your *prospect*, not for the general population.
- Keep an eagle eye on your prospect's eyes, teeth, and hands. If the prospect is looking around rather than at you, you've got to say something to regain attention. If your prospect is not smiling, you are being too serious. Say something to earn a smile. Most important, smile yourself. That will get your prospect to smile. If your prospect is wringing his or her hands, your prospect is bored. Say something to ease the boredom and spark more interest.
- A sales point made to the eye is 78 percent more effective than one made to the ear. So show as much as you can: photos, drawings, a circular, a product, your sales video, *anything*. Just be sure that it relates to your presentation.
- Sell the benefit along with the feature. If the feature is solar power, for instance, the benefit is economy. If the feature is new computer software, the benefit is probably speed or power or profitability.
- Mention your past successes so the prospect will feel that the key to success is in your hands and there is little chance of a rip-off.
- Be *proud* of your prices, your benefits, your offering. Convey your pride by your facial expressions, tone of voice, and selection of words. Feel the pride and let it come shining through. There are 300,000 commonly used words in the English language, but there are 600,000 nonverbal methods of communication: stance, facial expression, hand gestures, eyebrow position, and 599,996 others. Learn them and use

them. They're completely free — another example of pure guerrilla marketing: no cost and high payoff.

- Throughout your presentation, remain convinced that your prospect *will* buy from you. This optimism will be sensed by the prospect and can affect the close positively.

Despite the importance I have attached to the contact and the presentation, I still reiterate that all the marbles are in the close. Effective salespeople and canvassers are effective closers. Aim to be a dynamite closer and your income will reflect this. To close effectively, try to close immediately rather than in a week or so. Keep these points in mind.

- Always assume that your prospective customer is going to do what you want. Close with a leading question, such as, "Will it be better for you to take delivery this week or next week?" "Do you want it in gray or brown?"
- Summarize your main points and confidently end with a closing line, such as, "Everything seems to be in order. Why don't I write up your order now?"
- Ask the customer to make some kind of decision, then close on it. Typical points that must be agreed on are delivery date, order size, and payment method. A good closing is: "I can perform this service for you tomorrow, the eighth, or the fifteenth. The eighth would be best for me. Which would be best for you?" Attempt the close as soon as possible by easing your prospect into it. If that doesn't work, try again, then again. Continue trying. If you don't, your prospect will spend his or her hard-earned money elsewhere — with someone else. Count on that. Remember: People *like* to be sold to and *need* to have the deal closed. They won't make the close themselves. So you are performing a service when you sell and close. Always be on the alert for signs that the time is right to close. The prospect will hardly ever tell you when the time has come. You must look for hints in the prospect's words *and* actions. A mere shifting of weight from one foot to another may be a signal to close.
- Try to give your prospect a good reason to close *immediately*. It may be that you won't be back in the neighborhood for a long time or that the prospect will wish to use your product or service as soon as possible or that prices are expected to rise or that you have the inventory available now but might not have it later.
- Let your prospect know of the success of your product or service with

people *like* the prospect, with people *recently*, with people in the community — with people *with whom the prospect can easily relate.*

- Be specific with names, dates, costs, times, and benefits. Evasiveness in any area works against you.
- If the prospect likes what you say but won't close now, ask, "Why wait?" The prospect may then voice an objection. And you may close by saying, "That's great, and I understand." Then you can solve the objection and close on it. In fact, one of the easiest ways to close is to search for an objection, then solve the problem and close on it. If you have not yet completed your presentation but feel the time may be right to close, attempt to close on the most important sales point you have yet to state. Always remember that a person knows what you want him or her to do, that there is a reason for your meeting, and that your offering does have merit. If you remember these points, it will be easier for you to close. A prospect who says, "Let me think it over" means no.
- If you don't close just after your presentation, you will most likely lose the sale. Few prospects have the guts to tell you that they will definitely not buy from you. They search for excuses. So do everything you can to move them into a position where they will buy from you. If you don't, a better salesperson will.
- Tie the close in with the contact. Try to close on a personal note. Say something like, "I think you'll feel more secure now with this new security system, and that's important. Shall I have your smoke alarm installed tomorrow or the next day?"

Some canvassers are lucky — those who talk only to people who are honest-to-goodness leads, who have actually demonstrated an interest in the product or service. But most canvassers have to make cold calls. Brr! A pundit once observed, "Throughout history, the most common debilitating human ailment has been cold feet."

Guerrillas, however, aren't troubled by this ailment. They thrive on cold calls. They need no introduction, referral, or appointment. They know that the key to success is to *make the most of the short time they have to attract their prospect's attention.* Here are six hot tips on cold calling.

1. *Do your homework.* Learn as much as possible about the company that you'll visit. The more you know, the better you can tailor your presentation to the prospect.
2. *Start at the top.* Ask for and speak with the person in charge, the one

who can say yes. Before you begin, do what you must to find out this person's name and title. Anything you can learn will prove to be very helpful to you.

3. *Be brief.* Don't waste anyone's time. Keep your message concise. Brevity in cold calling primes you for success.

4. *Get to the point.* Tell whether your offering does the job faster, easier, lasts longer, saves time, saves energy, or whatever. Zero in quickly on the prime benefits of your product or service.

5. *Give references.* Give names of satisfied customers, names that your prospect will recognize and respect. If the prospect doesn't know the name, he or she may know the company.

6. *Close the sale.* Make an appointment. Schedule a full presentation or a demonstration. Before you begin, know exactly what you wish to achieve, and close on that objective.

Whatever you do, *ask for the order.* If you don't feel comfortable with ABC (always be closing), you should learn to feel comfortable with ATC (always *think* closing). If you think closing, your thoughts will carry over to your prospect. And you'll close more as a result. Eventually, you may want to exercise your powers of selling on larger groups of people. The inner core of what you've learned about canvassing can be applied to mass marketing.

A shortcut to credibility in the canvassing game is a handsome, up-to-date business card.

Business Cards

Business cards have all the information they used to have, as well as your fax number, e-mail address, Web site, pager and cellphone numbers, and a lot of data about your company. Sure, they have your meme and your theme line on the front. But they also can market from their reverse side — extolling the benefits you offer, enumerating the services, and perhaps fitting in a bit about your history or even a special offer. A business card can double as a circular or wallet-sized advertisement and can even open up to become a minibrochure. Customers appreciate such minibrochures; their space is at a premium, and your card tells a lot while taking up little space. A guerrilla business card manages to present a lot of valuable information. To stand out, it's in color; the paper stock is unique and thick; and the card is readable horizontally. It's a mistake to print yours vertically. Most people store their cards horizontally. Some staple business cards into their Rolodex, so don't make your card oversized. Don't overlook the marketing power of a business card. A good one costs only a tiny bit more than a bad one — and you know what they say about first impressions. A business card is often the first thing a person will learn about your company.

Personal Letters

The writing of personal letters — not direct mailings of large quantities of letters and brochures but simple, personal letters sent by surface mail or e-mail — is one of the most effective, easy, inexpensive, and overlooked methods of marketing. The large corporations certainly don't use this type of communication, for it doesn't reach enough people to enrich their coffers. However, it's just the ticket for many an individual businessperson. If you can write clear English, spell properly, and keep your message brief, you should develop enough business through this mode of marketing so that you need not use many other methods. If you're a dismal grammarian, many computers can usually help you put your ideas into acceptable form on the printed page. Also, computer software corrects grammar, spelling, and word repetition.

The primary value of a personal letter is that it enables you to convey a truly personal feeling and reach a special place in the mind of the reader. In personal letters, you can relate specific thoughts that are simply not practical in any other medium, except for certain kinds of telephone marketing.

For example, you could write, "Ms. Adkins, your gardenias and carnations look wonderful this year. However, your roses look as though they can use a bit of help. I can provide that help and bring your roses back to glowing health." This is much more personal than to write, "Dear Home Gardener, perhaps your garden isn't as beautiful this year as usual. We offer a full range of garden supplies and expertise to aid you."

In a personal letter, you can, should, and must include as much personal data as possible. Computers make it easy to do so.

Type the person's name, of course, in your personal letter. You want to write about the person's life, business, car, home, or, if you're in the gardening business, garden. By doing so, you are whispering into someone's ear rather than shouting through a distant megaphone. Naturally, you can't mention personal things — or use the person's first name — unless you know the person. Therefore, you need to do your homework and learn about your prospective customers — their working and living habits, hopes and goals, and *problems*. In your customer questionnaires, ask about people's problems — this will help you learn important things about them.

The ability to solve problems and to save time are growth industries today and probably forever. Businesses devoted to success are devoted to obtaining information about their prospects. You can get much of this information from your online or off-line questionnaire or through personal observation. Include your findings in your personal letter; you'll be dazzled by its effect.

After you send your personal letter, you can *double* its effectiveness if you do one of two things — or preferably both — write another personal letter within two weeks, and call the prospect on the telephone. Hey, I never said that guerrilla marketing is a piece of cake.

Your repeat letter can be brief: For the most part, it's a reminder of your original letter. However, it should provide new information and give more reasons to do business with you.

When you make the follow-up telephone call, refer to your letters. Ask whether the person read them. Take advantage of the fact that your letter has broken the "stranger barrier." You are now on speaking terms — ideally, on a first-name basis — with your prospect. Use the phone to develop a relationship. The stronger that relationship, the likelier the person is to do business with you. This relationship will intensify if your letter includes a number of specific *personal* references, demonstrating that you have not sent a clever mass-mailed flier.

You don't need me to tell you that people are bombarded with marketing in their mailboxes and e-mail boxes. Make your letter stand out by making it part of a three- or four-letter campaign. Multiple-mailing campaigns are more expensive than single letters, except with e-mail, but are incredibly effective. Many studies confirm that people patronize businesses with which they are familiar. One of the most enlightening studies was conducted to ascertain the factors that influence a buyer's purchase decision. Five thousand respondents indicated that confidence ranked first, quality second, selection third, service fourth, and price fifth. Don't be surprised by the fifth ranking — price ranked ninth in the 1980s. Price will always be of primary importance to a minority of people.

The truth is that the reasons people buy a product vary from industry to industry, age group to age group, target market to target market, and circumstance to circumstance. The leading appeal to a mother buying baby food differs from the appeal to that same mother buying a sports car.

If you don't have a clear idea of the leading appeal to your potential customers, forget personal letters altogether. You'll gain the greatest benefit from your personal letter if you know the leading appeal and as much personal data as possible. You've got to know what you want your personal letter to accomplish before you write it. And what might that be? It could be an order, a request for more data, or a meeting.

By sending out multiple mailings of personal letters, you build customer confidence through familiarity, paving your way to a relationship and a sale. Only an entrepreneur with a carefully targeted market can afford this luxury. A large company has too many prospects to engage in personal-letter campaigns.

There is a difference between a *personal* letter and a *personalized* letter. The latter is a rather impersonal letter with a person's name in the salutation and within the body of the letter, along with some personal references. The personalization is accomplished by means of a computer. A personal letter, on the other hand, is extremely personal. It is directed to one person and contains so many specific personal references and so much personal information that it cannot possibly be meant for anyone but the person to whom it is addressed. It is signed in ink — smearable, fountain-pen ink. It has a P.S., possibly handwritten. Naturally, it has a greater impact on the reader than a mere personalized letter.

It's possible to generate computer-printed personalized letters that look, act, and feel like a personal letter. Just make the changes on the computer, print it, and sign it by hand — and write the P.S. by hand.

E-mail does have a few shortcomings in the area of direct mail. For one thing, you can't handwrite the P.S. For another, P.S.s aren't as effective in e-mail as they are in surface mail. And then there's the touchy-feely aspect of an envelope with a commemorative stamp and the tactile substance of fine stationery — even one sheet of it.

A goal of your personal mailing is to make it *unnecessary for your prospect to respond*. Your letter might have an e-mail address or standard mail address or phone number but should not ask for a written reply or a phone call. It should not include a means for responding. However, it should whet the reader's appetite. It should tell the reader that you will telephone within a week to set up an appointment or firm up a sale.

The personal letter accomplishes several things: It forces the reader to think about your offer — because it tells the reader that you'll be talking with him or her about it soon. And it separates you from the writers who leave everything to the discretion of the reader and require the reader to take action. You ask the reader to wait for you to take action and provide the missing information. *And your letter prepares the reader for your phone call.* When you do call, you will not be a stranger but an expected caller.

This luxury to withhold a response mechanism in your letters cannot be practiced by big firms: It is inefficient on a large scale. It is the essence of guerrilla marketing, however, because it gives you an edge over the mass marketers. The personal letter goes to a unique extreme to gain attention.

The tone of your letter should incorporate business matters and personal feelings and should appeal to the reader's self-image. If written to the president of a company, for example, your letter should mention the responsibilities of a president, the importance of the job, and the problems encountered. Your letter should be well written, using a relatively sophisticated vocabulary.

How long should a guerrilla personal letter be? One page. Be sure to convey all the information you feel you must convey, but be as brief as possible. A good rule is to make your personal letter short unless it *must* be long. When I say *short*, I mean one full page of warm, personal, motivating, enticing copy. Because it is a personal letter, it need not have a brochure or circular enclosed — although it may. But be warned: If you add an enclosure, you lose the effect of an honest-to-goodness personal letter. Auntie Myrna never enclosed a brochure or a coupon, did she?

Your letter should give the reader relevant information — data that he or she might otherwise not have known. Occasionally, I will remind a prospective advertising client of an upcoming event or a promotion that worked well for another client. A gardener might alert prospects and customers of a coming season that is right for the planting of certain species. A tutor might talk of advances in education. *Give something to the reader rather than merely asking for something or selling something.* Impress a reader with your intelligence, insight, or personality. The prospect might use your information with no acknowledgment of you, but the rewards are usually worth the risks.

It is crucial to remember that the letter should not be about you. It should be about the reader. It should be in the reader's terms, about the reader's life or business. The letter should be loaded with potential benefits for the reader. The greater the number of benefits, the better. Remember the opera *Aida*, a memory crutch to remind you to get *attention* first, then *interest* the reader, then create a *desire*, then make a call to *action*. It may be simpler for you to remember to secure the reader's attention first, then state the benefits of doing business with you, and finally explain the specific action the reader must take — visit a Web site, make a phone call, write a letter, read page 15 of the Sunday paper, expect a phone call, or look for your product the next time the reader is at a Wal-Mart or a mall. Tell the reader exactly what you want him or her to do. Readers aren't going to spend much time trying to figure out what to do.

If you're a guerrilla, you'll treasure these personal letter gems.

- Keep your letter to one page.
- Make your paragraphs short — five or six lines each.

- Indent your paragraphs.
- Do not overuse underlining, capital letters, or writing in margins.
- Do everything you can to keep the letter from looking like a printed piece.
- Sign your letter in ink that is a different color than the type.
- Include a P.S. It should contain your most important point with a sense of urgency.

Studies reveal that when people receive personal, and even printed, letters, they read the salutation first and the P.S. next. Therefore, your P.S. should include your most attractive benefit, your invitation to action, or anything that inspires a feeling of urgency. There is an art to writing a P.S. I recommend that your personal letters — but not your e-mail — include a handwritten P.S. message, because it proves beyond doubt that you have created a one-of-a-kind letter that wasn't sent to thousands of people. In our age of technology, personal touches stand tall.

Here are ten sage suggestions for your P.S.

1. Motivate the prospect to take action. Tell that person to place an order now. Waiting is fatal to your cause.
2. Reinforce your offer. Make it the same as you made in the body of your letter, but make it more urgently, more cogently.
3. Emphasize or introduce a premium or a bonus. The power of freebies cannot be overestimated.
4. Introduce a surprise benefit. It might be just enough to get that prospect off the fence and onto your customer list.
5. Emphasize the price or terms of your offer. If that financial enticement is the heart of your offer, be sure to restate it in your P.S.
6. Stress the tax deductibility of the purchase. If this additional justification to buy is true, here's a good place to mention it.
7. Highlight your guarantee. Present it with pride and excitement, remembering that to your prospects, it removes all element of risk.
8. Tell how many customers you've satisfied in the past. Be specific so that readers will realize that buying from you is the normal thing to do.
9. If you're asking readers to call a toll-free number, repeat it in the P.S. to make it as easy as possible to respond to your offer.
10. Stress an element of urgency. Tell readers the date the offer expires, the limited quantities available, the reasons now is the time to order.

As with a great advertisement, a great personal letter should tell the reader what you are about to say, what you want to say, and, lastly, what you just said. This may seem repetitious, but it's *practical* in these days of mailboxes and e-mail boxes filled with pleas for you to spend your money.

I have written myriad personal letters. Five in ten probably get ignored completely. One in ten probably results in business. The business from that one, however, is usually so profitable that I can easily overlook the nine rejections. Ten percent is an excellent response rate compared with the 2 percent aimed for by many mass mailings.

To give you insight into how I create a personal letter, I provide one here, to which I clipped a crisp one-dollar bill. I mailed it twelve times, with zero business to me, then a thirteenth time, which resulted in enough business to keep me grinning for months. The idea is more than three decades old, yet versions of it continue to gain an impressive response. When I used the tactic of adding a million-dollar check (unsigned) instead of a buck, the letter pulled equally well. The gimmick is strong because it ties in with the letter's promise.

H. H. Thomas
Pacific Telephone
1313 53rd Street
Berkeley, CA 94705

Dear Mr. Thomas:

The dollar bill attached here symbolizes the thousands of dollars Pacific Telephone may be wasting by not utilizing the services of a prime quality freelance direct mail writer.

During this year alone, I have accomplished writing projects for Visa, Crocker Bank, Pacific Plan, Gallo, Bank of America, the University of California, and the Public Broadcasting System. Although these companies do not ordinarily work with freelancers, they did work with me.

In each case, the projects were completed successfully. In each case, I was given more assignments. There must be a reason why.

If you want to provide Pacific Telephone with the best freelance writing available for any type of project — or if you have a seemingly impossible deadline — I hope you will give me a call.

I have enclosed a description of my background — just to inform you that I have won major writing awards in all the media and that I have served as a Vice-President and Creative Director at J. Walter Thompson, America's largest advertising agency. I guarantee you, however, that I am far more interested in winning sales than winning awards.

By your company settling for mere competent writing, or by having your writing assignments handled by traditional sources, you just might be wasting Pacific Telephone's money. A good number of the Fortune 500 companies have already figured that out.

I'll call you Tuesday morning to set up an appointment for a pilot project. I look forward to meeting you.

Very truly yours,
Jay Levinson

P.S. If you are not the person who assigns work to freelancers, I would appreciate it if you would pass this letter (and this dollar) on to the person who does. Thank you very much.

It usually helps if you include a unique or informal enclosure with your letter. A newspaper article, trade magazine article (especially in your prospect's trade), or copy of your prospect's ad or a competitive ad helps a great deal, because the reader probably wants to read such material and will appreciate your sending it. In my case, the one-dollar enclosure served to separate my letter from the many others sent to the addressee. I'll bet that many of them spent more than a dollar on a brochure. And I figure I'm the only one whose mailing piece was printed by the U.S. Treasury.

Would this letter be effective today? Judging by the way it has worked so far, it will be effective until every direct mailer in America does the same thing. But I would make one change if there were a recession or economic downturn. After the fourth paragraph, I would write a separate paragraph, motivated by the recession: "My fees are not low. But in a recession, you can't afford to take chances with less than the highest possible quality."

Timing is very important. Be careful you don't mail when everyone else is mailing. Try to time your mailing to coincide with a particular season or the advent of a new competitor or when you hear word that your prospect may be in trouble and in the market for whatever it is you're offering. If there happens to be an ugly economic downturn for your offering, remember how guerrillas handle such opportunities during the bleak days of a troubled economy.

1. Market more to your customers and less to your prospects and the universe in general. Rely on, love, and make enticing offers to the people who have already learned to trust you: your customers.
2. Use the telephone as a follow-up weapon. We're talking relationships here, and if you've got one on paper, widen it to include the telephone, a potent weapon in tough times. When the going gets tough, the tough make phone calls.
3. Eliminate any perceived risk of buying from you. Do it with a guaran-

tee, warranty, deep commitment to service. Let the customer know that *the sale is not over until he or she is completely satisfied.* Guerrillas use this tactic to assuage skittish prospects.

4. Keep an eagle eye out for new profit centers, fusion-marketing opportunities, and cooperative ventures. Because others are also suffering through the dismal economy, there's a good chance that they'll be willing to go along with your idea for a collaborative effort.

5. Instead of shrinking your offerings, go against the grain and expand them. Do what you can to increase the size of your purchases, your selection of profit-producing items, the services you offer. Never forget that geometric growth comes from larger transactions, repeat business, and referral customers. Be geometric as often as possible.

6. Let your customers know that you are fully aware of the state of the nation economically and that you are basing your prices and offerings on it, making your business a more sensible place to patronize than ever before.

7. Tap the enormous referral power of your customers, knowing that your warm and careful follow-up to them will make them want to help you by giving you three, four, or five names of likely prospects.

During tough times as well as during healthier ones, it's important to mail your letter to the person who ought to be reading it. Find out who that is by studying the appropriate directories on the Internet or, better still, by phoning all the companies to which you hope to mail. When in doubt, mail your letter to the company president, who will either *be* the person you want to reach or will see to it that the right person does read your letter. It's worth a call to the company's phone operator to find out the president's name and the correct spelling. If you aren't willing to take the time to do that, you probably aren't meant to be a guerrilla. Take the time to attend to tiny details. You can be sure that if the president asks a subordinate to read something, it will get read.

With a computer and a printer, you can send out several thousand letters or even more if they're e-mails, all of which will appear to be personal letters, for all can be personalized with appropriate comments. But keep in mind that these are not personal letters unless they are written to sound personal and you take the time to learn personal details. Only a letter that is full of personal references is really a personal letter. It has nothing to do with technology and everything to do with psychology.

Personal letters can be sent out in smaller numbers. They will give you, the entrepreneur, a big advantage over the huge corporations. Take advantage of this valuable tool. If you do so, you are practicing guerrilla marketing with maximum skill.

Once you have a customer, do all you can to intensify the relationship. Do not treat all customers and prospects equally. Consider a menswear chain with a database of 47,000 names but whose mailings never include more than 3,000 pieces. Who receives the mail? Says the owner, "Only the people appropriate to mail to." When he received trousers of a specific style, he mailed only to those customers to whom he was certain they'd appeal. He enjoyed a 30 percent response rate.

Does it take extra time? Yes. Does it take extra energy? Yes. Does it take an extra dollop of imagination? Yes. Does it take extra money? No. But it earns high profits for you. And that's what makes it guerrilla marketing.

Telephone Marketing

Telephone marketing means picking up the phone, consulting your list, and calling one of your hottest prospects. My fellow guerrilla, Chet Holmes, refers to this list as your "Dream 100" — the 100 clients you'd most like to have. He recommends a laser focus on getting their business — not immediately, because life isn't like that, but eventually, because life is like that. I hope you follow his advice and get your Dream 100 on your customer list. But in the meantime, you should know some things about marketing on the telephone. For one thing, in 1982, telephone marketing surpassed direct mail in revenues spent, and the gap has been widening ever since. In 2005, well over half of all goods and services sold were sold by phone. Telephone marketing is used both by the big guys and by budding entrepreneurs. Telemarketing employs more than 12 million people, compared to 175,000 in 1983, when guerrilla marketing was invented.

Although Do Not Call lists have put a big damper on it, there's no question that telephone marketing has emerged as a prime marketing force, especially for business-to-business marketing, except for many of the telecommunications companies, which market to individuals — with special intensity, it seems, during the dinner hours.

Currently, there are three ways you can engage in telephone marketing. The first is individual phone calls, made by you or a member of your company. The second is mass telemarketing, which is carried out by firms specializing in it or by dedicated telemarketing departments and is directed at thousands of potential customers at a time. The third is by computer. Computerized calling machines call prospects, deliver tape-recorded sales pitches, and even pause during their messages so that prospects can answer questions and place orders. This method may be a bit impersonal, and many consider it an invasion of privacy, but it's commonly practiced. And for many a company, it works. Machines aren't hurt by rejection. A 1 percent or 2 percent response rate can be very cost-effective.

A telephone call takes less time than a canvass, is more personal than a letter, costs less than both (unless it's long distance), and provides you with fairly close personal contact with your prospect. It's difficult to say no to a person's face. It's less difficult to say no to a person's voice, and it's least difficult to say no to a person's letter or e-mail.

Guerrillas use telemarketing to make their ads and other marketing efforts work harder. They know that 7 percent of people hang up on all telemarketers, that 42 percent hang up on some telemarketers, and that 51 percent listen to all telemarketers. Bless that teensy majority. Even though most say no, each one should be appreciated for the clarity of their answer and for not wasting your time.

Experienced telemarketers realize that many calls are screened by secretaries or assistants and know that they must view the screener not as an enemy but as an ally. Screeners are given information, treated with respect, and informed of the results you are offering, not merely your product or service. When you enlist the screener as a resource, you'll find that the door to the boss's office opens more readily.

What kinds of companies use telemarketing? Mainly they are businesses that sell to other businesses. Often, though, they are businesses trying to sell directly to consumers, trying to sell anything from storm doors to automobile windshields to photographic services to chimney sweeps. An increasing number are charities trying to raise funds for their good works. My nephew George has raised so much money for the San Francisco Symphony that they ought to award him his own conductor's baton. The businesses that succeed plan the entire phone call: the objective, the words spoken, the mood and tone, and the follow-up.

Before calling a number, savvy telemarketers ask themselves what they know about the prospect, what they need to know in order for the prospect to take the action desired, what information might be obtained from a screener, what to say in case voicemail technology answers the call, what their opening statement will be, what questions they'll ask, and how they'll *end* the call (no matter what happens).

As with advertising, telephone marketing should be part of an overall marketing program. And it should be a continuing effort. One phone call isn't enough. If a member of your company makes the phone calls, certain incentive policies should be instituted. For instance, you should always pay your designated callers both by the completed call and by the completed sale. Even if you use a salaried employee, add incentive bonuses to the salary. Give an even higher incentive for first-time sales to new customers.

Regardless of who makes the calls, proper voice training is a good idea. Talk clearly. Use short sentences. Talk loudly but not directly into the mouthpiece; talking across the mouthpiece gives the most effective voice transmission. Your voice should project authority and warmth while instilling trust. Your message should be stated as concisely as possible. Whatever you do, don't read from a script. However, research shows that it's always a good idea to *memorize* a script, changing any words that feel "uncomfortable." The script must be so well memorized that the words sound as though you know them by heart, as natural as the Pledge of Allegiance. Find words and phrases that come naturally to you. Leave space for the person on the other end to respond. Guerrillas are in full control of their telemarketing and do not recite awkward speeches to their prospects.

Recently, I had an e-mail exchange with an old friend who told me that he tripled his income. "Cool, Jeff, how did that happen?" I asked. Jeff, who does voice-over announcing, said that he took voice lessons that enabled him to become two other people. He is the voice of many a movie trailer, a totally different voice for a big-city TV station, and a third voice for the on-hold marketing firm he runs. "Best of all," he wrote, "I do 99 percent of my work from my home studio."

Studies in varied industries consistently reveal that a memorized telemarketing presentation always produces better results than the same presentation from an outline. It may be more humanistic to let the caller use his or her own words, but few callers have the ability to summon the right ones. Gone are the days when it was recommended that callers use an outline, or "thought flow." However, the more naturally conversant you sound, the more sales you'll make. And that takes practice. Naturally, much of what you say will be in response to what the person being called says, but the best telemarketers are in full control of the call. They stay in control by asking questions, responding to the answers, and then asking more questions, directing the conversation toward the customer's needs.

If you are more comfortable using an outline to structure your phone presentations, be sure to heed the following guidelines. If the outline is longer than one page, you should try to streamline it. An outline creates a structure for your thoughts and ideas, and it keeps the call on track when the person at the other end redirects it. If you feel that you must work from an outline, it's a good idea to write a script of the phone call. After you write the script, you should do three things. First, record it. See what it sounds like. After all, you'll be using "ear" words, which are heard, rather than "eye" words, which are seen. There's a big, big difference. Words that callers unconsciously love to hear are *profits, sales, dollars, revenues, income, cash flow, savings, time, productivity, morale, motivation, output, attitude, image, victories, market share,* and *competitive edge.* What callers dislike hearing is jargon and new buzzwords. Second, make sure that the recorded script sounds like a conversation and not like an ad. Leave room for the person being called to talk. Third, make it a point not to restate the script but to rephrase it. State the same selling points. Present them in the same order. Use words with which you are comfortable. Your telephone outline should be able to accommodate several situations. After all, if your prospect decides to buy just after you've started, you should be prepared to close the sale and end the conversation.

Notice how your friends, and probably even you, assume different voice personalities when speaking on the phone. This is subtle, but it's there. Try to eliminate that telephone personality and bring out your most conversational qualities by practicing on the phone — talking to a tape recorder or to a friend. If you're going to do a good amount of telephone marketing, engage in role playing, with you as the customer and a friend or associate as you. Then switch roles. Role playing gives you a lot of insight into your offering and your message. Repeat this until you are completely satisfied with your presentation.

Many telephone solicitations crumble when objections are made. These objections are really opportunities in disguise. Many successful telephone salespeople (and nontelephone salespeople) are able to close sales when handling objections. In fact, "close on the objection" is a sales credo for many pro sellers. One way to handle an objection is to rephrase it. By doing so, you may be able to dissipate it. "We're already buying from someone else," says the person at the other end. "Oh, you're completely satisfied with the price, quality, and service you're currently receiving and feel there's no room for improvement?" By rephrasing the objection, you not only defuse it but also create an opportunity for yourself.

When calling a potential customer, try to establish a real relationship with that person. You may never speak to him or her again, but you should try to create a bond. Do so with a couple of personal questions or observations. Ask the person about a non-job-related subject. Relate as a human being before you relate as a salesperson. You probably have some interests in common. Meet on that common ground if possible.

Make no mistake: Your purpose in making the phone call is to make a sale. So go for it. A good opening that has worked for many guerrillas is straightforward:

> This is _____ with _____. We specialize in working with businesses, helping them to _____. Depending on what you're using in the area of _____, we might have something that could potentially help you to _____."

Another good way to open is to explain exactly why you're calling.

> Hello, Mr. Crain, my information shows me that you're driving a 2004 sports car. I'm calling because our company specializes in detailing sports cars like yours, bringing them back to their original glory and luster. Your car is on its way to becoming a classic. We'd love to contribute to its beauty. We're going to be in your neighborhood during the afternoon of Tuesday, November 2. What time would be best for us to come by and discuss the options available to you?

Think in terms of contact, presentation, and close. Remember, your contact should be brief and warm. Your presentation should be concise yet loaded with references to benefits. And your close should be clear and definite. Don't pussyfoot. In most instances, there is nothing wrong with asking for the sale. Just don't do it in such a way that a yes-or-no answer can be given. Close by saying something like, "What will be the most convenient way for you to pay for this: check or credit card?"

The following script is from a telephone marketing program that was used in conjunction with a direct-mail program. This makes for a potent combination. These days, as direct mail increases rapidly, it makes sense to follow up a mailing with a phone call. For guerrillas, it's almost mandatory with big-ticket sales. In this instance, the mailing was followed two weeks later by a phone call. A week later, another call was made. The program worked. Direct mail alone would not have worked.

> Hello, Mr. _____? This is _____. I'm calling for the Wilford Hotel in Los Angeles. Have you ever been to the Wilford? When was the last time you were in Los Angeles? Recently, we sent you an invitation. Did you receive it? Are you the person who makes out-of-town meeting arrangements for your firm, or is it someone else? Do you plan to take us up on our special offer now, or do you plan to request more information? As you may recall, we are offering special prices and complimentary services to companies that hold meetings at the Wilford between April 1 and June 30. Will your company be holding a meeting in Los Angeles during that time? Did you like the special offer we made to you? Do you have any questions about it? Do you usually have meetings in hotels such as the Wilford? How many people attend the meetings? Where do you ordinarily meet? I think you

might be interested in holding a meeting at the Wilford. Don't forget, during the period from April 1 to June 30, we're offering

- Special room rates
- Complimentary meeting room
- Complimentary wine with dinner
- One free room for every fifteen booked
- A complimentary coffee break daily
- Discounts on audiovisual equipment
- Preregistration for your people
- A suite for the meeting planner

Doesn't this sound good? You get all these benefits with a minimum of only fifteen guest rooms. Is there anything else we might offer you? When do you plan to hold your next meeting? When would be the best time to arrange a reservation for your group at the Wilford? Would you like to make the arrangements right now or later? When? Is there any other person at your company that you suggest I contact? Thanks very much for taking this time to speak with me. Good-bye.

As you can see, a good phone script calls for lots of questions, so that the person will feel he or she is part of the process and won't feel "talked at." What you say on the phone should be part of your overall marketing and creative plans, so measure your scripts against your marketing strategies.

An unfortunate aspect of telemarketing is that most calls are poorly scripted. It takes talent to create a good call. That means more than a way with words. A guerrilla telemarketing script helps telemarketers overcome employee turnover, despondent moods, lack of enthusiasm, and rejection daze. It keeps callers on track and ensures that prospects receive accurate data — all the while allowing for natural telephone conversation. It even raises and answers objections.

Most scripts fail because they don't give enough credence to the very important human element and because telemarketing is now regarded as suspicious by an increasingly sophisticated public. Be sure your scripts are tight yet loaded with warmth. Difficult to do? You bet it is.

Be sure your script has tons of humanity built into it, with room for give-and-take. Let the telemarketer add his or her own words and phrases to the script. The more comfortable the telemarketer, the more relaxed the prospect. Relaxed prospects are good to have.

Keep your script one page long, single-spaced. Paragraph 1 introduces the caller and the company. Paragraph 2 gives the reason for the call or makes the offer. Paragraph 3 highlights the benefits of the offer. Paragraphs

4 and 5 close the sale or set the stage for the next step — possibly a personal appointment.

Your script should contain a good reason for your call. You have fifteen to twenty seconds to gain or lose your prospect's attention, so don't waste one second or one word. Guerrilla scripts contain about four interest-creating comments and flow directly to the benefits. They build rapport immediately with questions.

Good scripts have systems to handle objections to the sale and to close the sale. You must be prepared for massive amounts of rejection when you embark on a telephone marketing program. For this reason, employee turnover in telephone marketing firms is tremendous.

One of the great advantages of telephone marketing is that you can obtain an instant response to your offer. You can deal with objections and overcome them. You can make contact with many people. In doing so, you can categorize the people you have called as customers, near customers, and noncustomers. In rare instances, you can accomplish all your marketing by phone. Some companies do. But even the great Dell Computer is learning the value of face time.

It's not difficult to see why such marketing works far better for businesses selling to other businesses than it does for companies selling directly to consumers. Consumers at home have little time for business, but businesspeople in their place of business do have a bit of time for business matters, even those that come by phone. High-ticket sales are one of the reasons for telemarketing success in business-to-business transactions; with individual consumers, profits tend to be far lower, making telemarketing to them less cost-efficient.

Be sure that you don't expect too much from your telemarketing campaign. A financial organization mailed a letter to its prospects, offering a free gift to those who requested a brochure. Telemarketing to the brochure requesters netted many personal appointments. It was during these appointments that sales were closed. Although sales may be closed on the phone, telemarketing is merely a crucial cog in a big machine.

When you telemarket, you must know which benefits turn on your prospective customers. Give prime emphasis to the benefits you feel have the most impact. Be sure you are speaking with the right person. Make a specific offer — preferably a special offer that is not available to all people at all times. And know how you'll handle objections, because they'll be as common as busy signals and answering devices.

The more people you call, the more sales you'll close. Of every twenty people you *call*, you'll probably make contact with only about five on your first try. The others will be busy, sick, away, on the phone, or otherwise indisposed. Of every twenty people you *reach*, you may close only one sale on the phone. You'll have to make about one hundred calls to close one sale. It may sound like a lot, but to a true telephone marketing pro, it means that a mere one thousand phone calls will result in ten sales. The top telemarketers cherish every *no* they get, because they realize that the ninety-nine are worth the one sale. Figuring an average of three minutes per call (some will take up to ten minutes, but most will take less than one minute), this means that fifty hours of calling will result in ten sales.

This also means that you'll either spend one hard workweek on the phone, or you'll hire someone to be on that phone for you. If your profit per sale is great enough, you should give serious consideration to this kind of marketing. If ten sales aren't nearly enough, perhaps you should think about using other marketing methods. For some entrepreneurs, ten sales in one week mean joy, wealth, and fulfillment. If you believe that telephone marketing makes sense for your offering, use it and take advantage before your competitors discover its powerful capabilities.

Look at the cost/return feasibility before starting a telemarketing campaign of your own. Only 3 percent of people called sit through a computerized telemarketing call, whereas 33 percent sit through a call from a live human being. A mere 4 percent of people reached by telemarketing place an order. To help you get your act together, find out what's new in telemarketing by contacting your local telephone company, which will probably tell you to test, test, and test: your scripts, your callers, and your target markets.

If you are pleased with the results of your telemarketing — and you will be if you combine it with other guerrilla marketing methods — remember that it can always be improved. That's why guerrillas never stop testing their scripts, continually experimenting with new words, phrases, and ideas. As a result, their response rates continue to rise.

In this chapter, I discussed only one aspect of telemarketing: outbound telemarketing. I didn't bring up inbound telemarketing — the taking of incoming calls — because it involves proper telephone demeanor and has long been in the domain of large businesses rather than small guerrilla businesses. But that is changing as small businesses are discovering the heady joy and nonstop excitement of home shopping channels.

If you deal only with local prospects and customers, do not establish a toll-free number, for people like to deal with local companies. It's the confidence factor again. If you feel that you must have a toll-free number, I must warn you that if it spells out a word, people probably won't write it down, because they figure they'll remember it. The truth is, they won't.

Telemarketing is a superb minimarketing weapon, already doubling as a maximarketing weapon. I encourage you to give it a try, especially if you're selling to businesses. In 2005, the average telephone transaction — contact to closed sale — was higher than $550 per call when one business telemarketed to another. Maybe you can improve on that figure. This guerrilla sure hopes so.

Circulars

There may not be much difference between a circular and a flier, but a brochure is a different kind of animal. Circulars and fliers are short and single minded; a brochure is longer and more detailed than either.

There are several ways to distribute circulars and brochures. They may be mailed alone or as part of a mailing package, placed in mailboxes, slipped under doors or windshield wipers, handed out at street corners and at trade shows and wherever lots of prospects congregate, given to prospects and/or customers, placed in racks that say "take one" or on counters for general distribution, posted on community bulletin boards, and placed in hotel rooms.

If you're going to distribute many pieces, make them circulars, because circulars are less expensive per piece. If you are distributing relatively few pieces, you might opt for the more expensive brochures.

The simplest form of circular is a single sheet of paper, printed on one side. Printing on both sides makes matters and format a tad more complex. Printing on both sides of two pieces of paper — each folded in half — makes a booklet, which I call a brochure if it is loaded with information, printed or visual. If it isn't, it's not really a brochure but a folded circular. Some brochures run as long as twenty-four pages.

A circular is considered by many astute guerrillas to be the purest of weapons. It gets instant action if used properly. It is astonishingly inexpensive, especially if produced on your own computer. It lets you use color in a sea of black and white. And it's the essence of simplicity and flexibility if you do it right. Your circular should

- Make a clear and persuasive offer
- Have an element of urgency
- Get right to the point
- Tell the prospect what to do next
- Tie in with your current identity

When planning to produce such materials, remember that when you fold a sheet of paper in two, you have a total of four pages (two on each side). So generally, you must think in terms of four-page units. Brochures are ordinarily four or eight or twelve pages. Some brochures have panels that fold rather than pages that turn. Usually, these are six-panel brochures: three panels on each side. If you start with a standard 8 × 11 piece of paper, folding it twice makes it ready to become a six-panel brochure and the ideal size for a standard #10 envelope.

The format isn't nearly as important as the content. And the content must be factual information, enlivened with a touch of style and romance. Unlike ads, which must flag a person's attention, a brochure or a circular already has that attention. Its primary job is to inform with the intention of selling. Most brochures, and some circulars, display artwork to keep the piece visually interesting. The purpose is to explain, inform, and sell.

When writing a circular, think first of the basic idea you wish to express. Then try to marry a picture (art or photograph) to a set of words. After you've stated your idea as briefly as possible, try to explain more fully what you are offering. *Always* be sure to include relevant information: your address and phone number. A circular is a headline. In fact, many guerrillas regard a circular as *all headline.* No need to attract attention; you've already got it. If you don't state your offer in a way that can be understood at a glance, I'm not too hopeful about your success. There's no need to list all your benefits — list your greatest benefit. My first boss and marketing idol, Howard Gossage, said, "You don't have to wound a charging tiger all over to stop him; one well-placed shot ought to do the job."

Let's talk about that entrepreneurial-minded contractor who calls himself Handyman Hero. He markets his services well, and he decided to improve business by distributing a circular or a brochure. This is how he proceeded. He first used a circular to see how this marketing vehicle would work for him. If it worked well, he might upgrade it to a brochure. On the circular, he included a drawing of a man (himself as a hero) doing five tasks at the same time in front of a house. Above the drawing, he listed his company name, which, incidentally, made a dandy headline for his circular: IT'S HANDYMAN HERO! Beneath that headline and picture, he briefly stated his offering:

He builds sun decks and patios.
He installs skylights and hot tubs.
He paints and puts up wallpaper.
He does masonry and electrical work.
He also designs and makes building plans.
HANDYMAN HERO DOES IT ALL!
Call him at 555-5656 any time, any day.
All work guaranteed. Contractor's License #54-45673.

Not very fancy but quite explicit. The cost for Handyman Hero to write this circular was nil. An art student drew the illustration for $50, and the cost to produce about 5,000 of the circulars, including paper, was another $100. It would have cost less if Handyman Hero had a computer on which to create the circular, but he didn't. So he spent about $150, which comes to three cents per circular. If printing costs had been higher — and they are higher now — he would have spent less than a nickel per circular. He didn't want to pay for color, but he was able to get a colorful circular by the ingenious use of colored ink on a colored paper stock — dark blue ink on light tan stock.

Handyman Hero then distributed his circulars by several methods: He mailed one thousand, placed one thousand on auto windshields (he hired a high school student to do some of this for him), distributed one thousand at a home show in his area, handed out one thousand at a local flea market, and kept one thousand to give to satisfied customers to pass on to their friends and neighbors. The enterprising handyman also asked each of his customers where they had heard of him. When they said, "I saw your flier," he asked where they had seen it. By doing so, he learned which of the five methods of circular distribution was most effective. That's guerrilla marketing! Not expensive but very effective. One job could recoup for Handyman Hero his entire marketing budget for circulars. And since five thousand circulars were distributed, you have to believe that he found more than one job.

Brochures

Perhaps he will decide to distribute a brochure someday. But would he distribute it or put it on his Web site and save on paper and printing costs? To plan a successful brochure for any purpose, he'd ask himself what the brochure is specifically supposed to do for him. Get leads? Close sales? Generate phone calls? Web site visits? People won't take the time to figure it out for themselves, so Handyman Hero has to do it for them.

My guess is that he'd think in terms of photography, so that he could show pictures of work he has accomplished. And because he has such a comprehensive offering, he'd figure that an eight-page brochure was needed to do the trick. Create a video brochure according to a strategy, just as you'd create a printed brochure. Say as much as you can *visually*. Realize that your visuals will communicate more powerfully than your verbiage, so keep the visual excitement to a maximum. Be sure the visuals pertain to your company and aren't merely special visual effects substituting for a solid idea.

A video brochure is jazzy and more dynamic than a printed piece, but its purpose is to make a sale: all by itself, in concert with a sales rep who is present during the viewing of the video, or in tandem with a direct-mail letter, card, or phone call. In numbers, there is strength. In visuals, there is strength. As wonderful as your video brochure may be, it is only as powerful as your idea.

Electronic and printed brochures are expensive. So don't say anything you'll want to amend within a year.

Follow up on everyone who requests any kind of brochure.

Unless the brochure was full color — a good idea because color increases retention rate by 57 percent and proclivity to buy by 41 percent — all type and photos would be in black ink. The paper stock, either glossy or not, would be white or a light color.

He'd plan to use the same drawing on the cover that he used on his circular. After all, if it worked once, it ought to work again. And it makes good economic sense. His cover would show his drawing, list his company name (which fortunately doubles as a headline and a brochure title), and maybe, but not definitely, list the other copy points from his circular. Let's say that he does list them, since he wants to impart as much information as possible. *Repetition in marketing is far more of a good thing than a bad thing.* And guerrillas realize that the real purpose of the cover is to give people a reason to read the rest of your brochure. The cover should go a long way toward answering the prospect's most important question: "What's in it for me?"

His second page might list pertinent information about Handyman Hero. It would list his experience, training, skills, and offerings and the jobs he has accomplished. It might even include a photo of him. The purpose of this page? To build his credibility. As a guerrilla, he knows that the more credible he is, the better results he will derive from his other marketing.

Page 3 might show photos of a sun deck and a patio and would give a description, about five sentences long, of the handyman's capabilities in this area. Page 4 would show photos of a skylight and a hot tub that he installed. Again, five or six sentences would indicate his expertise. Page 5 would show photos of a room that Handyman Hero painted and another room that he papered. It would also include a bit of copy attesting to his talent at painting and papering. Page 6 could feature photos of houses with masonry and electrical work he accomplished. One would be an exterior shot and the other an interior shot. Again, copy would describe the work accomplished. Each of these pages should repeat the short copy lines from the cover. For example, the seventh page, carrying a photograph of a gorgeous room addition that he designed and built, would carry the headline, "Handyman Hero also makes building plans and building designs." A few sentences of copy would follow the photo. The purpose of the brochure is to *inform*.

Finally, his eighth page, the back cover, would provide the name of his company, his phone number, fax number, Web site, e-mail address, contractor's license number, and a copy of the best photo from the interior of the brochure. Such a brochure might cost him as much as one dollar per unit. It's worth it, considering his profit per sale. He runs a relatively simple business, so his brochure is focused. If he had other special offerings, such as stained glass windows, he'd create separate brochures for those talents.

A solar-heating company for which I created a brochure had a problem. The company realized that a brochure would help its business, but the technology in the industry was changing so rapidly that the company was reluctant to commit itself to producing one. Solution: I created an eight-page brochure with a pocket inside the back cover. Within the eight pages, the brochure addressed all the aspects of solar technology that were not changing: its economy, cleanliness, responsibility to the environment, and acceptance and success in all parts of the world. In the pocket, the company inserts separate sheets that describe specific equipment as technology marches forward. These sheets are replaced at will. Price lists, also replaceable at a whim, are inserted there as well. This enables the company to have flexibility with its brochure.

Let's look at another example. A jewelry-making firm in San Francisco manufactured beautiful but very expensive jewelry. To add an element of value, the company produced a lavish brochure — full color, glossy, and photographed in the most glamorous parts of San Francisco. Each two-page spread contained one gorgeous photo of the San Francisco area and one photo of an item of jewelry. This lent to each piece of jewelry an air of value that could not have been created with a single photo. It connected the jewelry store with San Francisco, where tourism is the largest industry. A brochure was just the ticket.

One of my clients sent a photographer on a dream assignment to visit Mexico and shoot photos of a wide variety of villas and condominiums that my client was renting to people for vacation use. These photos were later made the basis for a colorful brochure. Without the photos, the brochure could have dealt with villa and condo vacations only in a theoretical sense. The photos brought the theory to vibrant life. The brochure helped the company quadruple its sales. Without a vehicle to show the many villas and condos, complete with beaches, pools, balconies, lush living rooms, and spacious bedrooms, the company could not have made its point. Less than a brochure could not have done the job.

Still another company was able to grow from tiny to tremendous merely by the proper use of a brochure. The company owned the patent on a new product that replaced the old-fashioned blowtorch. But the firm couldn't communicate all the advantages of its product with ads or letters or phone calls. Personal demonstrations were impractical because of logistics problems. A brochure was the answer. It was incredibly detailed, listing all the advantages of the product and all the famous-name companies using it and showing several exciting shots of the product in use. The brochure included a pageful of testimonials from satisfied users, and it described the technical data in such detail that even the most nitpicking engineer would be impressed. In addition, it was very handsome. This inspired confidence in the company. To this day, the company's primary marketing tools are its Web site and that brochure.

Many companies have a story that does not translate well in advertising but becomes brilliantly clear when the details, both verbal and graphic, are communicated in a brochure. You can afford to spend a great deal of your marketing budget producing a knockout brochure. The cost, including everything, runs anywhere from $500 to $50,000. But don't let the $50,000 figure scare you. That's only $4,166.67 per month, much less than many companies spend on media advertising alone. Perhaps you won't even need the mass media — perhaps a brochure will do the trick for you.

And then again, you'll begin to realize why so many companies now produce their brochures online. Changes are easy, paper costs are nil, and you don't get that messy ink on your hands.

Until now, you've read only the bad news about circulars and brochures. Here's the good news: They are more inexpensive to create and produce than ever before. Easy-to-use computer software is the reason. It lets guerrillas like Handyman Hero produce circulars and brochures at a fraction of what they used to cost. If you own a computer and current software, the figure of from $500 to $50,000 is more like $50 to $500 these days, an enormous difference, which is why guerrillas are so quick to embrace today's simplified technology.

Make no mistake: There is *no* room these days for a *trace* of amateurishness, sloppiness, smudges, poor grammar, misspelled words, typos, contradictions, or omissions. Use your computer's spellchecker and then hire a good proofreader to check anything you intend to expose to the public. Better that one friend or associate catch your goofs than five thousand prospects.

At the end of your brochure, be sure to tell people exactly what they are supposed to do — whether they should call you, visit you, visit your

Web site, fax you, or send you e-mail. Tell them exactly what you want them to do now that they know about you. Guerrillas assume nothing and test everything.

Although some businesses benefit almost every time they give away their brochure, there are instances in which you shouldn't give one away. If you have a store and distribute brochures to your potential customers, you are giving them an excuse not to buy. They can tell you that they want to look over your brochure before buying. I advise my clients, except those selling very expensive items, *not* to give their brochures to shoppers but to give them only to people who have purchased or to those who are on their way out. But do ask if they want one. Don't waste weapons.

I also advise people who run newspaper or magazine ads that convey a lot of information to consider using those ads as brochures. Reprint them and add front and rear covers by printing on the back of the folded-in-half advertisement. Often, the magazine will do this for you for peanuts.

If you don't have the budget for large ads, consider running small ads offering your free brochure. I know a man who earns his entire income (a six-figure income, I might add) by running tiny ads in myriad publications, offering his free brochure in each ad. Those who request the brochure are serious prospects: They took the time to write for the brochure. They are interested in what he's offering. My friend's brochure does his entire selling job for him. It describes his offer, gives the details, and asks for the order. His ads and his brochures are his only marketing tools, and he is very successful as a one-man show. This demonstrates how important a brochure can be.

Guerrillas consider their brochures to be part of a dance called the two-step. Step 1 is running a lot of little ads that say one salient thing about their companies and then have the magic line: "Call, write or send e-mail for our *free* brochure." You must give people a choice whether to call, write, or send e-mail, because a third of them won't call, a third won't write, and a third won't send e-mail. And you should highlight the absence of cost, because *free* is the most powerful word in the language of marketing.

When people call or write requesting your free brochure, should you send it to them all by itself? Of course not. Because people are bombarded with an estimated 4,700 marketing messages every day, contacting you for your brochures signifies a mighty powerful *act of intent* on their part. Acknowledge that fact by sending, along with your free brochure, a brief note thanking them for taking the time to request it. Sign that note in ink before mailing the brochure. Follow up with a card or a letter within ten days (a week is even better), taking the sale to the next level. If you do this, you can expect between 25 percent and 33 percent of brochure requesters to become paying customers. Brochures should be given only to people who really want them. Circulars and business cards can go to anybody.

If anything does a brochure's job better than a brochure, it is an *electronic brochure* — a five- to nine-minute version of a printed brochure.

If you don't require visual input to tell your business story perhaps you can do it with words. Put your words onto tape or a CD and offer an *audio brochure*. Approximately 97 percent of Americans have access to an audiocassette or CD player. A growing number of Americans commute for longer than thirty minutes each day. Instead of listening to the radio, they'll probably listen to your five- to fifteen-minute tape or CD. They know it's a way to learn while saving time.

Guerrillas rarely send brochures to anyone who doesn't request them. And when they do send brochures, they always include a brief note, signed in ink by them, identifying themselves as the president or owner of the company, thanking the person for requesting the brochure. They also send a follow-up note to these people within one week of mailing their brochure. Anyone who takes the time to ask for a brochure is really a torrid prospect asking for all the details. When's the last time you requested a brochure and received a note from the head of the company? Probably never. And that's why you will stand out so much when you do it.

Guerrillas go all out to convert curious prospects into paying customers. They do it with classy, professional, and inexpensive brochures; intensive, caring follow-up; and personalized service. Now it's your turn!

Classified Advertising

When you think of classified advertising, you probably think in terms of finding a job, looking for a car, selling a sofa, buying a boat, or locating a house or apartment. Think again. Classified advertising can also be used to support a business. And many a flourishing enterprise exists primarily on the pulling power of classified ads.

On a random weekday, my local newspaper's classified business directory, not in a major market, featured classified ads for 124 kinds of businesses. And this was a weekday paper — not a Sunday paper. I wouldn't even attempt to list the entrepreneurial enterprises using the Sunday classified section. Do your own homework and see for yourself — in your own community. Better do that homework on a regular basis, because the classified section is a living, growing thing that changes pretty darned quickly —

to the delight of the burgeoning number of small-business owners who profit from it.

If all these entrepreneurs and/or businesses use the classified section, it makes sense for you to consider it. Many of these advertisers have had ads in the classified section for more than twenty years. And I know that they wouldn't spend their money there if they weren't getting handsome returns.

Classified advertising represents a $28 billion to $30 billion business in the United States, including $16 billion in daily newspapers and an estimated $100 billion business internationally, according to a study by Classified Intelligence. That would make the overall classified revenues, print and online included, $17.1 billion. Obviously, classified sections are not nickel-and-dime ventures.

In my files, I have magazines that run far more classified ads than are in the newspaper just mentioned. And I'm sure you know of newspapers — many of them — that consist of nothing but classified ads. Obviously, classified ads work as a marketing medium. If you can see any advantage for your company in using this medium, a bit of investigation and investment on your part is worthwhile. If you visit Google, you'll discover in less than five minutes a treasury of opportunities to run ads in thousands of newspapers for free, as well as such sites as ZapMeta.com, which list the top thirty Web sites devoted to classified advertising. About a third of the money spent on newspaper ads is spent in the classified sections.

Among the fastest-growing segments of classified ads are those appearing online, many of them free. Generally, you can run classified ads in magazines, daily or weekly newspapers, classified-ad newspapers, and online. If your offering requires proximity to your customers, forget the magazines. And if your offering is national in character, forget the newspapers. There is little likelihood that you'll want to run classified ads in both local newspapers and national magazines — unless the papers you select are in localities spread throughout the country and you want to combine that advertising with national magazine advertising.

You are probably noticing that more and more magazines are offering classified advertising. They know that many of the new small businesses just plain can't afford a display ad, and they have this deep longing for revenue. So the magazines offer classified-advertising sections for entrepreneurs. Look deeply into this, for the cost is relatively low to get into a major magazine, because the classified section is generally at the back of the magazine.

You can cash in on this guerrilla hint: Because 61 percent of Americans read magazines from the back to the front, your economical classified ad will have a decent shot at being read. It's a glorious place to do step 1 of the two-step.

As you may have heard, it doesn't cost an arm and a leg to run a classified ad. And you'll usually be offered a frequency discount. This means that if your five-line classified ad costs you $20 to run one time, it will cost only, say, $18 per insertion if you run it three times and only $15 per insertion if you run it five times. The more frequently you run it, the lower your cost per insertion. This is called a frequency discount. Classified ad charges are based on the number of words, the number of lines, or the number of inches. It depends on the publication. The cost of the ad is also based on the circulation of the publication — in both quantity and quality.

Many people read the classified ads each day. Some read them to find specific bargains. Others read them merely to browse via the newspaper. And still others find them the most fascinating part of the newspaper. Check them yourself. See which ads and classified-ad categories draw your attention. By reading through the ads, you'll get a sense of whether your business can profit from this method of marketing. You'll also begin to learn, by osmosis, what to say in a classified ad and what not to say. Although classified ads are short, fraught with abbreviations, and devoid of illustrations, they aren't as simple as they may seem.

Online classified ads are the oldest and most widely used forms of online advertising. Say "eBay" or "Craig's List" to an entrepreneur, and you'll see their eyes flash with excitement. Many online services allow you to run your classified ad for free, and some offer video and audio capabilities, which means that your prospects can listen to soft jazz as they read about your consulting service. They can also listen to soothing symphonic music as they take a virtual tour through your facilities — all courtesy of classified advertising, twenty-first-century style. Some services, such as Classifind Network at classifind.com, provide a searchable database index and hundreds of descriptive words to help the right buyer find the right ad. Their multimedia advertising rates are less than the cost of most one-column-inch print ads. It's guerrilla marketing with sight, sound, action, technology, interactivity — at an extraordinarily low cost.

Classified ads of all kinds reach people who are *already shopping*. These ads are easy to create and run, can commence very shortly after you decide to run them, are simple to test, and have paid rich dividends to entrepreneurs for centuries. If you decide to use the classified-ad section, there are a few concepts that you should keep in mind.

For one thing, keep your headline short. You must have a headline, printed in capital letters. Don't use abbreviations unless you are sure that people will understand them. While living in England, my wife and I searched for an apartment by scanning the classified ads. Many said that the rental included CCF&F. We were thrown by that. Do you know what it means? Later, we learned that it stands for "carpets, curtains, fixtures, and fittings." We also found that most Britishers know that.

Don't use esoteric terms in your ads unless you're sure that most of your readers (99 percent) know the meaning. Write in short sentences. Try to sound more like a human being than a want ad. And include your phone number and address — more than once, I've seen an ad with no phone number or address.

Many publications have employees who can help you word your want ads. I suggest that you use these people as guides, but don't always follow their advice. If they were brilliant writers, they'd probably be paid for their writing. If you're a good writer, write your own classified-ad copy. If not, go to a pro. Don't rely on the person who takes the ads to write your copy.

Word your ad in such a way that it contrasts with other ads in the same section. And choose that section very, very carefully. Some newspapers have categories — such as attorneys, announcements, Christmas items, and computers — that don't appear in other papers. Advertise in the proper category. Make that plural. You may want to place your ad in more than one category.

Strange as it may seem, classified ads often outdraw display ads. So don't think that just because an ad has no picture and doesn't cost much, it's not going to be effective. Many companies run display ads and classified ads in the same newspapers on the same day and claim that the ads reach different classes of consumers.

I earned about $500 per month for at least a dozen years working about half an hour per month. I did it with a classified ad. I ran the same ad, with minor changes in wording, for twelve years. After I'd been working for a few years as a freelance writer, I'd learned quite a few important things about freelancing — things nobody had ever told me, things that weren't written in books. So I wrote a book and published it myself. I called the book *Secrets of Successful Free-Lancing*. And although it had but forty-three pages, I priced it at $10. The reason I charged $10 was that I sincerely felt that the book was worth it. The book cost me about $1 to print, including type and binding. Advertising ran about $3.33 per book. So I figured that I made $5.67 per book. Here's a sample of the classified ad I ran:

I EARN MORE AS A FREELANCER THAN I DID AS VP/CREATIVE DIRECTOR AT J. WALTER THOMPSON. I loved my JWT days. But I love now more. I live where I want. I work only 3 days a week. I work from my home and take lots of vacations. To do the same, read my incisive book, *Secrets of Successful Free-Lancing*. Send $10 to Prosper Press, 123 Alto Street, San Rafael, CA 94902. $11 refund if you're not completely satisfied.

Note that my ad used standard language rather than want-ad language. When I've run other classified ads using "people talk," I've also had good results. A regularly worded ad appearing in a sea of want-ad-worded ads tends to stand out.

The cost of the ad was $36 for one inch in the publication in which it originally appeared. And the entire ad fit in one inch in the classified section. For every dollar I invested in the ad, I averaged $3 in sales, $2.50 in profits. It cost fifty cents to mail it, envelope included.

For me, the biggest challenge was to find enough places to run the ad. After all, everybody isn't a prospect for a book on freelancing. I ran the ad in three advertising trade magazines, two art-director publications, two writers' magazines, the *Wall Street Journal,* and four opportunity magazines. Some of these publications drew a great response every time I ran the ad — and I ran it every three months. Others didn't pull well for me, so I withdrew them from my schedule. By sticking with the four publications that worked, I was able to bring in around $500 per month in profits — after paying for the ads, the books, and the mailing. I had all the orders mailed directly to a mail-order-fulfillment house that mailed out the books on the day orders were received, put the names of the people who ordered into a computer, and sent me the checks weekly — coded so that I knew which publications were working best.

People in the mail-order book business report that a 5 percent request rate for refunds is about par for the course. My requests for refunds were 1.2 percent. And don't forget, I offered an $11 refund for a forty-three-page $10 book.

The half-hour per month I spent on this business was used to keep tallies on the pulling power of the various magazines and to fill out deposit slips for my bank. And $500 per half hour isn't anything to complain about. And just think: My only method of marketing was classified advertising.

That book is no longer available by that title, because I expanded it to help others. It is available in two versions: *Earning Money Without a Job* and *555 Ways to Earn Extra Money.* (In fact, it was the response to those books that prompted me to write *Guerrilla Marketing* in the first place.) If financial independence and the freedom to enjoy it sound good to you, I unabashedly call your attention to *The Way of the Guerrilla: Achieving Success and Balance as an Entrepreneur in the 21st Century.* Enough about me and my books. Back to you and your marketing.

Some online guerrillas use classified ads solely to direct viewers to their Web sites. Many other marketers use the classified ads only to check out the pulling power of products, claims, prices, copy, headlines, and appeals. It's an inexpensive way to gain valuable information. Once you have a proven winner, you can then put forth your message in display ads if you wish. And keep in mind that classified ads sometimes pull better than display ads.

In your classified ad, don't use too many adjectives, but do use a lot of facts. Aim to be as clear in your message as you can. Remember that your classified ad is really your sales presentation. Don't hold back on features if your offering has features to boast about. You may end up spending several dollars more because your ad is longer, but if it brings you sales, this will easily outweigh the extra cost. *The cost of all advertising is measured not in dollars but in response.*

When thinking about classified advertising, think first in terms of clarity and then in terms of reader interest. You must capture your readers' attention. Do it with a catchy word — GHOSTWRITING! — or with a headline — NEED EXTRA MONEY? You have but a *fleeting* instant to gain attention. Get it with your short headline. The rest of your copy should follow directly from the headline. The GHOSTWRITING! headline might be followed with this sentence: "A professional writer will write, rewrite, or edit your letter, essay, manuscript, or advertisement so that it sings." NEED EXTRA MONEY? might be followed by copy that begins: "Obtaining the extra cash you need is not as hard as you think." If I needed money, I'd read on. Wouldn't you?

The idea in your classified ad is to maintain the momentum created by the headline. Write copy as though you are talking to one human being and not to a mass audience. Although you should mention as many features and benefits in your ad as you can afford, practice the selective withholding of information. Merely by omitting certain facts, you may generate phone calls, Web site visits, or other types of desired responses. The information you withhold may be the price, the location, or some other data the reader needs to complete the picture. Just be careful not to withhold so much information that you attract a horde of unqualified prospects.

A good exercise for classified-ad writing is to write your ad as though it were to be a display ad in a newspaper. Cut copy to make the ad shorter and shorter. Finally, you will be left with the pure facts. But remember *quality*. Pepper your facts with adjectives. "I can paint your house so that it gleams like the day it was built" sounds more appealing than "House painting at reasonable prices."

Although classified ads need not be as short as possible, they must nonetheless motivate your prospective customers — must create a desire to buy. One advertising genius who specializes in classified ads claims that the key to success in the classifieds is simplicity and tight copy. If you think that is easy to achieve, you are wrong. It's tough to be simple; tough to be brief. The writing of classified ads is a very special art. The ads must be well written; otherwise, they will not inspire confidence. Just because they're short does not mean that they can be shabby.

To gain insight into writing successful classified ads, look through current newspapers and magazines, studying the classifieds. Then look at one-year-old issues of the same newspapers and magazines. Check to see which ads are in both the new and the year-old publications. Those must be winners, or the people running them would not be repeating them. By studying them, you can learn what makes them so successful. Is it the headline? The offer? The price? The copy? Apply whatever you learn to your own business. You can't compare today's online classified ads with those of a year ago, but you can browse through the free and the paid online classified-ad sections to see who is advertising what. If you regularly surf online, you can spot the winners as the losers drop from sight and vanish.

The guerrilla Charles Rubin, coauthor of *Guerrilla Marketing Online*, tells us that online classified ads age quickly. If you're running a classified ad on an online service, you'll notice that most ad classifications have a few hundred ads, arranged chronologically from top to bottom in each category. This means that the latest ads submitted for publication are at the top of the list. Your posted ad, which appears on the first screenful of ads today may be three or four screens down the list tomorrow. To avoid getting lost, *resubmit your ad every day* to maintain its position near the top. You may have to use different titles for your ad to post it more than once. Still, most shoppers won't browse down more than three screens to view older ads.

Many large businesses that run high-powered advertising and marketing programs, making use of TV, radio, magazines, and other publicity, still use the classified section. They recognize that some people read classified ads when looking for, say, antiques or certain automobiles. Classified ads are not small potatoes. Some advertising consultants *specialize* in classified ads. You give them your ad copy, and they return it to you, improved, with a list of publications in which it is likely to elicit a response. If you will market a product or service nationally, consider newspapers in multiple markets as well as national magazines.

Classified ads in newspapers allow you to home in on a local audience. Classified ads in magazines allow you to home in on a more widespread audience. Online classified ads allow you to do both — proving once again the potential of online marketing. And all classified ads allow you to test your strategy, message, and advertising media. They're glorious places to say that magic sentence: "Call, send e-mail, or write for our FREE brochure."

Although classified ads are small and inexpensive, they *are* effective. A true guerrilla marketer tries to find ways to put the power of classified ads to work. Hardly any other medium enables you to talk to honest-to-goodness prospects and not only browsers. There's a huge difference between the two.

Gift Certificates

Nope. Gift certificates are not solely in the domain of department stores. More and more marketing guerrillas are learning that gift certificates work in virtually any business, especially in those in which gift certificates have never been offered.

The reason for this is that offering gift certificates plants ideas in the minds of your prospects and in the minds of their friends. When it comes to giving a gift, people are always on the lookout for new ideas. A gift certificate for your business may be a dazzlingly new idea.

To offer gift certificates, use your computer to prepare a few small signs that say, "Ask about our gift certificates." Then, print up a few certificates. Put your name at the top of your certificate, and leave room for the name of the recipient and the person authorized to sign the certificate, probably you. In all of your other marketing, say, "Ask about our gift certificates." When people ask, and ask they will, tell them that the gift certificate is available in any amount and that it is good for anything that you sell. Do not have a cut-off date on it. That's just tacky.

You'll be amazed at the number of people who *do* ask about your gift certificates, and you'll be delighted at the number of people who purchase them. Gift certificates make perfect gifts, are always affordable, and are almost always appreciated. I cannot for the life of me think of a time when they wouldn't be received with gratitude. Send one to me. See how grateful I am.

Gift certificates work their magic most when you market their availability — especially at gift-giving times, such as Christmas, Valentine's Day, and Mother's Day. Still, they do work all year long — if you let your public know that you offer them.

Add a few testimonials about your gift certificates to your Web site and in your next e-mail. That will make them work even harder for you, and more people than ever will purchase them. Remember: People are always on the lookout for new and unusual gift ideas. A gift certificate for what you sell might be just the ticket for them. If you can't wrap your mind around gift certificates, consider the Mercedes dealer who put up a sign for them in his service area, offering parts, accessories, or service. He wrote up over $100,000 in business in one year as a result.

Signs: Big and Little

Think of signs in two ways: those that appeal to people *outside* your place of business and those that appeal to people *within* your place of business. The first category consists of billboards, which we'll discuss in another chapter, small signs on bulletin boards, which are discussed in this chapter, window signs, store signs, banners, signs on trees, and poster-type signs. The second category is made up of interior signs, commonly called point-of-purchase (POP), or point-of-sale signs.

Whichever you use, or if you use both, be certain that your signs tie in as directly as possible with your advertising. The dictum, as stated by the late, great advertising pro Leo Burnett: "Plan the sale when you plan the ad." The dictum, as stated by Jay Conrad Levinson: "Signs trigger impulse purchases; guerrillas are trigger-happy."

Your ads will have made an unconscious impression on your potential customers, and your signs will awaken the memory of that advertising and might motivate a sale. Many people will patronize your business because of your ads. Your signs must be consistent with your advertising message and identity, or those people will be confused. If the signs are in keeping with your overall creative strategy, consumers' momentum to buy will be increased. About 75 percent of all purchase decisions are made right at the place of purchase. Most industry categories have increased their in-store sign spending during the past five years.

People enter a store with a vague notion of buying but no brand preference. They don't solidify their decision until they are *in* the store. And what do you suppose influences their decision? In many cases, a package. In many other cases, a sign.

Signs have exceptional power in malls, hypermarkets (a galaxy of malls), shopping centers, warehouses, supermarkets — large spaces where many businesses are competing for the eye and business of passersby. Many smart retailers have used their signs and their decor to tie in with the times. The idea is to match confidence in the offering — accomplished with mass marketing — with a reason to make an impulsive purchase. This is, in part, accomplished by the use of a sign. Make that match and — bingo! — you've made a sale.

Most exterior signs are there to remind, create a tiny impulse, implant inclinations a wee bit deeper, sharpen an identity, state a very brief message. As a rule, exterior signs should be no more than six words long. Some successful signs, but not many, have more than six words. Probably the most successful of all have no more than three words.

Now, since we're talking about the power of words — few words — let's examine some of the strongest words in the English language. Many are used in headlines; many are used in signs. Almost all are used in advertising and marketing.

Psychologists at Yale University tell us that the most persuasive words in the English language are

discovery	easy
guarantee	health
love	money
new	proven
results	safety
save	you

To that list, I would hasten to add

announcing	benefits
fast	free
how	now
power	sale
secrets	solution
why	yes

Now that you know these words, I'll bet you can come up with some dandy signs.

Frequently, motorists make abrupt decisions (and right turns) when they pass windows with huge banners proclaiming SALE! or FREE GIFTS! or SAVE 50 PERCENT! As you probably know, it doesn't take many words to convince some people that they ought to buy from you right now.

Many famous businesses were built with signs and signs alone. I instantly call to mind three: Burma-Shave, for which I had the privilege of writing two signs that were published, or shall I say "road-sided"? ("Keep World Tensions Spic and Span Send Fidel the King-Size Can" and "Our Shave Cream Fame Has Really Spread Nikita Puts It on His Head"); the late Harold's Club in Reno; and Wall Drug Store of South Dakota. These are nationally known businesses. Many locally famous concerns marketed their wares the same way. You can be sure that the Burma-Shave people, Harold, and Mr. Wall were all pioneer guerrillas, for they blazed trails that led directly to the bank. They also incensed coming generations of environmentalists, who claimed that the signs were encroaching on the beauty of America. Lady Bird Johnson spearheaded this movement, and it will never die. Be aware of it, and don't put up exterior signs that will be picketed by planet savers. As a guerrilla marketer, you must stay in touch with trends, and I, for one, am heartened by the nation's growing concern with the environment, as indicated by new marketing strategies, use of recyclable materials, and production measures to guide our species toward cosmic sanity.

Mike Lavin, a true "green guerrilla," searched for a unique way to promote his Berkeley business. A healthy combination of environmentalist and capitalist, Mike was able to have his cake and eat it, too, by erecting, in a field, a large sign frame with no sign inside the frame. Beneath his see-through creation was a smaller sign that said "SCENERY COURTESY OF BERKELEY DESIGN SHOP." His store, at the same location in Berkeley for more than twenty-five years, is now called European Sleep Works, but he still relies on signs to serve as silent salespeople, on and off the premises.

Other exterior signs that usually work well are those that say such things as VOTE FOR LEVINSON, GARAGE SALE, FLEA MARKET, PARK HERE, and GAS FOR LESS. Perhaps the most profitable investment a retail business owner can make is in a red neon sign that says OPEN. Not a lot of creativity in the copy for those signs, to be sure. Nonetheless, they work. Failure to make a sign investment early on may mean making a sign investment later on, putting your money into a GOING OUT OF BUSINESS sign.

Almost (but not quite) as important as the wording of the sign is the overall look of the sign. By this, I mean the picture or pictures, lettering style, colors, and design of the sign. A powerful graphic lends more power to the words. A sign that says FRESH DONUTS can be made doubly effective if it shows donuts growing in a meadow like flowers. If the sign says DELICIOUS DONUTS, it can be more motivating if it shows a picture of a grinning little girl or a big man holding a donut with a giant bite taken from it or a closeup of a donut in the process of being dunked.

It usually makes sense to use very light lettering against very dark background colors or very dark lettering against very light colors. One type of lettering is easier to read than several types. The words on the sign should be as large as possible while leaving room for the picture.

Although your sign should be expected only to remind and not to make an actual sale, go for the jugular, and try like crazy to make the sale from the sign. Large advertisers with humongous marketing budgets can use signs to remind only, but guerrillas have to get more mileage from their money. Although we know that signs remind, it is possible to sell *some* people with a sign, so go for the sale with the sign.

Consider also the clutter factor. Are many other signs nearby? If so, make sure that *your* sign stands out. If not, you can approach the creation of your sign with a different mindset. In England, when designing an outdoor sign campaign for a product that promised economy, we took the clutter factor into account and introduced black-and-white signs that contrasted with the surrounding sea of color signs. Our black-and-white beauties not only won awards but more important, also won customers. Had we used color with the same words and pictures, we would not have enjoyed such a high level of success. Our uniqueness, which tied in directly with our promise of economy, helped us stand out and make our point. Calvin Klein used the same technique on television: black and white in a color environment.

A powerful visual image should be created if you are going to use many signs. The Marlboro cowboy comes to mind immediately. Because you want your sign to be instantly identifiable with you, a graphic identity is highly recommended. The look should be unusual, connected with your company's identity, and suitable for being maintained over a long period of time. Consistency. Remember?

The only punctuation mark with which you need be concerned is the exclamation point. It lends a tone of excitement. Question marks, although of use in print advertising, take too much "reflection time" to be used on signs. Stay away from them unless you have a good reason to break that rule. Commas and periods usually are not necessary with six-word messages. And long words are to be avoided whenever possible.

In order to make a sale with a visual image plus five or six words, you'll need a great deal of thought and creativity. As with all other marketing devices, a great sign starts with a great idea. If you lack the idea, your words and pictures won't work. However, if you have the right words and the right pictures, along with the right idea and the right location, a sale can be made.

Interior signs require far more creativity than exterior signs, and you are allowed to use far more words. In fact, you are encouraged to.

Point-of-purchase signs are considered by those who use them to be extremely effective because they create impulse sales. They also put forth extra selling energy and cross-merchandising opportunities. A person comes in to buy a pen, sees a sign that says briefcases are marked down, and buys a briefcase, too. That's cross-merchandising.

POP signs make it easier for customers to locate and select products. The signs serve as silent salespeople, as aids to the real-life salespeople. They demonstrate product features. POP signs give customers product information, reinforce the ad campaign at the retail level, offer premiums and discounts, and generate sales all by themselves.

Many manufacturers offer free point-of-purchase materials to their customers. If you purchase from a manufacturer, you should ask whether POP materials are provided. If not, request some. Most manufacturers are happy to comply. They'll set you up with signs, brochures, display racks, window banners, display modules, counter cards, window cards, Plexiglas merchandisers, posters, display cases, stand-up signs, and more. Just ask.

The growth of in-store signs is causing the giant advertising agencies to change their attitudes toward this nonglamorous medium. They couldn't help but notice that during the 1990s, in-store media expenditures doubled, outgrowing more traditional vehicles, such as television and print. The in-store sign industry is growing. And growing along with it is couponing, part of the in-store experience with Americans. Approximately 63 percent of all cereal is now bought with a coupon, compared with less than 20 percent in 1987. But most ad agencies don't take in-store signs and couponing as seriously as they should. You, as a guerrilla, will not make the same mistake.

New video technologies are creating opportunities for in-store marketers. TV monitors are cropping up over product displays and store shelves, at checkout counters, and even on shopping carts. This very definitely is a happening medium, though it is not happening as rapidly as some experts predicted. As a guerrilla, you can get in on the new technologies while the big guys are waiting around to see how well they work. Many new marketing weapons, because of their low cost, nontraditional nature, and ability to let guerrillas market like the big dudes (and dudettes) before the biggies even get started, are ideal for guerrillas.

In the 1980s, telephone marketing was an emerging marketing force, according to *Forbes* magazine. In the 1990s, *Adweek* claimed that POP would be the emerging force. The twenty-first century is proving *Adweek* to be right. The money meets the merchandise in the supermarket aisles, they told us. Of course, it also meets and greets on the computer monitor. Still, the reason for POP advertising's popularity is its ability to connect mass-media marketing with the consumer at the time of purchase. This makes it cost-effective. Some surveys indicate that in the near future, POP materials will make up 80 percent of many advertisers' budgets.

As I mentioned earlier, the basic rule in creating any advertising is to plan the sale when you plan the ad. That means that you shouldn't think in terms of a person reading your ad or hearing your commercial. Instead, think of the person at the moment of purchase. Is your message designed to motivate the potential customer at that crucial moment? By nature, almost all POP marketing materials are. POP signs get to people when the getting is good. They are there. They are in a buying mood. They are thinking in terms of the type of merchandise or service you offer. POP advertising gives them many reasons to buy, or at least it should.

Many a smart guerrilla has run an ad, then blown it up into a five-foot-high poster, mounted it, and used it as a sign — inside the place of business, outside the place of business, and in the window. This is a way to market intelligently while saving lots of money, and it ensures that the interior signs will tie in with the ads.

Interior signs can be used to encourage customers to touch your offering, taste it, try it out, and compare it with the competition and also to explain complex points by means of clear graphics. Remember that 75 percent of all buying decisions are made right in the place of business, but even half that number would be impressive. It should cause any guerrilla to take the use of signs very, very seriously.

Today, decisions to buy are less casual than they once were, and people need to be convinced right there, at the point of sale. If your business is in a location where your customers will come to browse or buy, consider your aisles to be your "trenches" — where the true battle for customer dollars takes place. Since many battles are won or lost in the trenches, your point-of-purchase materials should be as potent as possible.

While the other marketing methods and materials create in the customer a desire to buy, as well they should, point-of-purchase signs promise instant rewards. Americans love instant gratification. True guerrillas recognize that people patronize their businesses on purpose, not by accident. And they capitalize on the presence of prospects by using motivating, informative signs. Some have lengthy copy. Some have brief copy. Some go into detail about product features and benefits. Some contain lists of satisfied-customer testimonials. Some display ornate graphics, some point out advantages of related merchandise. Each is there to move as much merchandise or sell as many services as possible.

You might want to walk the aisles of successful businesses in your area to learn how they use point-of-purchase signs. To learn even more about point-of-purchase signs, drop a line, requesting free information, to POPAI, the Point-of-Purchase Advertising Institute, 60 East Forty-second Street, New York, NY 10165.

Other types of marketing prime the public for the sale. The sign generates the purchase decision. Whenever possible, signs should be used to pull the trigger on the gun already cocked by aggressive guerrilla marketing.

Signs on Bulletin Boards

Guerrillas must fight their battles with every single available weapon. Small signs on bulletin boards have proved to be extremely effective weapons for many an entrepreneur. I'm talking about signs as small as 3 inches by 5 inches. Even business cards. A sign need not be big to attract customers. Little signs do the job, too.

What kinds of businesses and individuals might avail themselves of this medium? Tutors, gardeners, plumbers, typists, writers, baby-sitters, house sitters, movers, accountants, room renters, music teachers, nurses, answering services, pet groomers, cleaning people, painters, astrologers, mechanics, printers, seamstresses, decorators, Web site designers, dog walkers, tree pruners, entertainers. And a whole lot more!

If your business has any prospects who have occasion to see bulletin boards, perhaps you should use small signs on bulletin boards to promote your business. You'll find such bulletin boards on campuses and in libraries, cafeterias, dormitories, company rest rooms, offices, supermarkets, laundromats, locker rooms, bookstores, pet stores, sporting goods stores, barbershops, hairstyling salons, toy stores, RV resorts (my wife and I have patronized several businesses that marketed that way), and sundry other locations. Most major cities have hundreds of such locations; many small towns have as many as five or ten. Guerrillas post signs in places where there is high visibility and no cost:

- In front of their own business
- In front of neighboring businesses
- Subway stations
- School offices
- Senior recreational facilities and retirement homes
- College dormitories — in the community area, hallways, and bathrooms
- Fraternities and sororities
- Churches
- Other local community clubs and organizations
- Apartment buildings — in laundry rooms
- Community activity centers
- Grocery stores

- Shopping malls
- Car washes
- Condominium-complex party centers
- Hotel and motel lobbies
- Utility poles
- Military cafeterias and recreation centers
- Counters of public places
- Meeting convention centers and rooms
- Construction walls
- Libraries
- Union halls
- Chambers of commerce
- Medical or professional offices
- Roller rinks and bowling alleys
- Waiting rooms at auto repair and tire shops
- Liquor and convenience stores
- Company bulletin boards of friends and family
- Tourist information centers
- Highway rest stops
- Banks
- Factories
- Their cars — featuring a compelling sign, parked in a conspicuous place
- On the fences outside a construction site

The point here is that guerrillas are not very limited in their options. You can either post the signs yourself or hire companies that specialize in posting the signs for you. In the San Francisco Bay Area, a local company — Thumb Tack Bugle — provides this service. In 1981, it serviced eighty locations; now it services more than eight hundred locations in the Bay Area. Its chief rival is Your Daily Staple, a company that was spawned by the obvious success of sign-posting. The point is: This is a growing medium, and guerrillas must be aware of it because of its efficiency and low cost.

In most instances, your sign must be replaced on a regular basis (monthly or weekly). But sometimes, it can stay in place for years. In a few cases, you'll have to pay a tiny fee to post your sign, but often this method of marketing is free (if you do your own posting). The companies that post for you promise to place your sign on a guaranteed number of boards — a large number, I might add — and they'll also replace it on a regular basis. Unless you have the time to check your signs, look into these posting services. You can find them listed in your yellow pages under "signs" or "bulletin boards." If signs do work for you, consider hiring one of these companies to handle the work for you so you can concentrate on earning money.

A crucial point is to keep the lettering on your sign very CLEAR. Fancy lettering is out of the question. Typewriter type is fine. Other than the type-face in your handy computer, clear, handsome hand lettering is proba-bly best. If you haven't the proper calligraphic skills, ask a pro or a friend with immense talent to letter your sign for you. Remember to keep your copy short and to the point. Incidentally, it's fine to make copies of your signs. One original plus a slew of copies and enough thumbtacks, and you have the marketing tools to become a success. Once again, technol-ogy is your ally, because a wide variety of simple software makes it easy to create signs.

If Handyman Hero posted bulletin-board signs, they might say:

IT'S HANDYMAN HERO!
He builds super sun decks and patios,
installs skylights and hot tubs,
does masonry and electrical work,
and designs building plans.
Call Handyman Hero at 555-5656 anytime, any day.
All work guaranteed.
Contractor's License #54-45673.
E-mail: HandymanHero@hotmail.com

Handyman Hero probably wouldn't need a 3 × 5 sign. Instead, he could post his circular. Circulars double as small signs. Those created by guerril-las have precut strips at the bottom, each one with their name, Web site, and phone number. Five strips might do the trick for you. Readers can merely tear off a strip.

Amazingly, some businesses need promote only via this wonderfully in-expensive method of marketing. Perhaps you can be one of them. Although guerrilla marketers should use as many marketing methods as they can, they should save marketing money when they can do so intelligently. If you pro-mote your business with 3 × 5 cards, you truly save money. In fact, if you do the lettering, writing, and posting, it's free.

Desktop Publishing

If you own and operate a computer, you're now wondering whether you can use desktop publishing to help you produce and design signs. The answer is that you certainly can — and should — if you have the proper software, skills, and taste. If you do, you can use your desktop publishing prowess to produce newsletters, direct mail, brochures, and a host of other marketing tools. The technology is easy to use.

The opportunities for a business with desktop publishing capabilities are endless. There's a creative genius lurking within you! Desktop publishing can set it free. You don't have to draw things, merely select from things already drawn — a huge variety of dazzling graphics, just waiting for you to select, point, and click. Just be sure to devote your time to the areas where it can most help your business. If that includes desktop publishing, great. If you love it but should be doing something else, delegate it to someone else. A hallmark of the guerrilla is in the intelligent apportionment of time.

Ornate graphics are generally not necessary when marketing with small signs, though borders, typography, and little illustrations enliven most signs. If you post on a regular basis, it's a good idea to change the wording — but not the basic message — of your sign periodically. It's also a good idea to use different-colored paper so that your sign stands out from the rest. But be careful that your paper color does not impair the clarity of your ink color. Green ink on green paper makes for a very green but very unreadable sign. If you use green paper, make it light green — and make your ink a very dark color. Don't forget: Your major purpose is to motivate prospective customers, and if they can't read your message, they can't be motivated.

I suggest that you visit a few places where signs are posted in your region and notice the clever ways people are using this unique marketing method. A guerrilla marketer seriously considers such a method when developing an overall marketing plan: A true guerrilla doesn't think it at all silly to combine radio advertising, newspaper advertising, and bulletin-board advertising in his or her marketing strategy. Would the Ford Motor Company consider such a tactic? Is the Pope Buddhist?

Be sure to make your headlines large. Make plenty of signs. In fact, it's a good idea to make about ten at a time and staple them together. Tack the whole packet to a bulletin board and carefully letter the words "Take One" atop your signs. People can read your sign, and the serious prospects can take one home with them for future reference — and then pass it along to someone who is looking for a product or service exactly like yours.

If you place signs on ten different bulletin boards, do the same kind of research you would if you were testing any other type of marketing. Ask your customers, "Where did you learn of my business?" When they tell you that they saw your sign, ask, "Where did you see it?" This way, you'll be able to pinpoint your best sign-posting locations. The more you can zero in on your most productive marketing methods — including such subtleties as wording, sign color, sign location, and lettering style — the more successful you'll be.

It won't hurt for you to call some of the people who have posted signs in your area and ask about their effectiveness. Ask how long they've been posting signs, where they post them, whether the one you saw was typical, which locations seem best, and what success stories they may have heard. People are surprisingly open with information like this, and many enjoy being singled out as experts.

The Yellow Pages

If your business is off and running, you probably know quite a bit about the yellow pages. But if your business hasn't yet opened, it's a great idea to name it something that will appear as the first listing in its category in the yellow pages. For example, a new storage company called itself Abaco Storage and advertised only in the yellow pages. Success came to the company that first year, and phone inquiries resulting from the first listing in the yellow pages were clearly responsible.

The first thing to decide is whether your business can benefit from yellow pages marketing. Will people look there to find a product or a service such as yours, as they do for storage companies? If you are a retailer, chances are that people will consult the yellow pages phone directory and find out about you. But if you're an artist or a consultant, people will probably find out about you through other sources. Once you've decided you should be in the directory, determine which directory or directories. Will one be enough? Or, as is the case in large metropolitan areas, will you have to be in five or ten? The answer may be clearer after you've considered these findings by the Small Business Administration.

- The average independent store draws the majority of its customers from not more than a quarter of a mile away.
- The average chain store draws most of its customers from not more than three-quarters of a mile away.
- The average shopping center draws customers from as far away as four miles.

Some businesses draw customers from as far away as one hundred miles, especially in such wide-open areas as Montana and North Dakota. Furniture stores attract business from an average distance of ten miles away. One of my enterprises, Guerrilla Marketing International, draws business from around the world, living up to our name. How about your enterprise? If you think you should run yellow pages ads in a number of directories, decide whether the ads in other areas should be as large as or smaller than your primary area ad. Decide whether you should have an advertisement or a listing. Decide whether the listing should be in dark, bold type or in regular type. Choose the size, the colors you'll use, and whether you want to connect with the electronic portion of the yellow pages.

My publishing business was listed in but one directory, in normal type. It wasn't the kind of business that attracts yellow pages searchers. But some of my clients have large yellow pages ads in three directories, two with extra colors, small yellow pages ads in five more directories, and bold-type listings in six other directories.

The cost for a large number of listings is assessed monthly, and it's steep. Find out the names of other companies in your business category, and try to learn what percentage of their business each month comes from people who have located them through the yellow pages. I have some clients who obtain 6 percent of their business from people who first learned of them by consulting the yellow pages. Others obtain 50 percent of their business that way. And some received less than 1 percent of business from the yellow pages yet wish to continue advertising there. I am not in agreement. The yellow pages should be an investment that pays off every time.

You must do the groundwork to see how, where, and whether you should make use of a strong yellow pages program. Now you know some questions to ask and answer. Here's another: In which categories in your yellow pages directory will you list yourself? For example, if your sleep shop sells beds and bedroom furniture, should you list your shop under "furniture," "mattresses," or "beds"? Can you do with one listing, or do you need to pay for several? Answer: You'll probably have to list where people look. And they look in all three categories. One of life's necessary bummers.

A prime advantage of listing in the yellow pages is that you can appear as big as your biggest competitor, as large as the largest business of your type in town, and as well established as the oldest business of your type in town. Although directories differ from publisher to publisher (there are several), the largest-space unit you can usually purchase is a full page. In some cities, the largest-space unit you can purchase is a quarter of a page. Because these are also the largest ad spaces available to your competition, you can appear equal in size. Take advantage of this by running a more powerful ad than your competition. Often, the largest ads get placed first in the section, where customers will first see them.

Guerrillas have learned to control the page in their yellow pages directory — not by purchasing the largest ad but by running two different-dimension ads on the same page. This eliminates the possibility of anyone running a larger ad on that page.

Some bright entrepreneurs, who realize that a great deal of their business comes from people who consult the yellow pages, spend the majority of their marketing budgets on this medium. But here's a crucial truth: Unless you dominate your section of the yellow pages — I mean run the only large ad and the only good ad — you should never, in your advertising on radio and/or television, direct people to your store or phone number by saying, "You'll find us conveniently listed in the yellow pages." By doing so, you are wasting your media dollars by leading people to your direct competitors. Believe me, many people innocently do this. They run a fine radio commercial and tell listeners to find them in the yellow pages. But nothing happens. Why? Because in the yellow pages, the listeners learn of several other places where they can buy the product or service being advertised.

If you don't appear as the clear choice within your category of the yellow pages, don't recommend that people look there. Tell them, "You'll find us in the white pages of your phone directory." There, in the peace and quiet of the noncompetitive white pages, listeners and viewers can learn your phone number and your address, and they're not aimed in the direction of your competitors.

Now that that's understood, you'll need to view the yellow pages as a marketing vehicle, an advertising medium, an opportunity to sell. Many people think the yellow pages are merely a place to put their phone numbers in large type. Silly thinking! The yellow pages are an arena for attracting the business of active prospects, a place to confront prospects on a one-on-one basis. You are selling. Others are selling what you sell. The prospect is in a buying mood. Understand this opportunity, and you'll be able to create yellow pages ads that translate into sales.

Many yellow pages directories offer the option to use color. If you're springing for a large ad, or even a small ad, go for it. Clients from around the country tell me that it's worth the investment. Many directories also give you the option to participate in coupon promotions by placing coupons for discounts on your offering in the back of the directory. I recommend that you call some of the coupon placers and ask them outright whether it's working — because you're considering it and you're not a competitor. Maybe it's a hidden gold mine. Maybe it's a disaster area. A guerrilla would check into it.

A guerrilla would also inquire about the electronic yellow pages. The way this works is that each ad contains a toll-free number that prospects can call for further information. You can update the information on a monthly basis. Contact your local yellow pages rep to see whether the service is available to you and what kinds of results others are getting. Call the toll-free number of some of the advertisers and see whether it's a forum for your message. Then call some of the advertisers. I realize that what I'm asking is not all that easy, but it's a lot easier than losing money by latching on to a misguided missile or missing out on a rich opportunity.

If you decide to run one large ad in the yellow pages directory for your locality, you may want to run smaller ads in outlying directories. You may need a large ad and a small ad, and maybe more. At any rate, it's too expensive to run yellow pages ads that are poorly written. And most of them are. By putting thought into the content of your ad, you can greatly increase your yellow pages response rate.

I'm familiar with a local business that was attracting 2 percent of its sales with yellow pages ads. Two percent isn't all that good, but it does represent a fair sum of money at the end of the month, so the business couldn't eliminate that particular marketing tool. Instead, it changed its ad copy. That's all. The result was a 600 percent increase in business from yellow pages ads. The store then drew 12 percent of its sales from people who first learned of it through those pages of yellow.

What accounted for this dramatic increase? The owner of this store (the store carries a goodly selection of beds — by no means the largest in the area but big enough to enable her to promote her products seriously) understood the mindset of yellow pages readers. She realized that those people who consult the yellow pages are actively looking to find specific information. And she understood that one can usually motivate people more effectively by getting them to agree with what you are saying — to the point where they say yes to questions you are asking.

This store owner asked a question to which the person looking in the bed section of the yellow pages directory would always answer yes. The question was, "Looking for a bed?" Naturally, the answer was yes, and the reader read on. Whatever buttons the reader had regarding beds were intentionally pressed by the ad. The advertiser didn't feel self-conscious about putting forth a lot of information. She also recognized the nature of the medium and actively sought the business of her prospective customers.

See the two-column-by-five-inch ad above as it appeared in the San Francisco yellow pages. Other advertisers in the same directory used the same space to list their names, phone numbers, and little else. If your offering is suitable for yellow pages advertising, you have a splendid opportunity.

If you use the yellow pages, here are some tips.

- Do list a whole lot of facts about yourself.
- Do make your ad look and "feel" classier.
- Do treat it like a personal communication, not a cold listing.
- Do let folks know whether you accept credit cards or can finance.
- Do gain the reader's attention with a strong headline.
- Do let people know all the reasons they should buy from you.
- Don't let the yellow pages people write your ad.
- Don't run small ads if your competitors run big ads.
- Don't allow your ad to look or sound boring.
- Don't forget to use handsome graphics to communicate.
- Don't list your business in too many directories.
- Don't treat your ad less lightly than a full-page magazine ad.
- Don't hold back on the data; people are looking in the yellow pages for information. Give them lots of information.
- Don't fail to include your Web site in your yellow pages ad; people can learn a lot more about you online than in any directory.

Never fall into the trap of thinking that your yellow pages ad must dazzle the populace with beauty. Credibility, yes, but not necessarily beauty. If people want beauty, they go to national parks or art museums, certainly not to the yellow pages. They go there to get information and assist themselves in making a purchase. The more information you provide, the more purchases you'll stimulate at your Web site.

If there are several pages of yellow pages listings for your competitors, which is often the case, take heed of the chiropractic guerrilla who was in the same situation. There were five pages of ads where he wanted to run his. So he ran a smallish ad, clear yellow type reversed out of a black background. The copy stated:

FREE TELEPHONE CONSULTATION
ON HOW TO SELECT A CHIROPRACTOR
CALL 1-800-000-0000.

You don't need me to tell you who got the lion's share of the phone calls and the tyrannosaurus rex's share of the business.

PART III

Maximedia Marketing

10

Guerrilla-Style Maximedia Marketing

Maximedia marketing refers to the mass-market media, such as newspapers, magazines, radio, TV, billboards, and direct mail. The Internet is also part of maximedia marketing, such an important part that it is pivotal to almost every chapter in this book. Mistakes cost dearly in the area of maximedia marketing. The competition may be able to outspend you dramatically. But don't think of maximedia marketing as expensive. That is not the case. Expensive marketing is marketing that does not work. If you spend $10 on one local radio station to run one radio commercial but nobody hears it or acts on it, you have engaged in expensive marketing. But if you shell out $10,000 to run one week's worth of advertising on a large metropolitan area radio station and you realize a profit of $20,000 in that week, you've engaged in inexpensive marketing. Cost has nothing to do with it. Effectiveness does.

A guerrilla marketer who uses the mass media does what is necessary to make them effective and therefore inexpensive. A guerrilla is not intimidated by the mass media. Guerrillas must use the mass media with precision, carefully measure the results, and make the media part of an overall marketing plan. When they use the media, guerrillas must rely on intuition and business acumen. Maximedia marketing is about two things: (1) selling and (2) creating a powerful desire to buy. Also, maximedia marketing enhances the success of minimedia marketing — response rates to simple circulars jump when radio advertising blazes the way for them, and telemarketing results improve when TV spots presell the market. Guerrillas wage and win marketing battles by using mini- and maxiweapons. Maxiweapons make the other marketing weapons work more effectively and are coming down in price.

Since I first wrote this book, a marvelous revolution has taken place: Maximarketing is now more affordable and more sensible for very small companies than ever before. Responding to the growing number of small businesses — which comprise 98 percent of all businesses — the advertising media have bent over backward to attract business, offering far lower prices than ever before. Magazines and newspapers are available in regional and zone editions, and radio stations offer extremely attractive package rates. Postcard decks make direct mail extremely affordable and attractive to right-thinking guerrillas. The maximedia are within your reach and right up your alley because they allow you to advertise the way the big guys do *without* spending big.

Today, guerrillas compete in all arenas. Guerrillas take on the big players when it comes to attracting the attention — and the disposable income — of the American public. Change favors guerrillas because they use many weapons of marketing rather than a few: Customers are now in many places rather than only a few. In 1982, a TV spot on the top-rated *Cosby* show would reach one in four households. In 1997, a TV spot on the top-rated show *Seinfeld* reached only one in *seven*. In 2005, a TV spot on a top-rated show reached one in nine households.

In 1975, the three major networks attracted 82 percent of the twenty-four-hour viewing audience. In 2005, it had dropped to only 25 percent. And TV isn't the only maximedium facing a shakeup. The hottest magazines of today are titles you hadn't heard of yesterday. And they'll be different still tomorrow. Guerrillas know that the media never stand still and that prospects are moving targets.

Desktop publishing, laser printing, satellite TV, cellular telephones, fax machines, voicemail, and the Internet are now the arsenals of guerrilla *marketers*. Be aware of these technologies. Embrace them before the big corporations do. You're a guerrilla, lithe and agile. Large businesses may be bright and wealthy, but their marketers must maneuver through the molasses of bureaucracies, and meetings, committees, reams of memos, and layers of decision making make them clumsy.

Enter with confidence the world of the maximedia. There has never been a better time to be a guerrilla. So get 'em while the getting's good.

Newspapers

Whether you use the minimedia, the maximedia, both, or neither, you should be aware of the continual shifts in the U.S. marketplace. Because of the baby boom from 1946 to 1964, the median age in the United States is steadily rising, and people are living longer. In 1900, only 4 percent of Americans were older than eighty-five. Today, 12 percent of Americans are older than eighty-five — about 3.8 million people. According to the U.S. Census, this is the fastest-growing age group in the American population.

The population shift to the Sun Belt — Texas, Florida, Arizona, and California — will continue. Immigrants will account for 25 percent to 33 percent of our population, with Hispanics superseding blacks as the largest minority group. Ten percent of the population will be Hispanic. Minority groups will continue to move from cities to the suburbs. The Asian American population will rapidly increase.

Marketers must be aware of these trends as they begin to consider newspaper advertising and its place in their media mix. In most areas, a large number of newspapers are available. They all reach specific audiences. Which newspapers, which audiences, are best for you? There are metropolitan newspapers, national newspapers, local newspapers, shopper-oriented newspapers, classified-ad newspapers, campus newspapers, business newspapers, ethnic newspapers, and daily, weekly, and monthly newspapers. Your work is cut out for you: Make your selection skillfully.

When selecting your newspaper, you certainly need to know its circulation. When you hear a circulation figure, triple it to learn how many people are reading the paper. When a family has a subscription to the paper and two adults and three kids read each issue, this is counted as only one subscriber.

By far the major marketing method used by small business is newspaper advertising, though online marketing is in the process of eclipsing it. Of course, your type of business may not benefit from newspaper advertising. But if you think it may, pay close attention.

Newspapers offer a high degree of flexibility in that you can decide to run an ad or make changes in it up to a couple of days before the ad is to run. Radio gives you even more flexibility in that regard, allowing you to make changes up to the day your spot is to run. A Web site provides a great deal of flexibility; magazines and television marketing allow you the least leeway.

If you don't have a clear-cut favorite newspaper (defined as best targeted for your market and most appropriate for your ads), there is a test. Remember that there are most likely far more newspapers in your region than you ever imagined. Run an ad in as many of the newspapers in your area as you can — there may be as many as thirty. Use coupons in your ads. Have each coupon make a different offer, such as $5 off or a free book or a 15 percent discount or a free plant. In the ad, request that the customer either bring the coupon when coming to your place of business or mention the coupon when calling or sending you e-mail.

By measuring the responses, you'll soon see which newspapers work, which don't work, and which work best of all. You don't have to run ads in all thirty newspapers to learn which is the best paper. Maybe you'll have to test in only three or five or ten papers. *But you are nuts unless you test.* And be sure to determine what generated the customer's response: the offer or the newspaper. You can do this by means of a second test. Make a different offer in the most effective paper. If it still pulls well, you've got a horse to ride.

Don't forget, we're talking about advertising in terms of a conservative investment. So don't waste your money advertising in a paper that you happen to read or that your friends happen to recommend or that has a super salesperson selling ad space. The paper you eventually select will be the one in which you advertise consistently. That paper is the one to which you will commit your marketing program, your regularly placed ad, your money, your hopes. Select with the highest care possible. The paper must have proved itself in your coupon test and should be the one read by prospective customers in your marketing area. A monthly paper is not preferable. Use it if you wish, but be sure that your major newspaper is at least a weekly, if not a daily.

Marketing is part science and part art — and the art part is very subjective. The artistic end of marketing is not limited to words and pictures; it involves timing and media selection and ad size.

The importance of your ad's appearance is not to be underestimated. Far more people will see your ad than will see you or your place of business, so their opinion of your business will be shaped by your ad. Don't let the newspaper people design your ad, and don't let them write the copy. If they do, it will look and sound like all the other ads in the paper. *Your competition is not simply the others in your business but rather everybody who advertises.*

You're vying for the reader's attention with banks, telecommunications companies, airlines, car companies, cigarette companies, soft-drink companies, and who knows what else. You must give your ad a distinct style. Hire a professional art director to establish the look for your ad. Later, you can ask the paper to follow the design guidelines created by that art director. At first, however, you or a talented friend or a gifted art director should make your advertising identity follow your marketing plan — and do so in a unique manner. You won't win customers by boring them into buying. You've got to create a desire, and a good-looking ad helps immeasurably, even measurably, if you do your tracking.

I must caution you that perhaps one in twenty-five newspapers has a first-class art department that can design ads with the best of the expensive graphics companies. Put another way, twenty-four out of twenty-five newspapers have art departments that can help you waste your marketing money by designing ordinary-looking ads. The same goes for copy. Newspapers will help write your copy — because they want you to advertise. Give your marketing money to charity instead. Or spend it on a great ad writer who can make your ad sing, motivate, and cause people to sit up and say, "I want that." If you have a winning ad, your marketing money can be safely invested in newspapers with the expectation of a high return.

Select the type used in your ad on the basis of readability and clarity. Don't use a type size that is smaller than the type used by the paper. (In fact, even type that size is too small.) Make it *easy* for the reader to read your ad. If you decide to reverse the type (a black background with the type appearing in white), be sure that the black ink doesn't spill over into the white letters, obliterating them. It happens every day. Don't let it happen to you. Newspapers are notorious for running ads that look faint and unreadable (as a result of their particular printing process, though those processes are giving way to digital printing, which gives you more clarity and control over the finished ad). You or your art director should discuss your ad with people in the newspaper's production department to confirm that the ad will print well.

Then there's the matter of size. Of course, a full-page ad is probably best if you want to make an impact. But you won't want to pay for a weekly full-page ad, so you must make do with something smaller. What size can you comfortably afford?

Newspapers charge you by the line or by the inch. There are fourteen lines to the inch. If the newspaper charges, say, $1 per line, you are paying $14 per inch. If you want your ad to be fifteen inches high and three columns wide, you multiply $14 by fifteen, coming out with $210, then multiply that by three, for a total ad cost of $630. If you run an ad that size weekly, it will cost $2,709 per month. (I multiplied the $630 by 4.3 because that's the approximate number of weeks per month.) If the figure is too high, run a smaller ad — one you can afford. Some people can run a weekly ten-inch ad (two columns by five inches) all year every year and enjoy a 25 percent sales increase each year. Others want a greater increase, so they design a larger ad and run it two times a week. A lot depends on the cost of advertising in the particular paper.

Most full-size newspapers are twenty-two inches high. If you can afford it, run an ad that is twelve inches high or higher. That way, you'll be sure that your ad is above the fold. Most full-size newspapers are six columns wide. So you can be certain of dominating the page with an ad four columns by twelve inches high.

That's a great tack, and if you use it, you won't be wasting your money. But you can save a bit of money if you run a smaller ad with a powerful and unique border. An ad does not have to dominate a page to be seen. It merely has to interest the reader, create a desire, and then motivate the reader to do something you want him or her to do.

If you run your ad in a tabloid-size newspaper rather than a full-size newspaper, you can save money by running a smaller ad. A ten-inch ad may appear to be buried in a large newspaper but stands out in a tabloid. Many Sunday newspapers have tabloid-size sections, and you can save money by using them. But don't use them for that reason only — be sure that your prospects read that paper and that section.

Some guidelines will help you decide whether to run large or small ads. Consider the advantages and disadvantages of small ads. Small ads don't

- Impress as much as large ones
- Allow you to include long lists of names or lots of information
- Enable you to use color
- Provide enough space for photos or drawings
- Generate high-volume sales
- Allow you to have the position you want in the newspaper

But small ads do

- Allow you to run several for the cost of one large ad
- Let you feature samples of your selection in each
- Let you run them in several publications for valid test results
- Allow you to offer free brochures, samples, or catalogs
- Enable you to compile a database from the leads you get from inquiries
- Serve as logical places to advertise single items or announce new ones
- Let you run in the middle of the classified section, where the serious shoppers look

- Include your Web site, where potential customers can get a lot more information

What are the best days to run your ads? It differs with different towns and different businesses. Ask your local newspaper's space salesperson for a recommendation. Generally, Sunday is the day that the most people read the paper and spend the most time with it. But can your business succeed by running ads on days your doors are closed? Some businesses can. If yours can, give a nod to Sunday.

Guerrillas favor Sundays because there are more employment-opportunity ads, resulting in a higher readership of the newspaper — especially the classified section. People who are often on the road are usually home on Sundays and have more time to spend with their newspaper.

Monday is a pretty good day if your offering is directed to males, because many males read the Monday papers carefully to learn about the sports events of the preceding weekend. Saturday is also a fairly good day, because many advertisers shy away from it, and you'll have less competition. Some papers make Wednesday or Thursday their food day, so the papers are loaded with food and grocery ads.

You'll have to observe the papers yourself, then ask the person who will be selling the ad space to you. That ad space comes a lot cheaper if you sign a contract for a given number of lines or inches per year. Ask about the discounts you can receive for volume usage. They are quite substantial — a fringe benefit of consistent advertising in the same paper.

It's usually best if your ad appears as far to the front as possible, on a right-hand page, above the fold of the paper. But few, if any, papers will guarantee placement unless you sign a giant contract. The main news section is also considered to be an optimum place for an ad because of high readership by a large cross-section of readers.

Because of the nature of your product, you may want to run your ad in the business section, the sports section, or the entertainment section. Run your ad where competitors run theirs. If you have no competition, run your ad where services or merchandise similar to yours are being offered. Why? Because that's where readers are conditioned to look for offerings such as yours.

Incidentally, readers most likely will read your ad. Study after study reveals that newspaper readers read the ads almost as intensively as they read the stories. And because of the power of graphics, some ads attract more attention than do the news stories. Use graphics in your ad (but go easy!). Generally, more than three or four pictures — whether art or photography

— is too many. But that's a rule that is both useful to know and useful to break; I've broken it on purpose and with good cause more than once. I've also run very successful ads that have only one illustration or photo. Lack of an illustration or photo means that the ad will be 27 percent less effective.

Another rule to know in case you want to break it intentionally is that one of the great powers of print advertising is that it easily enables you to repeat your message three times — in the illustration or photo, the headline, and the copy. Illustrations that relate directly to the message work 32 percent better, unless they're a cliché.

Long copy works as well as short copy and better, in many cases, when serious prospects are looking over your ad. Vague headlines reduce the effectiveness of an ad by 11 percent; humor can add 10 percent. Celebrities add another 25 percent to the power of the ad, though it's not guaranteed. Recipes can add 20 percent and coupons 26 percent. If you also use TV, including just one frame from your commercial will boost the power of your newspaper ad by 42 percent. See? There is a lot of cross-over value from one medium to the next.

If you have a truly good ad — one that states all the features and benefits of your offering — consider making multiple reprints. Use the reprints as circulars, customer handouts, mailing pieces, or interior signs. Their true cost was incurred when you originally produced the ad. Remember, you can enlarge the ad and make it a poster.

To increase the number of inquiries you receive through newspaper advertising, *always* remember to consistently state your name and primary message throughout your ads. In addition, put these ideas into action.

- Mention your offer in your headline.
- Restate your offer in a subhead.
- Emphasize the word *free* and repeat it when possible.
- Say something to add urgency to your offer. It can be a limited-time offer. It can be a limited-quantities offer. Get those sales *now*.
- Run a picture of your product or service in action.
- Include testimonials when applicable.
- Do something to differentiate yourself from others who advertise in the newspaper. That means all others — not only your direct competitors.
- Put a border around your ad if it's a small ad. Make the border unique.
- Be sure that your ad contains a word or phrase set in huge type. Even a small ad can "act" big if you do so.
- Always include your address, specific location, phone number, e-mail

address, and Web site address. Make it easy for readers to find you or talk with you.

- Create a visual look that you can maintain every time you advertise. This clarifies your identity and increases consumer familiarity.
- Experiment with different ad sizes, shapes, days on which you run the ad, and newspaper sections.
- Consider free-standing inserts in your newspaper. These are increasingly popular and may be less expensive than you imagine.
- Try adding a color to your ad. Red, blue, and brown work well. You can't do this with tiny ads, but it may be worth trying with a large ad.
- Test several types of ads and offers in different publications until you have the optimum ad, offer, and ad size. Then run the ad with confidence. It's very unusual to get everything right the first time.
- Be careful with new newspapers. Wait until they prove themselves. But once they do prove themselves, think of yourself as married to the newspaper — you're in it for the long haul.
- Do everything in your power to get your ad placed in the front section of the paper on a right-hand page above the fold. Merely asking isn't enough. You may have to pay personal visits. Be a squeaky wheel.
- Don't be afraid of using lengthy copy. Although lengthy copy is best suited for magazines, many successful newspaper advertisers use it.
- Run your ad in the financial pages if you have a business offer, in the sports pages if you have a male-oriented offer, in the food pages for food products. The astrology page usually gets the best readership. In general, the best location for ads is the main news section, as far forward as possible.
- Study the ads run by your competitors. Study their offers. Make yours more cogent, concise, sweeter, different, better.
- Keep detailed records of the results of your ads. If you don't keep track of your experiments, you won't learn anything.
- Be sure that your ad is in character with your intended market, product or service, and the newspaper in which you advertise.
- Use short words, short sentences, and short paragraphs.
- If you distribute a coupon, make sure that your address appears on the coupon and also next to the coupon so that if the coupon gets clipped, your name and address still appear.
- Use photos or illustrations that reproduce faithfully in newspapers.
- Always put the name of your company somewhere at the bottom of your ad. Don't expect people to get the name from the copy, the headline, the picture of the product, or the picture of the storefront. And it's

a good idea to put your name in your headline. At least put it in the subhead.

- Include your Web site address at the top of your ad. Place it prominently. Invite people to visit you there.
- Say something timely in your ad. Remember, people read papers for news. So your message should tie in with the news when it can.
- Ask all your customers where they heard about you. If they don't mention the newspaper, ask them directly, "Did you see our newspaper ad?" Customer feedback is invaluable.
- *Aim your ad to people who are in the market for your offering right now.*
- If you don't plan to use newspapers to support your other marketing efforts, use them weekly or stay away from them altogether. Occasional use doesn't cut it.

These tips, your common sense, the quality of newspapers in your community, the newspaper production department, the newspaper representative calling on your business, and the presence or absence of your competitors in the newspaper should be prime considerations in your decision to advertise in newspapers as part of your guerrilla marketing mix. To many guerrillas around the world, a newspaper looks like a meal ticket!

Magazines

Whoever heard of a small-time entrepreneur advertising in well-known and respected national magazines? You have now. Magazine advertising has been the linchpin for many a successful small business. Remember, the single most important reason people patronize one business over another is confidence. And magazine advertisements breed confidence by instilling familiarity and giving credibility. *A properly produced magazine ad, preferably of the full-page variety, gives a small business more credibility than any other mass-marketing medium.*

You will not necessarily gain consumer confidence from a single exposure to your magazine ad. But if you run the ad once, you can use the reprints of that ad forever. One highly successful company ran a single regional ad in a single issue of *Time* magazine, then used reprints of the ad (reprints are available at a fraction of a cent each) in its window and on its counter for nearly thirty-five years afterward. Reprints were also sent in direct mailings. His mailings in 2006 could even run a reprint that stated, "As seen in *Time* magazine" — heavy-duty name dropping from an ad run once in 1973. That's getting mileage out of magazine advertising!

The magazine ad that you run in 2007 can bring home the bacon for you in 2027. The investment isn't very high. Several bright entrepreneurs have run an ad one time in a regional edition of a national magazine, then mailed out reprints in all direct mailings — each time gaining the confidence that prospects ordinarily placed in the magazine itself. This is the *point* of magazine advertising for small business. It gives them a great deal of credibility, which creates confidence, which translates to sales. And profits. If people feel that *Time* magazine is reliable, credible, trustworthy, and solid, they'll feel the same way about the companies that advertise in *Time*. So if you wish to gain instant credibility, advertise in magazines that will give it to you.

I'm talking about running your ad in your regional edition *only*, only one time. Not all magazines have regional editions. But those that do have regional editions can save you a fortune.

The number of publications offering these affordable methods of reaching target audiences is growing quickly. It takes a media-buying service to keep up with the maximedia's efforts to woo budgets from small businesses. That's one reason guerrillas use them.

Most people don't realize that regional editions exist. When they see your full-page (or smaller if you engage in fusion marketing and split the cost of the page with one, two, or three others) ad in *Time* magazine, they'll be quite impressed that you are advertising in a respected national magazine. And they'll turn that state of being impressed into a state of confidence in your offering. Check your library or the Internet for the latest issue of *Consumer Magazine and Agri-Media Rates and Data* (published monthly by Standard Rate and Data Service, Inc. — known as SRDS), and you'll learn which magazines have regional editions and how much they charge for advertising in them.

If you run a small display ad for a mail-order venture in a national publication, you should do as much testing as possible. An inexpensive method of testing is to avail yourself of the split runs offered by many magazines. By taking advantage of them, you can test two headlines. Send your two ads to the publication, being certain to code each ad for response so that you'll be able to tell which of the two headlines pulls better, and ask the publication to split-run the ads. One headline will run in half the magazines printed; the other headline will run in the other half.

For example, a manufacturer of exercise equipment once ran a split-run ad with a coupon. One headline said, STRENGTHEN YOUR WRISTS FOR BETTER GOLF! The other said, STRENGTHEN YOUR WRISTS IN ONLY TWO MINUTES A DAY! The coupon in the first ad was addressed to Lion's Head,

7230 Paxton, Dept. G6A, Chicago, IL 60649. The coupon in the second ad was addressed to Lion's Head, 7230 Paxton, Dept. GOB, Chicago, IL 60649.

Although the coupons looked alike, it was easy for the advertiser to tell that the appeal of two minutes a day was stronger than the appeal of better golf, even though the advertiser had guessed that the golf headline would attract the better response. How could the advertiser tell that his guess was wrong? Because the responses to Dept. GOB ran four times higher than those to Dept. G6A. Incidentally, the advertiser could also tell by referring to those responses that they came from *Golf* magazine (G) in answer to an ad run in June (6). The code indicated three points: the publication, the month in which the ad ran, and which of the two ads drew the better response.

Codes can also tell you the year, ad size, and other information. Some publications allow you to do a triple split-run and not just a double, enabling you to test three headlines rather than two. If you can test three headlines, do it. Let your audience make your judgments for you when possible. After you count the coded responses, you'll know which headline is best, and the cost of the test itself will have been minimal. The magazine's split-run capability will have saved money for you while giving you valuable information. Now you can run the successful ad with boldness and confidence.

Don't count yourself out of advertising in national publications because of the cost. You can cut down on that cost by establishing an in-house advertising agency, purchasing remnant space or space in regional editions, and purchasing a tiny space unit — say, one column by two inches. Or you can advertise in the classified section that is available in many national magazines. Also, many magazines offer enticing discounts to mail-order advertisers. And virtually all magazines offer impressive merchandising materials: easel-back cards, reprints, decals with the name of the magazine (for example, "as seen in *Time*"), and mailing folders. The magazine's advertising sales representative will be happy to tell you about all the merchandising aids offered. Take advantage of them. They'll be useful at your place of business, on your Web site, in your window (if you have one), and in your other modes of advertising.

Your business will be helped if you simply mention, "You've probably seen our ad in *Woman's Day* magazine." Put that ad on the front page of your Web site for a month. Milk it for all it's worth, and realize that it has a lot of milk in it. Materials can be used as enclosures in direct mailings and with personal letters; as signs on bulletin boards; as counter cards and display pieces at trade shows, exhibits, or fairs; and in a brochure or a circular. The cost of these powerful guerrilla marketing aids is ridiculously low, sometimes even free. Use them to the fullest extent. Magazines can help you market your offering immediately and in the years ahead. It's the years ahead that will result in profitable business for you.

Magazine advertising offers other attractive advantages. You can target your market better with magazines than with newspapers. Also, you can reach a specific circulation rather than a general circulation. You can reach people who have demonstrated an interest in skiing, gardening, do-it-yourselfing, snowmobiling — you name it. Little waste circulation. Everyone who sees your ad is a prospect. And one of the basic tenets of guerrilla marketing is to talk primarily to prospects and not to browsers.

A good guerrilla marketer also considers advertising in magazines other than consumer magazines. A whole world of trade magazines is out there. Almost every trade and profession has its own publication or, more likely, group of publications. Because you want to focus on prospects, consider advertising in some of these trade publications, because they are subscribed to and read cover to cover by many prospective customers. This is especially true if your product is at all business oriented.

Research your options online or at the library. Visit MediaFinder at mediafinder.com. Most likely, you'll want to subscribe to at least one trade magazine to keep abreast of new developments in your field.

Standard Rate and Data publishes a host of directories that may be of use in your business. If I ran a business school, I'd make it mandatory to spend a day looking through SRDS publications. Success-bound students would petition for more days. If you want to subscribe, write to Standard Rate and Data Service, 5201 Old Orchard Road, Skokie, Illinois 60077, or call 708-256-6067. Naturally, they're online, at srds.com.

Another important advantage of advertising in magazines is that you can use color much more effectively than you can in newspapers. If your offering is oriented to color — if you're marketing fabrics, for instance — consider advertising in magazines to show off the hues and tones.

Magazines are better suited than any other medium, except for Web sites, to lengthy copy. People buy magazines with the idea of spending time with them, unlike newspapers, which are read quickly for news. Magazines involve their readers, and your ads may do the same. Studies reveal that nonprospects screen themselves out voluntarily and that hot prospects read every single word.

Use subheads. Figure on using three of them for an ad in which 33 percent to 50 percent of the total space is devoted to text. If it's less than that, one or two subheads will do the trick. Write your subheads in upper- and lowercase letters and boldface type. Keep them short — people read them *before* they read your copy.

It is primarily because of guerrilla marketers that magazines now publish so many regional editions. Now that you know this, look through your local issue of *Time, TV Guide, Sports Illustrated,* or *Better Homes and Gardens.* How many regional advertisers are using those media? How many use color to show off their products? How many run long-copy ads? Which ones share the cost of a full-page ad even though they run different half-page ads? Most important, remember that in all likelihood, these advertisers could never afford a national ad in the same magazine. But the growth of the entrepreneurial spirit in America has necessitated an increase in regional editions. Advertisers in these regional editions know that by advertising in a major magazine, they are putting themselves in the big leagues. Their ad might run on the page next to an ad for Bank of America or Rolls-Royce or IBM. Not bad company for a guerrilla, no? Guerrilla marketing lets you play in the big leagues without first struggling in the minors.

Many major magazines have been available to minor advertisers for longer than forty years. Guerrillas avail themselves of major magazine opportunities and of their merchandising aids as a key to successful marketing. This gives you credibility within your community, and it gives you respect in the minds of your sales staff, suppliers, and even competitors.

If you're a thinking entrepreneur, you'll use magazines in several ways. You'll advertise regularly in a magazine that hits your target audience right on the nose. You'll advertise only one time in a prestige magazine, so as to use its merchandising aids. You'll use the classified sections of national magazines if you are in the mail-order business. And you'll use the display sections of national magazines if what you sell is too big for the classified sections or if your chosen magazine doesn't run classified ads.

It may be that you want to advertise in a national magazine because of the status, huge circulation, and easily identifiable audience but don't have the money for a large ad. No problem.

Go little instead of large. If you're practicing guerrilla marketing to the hilt, you will mention your national magazine advertisements in the other media you use: on the radio, in your direct-mail advertisements, on your signs, in your yellow pages ads, in your personal letters, in your telemarketing, at your Web site, in your e-mail signature — wherever you can. "As seen in *Fortune*" carries a lot of prestige. Size really doesn't matter in this scenario.

If you come up with a winning magazine ad, you may be able to run it in a multitude of magazines. The result can be a multitude of profits. You can run your proven money maker for years and years in a wide selection of publications. To a guerrilla, few marketing situations are as delightful.

But the prime reason for using magazines is the lasting value of the ad. I recall placing a full-page ad in *Newsweek* for a client. After the ad was run, the client asked each customer where he or she had heard of his company. At the end of one week, only five people claimed to have seen his ad in *Newsweek*, where it had run only one time. At the end of one month, that number had climbed — to eighteen people. And after a full year, a total of sixty-three customers had said they had first heard of the company through its ad in *Newsweek*. And that's not even the impressive part! The really significant aspect of this story is that the entrepreneur blew up a reprint of the ad to the size of an enormous poster — five feet high — then mounted it and placed it outside his place of business. Thousands of customers patronized his business because of that poster.

Newsweek turned out to be his most effective advertising medium that year — and yet he placed but one ad there. To make matters more wonderful, the *Newsweek* page was purchased at less than half the going rate, because it was remnant space. The magazine had sold three full-page ads to regional advertisers and had one page left over — a remnant. So my client was able to buy the space for a fraction of its original price.

If you're interested in advertising in any particular magazine, call the local representative of the magazine and say that you are definitely a candidate for any remnant space and that you should be phoned when it is available. You may wait a bit, but it will be well worth the wait. Do Coca-Cola and AT&T practice this tactic? No. Do successful guerrilla marketing people practice it? You bet their bank balance they do!

Most small-business owners never even consider advertising in magazines. That's because they don't know about regional editions, remnant space, in-house agency discounts, the power of a tiny ad, and valuable merchandising aids. Now that you do know about these lovely aspects of magazine advertising, give serious consideration to the medium.

Radio

Unless you have a good friend who owns a radio station, most of your radio marketing will be of the paid, rather than free, variety, though remember that in 2005, more than 50 percent of all media was obtained via barter, according to the head of one of the nation's largest media-buying services. It is possible to have stories or interviews about your product or service on the radio, and it may be that those will cost you nary a cent. Free and valuable publicity is not that difficult to come by on the radio. But as far as this chapter is concerned, you'll have to pay or trade for your radio marketing. For purposes of simplicity, let's talk paying.

Although newspapers are the primary marketing medium for most small businesses and direct mail has taken over second place, with online marketing coming up slowly on the rail, radio still does come in a strong third. Radio advertising can be used effectively by a company with a limited budget. And radio can help improve your aim when you're trying to reach your target consumers. Radio helps you establish a close relationship with your prospects. Consider this: Because of its intimate nature, radio brings you even closer than newspapers do. The sound of an announcer's voice, the type of musical background, the sound effects you use to punctuate and enhance your message — all these are ammunition in your radio-marketing arsenal. All can help win customers and sales for you.

Although it's true that you can, if you try, pay $1,500 or more for the airtime for a single thirty-second radio commercial on a large commercial radio station, you can also, if you try, pay $5 for a single radio commercial on a smaller, less popular station. You'll certainly talk to more people with the $1,500 spot, but you will reach more than a few people with your $5 commercial.

Don't think, however, that you can spend $5 and be involved in radio marketing. But if you spend $5 for five spots per day ($25) and you run your spots four days a week ($100) three weeks out of four, you may say that for $300 a month, you are adequately covering the listener profile in the community that the particular radio station covers.

Because radio listeners often change stations, you should run radio spots on more than one station. This is a rule to know and to break. But know it. One station does not a radio campaign make.

How many stations do you need? Well, you may need only one. But you'll probably need three or four or five. It may also be that you have the type of offering that lends itself so well to radio that you'll need no other ad media and can dive headlong into advertising on ten stations. Some of my clients have. One of the advantages to being on so many stations is that by carefully tracking your audience response — that is, learning which stations are bringing in the business — you can eliminate the losers and narrow your radio marketing down to proven winners. You can also use the coupon-type testing we explored in Chapter 9. That means you pick, say, five stations and run commercials on all five. In each commercial, make a different offer — a discount, a free gift, a 50 percent reduction — and ask listeners to mention the offer when they contact you. By keeping assiduous track of the offers mentioned by your customers, you'll know which stations to drop (maybe all of them) and which to continue with (maybe all of them).

Unless you really keep track of all your media responses, you are not a guerrilla. If you run your ads and keep selecting media on blind faith, you are closer to a lemming. You've got to make your marketing as scientific as possible. This is one of those rare instances in which you can measure the effectiveness of your media scientifically. Avail yourself of it.

If you have salespeople, ask them to track responses. If you're the person taking orders from customers, you must track responses. Ask the customers, "Where did you hear of us first?" If they say radio, ask "Which station?" If they name a station that you don't use, ask, "Which stations do you ordinarily listen to?" If that doesn't net a solid response, prompt the customer, naming a few stations (one of which you do use). It's a drag to do this, but it's a bigger drag to waste marketing money and bankrupt a business. Do everything you can to learn which stations are pulling in customers and which are not. After you've been marketing seriously for a year or three, you can cut down on your media tracking, though I don't suggest that you do. If you start learning for sure which stations pull best, you may feel that you need no longer ask. But until you're certain, you must ask. Because stations and people change, keep track consistently.

There are many types of radio stations: rock and roll, rap, hip-hop, middle of the road, country, public, all news, talk show, drama, Spanish language, religious, black, top 40, bubblegum rock, jazz, oldies, intellectual, avant-garde, local interest, farm oriented, progressive rock, reggae. Public radio and community radio do not run commercials, but they do make public service announcements for free. Which stations do your prospective customers listen to? Although it's possible to divide radio stations into twenty-three categories, as I've just done, it's advisable to divide them into two categories: background stations and foreground stations.

Some radio stations play *background* programming, playing music that is generally a background sound. People talk, converse, work, play, iron, cook, and do myriad other things with background radio sounds. The music does not get in the way, command attention, distract. Unfortunately, because people are not actively listening, the commercials also are in the background. Sure, when a person is driving home with the radio on, all alone, the commercials — and the music — move up from the background. But in general, all-music stations are background radio stations. And many music and knowledge lovers have CD players or cassette decks in their cars, not to mention their homes.

Sports, religion, all-news, and talk stations are *foreground* radio stations. They are in the foreground of people's consciousness. They command attention. They are poor stations to have on when conversing, working, or concentrating. As a result, the commercials that these stations broadcast are likely to attract more active listeners. These people pay closer attention to commercials because they are actively listening to the radio. This is not to say that foreground radio is better than background radio for advertising. But be aware of the difference.

There are other differences as well. Talk radio is hosted by personalities. Disc jockeys at music radio stations tell what music has just been aired and what music is about to air. Sometimes, this is on tape. Talk radio involves listener rapport, more informal utter, and more personal asides.

Here's a guerrilla tactic that works gloriously well on foreground stations when it is appropriate. Suppose that you have a new company that sells, say, computer instruction. Invite a talk radio personality to take a few lessons. Then buy time on that personality's station. Rather than provide a sixty- or thirty-second script for your commercial, which you might ordinarily do, provide an outline and invite the personality to ad-lib. The result is usually a sincere commercial, far longer than the commercial for which you have contracted, that has loads of credibility. If your product or service is worth raving about, you can count on most personalities to give it their all. You have to pay for only a sixty-second spot, but you may end up with a three-minute spot at no extra cost.

That is about the only instance in which I'd advise you to put your message into the hands of the radio station. In virtually all other instances, I suggest that you provide recorded commercials, which you can tape at an independent facility or at the station itself. Do not furnish scripts to the station. Although some of their announcers may read them well, other announcers may make mincemeat out of them, may read them with no conviction and no enthusiasm. Murphy's law has a way of asserting itself at radio stations: If the commercial can be messed up, it will be. Protect yourself by supplying finished tapes only — unless you can get a personality to breathe true life into your script.

Just as it is bad business to let a newspaper write your newspaper ad copy, it is also a grave error to let a radio station write your radio ad copy. Most stations will be all too willing to volunteer. Don't let them. If you do, your commercial will sound just like everyone else's commercials. One of the most asinine methods of saving money is to let the station write your advertising.

If the station offers to produce your spot, that's a different story. Check out the equipment. It's probably all right. Listen to the station's announcers. If you trust the equipment — as measured by the sound of finished commercials produced on it — and you like one or more of the announcers, allow the station to voice and produce the commercial on tape for you. Generally, there is no charge or a low charge for this service. In most, but not all, cases, it's worth the price.

Whichever format you select as the home base for your radio marketing program, should you run thirty-second spots or sixty-second spots? A thirty-second spot is usually far more than 50 percent of the cost of a sixty-second spot. In most instances, what you can say in sixty seconds can also be expressed in thirty seconds. So go with the shorter spots even though they are not great values. In the long run, they'll give you more bang for your budget. If, however, you have a complex product or service, you'll have to run a full sixty-second spot. Some advertisers achieve superb results with two-minute commercials. Take as long as you must to state your message, but make it thirty seconds in length, if possible.

A long-time radio pro once told me that if he had to cut 33 percent of his radio advertising budget but could spend that 33 percent on a music track for his commercials, he'd gladly do it. He believes that the presence of music lends a powerful emotional overtone to the commercial. I agree. Music can convey what words frequently cannot, and music can be obtained inexpensively. You can rent it from the station's rights-free music library. You can have a music track made by hungry musicians who will record a track for very little money, appreciating the exposure they will receive. Or you can purchase an expensive music track — made expressly for you or taken from a hot record — and use it so much that the amortized cost is mere peanuts.

I know an entrepreneur who made a deal with a composer who had recently released a record album. The entrepreneur, on learning that the particular music he liked would cost $3,000, said that he'd pay the composer $100 per month for a full year. If, at the end of that period, he was still in business and wanted the music, he would then pay $3,000 in addition to the rental fees he had paid. If he hadn't been successful, he would be out merely the rental fees, and the composer would still have the music. It sounded like a fair deal for both parties, so the composer agreed. At the end of one year, the composer did receive $3,000 in addition to the $1,200 he earned for renting his music. His total gain was $4,200. The entrepreneur, who at the time could barely afford the $100 rental, could later easily afford the $3,000. Everyone came out a winner.

If you have to use announcers and musicians who are members of the various unions (Screen Actors' Guild and/or American Federation of Television and Radio Actors), be wary. Union costs and paperwork are overwhelming, and you might be better off to avoid unions. I work with unions only when I absolutely must, and when I do, I see that all the paperwork is handled by an independent party. Unions and guerrillas mix like gasoline and Gatorade.

As music adds new dimensions to your selling message, so do sound effects. Use them when you can; radio stations (and most production facilities) have libraries of them and rent them at nominal costs. Just be careful that you don't get carried away with their use.

You have but three seconds to catch and hold the attention of the listener. Be interesting during those first three seconds and say what you have to say, lest the listener's attention stray. Be sure to use "ear" words rather than "eye" words. Whatever you do, repeat your main selling point. Also, repeat your company name as many times as you possibly can.

A good idea for a radio commercial: Put the president of the company into a recording booth and interview him or her. The interview should last for thirty minutes or longer. Then use small sections of the interview as ingredients — sound bites — in future commercials. Sound bites are ideas expressed simply and briefly. The concept was spawned for the political process by public relations pros, who are called "spin doctors" by the media, based on their ability to give the proper "spin," or public perception, to the activities of the firms they represent. Spin doctors can create the perception that an oil company is a group of ardent environmentalists. The 1998 movie *Wag the Dog* was an accurate if exaggerated demonstration of the power and skill of spin doctors as they manipulate public opinion from Washington. But our government isn't the only one to employ spin doctors. They have long been functioning in the capitals of nations around the world.

As a guerrilla, you can be your own spin doctor. Select your own sound bites from the interview for your marketing. But you never want to be *perceived* as a spin doctor; you want to put the right "spin" only on your marketing.

Although most announcers can easily fit seventy words into a thirty-second spot, studies indicate that people listen more attentively if the announcer talks faster and crams more words into a short space. Columbia University conducted the study, which gave speed-talk a shot in the arm. Here are a few radio hints for guerrillas.

- Save money by running ads three weeks out of every four.
- Concentrate your spots during a few days of the week, such as Wednesday through Sunday.
- Try to run radio advertising during afternoon drive time, when people are heading home. They're in more of a buying mood than in the morning, when work is on their minds.
- When listening to the radio commercials you've produced, listen to them on a car-radio-type speaker, not on a fancy high-fidelity speaker like the ones production studios use. Many an advertiser, dazzled after hearing his or her commercial on an expensive speaker system, has become depressed when hearing what the commercials sound like on a typical car stereo system.
- Consider radio rate cards to be pure fiction. They are highly negotiable.
- Study the audiences of all the radio stations in your marketing area. Then match your typical prospect with the appropriate stations. It's not difficult.
- If you want to reach teenagers, advertise on the radio, not in the newspaper.
- Mention your Web site in your radio commercial. You have only a minute or less to convince listeners to buy from you on the radio, but you have unlimited time online.

One of radio's surprises is its power as a direct-response medium. Many companies spend twenty-five seconds delivering their sales pitch and five seconds providing their toll-free number. Because companies are advertising on radio and realize that people can't write the number on a piece of paper, they spell a word with their phone number. Response rates are equivalent to those on TV, and the cost is usually much lower. The influx of car phones can't be a hindrance to the use of radio for direct marketing. But please don't make a call while you're heading in my direction on the highway.

If you plan to use radio for your direct-response offer, repeat your phone number at least three times. Use a high-quality voice. Take advantage of the intimacy of radio. Air your spot on weekends and during evenings, and figure on receiving responses within three to four days. Change your copy immediately if you get a poor response, and change your product if new and improved copy doesn't help. Before you change your product, however, be absolutely certain that your offering matches the tastes of the listening audience.

Unless you simply cannot see your way to using radio, do give it a try. You'll appreciate its flexibility, ability to allow you to make last-minute changes, and the opportunity to home in on your prospects on the basis of station format, time of day, and day of the week. I have a very successful client who owns a furniture store. Although he uses many marketing media — newspapers, yellow pages, billboards, point-of-purchase signs, and direct mail — he spends 90 percent of his marketing money on radio advertising. With such a high concentration of dollars in only one medium, does he qualify as a true guerrilla? He sure does! He has learned through the years that radio reaches his exact audience and motivates them to come into his store. He runs his commercials on anywhere from six to ten stations, and he often runs the same commercial fifteen times in a day. What's more, he's never off the radio, using it fifty-two weeks per year. Because he learned to use this medium to the benefit of his bottom line, he is a true guerrilla marketer. After experimenting with all kinds of marketing mixes, he finally decided that radio was the medium for him. He uses it with music. He uses it consistently. And he makes so much money that he lives a luxurious life in Hawaii while his business, located in the Midwest, continues to flourish. Although many factors are responsible for his success, he gives most of the credit to radio advertising. He is living proof that you can prosper in style as a one-medium guerrilla.

Television

Television is the most effective of all marketing vehicles, the undisputed heavyweight champion and the American Idol, though online marketing is becoming a contender for the title and should hold it before long. But television is also the most elusive and easiest to misuse. It's elusive because it's not as simple as it seems, because it requires many talents, is not normally associated with small businesspeople, and is dominated by giants that give entrepreneurs a mistaken impression of how it should be used. You cannot use TV as Nike, Coca-Cola, Ford, and McDonald's use it unless you have their money.

Television is easy to misuse because it does seem straightforward, affordable for almost anyone to run one or two television commercials, and readily available. It has more options than ever, is the medium that strokes the entrepreneur's ego the most tantalizingly, and requires a whole new discipline. *Television is not, as some believe, radio with pictures.*

Americans watched more TV in 2005 than in any other year since Nielsen Media Research started tracking it in the 1950s. The average American household watched 8 hours and 11 minutes of TV per day, up 2.7 percent from the year before and 12.5 percent from ten years ago, according to data released recently by Nielsen Media Research. Individual viewing habits were about half that, with the average American TV viewer watching 4 hours and 32 minutes daily, the highest in fifteen years, according to Nielsen. There were also slightly higher viewing levels during summer 2005 than in summer 2004 and in the first week of the new TV season.

Television has changed in many ways, all of them favoring guerrillas. Advertising costs have plummeted to the point that a thirty-second prime-time commercial costs $20 or less, even in major markets (this is for cable, not for network programming).

Targeting ability has improved: You can run commercials in specific city neighborhoods, selected suburbs, your community. You can run them in affluent zip codes that may not even be in your community — if you offer things that affluent people want. Also, satellite and cable TV allow you to pick TV channels that hit your prospects smack-dab in the middle of their viewing patterns. With a dish called an uplink, satellite TV is broadcast upward to one of thirty communication satellites. The satellite then sends the TV signals back to Earth, where they are picked up by people who have conventional home satellite dishes and those who subscribe to direct broadcast satellite services. Add to that the many cable stations that transmit satellite broadcasts to umpteen million more homes. You probably know that many communities today receive more than seventy TV channels. Oh, some now receive more than seven hundred? Better read fast before my updated information becomes outdated.

Whether your interest is education, international news, movies, adult programming, network TV, kids, business, animals, game shows, romance, history, crime, science, information, shopping, religion, sports, travel, or weather, chances are that it's on satellite. Because satellite dishes are sold in different sizes, the cost of ownership is quite low, attracting more viewers and making the television medium more enticing to guerrillas. One of the fastest growth areas is in home shopping channels.

As TV technology, cable systems, satellites in orbit, and videocassette/ DVR ownership — now above 90 percent — have changed, so too have viewing patterns. Of the ten prime uses of TV sets, three do not allow commercials: rented tapes/DVDs, video games, and the TV as a monitor for a computer. PBS, the third most popular use of TV, may be a good station on which to market, and you shouldn't overlook it if your target market watches it. If you sponsor a PBS program, you'll create as much awareness as you would with a commercial on CBS. But you'll get a heck of a lot more credibility.

When you were a kid, network TV ruled the roost. Today, it's hanging in there but is not enjoying a growth spurt. Cable and satellite TV are growing at a much healthier rate.

Another new option is the increasingly ad-friendly Public Broadcasting System. Many local affiliates now accept sponsorships that look and feel — and sell — much like standard TV commercials. One guerrilla, Jerry Baker, who calls himself America's Master Gardener, participates in PBS fund-raisers by giving gardening advice during pledge breaks. The stations then offer his books and videos as premiums for donations. His success on PBS has been translated to QVC, one of the shopping channels, where he sells thousands of videos each time he appears. If you can't give gardening advice, perhaps you can give your local PBS station something that it can auction at a fundraising drive.

The TV market is becoming fragmented, just as is happening with all media. The Internet seems to be the only place where all the fragments can and do come together.

TV viewers are now more sophisticated than ever. They've been around the block when it comes to TV advertising spots and have opinions that you should know about the spots: 31 percent find TV advertising spots to be misleading; 24.3 percent, offensive; 17 percent, informative; 15.9 percent, entertaining.

If you're planning to test TV for advertising to your market, give cable serious consideration. Cable TV is growing and is becoming more and more affordable. But don't be deceived by the low cost. For the tiny sum of money it costs, expect it to deliver a tiny audience. Experts say that it's best suited for marketers with small trading areas where other media alternatives charge you for a lot of waste coverage — meaning that they reach people not in your trading area.

Nonetheless, small-business owners can now advertise on TV, on any satellite-delivered cable show, for prices even the smallest can afford. The twenty-dollar figure I mentioned was on the high side for cable. Most slots are considerably less than that. Think single digits. You can advertise on prime time; cherry-pick the subscriber neighborhoods and suburbs in which your spots appear; pick such stations as CNN, ESPN, MTV, the Nashville Network, Arts and Entertainment, the Discovery Channel, Court TV, Animal Planet, and loads more — *for not much more than the cost of a radio commercial.* Never before has TV been more available and desirable to owners of small businesses. Guerrillas in droves are, at this very moment, discovering the awesome power of TV, and I suggest that you do the very same.

Television is effective only if you use it enough. And enough is a lot. Enough is expensive. How much is enough? Many experts say that you can measure how much enough is by understanding rating points. A GRP (gross rating point) is calculated on the basis of 1 percent of the TV households in the TV marketing area. If 1 million TV sets are in the area, one rating point equals 10,000 TV households. The cost of TV advertising is determined by the size of each GRP in the marketing area, and advertisers pay for a given number of GRPs when they buy advertising time. The experts advise, and I agree, that you should not consider TV advertising unless you can afford to pay for 150 GRPs per month. Those can come in the form of 75 GRPs per week every other week or 50 GRPs for three weeks out of four, or even 150 GRPs for one week per month. How much a single rating point costs in your area depends on the size of the area, the competitive situation, and the time of year. Points tend to cost more around Christmas shopping time — October through late December — and less during the summer, when reruns are being shown. Rating points in small towns cost far less than in big cities. The price ranges from about $4 per GRP in a small city, such as Helena, Montana, to about $2,000 per GRP in a big city, such as New York or Los Angeles.

Can you start small in TV and then build up? Only if you start out by buying 150 GRPs for one month and have the funds and emotional endurance to tough it out for a minimum of three months. If you can't do that, don't fool around with TV. If you can afford to pay for the proper number of rating points — and you can if you live in a low-cost TV marketing area, such as those found in many rural sections of the United States, or if you are well funded — you'll find that TV can do many things the other media cannot. Television allows you to demonstrate, act, dance, sing, put on playlets, show cause and effect, create a lively identity, be dramatic, reach large numbers of people, zero in on your specific audience, prove your points visually and verbally — all at the same time. You can not only provide your Web site address but also show your Web site. No other medium provides so many advantages to the advertiser at one time.

Of the various times you can advertise on the tube, steer clear of prime time — 8:00 P.M. to 11:00 P.M. (unless you're going to economize by advertising on cable channels). You can realize better values — more viewers per dollar — by using fringe time (the time before and after prime time), especially on local affiliates of the big networks. You might also look into daytime TV, which attracts many women viewers. The audience size is smaller and so is the cost. The time period past midnight, when few people are watching, is very inexpensive and can prove a springboard to success. Some shows have ratings so low that they are unmeasurable. This means, happily, that air time is inexpensive. If you truly want to advertise on television, learn which shows your prospects watch, then run commercials on those shows.

Many of the shows are available on cable. For example, when the solar energy industry was in its infancy, aggressive marketing people soon learned that the same people who watch *Star Trek* tend to buy solar energy units and that men who watch science-fiction movies, not sports, have a proclivity toward solar power. Some solar energy companies went to the bank as a result of that fascinating information. Even though *Star Trek* was in its tenth series of reruns, it still proved to be a marvelous and inexpensive vehicle for solar heating marketers. Talk shows, which frequently attract an older audience, were determined to be poison for solar energy sellers. Their product simply did not appeal to seniors — at least it didn't at first. Today, solar energy is more acceptable as an alternative source of power, and media coverage of solar applications is generous, appealing to the increasing number of environmentally aware citizens. Is that your electric car I hear (barely) pulling into my driveway?

To get the most out of TV, keep in mind that TV rate cards, like radio rate cards, are established as the basis for negotiation and are not to be taken as gospel. In fact, if you're going to go on television, you should consider retaining a media-buying service to make your plans and buys for you. The service will charge about 7.5 percent of the total but will save you more than that. Many small businesspeople make their own buys, thinking that they are getting good deals. But the media-buying services, which purchase millions of dollars' worth of TV time monthly, get bargains that would shock the small businessperson.

Another warning about buying your TV directly: TV salespeople have a powerful way of putting the egos of their commercial clients to work for them. Some convince an advertiser that he or she would be a terrific spokesperson. The advertiser, enjoying the strokes to his or her ego, then goes on TV and presents the commercial in person. Sometimes, but rarely, this is effective. Generally, the advertiser loses as many sales as he or she gains. Frequently, the advertiser becomes a laughingstock but continues to present the ads because his or her TV salespeople wouldn't dream of risking their sales by telling the truth. Don't let your ego get in the way of your TV marketing when it comes to buying the time or presenting the information. If you've watched enough TV, I'm sure you get the gist of what I'm saying.

A guerrilla I know used to offer to buy any unsold TV time from 6 A.M.

through midnight from a TV channel. He purchased the time at far below market rates. You can afford prime time on a network affiliate if that station is willing to sell the prime-time slots at the same cost per rating point as after-midnight time slots.

Guerrillas never fail to check into cable TV and satellite TV. It just may be that you can afford to market your offerings on television because of the new cable availabilities. Instead of going on TV and reaching the 90 percent of the audience that is out of your marketing area, you can telecast only to people within your marketing area. As cable and satellite TV are making television advertising more and more affordable to more small businesses, the networks are losing their shirts to cable — billions of dollars each year. And TV is still in a state of flux — all favoring the guerrilla. So be one! And get yourself onto the tube.

Test TV for yourself. Put an offer into your commercial so that you can track the results. Perhaps you'll offer a free brochure. Maybe a special discount for people mentioning the commercial. Possibly a sweepstakes. Run your spots on different stations, cable and broadcast, and use a different phone number for each channel, enabling you to track easily. You might hire a seven-day, twenty-four-hour telemarketing service to take your phone calls and report the results for each station.

Also, DVR sales are skyrocketing — more than 90 percent of Americans have access to one, letting audiences view postmidnight programming anytime the next day.

Many guerrillas have discovered the joys of direct-response television, allowing people to order immediately after viewing the commercial. They do this because you furnish a toll-free number and accept most credit cards. Products that move well with direct-response TV are cooking and kitchen appliances, books and videos covering a wide range of topics, health and beauty aids, cosmetics, exercise equipment, and CDs and tapes. I'm sure that many items can be added to that list. Once, I ordered a buckwheat husk–filled pillow because of a direct-response TV spot that caught my fancy just when I was contemplating the purchase of a new pillow. I'm always floored when guerrilla marketing works on me. But it does!

A soul-satisfying aspect of direct-response TV is the brief wait before knowing whether you have a hit or a miss. Usually, you can tell within a week whether you've got a winner, and then you begin narrowing down the factors as to what channels work best, what time slots, what days of the week, how often, what times of the year, and how long it will continue serving as a cash cow. You might run it six months and wait two months.

The yardstick by which you measure your success or failure is your CPO (cost per order). If you can gain $2 in sales for every $1 invested in TV, your cost per order is $1, and I'm hoping that your profit is healthy. If you earn $2,000 in sales for an investment of $1,000 in TV time, don't forget your investments in producing the commercial and the cost of your product. The money left over after those are deducted is your profit. If you don't have money left over, you need a lower CPO, often possible by changing your pricing.

One of the most lovable parts of direct-response TV is the low cost of failure and the high payoff for success. If your venture fails on cable TV in Olympia, Washington, it won't hurt you too much. But if it succeeds, many cable stations out there will want to run your spot. If you can make an offer that makes a profit for you, try making it on television.

Some direct-response advertisers avoid cable like the plague unless they can buy their spots on a per inquiry or per sale basis, which means that they pay nothing up front and pay based only on how many inquiries or sales they make as a result of the TV spot.

If you do decide to invest in television marketing, there are many methods by which you can cut down drastically on the cost of producing TV commercials, which in 2005 ran over $210,000 for a thirty-second spot. Truth is, you can turn out a very good thirty-second spot for about $1,000. And even that figure can be reduced as you increase your TV savvy.

First of all, let your TV station provide all the *production* assistance. Not the writing. Let *it* put up the equipment and furnish the camera people, lighting experts, director, and all-important editor. Don't let the station write the spot. If you do, it will look like all the station's other homegrown TV commercials. Instead, either you or a talented individual you coerce, barter with, or hire should write a tight script. The left side of the sheet of paper on which the script is written is reserved for video instructions. There, describe every single action, numbering each one, the viewers will see. The right side of the script paper is for the audio portion. These are the sounds the viewers will hear. Again, number each audio section, matching it with the appropriate video section so that the audio and video make a team.

If necessary, and it usually is not necessary, make a storyboard, or pictorial representation of your script. A storyboard consists of perhaps ten frames, or pictures. Each frame contains a picture of what the viewers will see, a description of what will be happening, and the message that will be heard while the action is taking place. Storyboards tend to be taken too literally, however, and do not allow you the leeway to make changes during production. Those little changes are often the difference between an ordinary commercial and an extraordinary one. Most (but not all) people have the imagination to understand a commercial from a script alone. If the people you are working with don't, you may have to resort to a storyboard. Artists charge from $10 to $500 per frame, so you can see how storyboards make costs rise.

While working in major ad agencies, I had to prepare a storyboard for every commercial I wrote. And I know that I wrote more than a thousand. Many art directors enjoyed gainful employment because of my active typewriter and the traditions of advertising agencies, which called for storyboards. Since I've been working on my own, I have written well over another thousand commercials. Only five required storyboards. Yet the commercials were no less successful than those I made using storyboards.

You can also save money by scheduling preproduction meetings with all who will be involved in the production of your commercial. Meet with the actors, actresses, director, lighting person, prop person, and anyone else involved. Make sure that everyone knows what is expected and understands the script. Make sure that the timing is on the button. Leave not one detail unexplored. Then hold at least one tightly timed rehearsal. Have the people involved go through the motions before the cameras are running. By doing so, you can produce two commercials in the time usually necessary to produce one. You'll even be able to fit three commercials into the same production time, if you're good enough. When you are paying $1,000 per day for equipment and crew, that comes to $333.33 per commercial when you do three commercials at once. A far cry from the average cost of $210,000. That $333.33 figure was true in the 1980s and remains true today. All it takes is shopping around plus the attitude of a guerrilla.

To keep the cost down, which is one characteristic of a guerrilla, avoid expensive union talent and crew whenever possible (in some union cities, such as Los Angeles and San Francisco, this is not easily done). Get everything right by planning rehearsals and preproduction meetings, and plan the editing when you plan the spot. Editing videotape can be very expensive, so plan your shooting so that little editing will be necessary. Experts say that the commercial is really made in the editing room. So make it a point to be there watching — and commenting — when the editing takes place. It's an important process of guerrilla learning.

The use of film or tape or digital recording usually won't make a great difference in your final cost. Film allows you to use more special effects, has more of a magical quality because it has less "presence" than tape, and allows for less expensive editing. But with film, you have no instant feedback. If someone goofed, you won't know it until the film is processed. With digital, you can replay what you have shot immediately, and if anything is wrong, you can redo it. No processing is necessary. As to which is better, there is no correct answer. Both can be ideal, depending on the circumstances. But if you are planning to have the station help with production, better plan on digital. Stations don't usually film for you. That's OK; guerrillas seem to opt for digital.

What makes a great TV commercial? Well, Procter & Gamble, one of the most sophisticated advertisers in the United States, frequently uses "slice of life" commercials, which are little playlets, the type that seem boring and commonplace. But with the big bucks P&G puts behind them, they work extremely well. And many companies have made a bundle copying this format. So don't knock them if you are considering TV as a marketing vehicle. You can learn plenty from P&G. I certainly did. Here are some other guidelines that will help you, regardless of the type of commercial you wish to produce.

Remember that television is a *visual medium with audio enhancement*. Many ill-informed advertisers look on it as the opposite. A guerrilla marketer knows that a great TV commercial *starts with a great idea*. Try to express that idea visually, then add the words, music, and sound effects to make it clearer and stronger. Try viewing your commercial with no sound. If it's a winner, it will make its point with pictures only.

Again, go with thirty-second spots rather than sixty-second spots. If you are using TV for direct response, such as for ordering by toll-free number, try two-minute spots. They're very effective. Say that phone number at least three times, and show it as much as you can.

Keep in mind that, as with radio, you have three seconds to attract the viewers' attention. If you haven't hooked them right up front, you've probably lost them. So say what you have to say in a captivating manner at the outset. Say it again, in different words, in the middle of your spot. Say it a final time, again in different words (or maybe even in the same words), at the end. Don't fall into the trap of making your commercial more interesting than your product. Don't allow anyone to remember your commercial without remembering your name. There are bushels of sob stories about commercials that won all sorts of awards while the products they were promoting died horrible deaths. You want sales — not awards, praise, or laughs.

To my mind, many TV commercials these days are created by people who hate advertising and are ashamed of it. This explains why many TV spots are visually dazzling but give no clue as to who is advertising. You've got to pay close attention to see who you should purchase from, and guerrillas know that people don't pay close attention to TV commercials. My wife calls this the "by the way" school of advertising, as in, "Let us entertain you and amuse you, enthrall you, and delight you. By the way, we're also hoping you'll buy our beer."

When you can, *show your product or service in action*. People's memories improve 68 percent when they have a visual element to recall. So say what you have to say verbally and visually, especially visually.

The following thirty-second commercial won first prize at the Venice TV Film Festival. The advertiser then had to withdraw it from the air because he could not keep up with the demand for his product. The idea conveyed in the commercial is that this particular cookie, known as "Sports" and manufactured by a company called Carr's, has more chocolate on it than any similar cookie. Simple enough? Here's the script:

Video	Audio
1. Open with two slapstick characters facing the camera. One is tall and one is short. Tall one speaks:	1. (Tall man) Good evening. Sidney and I would like to prove that Carr's Sports have the most chocolate — by showing you two ways to make chocolate cookies.
2. Short man smiles when his name is mentioned, but loses the smile when he hears that he is a cookie.	2. Imagine Sidney here is a cookie.
3. Tall man lifts huge container marked "chocolate" and pours real chocolate fluid onto short man.	3. Now take your cookie. Cover it with chocolate.
4. Camera tilts down to show pool of chocolate at short man's feet.	4. Effective, but not much stays on. Carr's makes Sports a better way.
5. Cut to the two men. Tall man now carries short man, holds him above a tub marked chocolate. Tall man then drops short man into the tub.	5. Pop the cookie in chocolate.
6. Cut to short man's head surfacing from the chocolate. As it surfaces, more chocolate is poured on it.	6. Top it up, and when it is set . . .
7. Dissolve to short man, now encased in chocolate. He is lying down. Tall man stands proudly above him.	7. You have your cookie with all your chocolate on it.
8. Tall man molds out a Carr's Sports package as camera zooms to closeup of it.	8. That's how Carr's makes Sports.

Because so many people have remote controls with both their TV sets and their DVRs, there's a great chance (estimated at 70 percent) that your commercial will get zapped — fast-forwarded or muted. Does this steer guerrillas away from television? No.

Instead, guerrillas take heed of this ugly reality by working with it, not against it. They mute-proof their TV commercials by telling their stories visually, using words and music, but not really requiring them, because their pictures make their point. They show their names — often throughout the commercials — by superimposing them in the lower corner of the screen, à la CNN. Notice how many networks have climbed aboard that particular bandwagon, finally realizing the visuality of their medium.

TV guerrillas show their commercials enough times to their target audiences that they begin to see the results of this powerful guerrilla marketing tactic after a few months. A few months? Why not instantly? Because TV, as high potency as it is, does not bring about instant results unless you are having a limited-time sale, making a limited-time offer, or using TV as a direct-response medium, providing viewers with a toll-free number and enough information to make the decision to buy from you.

You're going to be a happy guerrilla if you *lower your expectations for TV in the short run*. Over time, TV will work its miracles for you. Only they won't be miracles. They'll be the result of your patience combined with your knowledge that no medium does as much to sell your offering as television. Don't think that you can make TV prove itself to you with limited funds. As low-cost as a spot may be, you still must have a decent-size war chest to use it. One expert for whom I have a lot of respect counsels his clients that if they can't stand to lose their TV investment, they should try something else. But if you can test it and make it work for you, you'll be one very happy guerrilla.

A goodly number of small-business owners shy away from the tube for several reasons, foremost of which is that it's too expensive to afford a thirty-second spot, let alone one hundred thirty-second spots. What then? Well, if you've ever watched *Survivor*, you've seen the clever placement of soft drinks under the palms or the use of cars as prizes. If you've seen *American Idol*, you've seen Ford cars and Coca-Cola integrated into the shows — not as commercials but as what is termed *product placement*. An early example of product placement in movies is the 1949 film *Love Happy*, in which Harpo Marx cavorts on a rooftop among various billboards and at one point escapes from the villains on the old Mobil meme, the "Flying Red Horse." Clorox didn't get all that camera time in *Million Dollar Baby* by accident. And box after box of Kleenex adorning the set of *The*

Aviator was no coincidence. And let's not forget AOL as the technostar of *You've Got Mail* or Reese's Pieces as a star of *E.T.* It's happening. Get to know it.

If you're going to give it a try, keep in mind that the best product placement in a film or a TV show incorporates the product or service into the film so that it is central to the plot and not obvious commercialism. Speaking of that topic, Ford was the king of the road in 2005, with its vehicles being showcased in nineteen films. But the king of product placement seems to be Gatorade, which seems to love show biz and sports biz.

Product placement seems to be a clever way to bypass TIVOing and taping and other forms of commercial avoidance. As those forms proliferate, you'll be seeing more product placement — to the point that eventually, you'll become immune to seeing it. To some marketers, that means disaster; to others, that their product is now part of the cultural landscape.

Do keep in mind that you must have a great product or service for TV to do its job for you. This century appears to be shaping up as one that responds most to the basics. The hot buttons will be the functionally elegant, plain and simple, healthy and sensible, politically correct, environmentally responsible, what is good for America, and what is solidly positioned as midprice.

Once you have offerings that live up to these consumer demands, TV can be most effective for you, the guerrilla. That's when to use and not to abuse TV.

Outdoor Advertising

Outdoor advertising consists of billboards, bus ads, taxi signs, painted walls, and outdoor signs. I guess it also includes skywriting, since that never occurs indoors. Still, let's deal with billboards first. Rare is the entrepreneur who can survive on billboard advertising alone — although it can be done. Billboard advertising — and to use the term *advertising* is somewhat of an overstatement — is really reminder advertising for the most part. It works best when combined with advertising through other media.

Each year, a Des Moines, Iowa, entrepreneur runs a month-long, one-cent-sale promotion on the radio and in newspapers. He also supports the radio and newspaper advertising for a month each year with billboards. His sales rise an average of 18 percent. With billboards alone, this would never happen. But the billboards add an important ingredient to his marketing mix. He uses them only once a year to promote his furniture business. They work wonderfully.

Billboard advertising doesn't have to be strictly reminder advertising. In some instances, it can lead directly to sales. In regard to this, let me tell you the two most important words you can use on a billboard. They aren't at all like the high-motivation words discussed earlier — not that obvious. The two magic words that can spell instant success for you if used on a billboard are *next exit*. If you can use them on your billboard, they may do a great job of marketing for you. For example, a new store in the San Francisco Bay Area could afford only one billboard. That billboard, fortunately, was able to display the words *next exit*. Success came rapidly and overwhelmingly. Of course, the store had to do everything else right to succeed, and it did. But the billboard gets the prime credit. If you can't use these two words, these three also work well: *two miles ahead*.

Most of the time, you cannot lease only one billboard. You will usually have to rent ten or twenty billboards at once. Some are in winning locations; some are sure-fire losing locations. You must take the bad with the good. However, through cogent arguing or a loophole in the billboard firm's policies, you may be able to lease just one beautifully located billboard. If ever you can, do it. Otherwise, be careful. Consider using billboards if you have a restaurant, tourist attraction, garage, gas station, motel, or hotel. Be wary of billboard advertising if your business doesn't have instant appeal to motorists. If you have a car wash that is at the next exit, a billboard might just be the ticket. If you own a computer-education firm, forget it. A billboard can, however, help you maintain your identity if your identity is established.

McDonald's maintains its golden arches identity with billboards. Words aren't even necessary. If you're thinking about using billboards simply as reminders and haven't invested a lot in your identity, as McDonald's has, scratch the idea from your marketing plan.

To ascertain whether a billboard might work for you, find out how many cars pass the billboard site each day. This is known in the business as the traffic count. Billboard firms have the data at their fingertips. What type of traffic passes by? Trucks won't be able to patronize your car wash. On the other hand, homeward-bound affluent suburbanites may be interested in your take-home restaurant.

When planning a billboard, keep the rules for outdoor signs in mind. Rarely use more than six words. Remember that people are probably driving around fifty-five miles per hour or are negotiating in traffic when they glance, if they glance at all, at your billboard. Keep it simple for them. Give them one large graphic on which they can concentrate. Be sure that the type is clear and large. If the traffic count remains more or less the same at night, be sure that your board is illuminated. That costs more than a non-illuminated board but may be worth the extra bucks.

Billboard companies are open to price negotiation, although they may not appreciate my putting that in print. They are also amenable to location negotiation. Once I wanted a specific location and was told that in order to get it, I'd have to rent nine other billboards — all in dismal locations. I said I wasn't interested.

A couple of weeks later, I was offered the billboard along with only four other locations, also dismal. Again, I said no. Finally, the sales rep called me to say that I could have the one location I wanted but that the price would be significantly higher than originally quoted. It would have been a good deal, and I wished I could have said yes. But by this time, my client's monies had been committed. So we all lost out. Too bad the rep hadn't made me the same offer in the beginning. I could have used "next exit" on the billboard and had one more success story to report here.

Billboards can do more than attract direct sales on occasion. Billboards also help when you are new to an area and want to make your presence known and when you want to tie in with a unique advertising campaign or promotion.

One of the more attractive aspects of billboard advertising is that if you supply the design, the billboard company will produce the billboard for you, blowing the artwork up to a size that will fit on the billboard. Billboard sizes are measured in sheets. The usual size is a twenty-four-sheet, with one sheet approximating the size of a large poster.

Whatever you do, make sure that your billboard fits in with the rest of your advertising campaign. The Iowa man was able to present his message in six words on his immensely successful billboard only because the message had been explained more fully elsewhere. A guerrilla uses billboards like darts. A guerrilla says "next exit," "two miles," or "five minutes ahead"; ties his or her billboard in directly with a strong campaign; or uses a single billboard with surgical precision. No guerrilla uses a "next exit" billboard for the usual one month or three months. After testing the merits of a billboard, a guerrilla signs a one-, three-, or five-year contract for such a board. A guerrilla contracts with a billboard company to erect a billboard in a place where "next exit" can be used, if one does not yet exist there. And a guerrilla still realizes that a great billboard isn't much more than a great reminder.

I suggest that you avoid the use of billboards unless there is a compelling reason to use them. Drive around your community and carefully note the local companies that use billboards. Then talk to the owners of those companies and find out whether the billboards work. Unless you are in a business that competes with theirs, you'll probably get a straight answer.

Call the billboard representatives in your area and listen to their sales pitches. Perhaps they can enlighten you as to special opportunities, new boards to be erected, or chances to go in on billboards with other companies. Maybe you won't be persuaded to use even a small billboard in your marketing plan. But you've nothing to lose by talking with them. So do it. Better yet, listen to them. If you have a well-known theme, billboards might be for you. As with many other marketing media, it may be worth your while to test their efficacy. Different towns respond in different ways to billboards. Maybe you live in a town that gets motivated by billboards. Los Angeles seems to be the billboard capital of the universe, with a multitude of ornate moving billboards in high-traffic locations — all heralding movies, stars, shows — but never Preparation H. Maybe you are located near a street that is ideal for a billboard. If that's the case, I recommend testing. If you test a billboard for a month or two and nothing happens, you're not out all that much money. But if you never give it a try, and then your biggest competitor tries billboards and goes to glory with them, you'll kick yourself from now till Sunday.

Billboard marketing is, almost without exception, *share-of-mind* advertising. This type of advertising attempts to win sales down the road by implanting a thought or establishing an identity. It tries to win for you a continually increasing share of the minds of the people in your marketing area. It does not normally prove effective in a hurry, cannot be translated into results, and is profitable only in the long run, if ever.

Share-of-market advertising, on the other hand, attempts to win instant sales. It tries to win for you a continually increasing share of whatever market your offering belongs to. Share-of-market advertising is the most effective, the most instantly translated into results, and the most profitable in the short run. Most entrepreneurs are a bit too concerned with cash to worry about shares of minds. They want increased shares of markets, and they want them right now. So consider using billboards, but don't expect to attract highly motivated prospects through them.

You can expect about the same, perhaps a little more, from bus signs, both interior and exterior, and interior or exterior taxi signs. Such signs may be used as part of a marketing plan that calls for the use of signs in targeted urban areas. These moving signs are seen by many people, many of whom may be serious prospects. Taxi signs are seen by people throughout the metropolitan area. Bus signs are usually seen by the same people — bus riders and people who live along the route. Of course, taxis don't always travel the same routes buses do. But this should be kept in mind if you're thinking about using both bus signs and taxi signs.

A client of mine enjoyed a great deal of success attracting temporary office workers with signs placed inside buses. The client was an agency that supplied these workers for large employers, and the signs were designed to appeal to both the workers and the employers. If your product or service is located near a bus line, you should consider placing signs on that particular bus line — on the exterior of the buses. Such signs will not serve as a complete marketing plan, but they can be an effective part of one.

We have already chronicled the successes of Harold's Club, Wall Drugs, and Burma-Shave, enterprises that used outdoor signs. What makes a good outdoor sign? Readability. Warmth. Good location. Uniqueness. An identity that matches that of your business. Clarity from afar, from moving vehicles, on dark nights. Good colors. Clear and unmistakable connection with your other marketing.

Make certain that your sign communicates what your business is all about. For instance, "Moore's" tells us a lot less than "Moore's Stationery." To gain community acceptance, try to have your sign designed so that it fits in with the character of the community. Garish signs may be dandy in some locations and horrid in others. A large neon sign, like one you'd see in Las Vegas, would win nothing but enemies for the advertiser in my community. Conservative signs may be just the ticket on some streets but a ticket to doom on others. Be sensitive to the tastes of your community.

What makes a bad outdoor sign? Lack of clarity. Lack of uniqueness. Fancy lettering. Bland colors. Tiny words. Improper placement. Little connection with your other marketing.

Don't allow yourself to be hemmed in by a small imagination. But remember that advertising seen by speeding motorists has less impact than advertising seen by relaxed prospects — the type that might take the time to read a direct mailing from you.

Direct-Mail Marketing

Attention all guerrillas! Direct marketing is where it's at. Direct marketing is the name of your game. Direct marketing has a built-in mirror that reflects the true effectiveness of your advertising message. All other forms of marketing have much to be said for them, but direct marketing has more. All other forms of marketing can help you immensely, but direct marketing can help you more.

Direct marketing refers to direct-mail, e-mail, Web site, mail-order, or coupon advertising, as well as to telephone marketing, direct-response TV, postcard decks, door-to-door salespeople, home shopping TV shows, or any method of marketing that attempts to make a sale right then and there. Direct marketing doesn't require a middleman. It doesn't require a store. Because direct marketing requires only a seller and a buyer, much unnecessary game playing is removed from the marketing process, leaving only accountable results. Let me repeat that word: *accountable*. When you run a radio commercial or a newspaper ad, you do all in your power to make sure that it works, but you don't really know whether it does. But when you engage in direct-mail advertising, you'll know clearly whether your mailing worked. If it worked, you'll know how well it worked. And if it failed, you'll know how dismally it failed.

Direct mail doesn't always make the sale all by itself, but it obtains crucial leads that result in sales. A huge 89 percent of marketing directors use it to generate leads; 48 percent use it to generate sales.

Along with its all-important accountability, direct marketing has some other advantages over other advertising media.

1. You can achieve more accurately measured results.
2. You can be as expansive or as concise as you wish.
3. You can zero in on almost any target audience.
4. You can personalize your marketing like crazy.
5. You can expect the highest of all response rates.
6. You can use unlimited opportunities for testing.
7. You can enjoy repeat sales to proven customers.
8. You can compete with, even beat, the giants.

Along with those eight advantages come eight rules of thumb.

1. Concentrate on the most important element: the right list.
2. Make it easy for the recipient to take action.
3. Keep in mind that letters almost always outpull mailing packages with no letters.
4. Understand that the best buyers are those who have bought by mail before, a rapidly growing number.
5. Do anything to get your envelope opened.
6. Make sure to keep good records.
7. To improve your response rate, use testimonials.
8. Remember that *nothing is as simple as it seems*.

In true guerrilla fashion, I also offer you seven tips for gaining the response rate you want with direct mail.

1. The headline of your brochure should ask for the order.
2. The copy should always tell the person what to do next.
3. Blue is a dandy second color, but red with black is generally the best-pulling direct-mail combination.
4. Red can be overused; use it primarily for highlights.
5. Experts say that *the four most important elements in direct mail are the list, the offer, the copy, and the graphics.* Guerrillas pay close attention to each.
6. The fastest-growing segment of the direct-mail industry is nontraditional mailers — those who haven't used direct mail in the past.
7. Direct-mail success comes with the cumulative effect of repeat mailings. Make them repetitive yet different from one another.

Guerrillas realize that when it comes to determining the normal percentage of return on direct mail, *there is none.* You'll have to determine your own, then go about improving it — the name of the game in direct mail.

Keep in mind that with postal rates rising, amateurs are being forced away from direct mail and opting for e-mail, leaving a lush new universe for guerrillas.

To a guerrilla, marketing is part art and part science. Direct mail is more science than art. This is not to downplay the art of creating a successful direct-mail package. But let's focus on the science, the things we already know. For instance, we know that the three most important things to do if you are to succeed at direct marketing are to test, test, and test. If you know that and do that, you are on the right road. If you play it by ear, you will probably fall on your ear. With a mailing, you *have a good chance of getting through* to people. Studies reveal that 60 percent of people say of direct mail, "I usually read or scan it"; 31 percent say, "I read some of it, don't read some of it"; 9 percent say, "I don't read any of it." The bottom line: You have a shot at reaching 91 percent of your audience. That's a healthy number.

Current estimates say that people get twenty direct mailings each day and that only 50 percent of direct mail gets through to the boss; the other 50 percent is handled by assistants — the gatekeepers of industry. Guerrillas know how gatekeepers make their decisions. Those protectors of the boss's time want to know whether (1) it's a credible offer from a credible firm, (2) the subject matter is relevant to the boss and the company, and (3) the mailing is personal or business.

Guerrillas know to shorten their copy when writing to high-level executives (two or three paragraphs maximum). Guerrillas also make sure that a high-level executive signs any letters directed to other top execs. The title "account executive" really doesn't cut it anymore. Sometimes, guerrillas send a mailing in a box because it is just too tempting to ignore. And when they absolutely positively want their mailing to get through to the recipient, they pop for the cost of Federal Express, UPS, or DHL.

More on the science of direct mail is embodied in the *60-30-10 rule*. Sixty percent of your direct-mail program depends on your using the right list of people; 30 percent depends on your making the right offer; 10 percent depends on your creative package. You can make it creative if you take to heart these three tips.

1. Brightly colored envelopes grab attention. Although red and blue are time-honored direct-mail colors, the twenty-first century is proving that silver, gold, mauve, yellow, orange, and pink merit consideration, too. But white is always a safe, good bet.
2. Oversized addressing stimulates the unconscious pleasure people gain from seeing their name in print. The larger, the better.
3. A white #10 (business-size) envelope with a first-class stamp and no return address is especially intriguing and gets rave notices when it comes to response rates. Look into it (that's a guerrilla hint to test it).

There are many reasons to do a direct mailing. And when you think of mailing, don't always think of mass mailing. As a guerrilla, you write letters to

- Follow up on a salesperson's call
- Set up an appointment
- Apologize for something you may have done wrong
- Compliment someone for something
- Recognize an anniversary of almost anything
- Celebrate holidays — Christmas, Hanukkah, Thanksgiving, Valentine's Day, Passover, and Easter, for instance
- Solidify telephone contact
- Thank someone for seeing your demo or hearing your presentation
- Thank someone for making a purchase
- Thank someone for his or her time, even if the person turned down your offer
- Thank someone for giving you a referral

- Welcome someone to anything at which he or she is new
- Applaud someone for a job well done
- Reiterate how much you've enjoyed working with someone
- Congratulate someone on a promotion or a new job
- Mention that you saw the person in the news (enclose the clipping)
- Congratulate someone on a special achievement
- Thank a person for doing a favor
- Thank someone for exceptional service
- Let a person know that you appreciate his or her product or service
- Thank a person for his or her time or effort
- Express regrets if they are merited
- Thank someone for inviting you to something
- Tell somebody you hope that he or she gets well
- Express condolences
- Congratulate someone on a new baby, marriage, or new home
- Recognize a person's birthday
- Announce a new product or service
- Give advance notice of a discount
- Sell something

If you send a letter about these topics, this letter will be more warmly received.

The complete honesty that results from direct-mail marketing is invaluable. Because it is so accountable, it lets you know whether you have done a good job making your offer, pricing your merchandise, constructing your mailing package, writing your copy, timing your mailing, or selecting your mailing list. Soon after you have accomplished your mailing, you learn whether it worked or failed. That's what I mean by accountability.

Before studying the secrets imparted in these pages, you must honestly ask yourself whether your product or service lends itself to direct marketing. Only after you are satisfied that you ought to proceed into the world of direct marketing should you take the next step — understanding the relationship of direct-response advertising to non-direct-response advertising.

If you don't know about direct-response marketing, you don't know about marketing. According to technical experts in the field, direct marketing is not a fancy term for mail order but rather is an interactive system of marketing that uses one or more advertising media to effect a measurable response and/or transaction at any location. We have the magazine *Direct Marketing* to thank for this definition.

The same publication reminds us that marketing is all the activities involved in moving goods and services from seller to buyer. Then *Direct Mar-keting* makes a crucial distinction. It says that *direct marketing has the same broad function as standard marketing but also requires the maintenance of a database*. This database records the names of customers, prospects, and for-mer customers. It serves as a vehicle for storing, then measuring, the results of direct-response advertising. The database also provides a way to store, then measure, purchasing performance. And finally, the database is a way to continue direct communication by mail and/or telephone.

Risk-wary advertisers are shying away from the mass-market media, choosing instead to target their prospects directly. These advertisers might have invested $0.50 a person to reach a general audience in the past, but in the first decade of the twenty-first century, they're putting up $1 or more for someone whose demographic and economic profile indicates predisposi-tion to making a purchase. Literally hundreds of millions of people watch Home Shopping Network, Cable Value Network, QVC Network, and a host of others. And those numbers are growing, along with the mailing lists compiled by the home shopping networks.

If you have the soul of a guerrilla, you will have been compiling your own mailing list from the day your business began. The list should naturally start with your own customers. From there, expand it to include people who have recently moved into your area and those who have recently been mar-ried or divorced or become parents. Eliminate people who have moved away — a full 25 percent of Americans, nearly one in four, moved in 2005.

You might engage in a simple direct mailing of postcards to customers, informing them of a sale you'll have the next week. They will appreciate the early notification and might show their gratitude by purchasing from you. You might also engage in a full-scale direct mailing, using what is known as the "classic package," which consists of an outer envelope, a direct-mail let-ter, a brochure, an order form, a return envelope (maybe postpaid, maybe not), and other marketing materials.

In the interest of making direct mail a money maker for your company, I offer these insights.

- Print your most important sentences in a second color to increase sales enough to warrant the extra money. Be sure to choose a bright, pleas-ing color.
- Restate your main offer on your response form. The repetition will motivate the reader.
- Use illustrations or photos in your letter to improve your response rate. Just be sure that the graphic element adds to the offer or the promise.

- Avoid the worst months for direct mail: March, May, and June; the best months are January, February, and October. The period January through March is best for business direct mail.
- Juice up your offers — and response rates — with free gifts for ordering, a photo of the free gift on the envelope, or a free trial of their product or service. Something free always aids in marketing.
- Update your mailing list. If it hasn't been updated in two years, you've got to figure that 20 percent of it is probably decayed or out of date. Assume that 10 percent of addresses go bad every year.
- Always do a few intensive hours of research before you write even the first word of your letter. Ask some current customers what they like about doing business with you, and begin your letter with those benefits.
- Find a new and appealing way to bundle your products or services. Offer special payment terms or a unique guarantee. One guerrilla offers a five-year guarantee in a field where others offer a one-year guarantee. It pays off handsomely in his response rates and doesn't come back to haunt him.
- Think short. Use short words, short sentences, and short paragraphs. Author James Michener, among others, said that the job of the writer is to use ordinary words to convey extraordinary ideas. People won't read a letter that is not easy to read. Life is tough enough without your letter contributing to the complexity.
- Count the number of *you's* and *your's* in the letter. It should have at least twice as many *you's* and *your's* than *I's* and *me's*. A ratio of four to one is even better.
- In your letter, write about your customers' dreams and problems. List the solutions you can provide to those problems and benefits that you offer.
- Don't mail your letter right after you write it. Let it sit a day or two. Then rewrite it. Make it shorter, simpler, more clear, and more compelling. Show it to customers. If they say, "Wonderful letter," thank them politely. If they say, "Where can I get one of these?" you know you've got a winner.
- Be brutally honest with yourself in determining whether you vividly state what it is you are offering and how a reader can accept your offer. Some guerrillas show their letters to a child because kids can often see the obvious before adults can.
- Send a test mailing and measure the results. A few dozen or a few hundred letters will give you a good feeling for the response you can ex-

pect. You'll get it — or not get it — in a hurry. If the mailing earned more profits for you than you would have earned if you had spent your time and money in other ways, smile widely and accept my congratulations.

In the old days, a direct-mail campaign meant a letter. Today, it means a letter, two or three or five follow-up letters, two more e-mails, perhaps a follow-up phone call or two, and finally, one more direct-mail letter. Many entrepreneurs engage in weekly or monthly direct mailings.

You have a multitude of decisions to make when you embark on a mailing, so it is crucial that you know the right questions to ask. In addition to deciding about your mailing list, offer, and financial projections, you'll have to decide whether to mail first class or third class. Will you personalize your mailing? Will you have a toll-free number available for ordering? Which credit cards will you accept? Will you need to alter your pricing because you'll be selling direct? This seemingly simple subject becomes more complex as you learn more about it.

Envelopes

The envelope for a direct mailing merits a chapter of its own. Executives should not be sent envelopes with address labels. For maximum response, their names must be typed on the envelope. And for selling stationery, feminine products, or political candidates or causes, a handwritten envelope provides a wonderfully personal tone. Envelopes can be standard size (#10) or oversize (6 inches by 9 inches), manila, covered with gorgeous art, foil-lined, or window-type. They can have a return address, or, to pique curiosity, omit the return address.

One of the best devices you can use on an envelope is a *teaser* — a copy line that compels the recipient to open the envelope. Examples of successful teasers are:

FREE! A microcalculator for you.
Want to get your hands on $10,000 extra cash?
The most astonishing offer of the year. Details inside.

As you can see, there are myriad ways to get a person to open an envelope. And that is the purpose of the envelope: to interest the recipient so that he or she will open it and read the contents.

Guerrillas know that people read the addressee name first, then they look at the teaser copy, and finally they read to see who sent it. Was it the

Office of the President? The Awards Committee? The IRS? If it has the name of the person's bank, it usually gets opened. No teaser is needed. I doubt that the IRS needs one, either.

When planning your envelope, determine the needs and wants of your target audience. Remember that you can use the *back* of the envelope; 75 percent of the people holding it will read it. Figure that you have three seconds to get them to open it. Say something *enticing* to *motivate* that action, such as

- Free gift enclosed
- Money-saving offer inside
- Wealth-building secrets for the new millennium
- Private information for your eyes only
- Did you know you can double your profits?
- What every business like yours needs to know . . .
- How to add new profits for only six cents a day
- See inside for exciting details on [virtually anything]
- Read what's in store for you — this week only!

The idea of teaser copy is not to be cute, clever, or fancy. The job is to be provocative, to entice the recipient into opening the envelope. Yes, it's only an envelope, but guerrillas know that it's often the key to a successful or a failed mailing.

Naturally, people are quick to open priority and express mail. But it costs a lot to send — unless you're a guerrilla. Envelopes that look like priority and express envelopes and that are approved by the U.S. Postal Service are available to be sent first class or bulk rate. To get a free sample, call Response Mail Express at 800-795-2773. If it's important to you to get your envelope opened, you'll call that number.

Some guerrillas call attention to their mailings by printing them on pieces of wood, jewelry boxes, CD cases, brown bags, greeting cards, pieces of plastic, or paint cans. Others include something bulky in their envelopes: an audiotape, a coin, a piece of gum, a magnetic business card, a balloon. However, when all is said, done, and mailed, you must get the order with the letter you've written when your envelope is opened.

Include a P.S. in your letter. The P.S. is read with regularity (more often than is body copy). Many direct mailings now include what are known as *lift letters* — little notes that might say something like, "Read this only if you have decided not to respond to this offer." Inside is one more attempt to make the sale, probably a handwritten message, called a *buck slip*, signed by the company president.

Adding a P.S. can be used in these seven ways.

1. *Motivate the prospect to take action.* Do all you can to overcome procrastination and get the person to order this very moment.
2. *Reinforce your offer.* Make the same offer you made in your letter, but do it more cogently and urgently. If you have a solid offer, this is the safest use of a P.S.
3. *Emphasize or introduce a premium or bonus.* This might get folks off the fence and right onto your customer list. People love freebies.
4. *Emphasize the price or terms of your offer.* If your price or payment plans are the heart of your offer, dramatize them in your P.S.
5. *Introduce a surprise benefit.* This might be just the ticket to move people from apathy to enthusiasm. It's also a place to restate the primary benefit you offer and why it's so darned important.
6. *Stress the tax deductibility of the purchase.* Everybody loves a good deduction, so if your product or service cost is honestly deductible, say so in the P.S.
7. *Highlight your guarantee.* Don't take it for granted, but instead, present it with excitement and enthusiasm.

Guarantee what you are selling, because you are not as in touch with customers as you would be with a store-sold product or service, and they will want the reassurance of a guarantee. You've got to do all you can to remove any possible perception of risk.

The most effective direct-mail efforts allow people to buy with credit cards. "Bill me" also works well as a rule. An element of urgency, such as "offer expires in one week," increases the response even more. Guerrillas always put a time limit on their direct-mail offers.

Whatever you do, make your offer clear, repeat it several times, keep your message as short as possible, and ask for the order. Don't pussyfoot around. Ask people to do exactly what you wish them to do. Then ask them again.

I also recommend listing toll-free phone numbers, which can triple the response rate or even better. Every day, three-quarters of a million Americans order $225 *million* worth of merchandise by phone!

When you create a direct-mail ad with a coupon, make it a miniature version of your ad, complete with headline, benefit, and offer. In short, make it a brief summary of the advertisement. Some direct-mail pros write their coupons or response devices before they write their ads. This is called *working backward*, and guerrillas see the wisdom in it. Working backward helps you immensely when you write the letter or brochure, because it helps you remember what you want the recipient to do.

If you're up and running with direct mail, you know the importance of delivering orders within one week of receiving the order (and less time than that for phone, fax, and online orders).

Answer all customer inquiries within one week (again, faster if they used a speedy technology; autoresponders let you respond within seconds to Internet orders). Guerrillas never offer merchandise that isn't in stock and on hand for instant delivery. They want profits, not enemies. And they also have on hand the information that customers need. Every order is treated like a rush order. Most guerrillas are able to handle calls without putting people on hold. I recently received a postcard informing me of a special rate if I resubscribed to a magazine. I called the 800 number to sign up and was put on hold. I tossed the postcard and hung up the phone.

Where should your mail-order ad appear in a publication? The best place, although relatively expensive, is the back page of a newspaper or magazine — where response can be as much as 150 percent greater than from the same ad inside the publication.

When you consider direct marketing, always consider including an insert with your bill. People certainly open bills, so they'll probably see your insert. And you'll get a free ride, because the bill is paying the postage for the insert. Another type of insert is the freestanding type that often appears in newspapers or magazines. These are known to be effective. Check with your newspaper or magazine rep to find out about their services with regard to inserts.

Postcards

What's even more effective than a direct-mail letter? A direct-mail postcard — because people don't get to decide whether to open the envelope and because you can make the offer so concise that they don't get to decide whether to read the copy. Guerrillas also like postcard mailings because they cost nearly one-third less than letter mailings and because their computers can churn them out in a manner some people find akin to printing money. Postcards are great for saying thank you, reminding customers of their next appointment, and announcing a killer discount, new product, or valuable service. Consider using oversized (6 inches by 9 inches) postcards as well as high-impact full-color postcards. They should convey your identity and your attitude. Psssst: Do yourself a favor. Look into audiopostcards, talking postcards sent via e-mail. They're enticingly described and demonstrated at audiogenerator.com.

Dare I add tips to help you succeed? Of course I dare. Take heed of these pointers, and see the difference in your response rate.

- Decide exactly to whom you should be mailing. Do this first and do it right; if you do it wrong, nothing else will go as you wish.
- Decide which specific action you want your recipient to take.
- Create an outer envelope that will get opened.
- Come up with an offer your prospects can't possibly ignore.
- Write a first line and a P.S. that compel your prospect to read your letter.
- Describe your offer in the most enticing terms possible.
- Explain the results your offer will deliver, focusing on the main benefit.
- Explain why your offer makes so much sense to your prospect.
- Give your prospect other key benefits of accepting your offer.
- Show that you know who your prospect is.
- Describe the key features of what you are offering.
- Make it irresistible to take action right now.
- Tell your prospects the exact steps to take.
- Set measurable goals for yourself.
- Make a plan for your follow-up — by either mail or phone.
- Track your results precisely.
- Improve your results by increasing what's working and eliminating what's not.
- Consider bolstering your mailing with an e-mail or fax or with overnight mail.
- Identify new markets that you can tap.
- Increase your sales and profits by improving all your copy.

I'm certainly not suggesting that you give your prospects your home phone number. I do know a guerrilla who includes hers on her business cards — and she encloses a card in every piece of mail she sends. She sends a personal letter to 25 customers each week and a warm and friendly form letter to 1,500 customers each month.

Catalogs

Catalogs are a different ballgame — part of direct mail, to be sure, but a very different part. As your business grows, you may want to send a catalog to spur your direct marketing. When you do decide to market with a catalog, be absolutely certain that it has the right positioning, the right merchandise selection, the right kind of merchandise, the right graphics, the right use of color, the right size (thirty-two pages is considered optimum), the right headlines, the right subheads, the right copy, the right sales stimulators, and the right order forms. Formulate your projections correctly. Other than this, direct marketing with catalogs is a piece of cake.

Direct mail via catalogs does mean higher costs for both paper and postage. Be sure to factor in all the numbers when you decide to publish and distribute a catalog.

If you run a mail-order business, your catalog will be the heart of your business — it will be a mighty contributor to your bottom line. The success of your mail-order catalog will depend on customers with whom you've already had one or more satisfactory transactions. Those customers, when they receive your catalog, will trust you and will have confidence in your offerings.

Be prepared to invest in your catalog. A friend of mine who ran a successful mail-order company ($2 million in sales, with $500,000 in marketing expenses) spent 50 percent of his marketing money on direct mail, 30 percent on catalogs, and 20 percent on mail-order ads. Did he believe in catalogs? You bet! He changed his marketing budget so as to spend 15 percent of his marketing money on mail-order ads, 20 percent on direct mail, and 65 percent on catalogs. He learned that his catalogs were the most important selling tools he had. In fact, he used to say that he was in the catalog business rather than the mail-order business. My friend became a millionaire in the business, so take heed.

Think of your catalog as a specialized form of direct mail. It's a store on paper — a complete presentation of your merchandise. The items in your catalog should reflect the interests of your audience and should be similar in nature.

To print a catalog, you should have about 25,000 customers. That's a lot. But if you want to earn a whale of a lot of money, you'll have to start developing a customer list that long. The big money — the truly large sums — will come to you when you send those customers your catalog. What if you don't have 25,000 customers? Create an inexpensive catalog, perhaps a minicatalog of eight pages with black-and-white photos.

Once designed, a catalog can be printed for 5,000 customers or 5 million customers. However, the amount of work required to prepare the catalog for the printer makes it cost-ineffective unless you print 25,000 copies. It's only a rule of thumb, but it's a good one.

If you purchase outside lists, even exceptional ones, don't figure on a return that is more than 85 percent of that realized from your own list. Test other lists *carefully* before plunging in. And whatever you do, mail your catalog before Christmas. People want to buy at that time, and you've blown an important opportunity if you don't mail then. Everybody mails their catalogs at that time, but they do so because people are *buying* before the holidays. The infamous bank robber Willie Sutton said, when asked why he robbed banks, "Because that's where the money is." Holiday time is *when* the money is.

Your copy should be simple, straightforward, and concise. Provide the *facts* and the *benefits*. Describe the features. It's better to answer any questions that may come rather than to be too brief. If you can write the copy yourself, do so.

What do people like about catalogs?

- *Convenience* (36 percent)
- *More variety* (19 percent)
- *Low prices* (17 percent)
- *High quality offered* (6 percent)
- "Other" or nothing listed (22 percent)

After the 78 percent who have good things to say about catalogs finish reading or ordering from them, what do they do with them? Forty-two percent save them; 41 percent toss them; 10 percent pass them on; 7 percent say "it depends."

If you're thinking of mailing a catalog, follow these guerrilla guidelines.

- Set specific objectives on what the catalog should do for your business.
- Define your audience so that you know who will receive your catalog; that helps in creating and producing it.
- Preplan all the elements of your catalog before going into production: products, prices, fulfillment, and more.
- Make all the hard decisions up front: which products to include, which to exclude, how production will be handled.
- If possible, group your offerings into clearly defined categories so that the catalog is not a hodgepodge.
- Make a rough outline of the contents of your catalog, including everything you wish to have in it — everything.
- Determine the exact format you want: size, typeface, color or black and white, paper stock, binding.

- Make a layout that is organized, logical, and pleasing to the eye of your target audience. Think of their eyes only.
- Plan, write, and perfect the copy. Then set up a timetable and stick with it.

As you can tell, the business òf producing and mailing catalogs is complex. But after the first year, it is exceptionally profitable — if you do it right. If you think that you might ever offer a catalog, start putting your name on as many catalog mailing lists as possible. Then you can expect your mailbox to be filled with five examples every day but Sunday.

Keep in mind that the number of Americans ordering at least one thing from a catalog is fast approaching 97 percent, and the percentage continues to grow. There must be a reason.

American catalog companies are now being counseled that if their catalogs draw 1 percent or 2 percent in the United States, they can draw between 10 percent and 20 percent in new markets where competing catalogs aren't around and catalog glut is no problem. If this helps you think more globally or give more serious consideration to putting a catalog up on the Internet, you're thinking like a guerrilla. You can also inexpensively create a catalog on your Web site.

Direct-Mail Wrap-Up

Even if it isn't practical for you to use catalogs, I hope that you will try direct mail if it is at all feasible for your business. Try a small number of mailings first. Test always. Learn from each test. In truth, if you break even while testing, you are doing fine. The goal is to come up with a formula that can be repeated and expanded. If you ever obtain a publicity story about your business, consider enclosing reprints of it in a mailing.

In my own experience as an entrepreneur and as a direct-response specialist, I have found that envelopes with teaser lines get a better response than those without. I have found that short letters work better than long letters, that long brochures work better than short brochures, that postcards often make superb mailers all by themselves. I have learned that it is worth the time to check out many lists before selecting one and that one's own customer list is a gold mine when it comes to direct mail. I know that a single mailing isn't nearly as effective as a mailing with one, two, or more follow-ups and that a mailing with a phone follow-up is frequently best of all.

A guerrilla will either realize that direct marketing is not the way for his or her business to proceed or will use direct marketing with intelligence, reading books about it, talking with direct-marketing pros, and making it his or her most cost-effective marketing method. Strange as it may seem, the majority of people like to receive mailings from businesses; don't feel self-conscious, and put the U.S. Postal Service to work for you.

If you've got this feeling that all direct marketing is going to be changed by the Internet, you're thinking the right way. In fact, to alert you to more valuable information about direct mail, I call your attention to Direct Mail News on the Internet at dmnews.com. Then, I rest my case.

PART IV

New-Media Marketing

11

E-Media Marketing

Since I wrote the first edition of this book, the world has learned to buy things a new way. People used to come into stores or make a phone call and make their purchase. Now, they go online to learn more about what they're considering buying. Sometimes, they make the purchase online. But more often than not, they continue to shop around, online and off line; then they make the purchase somewhere, possibly other than the Web site they first visited.

If there's one thing for certain about the Internet, it's that nothing is for certain about the Internet — except that you'll have to continue learning new things about this fascinating method of commerce. Before entering the world of online marketing, you need to know two things. The first is the size of e-commerce: Forrester Research predicted that online retailing will grow from $95.7 billion in 2003 to $229 billion by 2008 and will account for 10 percent of all retail sales. Note that growth curve.

According to Jupiter Communications, U.S. online consumers spent in excess of $632 billion outside of the Internet as a direct result of research they conducted on the Web. Many people first visit your Web site, then purchase by calling, mailing, faxing, or placing their order in person. I have a client who reports that the Internet is by far his most profit-producing marketing weapon in his arsenal. Yet he has never sold one thing online. He merely describes his merchandise, directs people to his store, and marvels at how transactions that used to take an hour now take fifteen minutes. That gives his salespeople more time to sell more merchandise. Do the profits from those transactions get credited to the Internet? In my book, they do.

According to IDC, a subsidiary of International Data Group, Inc., a leading provider of market intelligence, nearly 1 billion people, or about 15 percent of the world's population, used the Internet in 2006. I sense that I don't have to tell you much more to convey the size of online marketing. Yet it is still in its infancy. There's a lot of room for it and you to grow.

The second thing you need to know at the outset is that the Internet is a direct-marketing weapon. The tactics and nuances of direct mail definitely continue to apply to Internet marketing. After all, the Internet did not repeal the laws of human nature. Some Internet marketers fail because they were never involved in direct marketing, so they weren't playing with a full deck when it came to the human touch. Guerrillas succeed online because regardless of their background, they make it a point to learn the art and science of direct marketing, providing them with crucial insights about people. E-mail marketing is all about people, just in case that has slipped your memory.

Given the dazzling array of Internet marketing knowledge, I'm going to try to focus primarily on the things we know for sure, the things that are not likely to change.

First of all, keep in mind that unless you know marketing, you're probably to going to thrive and flourish online. The Internet is only one of one hundred marketing weapons. True, it's the fastest growing. True, it's the most comprehensive. True, it's the most rewarding if you do it right. But unless you know how marketing works, you won't have much of a chance to do it right.

The World Wide Web can certainly help you with your job of effective marketing. It can help in ways that didn't even exist in the fertile imaginations of the marketing professionals of the twentieth century. But can the Web *do* the job for you? Plain and simple, no. You can automate an online business to the point that it does almost everything for you. But the success of the business is hardly the domain of the automation process. That's *your* turf.

If you've decided to market online, the first rule of which you should be aware is the *rule of thirds:* You should determine the budget you'll have for online marketing, then invest one third in developing your site, one third in promoting your site, and one third in maintaining your site. Most ill-advised online marketers invest three thirds in developing their site, then wonder why they aren't earning landmark profits.

Guerrillas know that no matter how brilliant their site, it's invisible and powerless unless people know it's there. That's why the moment they think of going online, they think of how they'll promote their online *and* off-line presence. And once their site is up and running, they think of it as an infant who needs constant maintenance, constant attention, and constant changing.

They delight in the truism that their Web site now makes their advertising job a whole lot easier. Before, their advertising had to sell a product or a service. Now, all it has to do is get people to visit their Web site. That gives their advertising a whole new power and an ultra clear goal.

Before I hunker down with you in cyberspace and go deep on the most important new e-media topics — list building, e-mail, subject lines, landing pages, autoresponders, automated marketing, search engine wisdom, blogs, podcasting, RSS, audio- and videopostcards, webinars, joint ventures, affiliate programs, standard Web sites, subscription Web sites, viral word-of-mouse marketing, e-zines, and e-books — I want you to realize that the Internet is the best relationship builder since the Garden of Eden.

I just gave you a brainful of Internet topics. The one to remember above all is the one about relationship building. The Internet is the pure distilled essence of building a relationship with a person. Although you may be building thousands with each mailing, you are building them one person at a time. At least, that's how your prospects and customers feel.

Although things that fit into nutshells probably ought to stay there, in a nutshell, here's the three-step skinny on Internet marketing.

1. Begin with a wonderful product or service.
2. Create a motivational Web site.
3. Send e-mails with hyperlinks (click and you're there) to your Web site.

The easiest part of this process is the wonderful product or service part. That can be yours or someone else's. Creating a Web site that results in sales is not an easy job. But it's a cinch compared with the difficulty of compiling a list of people who want to hear from you, know your name, have had contact with you before, are cool with the process of checking your offers. How, in heaven's name, do you generate such a list?

List Building

You can purchase or rent millions of lists, but the best list of all is the one you compile yourself, a list of your own past and satisfied customers. So save your money and roll up your sleeves. List building is a process of defining your market, setting your objectives, and then figuring how to establish warm and trusting relationships with the people on your list.

Don't simply add names. Anyone with a phone book can do that. Instead, get permission from people to be on your mailing list. The term for this process is *opt in*. Let your prospects decide whether they want to be on your list. If they opt out, bless them — because you won't have to waste time, money, or hopes on them. If they opt in, they want to hear from you, and they'll anticipate each contact from you. People who opt in will never consider your e-mail to be spam.

Get some of those names by offering a free newsletter subscription on your site. Get others with the offer of a free report or two. Get even more by offering a free e-book. The idea is to offer valuable free information — especially data that is not available elsewhere — and keep a list of the people who sign up or order your freebie. You'll get perhaps ten names at first. Keep it up, and you'll get 10,000. People aren't changing that fast. They still love valuable free information.

Contests, sweepstakes, free e-zines, joint ventures — those are more obvious ways to add names to your list. You'll get a lot more with your blog and your participation in forums, not to mention chat sessions. Lists can grow in many different ways, but they should all start in the same place: at every significant touch point with your current customers. Be sure to ask for business cards at networking functions. Then use a scanner to transform those cards and put their e-mail addresses into a digital format.

By the way, do you know when to begin compiling that list? I'll wait here while you begin right now.

A good way to get quite a few names on that list for no financial investment is to write a brief column on your field of expertise, then offer it to newsletters devoted to that topic. Charge nothing, but be sure they include a paragraph at the end with your contact information, an especially sweet situation for you if they give you a hyperlink. Can you offer a free report to people who send you an e-mail? I don't see why not if you're really serious about this business of list building.

If you are, you'll appreciate these eleven techniques used by people who have amassed large mailing lists.

1. Gather e-mail opt ins throughout your Web site: Ask for e-mail opt ins on every page of your Web site. The more frequent and convenient you make your opt in, the more people will use it. This may seem an obvious point, yet many companies bury their e-mail opt-in forms deep within their sites. Or they grant only one or two chances to opt

in. According to Silverpop's "2005 Retail Email Marketing Study" of 175 Internet retailers, 23 percent didn't even offer an e-mail opt in on their homepage.

2. Keep your e-mail registration forms short and sweet: The more questions you require at registration, the fewer the number of consumers who will complete it. A test conducted by MarketingSherpa and Netline showed a substantial increase in registration completion — from 50 percent to 75 percent — when the number of questions was reduced from twenty to six. As all guerrillas know, time is *not* money. It is far more precious. So don't be wasting the time of your potential customers. And respect their need for security. Six questions respects it. Twenty questions doesn't.

3. You've already got a list! Building a list of responsive people is one of the biggest challenges facing you. The good news is that you already have a receptive audience — your current customers. The bad news is that you may not have an e-mail address for each customer. But a host of service firms, called append services, will take your off-line or postal customer list and append e-mail addresses to it from their customer data records. These append services vary greatly, so if you decide to go this route, do your homework. Start with Google, where a list of over 8 million such services awaits you. Make your expectations clear up front when you talk to the one you choose. Make sure it's reputable.

4. Consider coregistration: Allow customers to opt in via a fusion-marketing partner's Web site. Coregistration is one of the fastest-growing areas for list development in the e-mail marketing industry. When users register for the Web site's e-mail list, they'll see your offer and, by merely checking the box next to it, coregister for your opt-in list along with the site's list. Too cool.

5. Viral marketing can help you build your list simply by encouraging the folks on your list to forward your messages to friends and coworkers. They had better be cogent, fascinating, informative, funny, or unique messages.

6. E-mail change of address is quite common. Keep your list of e-mail addresses up-to-date as customers change Internet service providers (ISPs) or companies. Many firms can scan your bounced customer records and provide you with updated e-mail addresses.

7. Direct marketing can also add names to your list. Be sure to include your e-mail registration Web page URL on all your traditional direct-marketing campaigns. The same goes for TV, radio, and print

advertising. Lots of guerrillas include it on their phone answering message.

8. Create a point-of-sale sign-up form. Capture e-mail addresses with a sign-up form at cash registers and other visible locations in your stores. Customers making a purchase are already interested in your brand. What's more, you have their undivided attention. They are presenting you with a perfect opportunity to get them on your list. So, what are you waiting for?

9. Use real live customer service representatives. Have your sales, customer service, and technical-support people ask for e-mail addresses in the course of customer communications. A 2004 Shop.org study by Forrester Research found that only 50 percent of catalog retailers have their customer service representatives ask for e-mail addresses — a "shocking oversight," Forrester said. Guerrillas should never fail to ask for an e-mail address.

10. Capitalize on product registration. Ask for e-mail addresses on your standard product registration mail-in card or Web pages.

11. Become an expert in Web traffic conversion. It's great if you have a gargantuan mailing list. It's terrific if you can draft compelling e-mails that get your opt-inners to speed-click their way to your Web site. But it's depressing if you can't do something, sell something, establish something with all those people who visit you. If you can't convert those people to paying customers, you'll have failed at one of Internet marketing's necessities — converting visitors to customers. Online marketing may be fun, and it is a game, but it's a game you play for real money, and you won't get your fair share if you can't play by the rules the grown-ups use.

Not every method outlined here will work for your company. Try several elements from various approaches until you find the list-building techniques that best complement your brand strategy. Don't rely on any one of them. Use them all.

Great lists aren't built in a day. List building takes time, and it requires integration with every one of your endeavors both online and off line. As you gather names and ask for permission, you not only add to your list but also preserve it. E-mail addresses "churn" continually, and as soon as you stop building your list, it will begin to shrink.

Marketers who invest in their own lists reap the rewards. According to October 2004 Direct Marketing Association figures, the response rates for e-mail sent to a house list outstrip those for prospect lists across direct mail and catalogs. *The return on investment for e-mail has eclipsed that of every direct-marketing medium except telemarketing.* I hope that single salient fact motivates you to compile a large and responsive list. You often hear of six-figure incomes. Many of them come from six-figure mailing lists.

Blogs

A list is a wonderful thing to build. But a blog is a more enjoyable word to say. In simplest terms, a blog is a Web site in which items are posted on a regular basis and displayed in reverse chronological order. The term *blog* is a shortened form of Weblog, or Web log. Authoring a blog, maintaining a blog, or adding an article to an existing blog is called *blogging*. Individual articles on a blog are called *blog posts*, *posts*, or *entries*. A person who posts these entries is called a *blogger*.

A blog comprises text, hypertext, images, and links to other Web pages and to video, audio, and other files. Blogs use a conversational style. Many of them are not only informative but also entertaining. As good as a book or movie? Sometimes better. And less costly. So don't look shocked when you learn that blogs are revolutionizing the publishing industry. Everybody can be an author and a publisher, an editor and a reviewer. Everybody can market intelligently and establish many rewarding relationships with a good blog.

Usually, blogs focus on a particular area of interest, such as the political goings-on in Washington, D.C. Blogging has emerged as an increasingly popular and important means of communication, affecting public opinion and mass media around the world.

Some blogs discuss personal experiences. I'm tempted to write one about living in an RV full time, but I'm too busy marveling at it. If you haven't got the time to author a blog, don't even think about it. But if you have the time, expertise, and writing ability to sell powerfully but subtly, on a regular basis, have a go at writing a blog. It can be a highly enjoyable way of generating income by providing readable information.

Blogs can be hosted by dedicated blog-hosting services, or they can be run using blog software on regular Web-hosting services.

A blog entry typically consists of the following:

- Title — main title of the post
- Body — main content of the post
- Permalink — the URL of the full, individual article
- Post date — date and time the post was published

A blog site typically contains something called *blogroll*, which are other blogs that the blog author reads or affiliates with. Unlike traditional Web sites, a blog allows for easy creation of new pages. Before blogging became popular, digital communities took many forms, including Usenet, e-mail lists, and bulletin board systems. In the 1990s, Internet forum software created running conversations with *threads*, topical connections between messages.

That was the birth of the blog. The modern blog evolved from the online diary whereby people would keep a running account, or blog, of their personal lives. The first of these personal blogs started in 1995.

No one knew it was a blog until the term Weblog was coined by Jorn Barger on December 17, 1997. The short form, blog, was coined by Peter Merholz. He broke the word Weblog into the phrase *we blog* in the sidebar of his Weblog in spring of 1999. In 2001, there was a revolution in consciousness and awareness of blogs. Daily, people around the world are learning more how valuable and versatile they can be — and how potent they can be as guerrilla marketing weapons.

In 2002, blogging helped to create a political crisis that forced Senator Trent Lott to step down as majority leader. The shaping of this story gave greater credibility to blogs as a medium of news dissemination.

Since 2003, blogs have gained increasing notice and coverage for their role in breaking, shaping, and spinning news stories. In 2004, the role of blogs became increasingly mainstream, as political consultants, news services, and candidates began using them as tools for outreach and opinion forming.

Around the beginning of 2005, amateur blogging took off in a big way. Well-informed bloggers soon shot into prominence by their sheer ingenuity and the clarity of their content.

In January 2005, *Fortune* magazine listed eight bloggers whom business-people "could not ignore"; 2006 was the year of years for blogging. And the blog beat goes on.

Blogging is becoming easier all the time. Cases in point: w.bloggar allows users to maintain their Web-hosted blog without the need to be online while composing or editing posts. Blog-creation tools and blog hosting are provided by some Web-hosting companies, Internet service providers, online publications, and Internet portals.

Cultural blogs, which are among the most read blogs, discuss music, sports, theater, other arts, and popular culture. Neighborhood reporting is ideal for blogging: Locals are the best witnesses of local events.

Topical blogs focus on a niche. For example, the Google blog covers nothing but news about Google.

The stock market is a popular subject of blogging. Both amateur and professional investors use blogs to share stock tips. Business blogs are used to promote and defame businesses, argue economic concepts, disseminate information, and more.

Many blogs are written by more than one person, often about a specific topic. Collaborative blogs can be open to everyone or limited to a group of people

An Internet forum is not a blog, but a blog can function as an Internet forum. Internet forums typically allow any user to post into the discussion. Blogs typically limit posting to the blogger and approved others.

Naturally, if you're devoting a few hours each week to your blog and want to make it profitable, you've got to make it popular. Guerrillas do that by

- Paying sites to put up links to their sites
- Getting noticed by Doc Searl (doc.weblogs.com/whoIsDoc)
- Mentioning their blogs in their URLs and on e-mail signatures
- Marketing their blogs as they market their Web sites

Guerrillas have learned that a successful blog needs these five attributes:

1. *Personality*. It must be clear. Readers must feel as though they know the writer or writers. Readers ought to get a feeling of intimacy that's missing from the mainstream media.
2. *Usefulness*. The information must be either useful or very enjoyable to read or both. It should make readers think, laugh, or click. It helps if there are handy links to other places.
3. *Writing style*. Be honest here. Your blog better not be a sales pitch disguised as a blog. It better be a concise, slightly informal blog and not a long-winded column. If it's news briefs, it better have analysis or insight, or you're going to lose readers with your shallowness.
4. *Usability and design*. Make sure that the typeface is easy to read. Be certain that readers can find links to archives. The writing should be easy to skim. Subheads help a lot. So do graphics that are either useful or fun.
5. *Return appeal*. Face up to the reality that your blog must be useful or engaging enough for visitors to visit it again. If they don't come back for more, maybe you ought to invest your time somewhere else.

If you can't commit to writing good, short posts two or three times a week, and if you're not open to inviting and continuing dialogue with your potential customers, blogging might not be for you. Better not to start than to create a blog that has only a few articles posted and lies dormant like an abandoned saloon in a ghost town. A neglected blog can make your company and your professional identity look like the doors and windows are all broken and no one cares. That transfers like quicksilver to your company. People without scruples, brainpower, or writing ability should forget the idea of writing a blog.

A blog won't be read if the writer can't get the message across clearly. If you treat an entire blog like a mini–press release, count on few visitors and maybe even blogosphere backlash. Many top-notch blogs are updated three times a week or more, which is why people refuse to clutter their reading lists with blogs lacking frequent new posts. A business that can't make the commitment to three entries a week doesn't need and shouldn't have a blog.

Podcasting

I see the future of guerrilla marketing, and podcasting looms large on the horizon. I hope that you have already added podcasting to your list of guerrilla marketing weapons. It's the cutting edge of guerrilla marketing and is one of the most powerful new tools for developing leads, increasing brand recognition, developing new customers and clients, expanding your reach, building customer loyalty, developing new sales channels, and launching a permission marketing program. You can get a preview of the future of guerrilla marketing by seeing how our Guerrilla Marketing Radio program is now being podcasted on Yahoo! and iTunes. Find it on our Web site at gmarketing.com. While you're there, learn how the process works by rating and subscribing to the program.

The word is out about podcasting. Twenty-two million American adults have MP3 players or iPods, according to a 2006 Pew Internet and American Life poll — a vast potential audience. Chris McIntyre, founder of Podcast Alley in Nashville, Tennessee, has seen double- to triple-digit growth over just a few months in the number of podcasts being produced and the number of people listening to them. "One of the most popular podcasts has about 28,000 subscribers from my site alone," says McIntyre.

Steve Rubel publishes a blog about persuasive technology (micropersuasion.com). He says that entrepreneurs may find value in creating their own broadcasts and sees multiple marketing opportunities in podcasting, including

- Sponsoring a popular podcast, much like a company might sponsor a radio broadcast
- Using giveaways, contests, and other promos that have proved effective in traditional broadcast media
- Incorporating short ads within podcast feeds, which would be visible as the program downloads

Podcasting is the distribution of audio or video files, such as radio programs or music videos, over the Internet, using either RSS or Atom syndication for listening on mobile devices and personal computers. Guerrillas already know that the essence of podcasting is about creating content — audio or video — for an audience that wants to listen when they want, where they want, and how they want.

Podcasters' Web sites also may offer direct download of their files, but the subscription feed of automatically delivered new content is what distinguishes a podcast from a simple download or real-time streaming. Usually, the podcast features one type of "show," with new episodes either sporadically or at planned intervals, such as daily, weekly, or whenever.

Subscribing to podcasts allows a user to collect programs from a variety of sources for off-line listening or viewing, whenever and wherever is convenient. Traditional broadcasting provides only one source at a time, and the time is broadcaster specified.

The word *podcasting* was coined in 2004 by combining two words: *iPod* and *broadcasting*. But neither podcasting nor listening to podcasts requires an iPod or other portable player, and no over-the-air broadcasting is required.

The editors of the *New Oxford American Dictionary* declared *podcasting* the 2005 word of the year in December, defining the term as "a digital recording of a radio broadcast or similar program, made available on the Internet for downloading to a personal audio player."

A podcast is analogous to a recorded television or radio series. Podcasting enables guerrillas to offer downloadable episodes that can be played, replayed, or archived as with any other computer file. I love seeing joggers wearing IPods and thinking that they're listening to my guerrilla marketing podcasts. We have enough of them and have been doing them long enough, beginning early enough, that my fantasy may be real in some cases.

The word about podcasting rapidly spread through popular blogs, and technology columnist Doc Searls began keeping track of how many hits Google found for the word *podcasts* on September 28, 2004. On that day, the result was 24 hits. There were 526 hits on September 30, then 2,750 three days later. The number doubled every few days, passing 100,000 by October 18. A year later, Google found more than 100,000,000 hits on the word *podcasts*.

The top podcasting programs gave further indication of podcast topics: four were about technology; three, about music; one, movies; one, politics; and — at the time number one on the list — *The Dawn and Drew Show*, described as "married-couple banter," a program format that *USA Today* noted was popular on American broadcast radio in the 1940s. In March 2005, John Edwards became the first national-level U.S. politician to hold his own podcast. In May 2005, the first book on podcasting was released, the award-winning *Podcasting: The Do-it-Yourself Guide*, by Todd Cochrane. Later in the summer of 2005, U.S. President George W. Bush became a podcaster of sorts, when the White House Web site added an RSS feed to the previously downloadable files of the president's weekly radio addresses.

Yet some experienced Internet users declared podcasting to be either nothing special — just a variant of blogs and MP3s — or already past its peak because of growing exposure and adoption by unsavvy Internet users. Time is already proving the naysayers to be short-sighted. In June 2005, Apple staked its claim on the medium by adding podcasting to its free iTunes software and building a directory of podcasts at its iTunes Music Store. The term *podmercial* was coined in early 2005; *poditorial*, in July 2005.

In February 2006, the first official *Guinness Book of Records* World Record for most popular podcast was awarded to *The Ricky Gervais Show*. The show maintained an average of more than a quarter million downloads per weekly episode. That's an impressive number if you're a guerrilla marketer.

Podcasting's initial appeal was to allow individuals to distribute their own "radio shows," but cutting-edge entrepreneurs see huge marketing potential there, and many guerrilla marketers have already embraced it as part of their marketing toolkit. They've invested a few hundred dollars and are already depositing the dividends.

"The marketing takes care of itself," says a podcaster, who as an attorney, has reaped new clients worldwide with his podcasts. He adds, "All the podcast does is give information. If you like the style of writing and speaking, then you're getting to know me. Then you might call me. It's not a hard sell." Heed well his words. People listen to podcasts to avoid the hard sell of the commercial media.

Podcasting has the unique ability to serve as a potent marketing weapon for businesses of all sizes. Some say that the technology may have the most to offer entrepreneurs. Small businesses can get their names before a world-wide audience, which can lead to financial fulfillment.

Podcasts provide businesses with fascinating marketing opportunities. Unlike traditional ads, which come with entertainment, podcasts must offer listeners educational or entertainment value in itself — or else they'll click it off and download a more interesting program.

Remember at all times: Your podcast is part of a permission marketing campaign. At first, you're not likely to send your sales curve skyward with your podcasts. But you are likely to plant the seeds of relationships, get names for your list, and cultivate candidates who will read your e-mail and who already demonstrate serious intent by listening to your podcasts.

In keeping with the tone of the medium, keep your podcasts listener friendly. Many listeners will play it while they multitask or during their commute or workout. All along, it will convey your personality more elo-quently than a conventional ad.

The medium can give potential customers a chance to sample your wares. When Jeff Kowal started a record label, he sought exposure for its growing list of artists in the progressive ambient music realm. But he sure couldn't afford expensive marketing.

He decided to start a podcast featuring chats with the label's artists, an-nouncements of forthcoming concerts, and music clips from CDs, as well as original music specifically made for the podcast. He describes it as an au-dio newsletter.

Mr. Kowal promoted his offering, dubbed LotusCast, with an e-mail campaign. He also posted the podcast on Apple's iTunes as well as other di-rectories and packed the description with such keywords as "ambient mu-sic," "relaxation," and "meditation" to make it easier for interested listeners to find. The result: Traffic soared at Lotuspike.com, and online sales of its CDs and other products doubled, Mr. Kowal says.

You're a guerrilla, so you probably want to get in on this medium before your competitors do. All you need is a good microphone, a computer, and podcasting software to capture the audio file. You can find a good tutorial on the process at PodcastTools.com, and you can download a free editing and recording tool from audacity.sourceforge.net.

With your few-hundred-buck investment, you can produce an info-mercial or broadcast and distribute it through aggregators, such as Ipodder and FeedDemon, or Web-based directories, such as Podcast Alley. These podcasts are sent via topic-specific feeds to subscribers, who can download them to their digital music players or computers.

The cost depends on what kind of microphone you choose. A good one will cost $100 or more. Because the choices are overwhelming, M-Audio, a unit of Avid Technology Inc., bundles starter kits for podcasters: The Podcast Factory, which includes a microphone, a host of software, and other features, retails for under $200.

You'll need a Web site to build your brand, post your podcasts, and give your listeners a central location for information about your company. A site will cost about $40 a month in hosting fees.

Have a structure for your podcast. Keep it brief — from five minutes to a half-hour, though some of mine are one minute. I advise writing a script beforehand to prevent awkward pauses and wandering from the topic. Ask yourself: Will the podcasts consist mostly of interviews, a monologue, or a panel discussion?

The big question is how to attract listeners. Start by making sure that your podcast has good sound quality. You may want to invest in a sound mixer that can eliminate crackles and pops.

Says one podcasting maven: "Your podcast needs to be educational, inspirational and entertaining — but stop yourself from selling too hard. Don't be an audio equivalent of a brochure. Forget it; nobody wants to hear that. It may be better to have two people be in a podcast, because a conversation sounds more natural than only one person reading copy."

Knowing what an earnest guerrilla you are, you will probably want to create an RSS, or Real Simple Syndication, feed, which *automatically* sends listeners new versions of your podcast. You can do this easily at such free sites as Feedburner.com or Odeo.com.

Post this feed on podcast directories, such as Yahoo's podcasts.yahoo .com, podcast.net, or iTunes at apple.com/podcasting. This step also involves supplying some information about your podcast, such as a description and contact information.

To get the most out of a directory site, you need to include the right keywords in your description — or else people won't find you when they search the site. To snare the most listeners, use lots of terms and keep them fairly general. Naturally, use your own site to promote the podcast — on the front page and on each interior page. Start a blog and mention the podcast frequently; this increases the chance that people searching on Google will find a reference to your offerings. In true guerrilla fashion, mention and recommend other people's podcasts, which will increase your chances of being cross-promoted. Make sure that your podcast is easily accessible and downloadable from your own site. Brand it. Create a meme for it. Let people know that it's a real thing.

Eventually, if your podcast becomes popular enough, it will reach the rankings of the most-popular podcasts posted at such sites as Podcast Alley.com. This will increase your visibility dramatically and drive up your listener numbers.

I'll be listening for you.

Nanocasting

Nanocasting is a model for commercial podcasting, based on established media and direct-marketing principles. I mentioned it in Chapter 1 but want to delve into it here because it's so important to guerrilla marketers.

Nanocasting differs from podcasting by beginning with a clear definition of the target audience, the business model, the revenue model, and the use of a system specifically developed for targeting commercial audiences called RTS (Really Targeted Syndication). There is more to commercial podcasting than selling advertising, sponsorships, or subscriptions. These business models are on the cutting edge of using podcasting commercially. "They're drawing from media fundamentals, marketing fundamentals and a decade of ecommerce experience," says Errol Smith, Emmy Award–winning founder of Jackstreet Media.

Nanocasting is a market-tested approach that blends podcasting, streaming, and e-commerce technologies into a market-tested system for using online radio commercially. "Until very recently, the term 'nano' had very little mindshare within the podcasting community, but when Steven Jobs introduced the term to the mainstream, he helped pave the way for the introduction of a commercial podcasting model that is supported by both research and real world business cases," says Smith.

"Nanocasting refers to the programming produced for the most narrowly but clearly defined target audience. This is the audience that is most interested in the type of programming, and from a marketing standpoint, the audience that is most likely to buy related products," according to Smith.

For all the buzz that podcasting is generating, it has been used largely noncommercially by frustrated wannabe talk-show hosts, garage shock jocks, and a wide cast of not-for-profit characters that make up the world of bloggers.

The commercial application of podcasting is called nanocasting. Although nanocasting uses all the same technology as podcasting, the aim of nanocasting is purely and unabashedly commercial.

Said simply, nanocasters focus squarely on how to use Internet radio to make money, expand a business, build a brand, secure new customers, market new products and services, and expand market share.

The International Nanocasting Alliance (INA) was founded by an A-list of media, marketing, academic and legal professionals, media entrepreneurs and advisers from the United States, the United Kingdom, and Australia. Collectively, the founding group has deep experience in the issues that are impacting this new media. INA has brought together the expertise of industry leaders with the creativity of a new generation of global media entrepreneurs to ensure that the highest level of talent is tapped to address the challenges this fledgling industry will undoubtedly face.

This whole evolution of Internet radio and podcasting is essentially a fast-growing guerrilla phenomenon. It is an unconventional way to disseminate information, entertainment, and education. You can learn more about the INA by going to nanocasting.org. As a guerrilla, you owe it to yourself to not only know what nanocasting is but also use it as much as possible. By its ability to target audiences more precisely, it can markedly decrease your marketing investment while driving up your profits. You watch a TV show about running the Colorado River. During the show, there's a commercial for a company that organizes Colorado River trips. That's nanocasting.

E-mail

No matter what happens as the Internet develops and matures, e-mail is always going to be one of its most important applications. You can have a star-studded Web site, a too-good-to-refuse offer, unbeatable quality, and a jaw-dropping price, but without e-mail, you'll be flailing in frustration. It's probably the e-mail that's going to get most of your customers to your site.

The idea is to have a wonderfully responsive list of people who opted in to your list, and then to send them a brief e-mail with a hyperlink to your Web site. That e-mail must be readable on one screen with no scrolling. Those who are not interested will quickly click on to something else. Those who are interested will click on over to your Web site. At that Web site, tell them immediately what they're going to get by visiting the site. There is a dire need for you to be brief with your e-mail. There is no such need at your site. Those visitors *want* information, which they've proved by visiting your site. They do not want glamour or glitter. They want to know how they'll benefit by taking you up on your offer.

You can't make all those salient points in your brief e-mail. If you try, you'll lose much of your audience, because people are busy and can't take the time to read every single e-mail that comes their way.

Your e-mail should even *feel* brief. Use short paragraphs, short sentences, and short words. Get to the point. The point is that readers will gain if they visit your Web site.

Here are two highly significant things that will *not* happen.

1. They will probably not visit your Web site — unless you convince them to go there with your e-mail — and they're probably strapped for time.
2. They will probably not read your e-mail — unless you have a subject line that compels them to open and read it. If you have their attention, can you hold it?

As you very well know, your prospects get a lot of e-mail and delete most of it without reading it. They do so because most likely, it looks like other e-mail subject lines, feels like spam, has hints of a high-pressure sales pitch, repeats what they've heard before, is exaggerated, is not what they want, or hints of something boring.

Your job: Create a short subject line that sets off no red flags. If they know you, be sure to mention your name in that subject line. Otherwise, they probably won't know that it's you. Think it's easy to create a short subject line that is different from all the others? You and I both know that it's not easy. But it is possible. Study the subject lines of the e-mail that is sent to you. Write down those that commanded your attention right from the get-go, those that aren't like others you've seen, those that make you want to click and open the e-mail that used them. If you're lucky and conscientious, you'll probably turn up two or three winning subject lines. If you're creative, you'll see a subject line that inspires you to create a similar subject line.

Check out these winning subject lines:

Frankie, seen this yet?
Amy, print this page.
Jeremy, what's your question?
Ginger, sorry you couldn't make it.
Make it this Thursday, Josh?
Christy, your courtesy reminder.
Seth, do me a favor?
Need your advice about this, Sage.
Ramona, all bets are off.
Frankly, James, I'm puzzled.
Remember this, Jeannie?
Steve, it happens in 72 hours.
Ruth, will you test this?

Do I have to stand on my head now to emphasize the point that each winning subject line is personalized with the recipient's first name?

One of the key arts of direct mail is to use an envelope that begs to be opened. One of the key arts of e-mail is to use a subject line that does the same.

Guerrillas know that they must become experts at marketing with e-mail. They realize that their competitors are doing or will do the exact same thing. Guerrillas have heard the reverberations of the huge explosion in e-mail — in both its efficacy and its economy. They're put off by the ever-increasing postal and paper costs. They love the lack of cost associated with e-mail. Don't forget: E-mail is a whole lot like direct mail but with no postage costs and no paper costs.

Unlike direct mail, e-mail does permit censorship in the form of the spam police. As part of a brave effort to protect the world from spam, spamblockers electronically scrutinize the e-mail you send. It will be unceremoniously deleted when the spamblockers examine the keywords in your subject lines and body copy and find any of these offending phrases:

Hello
Your family
Double your
Dear (something)
Online business
For pennies a day
No investment
While you sleep
Additional income
Financial freedom
Be your own boss
Money making
100% guaranteed
Starting now
Take action now
Requires initial investment

As I write this, most e-mail in America is sent on Tuesdays, followed by Wednesdays. Seventy-five percent of it is sent between 7 A.M. and 4 P.M. Wednesdays are the most popular "opening e-mail days," followed by Tuesdays. Very few people open and read e-mail on weekends.

A 2006 study to determine why people open and respond to e-mail listed these factors:

- Products or services featured (54 percent)
- Written copy (40 percent)
- Subject line (35 percent)
- Compelling offers (discounts, free shipping) (33 percent)

All four factors were topics of the subject line — except for the line itself. I still maintain the importance of subject lines; without a good one, the recipient wouldn't know what products or services are featured and what the copy says. I'm also a big fan of personalized e-mail, though barely 5 percent of it is personalized now. You also ought to know that most Americans check their e-mail first thing in the morning, though even more check it throughout the day. The most popular place to check it is in bed, according to Jupiter Research.

E-mail marketers seeking to increase their open- and click-through rates would be wise to keep subject lines short and hyperlinks plentiful, according to recent analysis by EmailLabs. The key findings tell us that subject lines shorter than 50 characters in length, as well as an increased number of hyperlinks, led to increased open- and click-through rates. Recipients comprehend shorter subject lines more easily and quickly.

E-mail penetration is at an all-time high of 91 percent among Internet users between the ages of eighteen and sixty-four, as reported by eMarketer. Shockingly, an even higher percentage of users sixty-five or older do the same. In the United States alone, 88 percent of adult Internet users have personal e-mail accounts, and 46 percent of them have e-mail access at work. eMarketer estimates that added together, 147 million people across the country use e-mail almost every day. The only other activity to even approach e-mail's popularity is using a search engine to find information. E-mail marketing is growing, and spam, I'm happy to say, is fading away.

I could fill an entire chapter, even a book, with insights into e-mail. But I've told you the most important things to know, and I'll simply hope that you remember those.

Your Web Site

Whenever business slows down or you find yourself with extra time, go through your Web site with the eyes of a cynic, a beady-eyed type who is visiting your site for the first time. The simpler and more user friendly your site is, the more sales it will generate, even from cynics. So always think of how you can remove unnecessary clutter, confusing links, or visual eyesores so that the main idea in your sales copy stands out.

Your site should include these ten critical elements:

1. *An attention-grabbing headline.* The first thing people see when they visit your site should be a compelling headline that describes the most important benefit your product or service offers. The headline is the key element of your site. It's what will persuade visitors to stick around and check out what you have to offer.

   Your headline should be clear, concise, and to the point. It should also be enticing — you want to pique your visitors' interest and make them eager to learn more about what you're selling. You can do this by emphasizing what your product or service can do for them. Don't forget, visitors to your site don't really care much about you, but they care intensely about themselves. That's their favorite subject. So talk to them about it.

   Start with your compelling headline. Be sure it stands out from the rest of the text. Use a large font size, bolding, italics, a different color — whatever suits the style of your site — and stand out.

2. *User-friendly navigation.* Nothing will drive customers away faster than confusing or complicated navigation. Your customers should be able to know where they are on your site at all times and should easily be able to find pages they've already visited.

   Make sure that your navigation bar or menu is clearly accessible and easy to understand. It should be exactly the same on every page of your site and be located in exactly the same place. Your customers shouldn't have to hunt for it. When it comes to navigation, consistency is paramount.

3. *Great sales copy.* The words you use to describe your product and its benefits are the key to the success of your business. Your sales copy is the only contact you'll have with the vast majority of your visitors. That's why you have to make the most of it. Your sales copy should immediately draw the reader in with exciting benefits and enticing copy so you can lead them toward the sale. It should establish your credibility — because nobody will buy from you if they don't feel they can trust you. Describe the benefits of your product or service and explain why your visitors need it. It's easy to be totally honest,

which you should be — but it's a bear to be believed. You've got to knock yourself out writing "shirtsleeve English," as ad great Leo Burnett used to say.

4. *A clear call to action.* If you want people to buy your products or services, you have to tell them how to do it, and you must tell them to do it. They probably aren't inclined to figure it out for themselves. Don't leave them guessing. You have to explain exactly what you want them to do, and you have to make it easy for them to do it.

If you want them to buy a product, present them with a call to action like this:

"CLICK HERE NOW to order your six-month supply of Product X." Say that more than once, more than twice, and say it throughout your site.

Provide your customers with clear, easy-to-understand instructions on how to make a purchase, and let them know what they can expect when they click on the link that leads them to the order page.

5. *Graphics with a purpose.* Graphics can help people visualize your products or services and their benefits. Be sure to include photos of every product you sell. Attractive product shots can boost your sales. Shots showing the product or service in use are generally very effective.

If you have a lot of products for sale, use thumbnails that link to larger images. This will make your pages load more quickly. If you're selling electronically delivered products, such as e-books or software, you may want to create simulated product shots to represent them. This makes your product more tangible to your visitors.

6. *A strong opt-in offer.* Most first-time visitors don't make a purchase. However, the fact that they've come to your site in the first place means that they're at least curious about what you have to offer.

In order to pursue a relationship with these potential customers, you should collect their e-mail addresses by encouraging them to subscribe to a free newsletter or a free download. This will give you the chance to send them updates and information, develop relationships with them, and enable them to trust you enough to buy from you.

Opt-in offers like this are a great way to turn browsers into customers and maximize your sales. Your opt-in offer should be clearly linked to each page of your site or, if possible, included on each page. One less click means losing fewer potential subscribers.

7. *Testimonials.* The best way to establish credibility is to provide evidence that your product or service really works. And the best way to do that is to include satisfied customers' testimonials that explain how your product or service has helped improve their lives.

   Be sure to include the names of your satisfied customers and where they live, possibly their vocation. Along with their testimonials, you should also post a small picture of them. This will personalize their messages, add credibility to their statements, and demonstrate that they're real people who've enjoyed real benefits from your product.

   For instant credibility, it's a good idea to have a few of your best testimonials featured right on your homepage. But you should also have a separate testimonials page. The more satisfied customers you can show to reluctant shoppers, the better.

8. *An "About Us" page.* People are often hesitant to buy things online, because they miss the personal interaction of doing business face to face. The best way to overcome their reluctance is to include an "About Us" page that provides information about you, your staff, and your business. Be sure to include pictures of yourself and your staff members. This shows your customers that they're doing business with real people and will help ease any worries they might have.

   But keep in mind that visitors to your site still want to read about themselves more than about you.

9. *A FAQ page.* It's a good idea to include a Frequently Asked Questions page on your site. This is where you'll list the questions most commonly asked by your customers and provide answers. It allows your visitors immediate access to the answers they need before they'll consider buying your product or service.

10. *Your contact info.* In order to close sales and establish your credibility, you have to provide full contact information on your site. This includes your mailing and e-mail address, as well as your fax and phone numbers. Businesses that post only e-mail addresses on their sites come across as unprofessional and possibly even disreputable.

    Make sure that your contact information is clearly visible on every page of your site. This will make it easy for customers to know how to reach you if they want to get more information or buy a product.

To keep your site in top form, review your site regularly, and create a list of must-do actions you can take to optimize its performance. Figure out where you can get rid of nonessential clutter and simplify the sales process. Don't forget: Streamlined sites generate more sales.

Take the time to browse through other sites, especially those of your competitors, to see how your site compares. What do you like about these other sites? What do you find annoying about them? These visits will help you get an idea of what to include and what to avoid on your own site.

After you've made improvements to your site, ask some friends to go through it. How difficult is it for them to get from page to page? Can they easily find their way back to pages they've already visited? Are they confused by any aspect of your sales process? Do they find your site appealing?

Subscription Web Sites

Running a subscription Web site can be your ticket to guerrilla profitability. It has been for others. After all, it's usually tough to sell anything anywhere. So you may as well sell a subscription to something on the Internet. Expend the effort once; reap the benefits for a long time, maybe even years.

The dot.com bust proved that you can't give everything away for free. At some point, you have to figure out a way to generate revenue if you hope to stay in business.

A lot of people learned this lesson the hard way. They spent millions developing grand Web sites yet never figured out a way to generate any revenue. And now the money spent and the sites themselves are mostly memories.

But not all Internet sites disappeared. Some discovered that their road to profitability lay in subscription sales. For many of these sites, the revenue generated by subscription sales kept them in business while sites that pursued other business models floundered.

A subscription Web site allows only those visitors who have paid a subscription or membership fee to access premium content on the site. It's the same concept as a newsletter or private club — only those who have paid to join can get in. The main advantage of running a subscription Web site is obvious — it allows the site operator to generate revenue to cover the cost of creating and maintaining it.

Many free sites have a high overhead because of the large number of visitors to the site. With a subscription Web site, you have only a fraction of the visitors using the site and much less maintenance. Fewer visitors sounds like a bad thing, but many site owners have discovered that it is far better to have lost 99 percent of your free visitors in return for the revenue that the 1 percent of paying members generate. What happens is that you lower your overhead and raise your revenue at the same time.

There are also advantages to subscribers, often called members, who join subscription Web sites. Much like an exclusive gated community or members-only country club, subscribers gain access to unique content within the members-only area, usually not available anywhere else on the Web. This content often includes exclusive articles, exclusive access to an expert, and exclusive access to software and file downloads not available to nonsubscribers.

Our subscriber site at the Guerrilla Marketing Association also includes a weekly telephone call with a top-flight author, a noted authority in a specific field, and me. Visit guerrillamarketingassociation.com to become a member. Be sure to say hi at our first telephone session.

Subscriber Web sites have a social aspect as well. Members find a community of like-minded people who come together with a common focus or goal. Often, members of subscription Web sites make valuable contacts and connections through the private discussion areas on the site.

Here I come with another twelve-step program, just what the world needs. But you do need it if you hope for success with your own subscription Web site.

1. *Your site must offer a unique experience and information unavailable anywhere else on the Net.* This usually means original material written from a unique perspective. If other sites offer free material recently written by the same author, that can dilute the value of your subscription site.

   The winning concept is this: If the visitor to your site wants to read this material, he or she must first become a subscriber to your site. If potential subscribers believe that this material is available free elsewhere, they won't join.

2. *Your site must target a very narrow niche market with very specific information on a tightly focused subject.* Our market is small-business owners. Our subject is guerrilla marketing. It is far better to have a topic that hits the hot button of just 5,000 people who are intensively interested, even emotionally involved, with your topic than it is to have a topic that everyone is interested in but that no one is emotionally involved with.

   Keep in mind that most people make buying decisions based on emotion, not logic. Make sure that your subscription Web site topic has a strong emotion — and logical appeal to potential subscribers.

3. *Your site must offer a sense of community.* Potential subscribers should be made aware that a strong community of people comes together at this one site to share information, thoughts, and opinions on this one

topic that they are emotionally involved with. They need to know that when they become members, they'll be able to network with others in this community.

4. *Your site must offer a sense of exclusivity.* Potential subscribers should feel that by joining the site, they will be joining a private club where only those inside the gates get to share the benefits of the community. Knowing that joining the site adds them to an exclusive club with benefits not available to the masses adds to the perceived value and appeal of the site.

5. *Your site must have a group leader.* The site needs a captain of the ship who pulls the community together, keeps it focused on the subject matter, and provides a continual supply of updated information that keeps subscribers coming back.

6. *Your site must have a compelling reason for people to join.* Even if you have all the preceding going for you, unless your site gives a potential visitor a compelling reason to join, he or she probably won't join. Ideally, you want your visitor to say, "This is exactly what I have been looking for! I want to join immediately!" If you can create that kind of feeling in your target market, you'll do well.

7. *Your site must follow a viable business model.* If your business model requires 5,000 paying members in order to break even, you are probably doomed to failure before you start. But if you have low overhead and need only a small number of members to be profitable, you have a much better chance of success.

8. *The look of your site must be immediately appealing to your visitors.* Too many sites are confusing, have no overall theme, are difficult to navigate, and scream out your amateurishness. When visitors reach your site, they should immediately feel comfortable with what they see. Anything else gives them a reason to head for the exits.

9. *Every element on your site should give visitors an unconscious reason to join the site.* Fine-tune the site so that every element — especially on the front pages — gives the visitor another reason to join and just begs to be clicked.

    Usually, visitors come to your site because they are looking for the information you offer. Make sure that your main page gives them a good impression of what's within your site.

10. *Your site must be easy for you to build and maintain.* If done by manual coding, maintaining a content-rich subscription Web site can be very time consuming. We use a Webmaster who charges by the hour. He's very responsive and conscientious — mandatory personal-

ity traits for anyone running a subscription Web site. Thank heavens we decided to pay a Webmaster rather than do it ourselves.

11. *Your site must have password protection.* If not, beware of hackers changing your site by adding or subtracting copy.

12. *Your site must have readily available reporting tools.* Knowing what is going on within your subscription Web site is the quickest way to find and resolve problems and to provide better content to current and potential subscribers. Reports should show you where your visitors are coming from, what they are looking for, what they search for, and in general, what is going on at any moment, as well as history and developing trends at your site. And you should be able to view all income transactions and activity records quickly. A good merchant account handles those details for you.

If you get those twelve items right, you'll greatly increase your chances of success with your own subscription Web site. But if you get only one of them wrong, you can expect some severe problems.

But the biggest mistake you can make is choosing the wrong topic. Avoiding this one mistake can mean the difference between success and failure. Make this mistake, and you may never overcome it. Whatever you do, don't select a topic based on what you think people need; focus instead on a topic on what people want.

People don't necessarily buy what they need, but they'll most always buy what they want. Most people who subscribe to your site won't be doing so because it's on a subject they need to know about. They'll be joining because you cover a subject they want to know more about. So clear your mind and think about the things people want, even lust after. Come up with a topic that helps people connect to their dreams, and you'll have more success than having a topic that connects people to their needs.

Teleseminars

Growing in popularity are teleseminars — live seminars conducted on the telephone. Unlike webinars, which are growing as rapidly as teleseminars, there is no visual support. Participants dial a conference-line number and then listen to the content presentation live from the comfort of their home or office, even their car. In many cases, participants may ask the presenter questions.

Because I enjoy my RV life, I enjoy teleseminars and webinars. They enable me to disseminate a lot of information, sell a lot of products, even make new contacts. And I don't have to pack, get to the airport an hour early, or go through airport security. No wonder they're growing in popularity. We've had nothing but good experiences with our "bridge line" conference company: accuconference.com.

Webinars

A webinar is a seminar conducted over the World Wide Web. In contrast to a webcast, which is transmission of information in one direction only, a webinar is designed to be interactive between presenter and audience. In contrast to a teleseminar, it has the added benefit of visual support. A webinar is "live" in the sense that information is conveyed according to an agenda, with starting and ending times. In most cases, the presenter speaks over a standard telephone line or through a computer, using Internet telephony to point out information being presented on screen, with a PowerPoint presentation, and an audience that can respond over their own telephones, probably using hands-free or speaker phones. Many times, a webcam is used so the audience can see the presenter.

One example of webinar hosting is Microsoft Office Live Meeting. You can find out more about them on its Web site: microsoft.com/office.

A key feature of a webinar is its interactive elements — the ability to give, receive, and discuss information. There is nothing to download. Just dial up the audio and go to the Web address provided to view the presentation materials. Because of its format, this live event will allow you to interact with others online, submit questions, and get clarification — all with the click of a mouse or touch of a button. (There is usually time allotted for questions and answers at the end of each webinar.)

Guerrillas like webinars for a variety of reasons.

- They can gain valuable information in a simple, easy, convenient, and cost-effective manner.
- There's no travel or out-of-office time; simply attend wherever you have a computer, Internet access, and a telephone.
- Webinars allow you to deliver an online presentation with Web-enabled text and visuals, along with voice.
- They are structured with predetermined presentation content and objectives.
- You can present to a few people — or a few thousand. I've conducted webinars for 8 people and for 1,400 people. As a presenter, it makes little difference.

Many successful businesses use webinars to

- Hold all-hand company meetings
- Train geographically dispersed customers and students
- Generate sales leads
- Give everyone a front-row seat at their next event
- Conduct sessions from intraoffice to international

RSS (Real Simple Syndication)

RSS is a family of Web-feed formats used for Web syndication. RSS is used by, among others, news Web sites, blogs, and podcasters. Web feeds provide Web content or summaries of Web content together with links to the full versions of the content and other data.

Since mid-2000, the use of RSS has spread to many of the major news organizations, including Reuters, CNN, PR Newswire, and the BBC. These providers allow other Web sites to incorporate their "syndicated" headline or headline-and-short-summary feeds under various usage agreements. RSS is now used for many purposes, including marketing. Many corporations are turning to RSS for delivery of their news, replacing e-mail and fax distribution.

As mainstream media attempt to realize the full potential of RSS, the new media are using it by bypassing traditional news sources. Consumers and journalists are now able to have news constantly fed to them instead of searching for it.

In November 2002, the *New York Times* began offering its readers the ability to subscribe to RSS news feeds related to various topics. To many, this was the tipping point in driving the RSS format's becoming an industry standard. Using an RSS reader, you can view data feeds from various news sources, such as CNN.com, including headlines, summaries, and links to full stories. Many people use RSS feeds by incorporating content into blogs. This is hardly a U.S. phenomenon. By spring of 2006, 34.4 percent of Chinese Internet users were using RSS.

MarketingSherpa, a lush and trustworthy online source of valuable wisdom, usually comes through with excellent practical tips and timely data, gathered from leading corporate marketers, and their piece on RSS is no exception.

- Despite the fact that marketers still aren't aggressively promoting their RSS feeds, they are seeing their RSS readership take off like crazy.

USAToday.com told MarketingSherpa that its RSS traffic is "rising month after month by orders of magnitude," even though it is barely promoting its RSS feeds.

- W. Atlee Burpee & Co., the garden seed company, saw its RSS strategy help increase November sales by four times — just from a trial RSS feed featuring a "seed of the day."

    In addition to this being yet another proof of RSS working for sales, it also gives some insight into what works. In this case, it was providing an e-commerce feed with a featured offering on a daily basis.

- RSS is now finally attracting the traditional online consumer, as noted by USAToday. It's now finally clear that you have to go a step forward in your RSS-promotion strategy and start using user-friendly subscribe buttons or face limiting your RSS accessibility to the cutting-edge crowd.

- Travelocity shares its data on its RSS feed promotional campaign to its existing e-mail subscribers, simply breaking down its e-mail list into Yahoo! e-mail users and MSN e-mail users, and then sending them an offer to subscribe to the RSS feed, using one of these online services.

The astonishing part is that two-thirds of the people who opened the e-mail subscribed. These eye-opening stats show that people are in need of the content consumption solution offered by RSS. *You simply have to present it appropriately.*

Information-packed ads work best. Inform rather than sell. The good news is that you can use images with your ads. The bad news is that there are still no best practices on ad length, except for trying to keep your ads shorter than the feed content.

Experiment with RSS and the Internet by offering an RSS feed right at your Web site. It might turn out to be a big traffic booster.

RSS is still nowhere near the penetration of e-mail. Keep your expectations low as to how many people you will reach. In most cases, you still won't be able to use RSS advertising to reach out to the masses. But if I know you, you'll come up with a way to make it work for you.

E-books

An e-book is a digital version of a book. Instead of appearing on paper, it appears on your screen. If you love paper, you can print the e-book and have lots of paper.

An e-book has a number of advantages over a printed book.

- Text can be searched, except when represented in the form of images.
- It takes up little space. Hundreds or thousands may be carried together on one device. In fact, approximately five hundred average e-books can be stored on one CD-ROM, which is equivalent to several shelves' worth of print books. This may be ho-hum to you, but as RV owners, it means a lot to my wife and me.
- Because they take up little space, e-books can be offered indefinitely, with no out-of-print date, allowing authors to continue to earn royalties indefinitely, copyright law permitting, and allowing readers to find older works by favorite authors.
- E-books may be read in low light or even total darkness, with a back-lit device.
- Type size and typeface may be adjusted.
- The book can be instantly copied.
- Once distributed, elimination is difficult to impossible.
- E-books can be distributed at low or no cost, instantly, allowing readers to begin reading at once, without first going to a bookstore.
- At the moment, e-books are commonly published by independent publishing houses, which can mean greater editorial and authorial freedom and more room for experimentation.
- E-books give you a fascinating and potentially profit-producing option: *viral marketing*. We'll get back to that in a moment.

But all with e-books is not rosy from the standpoint of the reader: They can be incompatible with new or replacement hardware or software, and reading them can be hard on or even harmful to the eyes.

Savvy guerrillas know that the way to grow massive traffic in a short time span is to have something on their site that is viral. It should be something that spreads across the Net on its own, with zero marketing dollars, like a virus, at an ever-increasing rate. That is how Hotmail, Blue Mountain Arts, Napster, the Blair Witch Project, Joke-A-Day, and others gained such large followings so quickly and with so little marketing. The mere act of using these products meant that you had to tell someone else about them, and so they grew. But how do you get the viral power on your site?

Granted, not all sites and products can be made viral. If your site markets tractors, you cannot make the use of a tractor viral. However, you can create something else that is viral. Every Webmaster can, and every site can.

You can create a viral and highly informative e-book. Good e-books, with built-in viral capabilities, keep spreading from person to person perpetually, without any end. In fact, the more time passes, the more they are spread around. Every reader gets to know about your site through your e-book. You can also use your e-book as a method of building your list. Moreover, it costs you nothing for this spreading to happen.

Basically, there are two kinds of e-books. The paid variety is up to 150 pages long and sells in the $10–$20 range. The free — or viral — variety is distributed for free — all 20 pages of it. One kind makes money for you because you are the author and, possibly, the publisher. The other kind makes money for you by establishing your credibility to a point that people want to buy other things that you offer for sale, usually information products. Viral e-books are a relatively new marketing medium, an older brother of special reports. Both have the capability of using their unique and desirable content to replicate all over the globe. But that doesn't happen automatically. You've got to do several things right.

The content is the most important part of a viral e-book. The golden rule is to make it relevant, informative, free, and useful. Do not make an e-book that merely advertises your products. No one finds that useful, and no one will pass it on. People, however, will always treasure and pass on information that is relevant and helps them with some aspect of their life. To make it viral, all you have to do is make that kind of information free and give an incentive for people to pass it on.

The idea is to keep your e-book closely related to your line of business so that it is passed on to people who would be interested later in your business. A viral e-book should be about twenty pages long. Don't worry if you are not a writer. Where do you get the content? Buy books on the topic or go to your library. Get magazine articles from the Web. Tap the treasury of public-domain documents, free for the asking. Let Google tell you the good parts. Compile your research in your own words, and that's it.

One way to find out what topic is popular in your subject field is to see what books are selling the most in that subject on Amazon.com. You must remember that to guerrillas, the end goal of creating this free e-book is to bring people to their sites. So have a descriptive link to your site at the footer of every page.

There are three main things that you will need to remember to make your e-book spread like a virus. *First, it has to be free.* You don't charge for any part of it. *Second, it has to be relevant, informative, free, and useful, not simply an advertisement of your products.* It has to be something people will read and feel glad and enlightened that they did. *Third, it has to offer an incentive to the reader to pass it on.* The fact that it is informative is already an incentive, but you need more than that. The most powerful incentive is money. And that's what affiliate programs are all about.

Affiliate Programs

If you can't beat 'em, join 'em. Two heads are better than one. United we stand. If you get it about those concepts, you get it about affiliate programs. If you are a business owner who wants to significantly increase market reach, break down barriers to entry in your market, or simply generate skyrocketing revenues in a shorter amount of time, these old adages are becoming more and more relevant.

Ask me how I earn my money. About a third comes from book royalties. Another third comes from speaking. The final third comes from joint ventures, also known as strategic alliances. When I first wrote *Guerrilla Marketing*, zero came from joint ventures.

According to the Commonwealth Alliance Program, businesses estimated that strategic alliances accounted for 25 percent of all revenues in 2005, a total of $40 trillion. Did I say *trillion?* I don't remember ever typing that word before.

This figure has been steadily growing over the past few years as more entrepreneurs and small businesses worldwide are uniting in a global environment. If you're an aspiring joint venturer who needs to acquire some key knowledge before making the decision to jump into this new world, or if you have already made the decision to start a joint venture but don't know where to begin, pay close attention.

To begin, get into your mind the eight ingredients that make up the recipe for successful joint venturing:

1. The right partner
2. Your timing and vision
3. The organization of the joint venture
4. The plan for your joint venture
5. Your and your partner's people
6. The execution of your plan
7. Open books so there are no secrets
8. Exit strategies

A joint venture is a strategic alliance whereby two or more parties, usually businesses, form a partnership to share markets, intellectual property, assets, knowledge, and, of course, profits. Companies with identical products and services can also join forces to penetrate markets they wouldn't or couldn't consider without investing tremendous resources.

A potential partner of mine sells valuable business education courses at

$6,000 each. He wants to offer it to the 40,000 people on my mailing list. For each one who buys it, he'll give me $2,000. We mail a letter written by my partner. Eleven people buy the course. He sends me a check for $22,000. Do I like joint ventures?

Some markets can be penetrated only via joint venturing with a local business. Sometimes, a large company can form a joint venture with a smaller business to quickly acquire critical intellectual property, technology, or resources.

The key to earning profits with a joint venture does not lie in the process itself but in its execution. There are no official statistics on the rate of success of specific strategic alliances, though studies from 2003 revealed that joint ventures fail about 60 percent of the time. Happily, things have changed. Experts today estimate that you have an 80 percent chance of success in a joint venture if you have the right partner and the right people.

If your joint venture fails, you trod the boulevard of dashed expectations just one time. If it succeeds, you can maintain it or repeat it for many years.

Automated Marketing

One of the more thrilling aspects of the digital age is the ability to kick back while your technology kicks in. I asked automation and coaching guru Mitch Meyerson (gmarketingcoach.com) for his take on this don't-do-it-yourself mindset. I speak his mind and paraphrase his words here.

Every guerrilla knows that gaining maximum exposure at minimum cost is the name of the game. With the explosion of the Internet, there has never been a better time or technology to do exactly that. Today's Internet technology allows every business — big or small — the opportunity to compete on a more level playing field. It's never been easier to use your time, energy, imagination, and information to automate your online business and increase your profits.

As you better know by now, making consistent money on the Web means excelling in three areas: building your online mailing list, converting prospects into customers and customers into repeat customers, and automating the process through *sequential autoresponders and online payment systems* to free up your time for other activities. Those are phrases you'd never find in any of my past guerrilla marketing books.

With new shopping-cart technologies, it is easier than ever to offer digitally downloaded special reports, e-newsletters, minieducational courses, or free trials the moment your visitors choose to share their names and e-mail addresses — thereby putting themselves in your gold mine. When their data is entered, it is automatically placed in your database and can be programmed to trigger autoresponders — e-mails that are sent to the subscriber automatically — which contain one or multiple messages.

Below your opt-in box, remind visitors of your privacy policy as well as your assurance that they can unsubscribe at any time. You should make sure that your opt-in box is in the top section of your Web page and is very easy to see. Online surfers have a short attention span, and that chance to make a favorable first impression is both precious and fleeting.

Recent consumer studies indicate that 48 percent of salespeople give up after their first unsuccessful contact and 25 percent after the second. Sequential autoresponders are a perfect way to make sure that your follow-up stays consistent and reaches your target audience. Even better, once you've completed the one-time initial setup, the work is done. Your programmed e-mail series will perform flawlessly for you for years to come.

Another proven way to increase the number of opt ins and build trust with your prospects is to offer a free minicourse that delivers content-rich, relevant information to your subscribers. These automatically distributed e-mail messages not only provide content but also motivate prospects to revisit your site for the latest offers and/or to buy your products and services. And, of course, once they click through to your Web site, you can invite them to purchase additional audio, video, and multimedia content, as well as other products and services. Viewing that process, you can see why you must give credit to automation for the warm relationships you're establishing.

Technology today allows you to set up online payment systems through PayPal or your own merchant account. Once you set up your payment account, it's very easy to sell products or services online by purchasing an online shopping cart. A shopping cart will allow you to capture e-mail addresses, automate responses, track leads, and then sell your product to customers around the world 24/7. Visit gmarketingcart.com for the best in shopping carts, Web automation systems, and merchant accounts. We practice what we preach.

When you automate daily tasks, you gain more time to focus on the essential strategic growth of your company. You can work *on* your business rather than *in* your business. You'll enjoy more free time without adding staff or worrying that you're interfering with your money-making activities. That's because *when your business becomes automated, your presence becomes optional.* With most systems, you can quickly and easily check your sales and orders from any Web browser — even when you're on vacation, though I'm not sure I approve of mixing profitability and pleasure. I just thought it over. I do approve, because automation makes it so painless.

The Internet is a competitive marketplace. The right strategy combined with powerful and practical systems gives you an edge over your competitors. Think about it: You'll attract more customers and spend less time, money, and energy winning them over. Automation services and software leverage the best technology available to make you money day and night, whether you're there or not. These days, the sounds of guerrilla marketing include snoring.

Search Engine Optimization

This is a simple little marketing book and hardly a comprehensive examination of online marketing, so I'll not dwell much on search engines. Still, I don't want you to go without knowing a few things.

Most Internet searchers visit and do business only with the Web sites that are listed in the top ten or top twenty of the sites in the major engines. Those companies enjoy qualified traffic and higher potential revenue. It is also true that the return on investment from a bright Internet marketing campaign is greater than most traditional marketing efforts. A lot of experts believe that *the longer your site isn't represented correctly on the search engines, the harder it will be to gain position later, because of the increased competition.*

You'll have to read and experiment your way around selecting the correct keywords, creating a winning title tag, dealing with metatags, your "alt" attribute, things to avoid, and how long you'll have to wait to be listed. You'll have to post articles on the Web sites and blogs of others, because every time those articles appear, you move up a notch on the search engine rankings. The higher you appear, the better — and the ways to climb are both paid and free. To learn what you absolutely have to know about search engines and search engine optimization, consult the two favorites of guerrilla marketers: Google and Yahoo! They're a good place to find your way around the search engine terrain. At this moment, out of 225 million Web sites on marketing, Google lists our dear own gmarketing.com fifth.

According to a recent Georgia Institute of Technology survey, 87 percent of Web surfers use search engines to find new Web sites. Over 100 million searches are performed every day on the Internet. If your Web site is not optimized to rank well within the top twelve search engines, some of your best customers may not be able to find you.

In addition, customers search for you using a wide variety of search terms, so you also need to rank well on a wide variety of search terms. Search engine optimization is the process of designing your Web site, then submitting it correctly to the search engines for the purpose of getting as much qualified traffic as possible from the search engines.

I'm an exception, but 80 percent to 90 percent of browsers do not look beyond the first page of results after a search, so your site must be returned in the first page of results after a search to get significant traffic. To get the most out of search engines, your site should be registered in all the top twelve search engines, where most of the search engine traffic is concentrated. Those twelve search engines change regularly.

A properly optimized site will provide motivated users — those actively looking for information or to buy. Visitors from search engines often convert to customers at ten to one hundred times the rate of banner advertising visitors. Unlike advertising or PR, which gives a short burst of traffic, search engine optimization can increase traffic to your site for months or years.

Search engine optimization can be a very inexpensive way to drive targeted traffic to a Web site. Search engine optimization is also complementary to other marketing you may use, helping customers who have seen your advertising connect with your site. Search engine optimization is a dynamic area and requires knowledge of how search engines work, as well as ongoing learning to stay on top of the way search engines rank results.

The number one factor in search engine optimization is the keyword you choose to optimize. The best keywords are the emotional benefit-filled terms that have such things as the following:

- The most number of searches
- The least amount of competition
- The ability to draw targeted traffic that is ready, willing, and able to spend money on your product or service

If you know what keywords people who want to buy your product are typing in, you are more than halfway done. Test your keyword conversion using a small Google Adwords campaign.

Getting good rankings on a wide variety of terms is worth the effort, however, and certainly a lot cheaper than using banner advertising. At a click-through rate of 0.5 percent, the industry average, and a $30 cost per thousand, visitors cost $6 each, using banner advertising. Search engine optimization can bring in traffic for as low as 1 cent per visitor — not free but very close to free. And many search engines will list you at no cost at all.

The best way to get listed in the major search engines is to have a link from a site that is already listed. When the search engine checks the links on that site, it will visit you and include you in its search engine results.

Here are some tips on what you need to know about search engine optimization.

- Have a unique title for every page.
- Make your title something that describes the benefits you provide and the needs you fulfill.
- Use keywords in your title.
- Get a domain name with your keywords in it.
- Put your keywords in the copy text of your Web site, and make them bold in a couple of places.
- Include your keywords at the very top and bottom of your page.

To be listed high on the major search engines, it's expedient for you to go to your own favorite search engine, type in the words "search engine optimization," then click your way to the best of the options in front of you. Although there are nearly 100 million options, you'll probably hang out at the first few pages, possibly only the first page. The same will happen with prospects for what you sell. They tend to linger at those first few pages, probably only the first page. That's your lesson on search engines for today.

Landing Pages

A Web site gives a lot of information that might lead to an eventual sale. A landing page closes that sale. An effective landing page for every special offer you make and campaign you launch can multiply your results. An ad attracts your prospect's interest, but your landing page picks up where the ad leaves off and leads the prospect to complete the transaction. Is that the name of the game or what?

The focused hours it will take you to perfect your landing pages are a significant investment in your success. Failure to invest enough brainpower in your landing pages, especially if you're direct marketing anything, is toxic to your overall marketing. It's very clear what a landing page must accomplish. It must get your prospects to complete their transactions and enable your advertising to do its job.

Although there is now a technical term for this process — landing page — you and I know it for what it really is: closing the sale. Although there are many new facets to marketing, most in the burgeoning world of the Internet, it continues to boil down to getting attention, making your presentation, and closing the sale.

12

Info-Media Marketing

A rich abundance of marketing weapons defy the standard categories of weaponry. Although many are devastatingly effective in helping you turn an honest profit, there is no way they could be considered minimedia, maximedia, or e-media. Sadly, this inability to fit neatly into a category has kept some of them out of standard textbooks on marketing, depriving many a business owner of a valuable asset for marketing forays.

Not to worry. That oversight is rectified right here. The info-media to be investigated have more in common than getting short shrift in past marketing books. These weapons also all provide information — the kind of information that, if disseminated properly, leads to a sale and a clanging of your cash register or its equivalent.

I hope you'll see the good sense of adding some of these tactics to your marketing plan. They're not going to tax your budget much, and they can become a beloved part of your long-term plan. Although these techniques are unquestionably devoted to imparting information, the real truth is that almost all the media have the same obligation and fulfill it admirably. But these particular marketing strategies have a bit more information and allow you to deliver it in a more fertile setting.

Free Consultations

I know that you'll want to open the door to long and lasting relationships. That's why I want you to know of one of the world's great door openers: a free consultation. When you offer it — by letter, phone, advertisement, or

Web site — it carries no pressure and requires little time. "Want a free sales presentation?" "Uh, no thanks." "Want a free thirty-minute consultation?" "Hmm, that sounds good. When can we set it up?"

A free consultation is a lot like a free sample in that it's a sample of how good you are. It's also like a free seminar at which you get to develop a personal, one-on-one relationship. It's even similar to a demonstration because it allows you to demonstrate how you can help your prospects. The offer of a free consultation is easy to accept, and the rules guerrillas follow are only five in number:

1. *You are not allowed to make a sales presentation.* You offered a free consultation, and that's what you've got to deliver.
2. *If you offered a thirty-minute consultation, you must offer to leave after thirty minutes.* Your prospect may ask you to stay and continue your consultation, and if you'd like to, fine. But you are honor-bound to offer to depart when you said you would. You prove in a consultation your professionalism, ability to listen and to help your prospect, reliability, enthusiasm, and maturity in a potential buyer-seller relationship.
3. *Your job in a free consultation is to prove how valuable you can be to your client.* Do it with sincere, valuable help. Don't worry about giving things away for free — that's the whole idea.
4. *Ask questions and listen carefully to the answers, responding to them the best way that you can.* The idea is not to hold things back but to give freely. If what you give is valuable enough, you'll be amply repaid.
5. *Follow up within forty-eight hours.* I know you're busy and may have other free consultations set up, but no matter what, you should thank the person for his or her time and restate the high points of the consultation. If you're not willing to follow up, you may be wasting your time during the consultation.

I know a Web designer who uses his laptop computer to show computer-illiterate prospects how simple it is for them to have a site on the Internet. If you can demonstrate while you consult, you can sign up customers in droves. To get the real lowdown on consulting, guerrilla style, read the Amazon #1 bestseller, *Guerrilla Marketing for Consultants*, by guess who and Michael McLaughlin.

Free consultations are one of my personal favorites because they're so effective, inexpensive, and quick to lead to the sale. Right up there with free consultations are free samples. Procter and Gamble, which has a market penetration of 97 percent in this country, claims that giving free samples is like buying a customer. Nipping at the heels of free consultations and free samples are free demonstrations and then free seminars. And don't forget free gifts. Do you sense a commonality in those phrases?

The F-Word

The f-word isn't used in the phraseology of these next weapons, but the spirit is definitely present. I refer to brochures and catalogs, newsletters, and e-zines. Two of the info-media are especially power packed, and I urge you to get past any hang-ups so that you can launch, then benefit from, them. One is writing an article or two for a local publication, which means that you'll have to get past that fear of rejection. And the other is speaking at community organizations, which entails quieting down those knocking knees and that palpitating heart. I'll give you a slam-dunk hint for jettisoning those jitters.

Even though some of these info-media are decidedly low profile, some have the potential to provide all the revenue you'll need for the rest of the life of your business. Enough of my chattering. Let's get down to your business.

As you know, guerrillas give things away. Giving and receiving are two sides of the same coin. The coin is called business. Guerrillas have learned, though they may have always suspected it in their bones, that the more they give, the more they receive. They are extremely imaginative about what they can give, shifting their generosity into high gear and seeing the world through the eyes of their customers. That's where to start when determining what to give away.

Gifts are given in the form of desk items and computer and personal trinkets. Guerrillas are also quick to give extra service, extra attention, extra value. Because we're in the middle of the information age, they also give away information. The information they provide will benefit their customers, help them succeed at whatever they are striving for. The information will make their target market smarter and therefore richer and happier.

Guerrillas give away their information in many forms. Some give talks at local clubs and organizations; some give free seminars and clinics. Some give free consultations and demonstrations; others host online conferences. Some guerrillas give tours of their facilities or the facilities of satisfied customers. And still others give valuable data in the form of columns or articles in publications read by their target audience.

Many guerrillas empower their generosity with technology. They use technology to help them in their quest to edify, educate, and enlighten their prospects and customers. They write articles for the Internet and are able to locate many Web site operators who are thrilled to get such worthy information at no cost. They create Web sites that brim with crucial content, that bring prospects back for more of the same.

These kinds of guerrillas sponsor forums, host conferences, and sponsor chat sessions for their prospects and customers. They produce CD-ROMs and DVDs to help their prospects see the light. Because they realize that technology can help them disseminate information and that information is a powerful marketing ally, they let their minds wander freely through the available possibilities.

They can produce newsletters on a regular basis. They can create information-laden brochures. They can give away information in the form of self-published booklets and pamphlets, catalogs and bulletins, even by daily or weekly e-mail communiqués and mouse pads and screen savers. Ask yourself what your prospects might want. *In many cases, what they want and need — what separates them from success — is information.* And it's information that you can provide. Are you the only company that can provide it? I hope you are.

Determine the best way to serve up that information. Perhaps you should do so with a meeting at which you enlist the hearts and minds of your prospects with technology — a multimedia presentation.

A presentation I attended by investment superstar Charles Schwab made such an impact that nearly a third of the audience signed up to invest. It felt like show biz, but it was sell biz, designed to look like an entertainment extravaganza. It's amazing that music and exciting graphics can be combined with content, thanks to computer technology. Just reminding you: You don't have to be Charles Schwab to do what he did that afternoon.

There is little doubt that your business strategy discusses what you can get and what you can earn. If you're a guerrilla, it will also include what you can give. These days, you can give a lot.

Free Seminars

I have a client whose business is computer education. His classes are unique, effective, and impressive. But standard marketing methods didn't attract many customers, so he decided to hold a free seminar on computers for people who knew nothing about them. He placed an ad, and more than five hundred people showed up for the seminar.

Had he teamed up with a great salesperson, he might have sold his program to as many as 50 percent of the people attending. But he'd never dreamed so many people would show up, so the number of people he sold on his series of lessons was closer to 5 percent. Next time he holds a free seminar, he'll be better prepared to close his sales. In fact, he might even hire a professional salesperson.

Many people who give paid seminars or courses for a living advertise free seminars with ads in the business sections of newspapers. One speed-reading school advertised its free seminars with television commercials. An income tax expert markets his free seminars by means of publicity stories coupled with radio commercials on talk-oriented stations. Many entrepreneurs earn a great deal of money with paid seminars and courses. But because they cannot attract large numbers of people to paid seminars and courses merely through newspaper ads, these guerrillas attract prospects to free seminars, then convert the attendees to paying customers.

As one guerrilla to another, I sincerely recommend the same tactic to you. If it is feasible for your type of product or service, I recommend that you use the newspaper to advertise that you are holding a free seminar on the topic most closely connected with your product or service. Get as many customers to come to your free seminar as you can. They may purchase your products or may sign up for your service. If you hold a decent seminar, they will probably do both.

When I say *seminar*, I really mean lecture. Give your audience valuable information and demonstrate your expertise or your product's efficacy for, say, the first forty-five minutes, using visual support if you can. It's easier these days than ever to put on multimedia presentations. Then spend the next fifteen minutes selling whatever it is you wish to sell. What I am talking about is a fifteen-minute, straight-from-the-heart commercial — delivered by you or by someone you hire. The entire process takes one hour. After that, sign up the prospects. Unlike professional seminar leaders, you probably won't be signing them up for a paid seminar (unless selling information is your business). But you will be allowing them to buy your offering. And they'll want it because your message, demonstration, enthusiasm, and proven expertise will have created within them a desire to purchase from you.

There is no question that an in-person commercial is better than a radio or TV commercial. Certainly, a fifteen-minute selling opportunity will pan out better than a thirty-second selling opportunity. For this reason, seminars and demonstrations are being used more and more to market products and services.

A lecture, consultation, or demonstration is very much like a sample. Your prospects get to see for themselves what you have to offer. They probably get to touch it, a very good thing, if it's a product, and they get to ask questions, whether it's a product or a service. They get to learn more about your offering this way than they do by standard marketing methods. And just as sampling convinces many people that they should buy a good product, so too can your seminar or consultation.

Before I write one more word, I should emphasize that a free seminar/consultation/demonstration amounts to marketing in a vacuum unless two other factors are present. First, your free imparting of information must be marketed and advertised so that you'll end up with a large group of prospects. Market in the newspaper, on the radio, or on TV. Use direct mail and telemarketing. Post signs. Go for the free publicity that is readily available when you're offering a free seminar. Tell the truth in your ads as to the contents of the seminar, and try to attract honest prospects, not simply warm bodies.

Second, be sure that either you or an associate can sell your offering to those prospects after the seminar is over. My client was a brilliant lecturer. People listened intently to his every word. They enjoyed looking at him and listening to him. He was a first-rate lecturer. As a salesman, though, he was eighth-rate: He hadn't an inkling of how to close. He had no instinct for blood. He didn't have a personality that could take advantage of the momentum he created in his lecture. Unfortunately, he signed up only 5 percent of the audience rather than the potential 50 percent.

If possible, demonstrate your product or service at your seminar. Although your offering is free, people *are* giving up their time; they are traveling to attend your seminar. And they have expectations, based on your ad. You must give them value in exchange. You must live up to their expectations and move beyond them. You must treat them as if they have paid to hear you. You should make sure that even if they do not buy from you, they still feel that their time was well spent. Perhaps they'll buy from you later.

Where should you conduct your seminar? At your place of business, if possible. Rent the chairs you'll need. Perhaps you'll conduct it outdoors, if you are demonstrating gardening skills or the like. Perhaps you'll conduct it in a gym, if you want to show and sell exercise equipment. Eventually, you'll be able to hold it on the premises of a "partner" with whom you have a *fusion-marketing arrangement* — a collaboration of marketing talent, money, and ideas. (Read more about the juicy topic of strategic alliances in *Guerrilla Marketing Excellence*.) Most seminars are held in motels or hotels where seminar facilities are readily available. If you have a store, hold a free seminar there — that will work best. Your prospects can learn where you are and what you sell. For instance, a decorating seminar in your furniture showroom is a natural.

People appreciate useful information. They appreciate it all the more when it is free. When you conduct a seminar or a workshop, give a lecture, demonstrate a product or service, consult with a prospect about that person's business, you prove your expertise. You establish yourself as an authority. You gain credibility. Even if people do not buy from you right then and there, they very well may buy from you later.

There is a tactic that some very successful (and high-pressure) businesses use to get the maximum number of people to buy right then and there at the seminar location. They establish three "sales points" on the way to the exit. At the end of the free seminar, the speaker tells the customers that they can either sign up for the paid seminar at a particular table or with specific representatives located throughout the room. Four reps are usually present to work with the potential customers. Prospects who do not buy must pass the three sales points before leaving the room. At each, the prospects are given a different sales pitch, each stronger than the one before. Some people sign up in the main room, others at the first sales point, and still others at the second sales point. Another group signs up at the third sales point. Only a tiny group — who have world-class sales resistance — leave the building without putting their hands to their wallets. Sounds a bit pressured for this guerrilla.

Free seminars, even without triple-teamed closes, can be a bonanza for you, and you should try to market with them if you possibly can. It may be that your business simply doesn't lend itself to seminars. If your business is window washing, car washing, or mail-order publishing, perhaps seminars are not for you. But if your business is income tax preparation, instruction, or retail furniture, perhaps they are.

Think about the field in which you operate. Can you give a lecture for forty-five minutes on any aspect of it? Which aspect? How will this tie in with your offering? Do you have the showmanship to lecture for forty-five minutes and hold the attention of your audience, or should you delegate that task to someone else? Do you have the salesmanship to close sales right then and there, or should that, too, be the job of an associate? What will you be selling at the seminar? Will it be products? Services? Books? Lessons? A paid seminar? Products or services of a fusion-marketing partner?

As with sampling, try, if feasible, to offer one free seminar to market your business. It can be a lot of fun. And it can be extremely profitable, with a lower cost per sale than advertising in any newspaper or on any radio station. It will give you both immediate and long-term benefits. You'll get to mention in future marketing that you have lectured in your field, led seminars in your area of expertise. Giving free seminars continues to be a very innovative way to market. Conducting a seminar that's not at your own place of business will run you about $50 to $500 for the room, plus whatever it costs to buy coffee or juice for your guests. If you will keep them for only an hour, you need not provide refreshments, but if you plan to go longer than that, it's a good idea to have them. Some morning seminars also offer free donuts. Even donuts are weapons in the arsenal of a practitioner of guerrilla marketing! Guerrillas know the dynamic power of small details.

To the cost of the room and refreshments, add the price of the ads you'll be running and any seminar materials you'll be handing out. After your seminar and sales pitch are completed, you can add up your receipts, then divide them by the total cost of the room, ads, refreshments, and materials. That will give you your cost per sale. If it is low enough, continue to market this way. In fact, it doesn't have to be low. Even if you sell ten people a $1,000 product that costs you $100 and it runs $1,000 for your room and ads and handouts, you will have earned $10,000 while spending $2,000 — a cost per sale of $80. This is a high cost, but it's minuscule when compared to your $900 profit on a $1,000 product. This is why so many free seminars are being offered these days. Also, you want the opportunity to talk to honest-to-goodness prospects, people who have already shown that they will expend time and effort to learn more about your field.

Free Demonstrations

Demonstrations can be given not only at seminars but also in homes, at parties (be sure you consider party-plan marketing for your business), in stores, at fairs and shows, in parks, at beaches, or almost anywhere. People are attracted to small crowds, and a free demonstration will almost certainly attract a small crowd. At a free demonstration, which is much shorter — no more than five minutes — than a seminar, be prepared to sell and take orders immediately afterward. Folks who give seminars and demonstrations often have cohorts all set to accept customers' credit cards, checks, and cash. The person giving the demo or seminar is usually too busy answering questions to take orders, so get that base covered.

A free demonstration need not be marketed in the same way as a seminar — simply showing up at a high-traffic location or placing a few well-conceived signs may do the trick. Of course, it's fine to advertise and distribute circulars, although they may not be necessary. It will be necessary to provide the showmanship and salesmanship.

Can you demonstrate your product or service effectively? Answer honestly. If you can say yes, by all means give it your best shot. Rarely will you be afforded so golden an opportunity.

Party-Plan Marketing

A few moments ago, I mentioned the idea of giving your free seminar or demo in a party situation. More and more items every year are being marketed through party-plan marketing. Here's how it works: A person becomes a party-plan representative for a company. Let's say it's an art gallery, since so many of them engage in this kind of marketing. Here's the deal: You throw a party for all your friends and close acquaintances, just as Tupperware party planners have been doing for decades, and very successfully.

At the party, serve coffee and pastries or maybe little sandwiches. You also give a well-planned sales spiel about whatever you are selling. You offer examples, conduct a brief seminar, distribute samples, or give a demonstration to the assembled throng. The lighting is optimum. Music selected especially for the occasion may be playing in the background. Your enthusiasm is bubbly and contagious. You're obviously proud of your offerings. Your friends start to like them, too. And the prices! They sound so low. A buying frenzy starts. Fifteen of your offerings are sold. They sell for an average of $100 each. But you purchased them for $25 each, including everything, from your supplier.

Each $100 sale results in a $75 profit. You should feel proud of yourself. You earned $1,125 for the night and spent only $50 for refreshments — a $1,075 profit. And that's just the start. Now you tell your friends that they can do the same. The word spreads. The parties spread. Soon they're being held in several towns. Naturally, you get the lion's share of sales from the parties thrown by the people you've signed up. You're raking in the bucks. Your buddies, along with strangers who are enthused about what you sell, are raking in the bucks. Your suppliers are doing very well, thank you. You are very, very happy that you engaged in party-plan marketing.

Can you? Here are the types of companies that do already: exercise-machine companies, art galleries, kitchen-equipment companies, women's clothing manufacturers, vitamin manufacturers, X-rated product companies (the "pleasure" industry), cosmetics manufacturers, computer companies, jewelry manufacturers, and lingerie manufacturers. The list is not shrinking.

Such parties are ideal places for demonstrations. And the people attending are already *conditioned* to buy. You can't beat that kind of situation if you're a practicing guerrilla. Of all the places at which free seminars or demonstrations can be held, parties certainly rank up there near the top.

The main disadvantage of free seminars, consultations, and demonstrations (except for parties) is that you must travel. You can't always hold free demos and seminars in the same area over again. You've got to hit the road and talk to fresh prospects. But you can make these free sessions part of your marketing plan and give one or two per year. A guerrilla would find some way to use them.

Newsletters

Half an hour. That's all it takes today to design a newsletter that would do any small-business owner proud. With easy-as-pie software, it's not a matter of creating new designs; you can choose from a generous selection of past designs. Select page designs, artwork, formats, mastheads, and typefaces by pointing and clicking. You'll be absolutely amazed at how creative you can be, at how much money you can earn by creating a broad array of weapons, and at how much money you can save by doing it on your own. Your kid can probably do it for you.

Of course, many newsletters today are sent digitally. Everyone knows that. But here's what people are just getting around to knowing: Time is too precious for long newsletters. So now there are one-page newsletters, an idea born in the mind of Roger C. Parker, and brought to vivid life at his Web site: onepagenewsletters.com.

As with standard newsletters, these should be sent at least once a month. Once every two months is the outside limit if you're publishing a real newsletter, the kind that habituates readers. And as with old-fashioned, longer newsletters, they should adhere to the 75–25 rule: 75 percent of your newsletter should give solid information of worth and value; 25 percent can give selling information. With public-domain materials so free and available, it shouldn't be difficult to fill a newsletter, even a long one.

Publishing on Demand

It's a lot easier, a lot faster, and a lot less frustrating to be an author now than at any time in the past. True, you've first got to write a book — not a piece of cake, to be sure. But once you've written it, you can bypass the hassles and joys of agents, publishers, editors, booksellers, and critics.

You can simply send your book to a publishing-on-demand publisher, such as one of the more than 70 million ones listed in your handy search engine. Keep in mind that when you write and publish a book, you are investing your time, energy, imagination, and information in a door opener, a credibility builder, and a book. My bet is that you'll make more money from door opening and credibility establishing than from the world of literature.

Still, if you write a book and decide to price it at $39.95, you can send it to an on-demand publisher, some of which will design, print, and mail your book to one person at a time at a cost of about $10.00 per book. After a few-hundred-buck one-time set-up fee, that's a $29.95 profit per book for you — more than the total selling price for the book you hold in your hands.

The main distinguishing mark for print or publish on demand is that a copy is not created until after an order is received. Although it is conceivable that one could print on demand using any printing, digital printing is so often used that the terms are often used interchangeably.

Print on demand (POD) with digital technology is used as a way of publishing books to order for a fixed cost per copy, regardless of the size of the order. Digital technology is ideally suited to publish small print runs of books and posters often as a single copy as and when they are needed. Although the unit price of each physical book printed is higher than with offset printing, digital print on demand provides lower per unit costs — when setup costs are taken into account — for very small print runs than do traditional printing methods.

Although the unit cost of a book or print produced using POD is usually higher than one produced as part of a longer print run, POD does bring some key business benefits: (1) large inventories of the book or poster do not need to be kept in stock, (2) the technical setup is usually quicker and less expensive than for traditional printing, and (3) there is little or no waste from unsold products. These advantages reduce the risks associated with publishing books and prints and can lead to increased choice for consumers. Although most print-on-demand services do ask an up-front fee for the creation of the digital masters, editing, and formatting services, it is likely to be less than the setup for traditional printing.

Profits from print-on-demand publishing are on a per sale basis, and the amount of commission will often vary, depending on the route by which the item is sold. Highest profits are usually generated from sales direct from the print-on-demand service's Web site or by buying copies from the service at a discount, as the publisher, and then selling them yourself. Lowest commission usually comes from sales from bricks-and-mortar bookshops, with online bookstores falling somewhere in between.

A POD book can be an excellent solution for writers who don't want to go through the submission process required by commercial publishers, feel that they've exhausted the possibilities of the commercial publishing market, or simply want to produce a few dozen copies of a family memoir or recipe book for private distribution. POD provides an attractively designed book at a far lower cost than traditional self- or vanity publishing and offers many of the same benefits, including guaranteed publication and lack of editorial interference. Also, since the book is produced only when ordered, you don't risk winding up with a garage full of unsold volumes.

But if you're a new writer looking to establish a career, a POD book is probably not a good choice. It's widely equated with vanity publishing; it's not likely that a book published this way will be considered a professional credit. Nor is POD a stepping stone to conventional publication. According to a 2004 article in the *New York Times*, out of the 10,000 or so titles published by Xlibris since its inception, only 20 had been picked up by commercial publishers.

Despite some highly publicized successes, the average POD book sells 150–175 copies, mostly to the authors themselves and to "pocket" markets surrounding them — friends, family, and local retailers who can be persuaded to place an order. According to the chief executive of iUniverse (quoted in the same *New York Times* article), 40 percent of iUniverse's books are sold directly to authors.

Booksellers don't like dealing with PODs. In order to sell books in significant numbers, you need bricks-and-mortar bookstore placement. Don't believe the hype about the power of the Internet: Less than 10 percent of all books are bought online. Bookstores are still where most people do their book buying. But listen up: Some authors have made good money by getting their books sold by Amazon, then doing mailings to both their lists and their fusion-marketing partners' lists. With cooperative list partners who have big lists, your book can move to number 1 best-seller status at Amazon, which has a very beneficial and long-term effect.

Authors who are willing to go door to door can often be successful in persuading local stores to stock their books — though often they must sell them on consignment, or agree to buy back the unsold copies.

I've seen some notable successes with POD books. But I must alert you to take the POD raves with a grain of salt. Many POD publishers portray the service they offer as a revolutionary new publishing model that's going to open up a world of opportunity for writers locked out of the market by the narrow standards of the monopolistic commercial publishing industry. Heady terms like *paradigm* and *democratization* are tossed around. But there's nothing new about paying to get published — or about the opportunity it offers, which is mainly for the publisher to make a profit.

The beauty of on-demand publishing is in the lack of risk. You don't have to print several thousand copies of the book, as my publisher had to do. You simply print them one at a time. If you love to write and need some doors opened, open your mind to on-demand publishing. Maybe I'll see you on the bestseller list.

E-zines

As you probably can figure from the title of this data snippet, an e-zine is a digital magazine. Like an e-book, it should be loaded with valuable information. Like a newsletter, it should be sent either weekly or monthly to those who opt in to receive it. You know, I feel I can go on and on about e-zines, but I also feel as though I'll be telling you what you already know. So I'll simply direct you to Google, ask you to enter the word *e-zines*, and let you read what you probably know already. There are nearly 6 million entries, so you may know a lot. But just in case you don't, Google is teeming with things you may not know. Just know this: An e-zine is a terrific way to drive traffic to your Web site, lift your search engine ranking, and use as a gold medal follow-up device, though device doesn't convey the humanity and warmth of an e-zine.

In addition to being what you think it is, a digital magazine, an e-zine is also a superb list builder. One way to build your e-mail prospect list is to write an article in two parts. Submit part 1 of the article to other e-zine publishers. Then include in the reference box in the bottom of the article a mention that part 2 is available at your Web site. Traffic will come from all over the place.

Columns in a Publication

If you enjoy writing, want a ton of credibility, and will appreciate a way to market extremely effectively at no cost, offer to write a column for free for a local publication — even a trade publication. Tell the editor to whom you make the offer that you'll charge nothing for your column and only want to be identified by your name, phone number, and Web site. Since editors are human beings and appreciate free things, you won't find it very difficult to find one who will take you up on your offer.

In your column, give valuable information that will be in the best interest of the readers, and don't try to sell your company's offering. Don't forget, the editor said yes to a column and not to a free advertisement. You'll be establishing yourself as the authority in your field — since everyone knows that columns are written by experts. You're writing a column, so you must be an authority.

Make reprints of your columns and post them on your Web site. Include them in your marketing materials. The fact that you're penning a column will add firepower and credibility to anything else that you might say.

In time, you might put together a collection of your columns and offer them as a free booklet to your prospects. Lean on those columns, realizing that people equate being published with being an acknowledged expert. The more solid information you impart in those columns, the more business you're going to attract.

Of course, you've got to enjoy writing and be fairly good at it before you offer to write a regular column. And you've got to restrain yourself from selling in all that you write.

You should refer to your column with your other marketing, realizing that it will add a large dose of integrity to those other marketing claims. You can offer to write your column weekly, monthly, or quarterly. You might also ask for a paragraph at the end of the column. That's where you are allowed, even encouraged, to toot your own horn. But do it there and not in the body of what you write.

If ever there was a win-win-win situation, this is it. The publication wins. The readers win. And you win. The cost of these victories? No cost at all.

Articles for Publications

Haven't got time to write a regular column? No problem. Write an article instead. Do it once, then reap the benefits for years afterward. Doing an article is a lot like doing a column, only you do it one time only.

Tell the editor of the publication you select to grace with your prose that you'll do it at no cost and that you won't try to sell anything to anybody. Ask to be identified by your name and phone number and Web site. Then, when your article appears, make 10,000 reprints. Maybe even 20,000. Use them all over the place — in e-mails, on your Web site, as handouts, wherever you can reach serious prospects.

As with a column, your article will establish that you're the authority, you're the person whose advice and information appears in print, you're the vendor of choice. Don't even try to sell a thing. Just give copious information and wise counsel.

How do you select a publication for your article? Pick the one in which you'd most like to advertise, then don't advertise but offer your article instead. Instead of a newspaper, you may select to write your article for a magazine or a newsletter. Don't forget: It's the reprints that will pave your way to the bank.

I suspect that you'll be happily surprised at the ease of getting your article published. If it's interesting to the readers of the publication, it might be published in more than one publication. If you're not a good enough writer, you can have your article ghostwritten. It's pretty simple to find ghostwriters if you peruse a copy of *Writer's Digest*.

Your single article can prove that you're the expert, a source of news, a person in whom they can be confident. And it can do this without costing you one cent. All this, along with the inner satisfaction of being published and seeing your wisdom in print. While you're feeling warm inside, your prospects will be impressed. That means they'll be more inclined to say yes to your offers.

Your article must do absolutely no touting of your skills or your quality. Bend over backward to prevent them from sounding like ads or infomercials. Let the quality of your data prove beyond words that you're the company with which to do business. Let your abilities tout themselves.

If you have the heebie-jeebies about writing, because you're cursed to be a perfectionist and you desperately fear rejection, heed the words of author Anne Lamott, one of the best writers I've ever read. In her book about writing, *Bird by Bird*, she reminds you that first drafts stink.

Speaking at Clubs

Of all the methods of marketing, this is the only one that some of my clients have begged me not to reveal to you. It's a lush marketing ground and relatively untapped.

A lot of organizations in your community would be delighted to have a lunchtime speaker come in and speak for thirty minutes at no cost. As with columns and articles, you're not supposed to use your speaking platform as a selling platform. You are supposed to give worthwhile information that will improve the lives or businesses of the members.

It's cool to give your Web site at the end of your presentation. If you provide valuable information during your talk and on your Web site, close to 50 percent of the attendees will eventually become paying customers. After all, you spoke to their club for nothing and didn't try to sell them anything.

I've got to caution you that if you do this, you must be a good speaker and carefully prepare your material. But you don't have to invest any money. I know that the greatest fear on Earth is the fear of public speaking. The second-greatest fear is the fear of death. Following this reasoning, you'd be better off at a funeral in the casket than delivering the eulogy. But you've got to brush aside those fears. To do that, don't focus on your audience, and definitely don't focus on yourself. Instead, focus on your material. Do that one thing, and those butterflies in your tummy will fly away. You can get a lot of valuable speaking support and advice by joining Toastmasters International or the National Speakers' Association.

I once had a client who planned a year of marketing. He wanted to spend half his budget on television and the other half on newspapers. I suggested that he contact a few local organizations and offer his speaking services. He was very fearful of public speaking, so he had a member of his business do the speaking instead. The results were so overwhelming that he hired two people to contact and speak to local clubs, then canceled his TV and newspaper plans. Can you do the same? I'm betting that you can.

To accomplish it, contact your local chamber of commerce to learn which organizations exist in your community. Then keep in mind that they'll relish the thought of having a free speaker deliver fascinating information.

As with columns and articles, you'll be establishing yourself as the authority in your field. Since you're the whiz — and you're local — don't be surprised at the customers you'll attract with your free information. But please, do my clients a favor — and don't share this tactic with others.

13

Human-Media Marketing

If you never give a thought to marketing — and most people don't — you wouldn't need the upcoming information. But if you are involved with marketing consciously and regularly, it's too important not to know.

Obviously, the human media are less about things and more about people and ideas. These media are available to all kinds of businesses, cost what you'd expect guerrilla human media to cost — nothing — and have the potential to transform a business, based on tiny details.

Much of life is being able to separate the winners from the losers. If you learn how to do that, you'll forget how to lose.

An investigation of the human media would start with the command center in the brain, then proceed to the human support systems. The allies of the guerrilla marketer are worth getting to know better than you do now. And there's never been a better time to hang out with them than now.

Marketing Insight

If you don't have a clue as to how and why marketing works, draw a blank at knowing what makes it different from what it used to be, and become a bit befuddled dealing with the whole process, perhaps you'll be better off getting a job working for someone who does have a clue. Having a clue means seeing everything from the customer's point of view. It's no surprise that guerrillas are extra sensitive to the economy, because they know that a bleak one is on the minds of their prospects and customers. Guerrillas have the insight to know how to cut their marketing costs without cutting their profits.

Guerrillas market more to their customers and less to their prospects and the universe in general. Follow their lead. Rely on and make enticing offers to the people who have already learned to trust you — your customers. Make this hidden method of economizing part of your daily existence, and stop wondering why marketing costs tumble as profits rise.

Use the telephone as a follow-up weapon. When the going gets tough, the tough make phone calls. Eliminate any perceived risk of buying from you. Do it with a guarantee, a warranty, a deep commitment to service. Let the customer know that *the sale is not over until the customer is completely satisfied.* Guerrillas know that this tactic assuages skittish prospects.

Keep an eagle eye out for new profit centers, fusion-marketing opportunities, cooperative ventures. Never forget that geometric growth comes from larger transactions, repeat business, and referral customers. Be geometric as often as possible.

Tap the enormous referral power of your customers, knowing that your warm and careful follow-up to them will make them want to help you by giving you three, four, or five names of likely prospects. In the battle for profits, guerrillas take names. They do it about once every two years.

Marketing insight is easier to come by now than ever before. Books galore are available, many of them terrific books. Marketing newsletters, often free, are disseminated all over the Internet. Insight-packed talks by traveling marketing gurus are given in major markets on a regular basis. And then there are webinars, bringing those gurus to a computer monitor near you.

An enormous number of people, many running a small business, and many in the field of marketing, don't understand what marketing is. Many who do understand are uninformed as to the powers and limitations of marketing. Insights into the way to play marketing like a Stradivarius are now presented most helpfully in the search engines you most like to visit. Simply Google around for about an hour and discover how many insights enrich your mind as well as your financial prospects.

You're not going to learn them in the real world — except slowly and painfully — but you can absorb them rapidly and painlessly by reading about marketing on a regular basis. The insights change so rapidly that I dare not give you a bibliography here and now.

Since you're taking the time to read this new edition of a book on marketing, you're proving that you understand the importance of keeping up. The point is — the point that you know — is that you've got to engage in continual learning if you're to stay ahead of your competitors. As soon as you think you know it all, more is revealed, and if you're not keeping up, you're falling behind. Hardly the hallmark of a guerrilla. Time is not money, but marketing insights are money. Going for the gold means keeping up-to-date on new revelations in this fast-changing field.

Yourself

You are your own marketing weapon — not only the things you say and do but also the things you are and believe. According to studies reported in *Time* magazine, *the best five personality traits for you to possess are extroversion, agreeableness, emotional stability, conscientiousness, and openness to experience.* It also helps immensely if you like and are fascinated by people.

An obvious truth to absorb is that *people like to do business with people they like.* Your job is clear: Be likeable. If you are, you'll probably be your best marketing weapon. If you're not, those other weapons may end up firing blanks.

People must buy you before they will buy what you are selling. They must buy your employees before they'll buy what they are selling. Business may appear to be about things, but it's primarily about people. If prospects and customers like you, they'll be far more inclined to buy from you. A client of mine had to fire an employee who was punctual, honest, efficient, and intelligent. But he had received more than a little feedback from customers and fellow employees that she was an unpleasant person and that they'd prefer to do business with anyone but her.

If you interface with prospects, you have to be good at people skills, which means being a good listener. It also helps immensely if you can view prospects first as people and next as prospects. If they like you, there's a good possibility that they'll buy from you, continue to buy from you, and recommend that others do the same.

Whatever you say to their faces means a lot more than what you say in a marketing context. Hey, the Internet is terrific, but I have a feeling that you're even more terrific.

I've coauthored, with Seth Godin, a book about being your own marketing weapon: *Get What You Deserve: How to Guerrilla Market Yourself.* The essence of the book is that you are the most important cog in your marketing machine. The cost of your having a sparkling and winning personality? It's zero. But the cost of your having a downtrodden or off-putting personality is depressingly high.

Let's get right down to it. Are you good enough to be a guerrilla marketer? Author/psychologist Mitch Meyerson and I devised a test that lets you score and track yourself in *sixteen guerrilla competencies.* Ready?

Read each statement and score each competency on a scale of 1 to 10 (1 = poor; 10 = excellent). Answer each question twice: once from your own perspective and then as a customer or client would answer for you.

1. I see every contact with my customers and prospects as marketing. My words, attitudes, and actions are intentional and based on my marketing goals._____

2. I look at my marketing activities from the customer's point of view. I consistently make time to ask my customers and prospects what it is they really want._____

3. I am aggressive in my marketing efforts._____

4. My marketing attack includes an assortment of strategies. I make use of many of the hundred marketing weapons available to me._____

5. If I surveyed my customers today, they would agree that I follow up in a timely and consistent manner._____

6. I consistently use a marketing calendar to track and measure the effectiveness of my marketing weapons._____

7. My friends, prospects, and customers would say that I am enthusiastic and consistently positive in all my interactions with them._____

8. I have a clearly defined marketing niche._____

9. I have a clear and specific marketing plan to guide my weekly actions._____

10. I use online marketing as one of my major marketing weapons. I use e-mail, a Web site, and the vast power of the Internet to reach new prospects and communicate with customers._____

11. I build strong one-on-one relationships with my prospects and customers, knowing that people buy from friends rather than from strangers._____

12. My business is oriented toward giving. I provide free consultations, tips, gifts, and information. I make generosity a part of my overall marketing plan._____

13. I look for ways to amaze my customers by providing exceptional service._____

14. I consistently use my imagination to develop marketing strategies that are unconventional and that will capture the attention of my target market._____

15. I actively work on developing strategic alliances with other businesses._____

16. I take consistent action on my marketing plan._____

The areas where you score low represent obstacles. Address them, or they will impede your progress. Raise the scores, and you're ready to be a super guerrilla marketer.

Your Sales Reps

It has long been known that the best salespeople do not work for a salary but instead for a commission. They are so confident in their sales ability that they want no paycheck, only a portion of the revenues that they earn. That's why in many organizations, the top salespeople earn more than the president and CEO.

Deep down, I'm hoping that you know some of these people, because they don't cost a cent to employ and can bring in untold numbers of dollars because of what they can sell. Some organizations have thousands of salespeople, none of whom are paid a dime. They earn their keep by the commissions they earn. Can you set up a similar network? It doesn't even take a network. One or two motivated salespeople can do the job for you. I know two guys, each running a different company, and each beholden to a single individual who racks up 90 percent of their sales. It doesn't take a huge sales force to generate huge profits for you. A single superstar can do the job.

You've got to support your sales staff with marketing firepower in the form of a Web site, a fact sheet brimming with benefits, and other marketing to help pave the way to the sales they'll be making. It helps if you offer a generous commission, which can range from 5 percent to 33 percent. But it's still free to you if you pay them based only on their performance.

Those who perform best should be given bonuses. Naturally, they'll need sales training, but frequently, they can do the training for you because of their inherent sales ability.

If you are looking for salespeople, you won't find it very difficult to find them. Many are employed selling for others. They may be happy as a clam at high tide to sell what you offer as well. They don't have to represent you and only you for you to profit from their sales skills. Success at marketing with commissioned salespeople doesn't depend on how many people are selling for you but on how good they are. In almost any sales organization, 20 percent of the salespeople make 80 percent of the sales. Your job: Determine who the 20 percent are, then use their talents to fire up and train the other 80 percent. If they're good at selling, there's a very good chance that they'll also be good at training.

Scan the classified ads in your newspaper to see the vast number of sales jobs being offered and the tremendous number of salespeople out there — all potential profit producers for you. If they want a salary or a draw, be nice to them but say no. If they want only a commission, I predict a happy and mutually rewarding relationship.

Employee Attire

This is not the place where you'll be advised to ask your employees to wear uniforms or for you to have a strict dress code. But it is the place where you'll be warned of the difficulty for your prospects and customers to make purchases from people with visible multiple body piercings and tattoos or wearing T-shirts heralding the Aryan nation.

Like it or not, your business will be judged by the employee with the tackiest and most in-your-face taste in clothing. If nobody wears outrageous attire or flaunts their individuality with nose rings and eagles on their forehead, you won't lose sales because of how they bedeck themselves. But you might lose sales if they do.

Fashion is a language of signs, a nonverbal system of communication, according to Alison Lure, who wrote *The Language of Clothes*. She adds that the vocabulary of dress includes not only your clothing but also accessories, hair styles, jewelry, and other "body decorations." The meaning is clear: Every part of your and your employees' personal presentation holds meaning.

Your employees' appearance includes their hair, car, energy level — every aspect of them that might attract notice. And believe me, people do notice. *Dress for Success* author, John Malloy, provides us with dress rules that always pay off.

- *If you have a choice, dress affluently.*
- *Always be clean. Obsessively neat is not necessary.*
- *Dress more conservatively than your prospects.*
- *Never wear anything that identifies you with a personal belief.*
- *Dress at least as well as the people to whom you are selling or meeting.*

In general, navy blue signifies authority; brown, a lack of sophistication. Black demonstrates almost too much power; red calls attention to the wearer more than to the content of what he or she says. People in the most chic styles draw attention away from their message unless their message deals with high fashion.

Guerrillas in a retail environment ask employees to wear company shirts with the company logo and the employee's name. This makes them more visible to customers. And if your male employees wear suits and ties and females wear dark suits or dresses with heels and hose, don't be surprised if your sales soar. It has happened before and will happen again.

Your Inner Circle

Everybody, even those in remote locations, has a circle of influence. This circle comprises your friends, relatives, colleagues, business associates, golf partners, poker game competitors, teammates, classmates, customers, suppliers, fellow White Sox fans (give me a break here), neighbors, fellow church members, fellow club members, and even acquaintances.

These people are usually the first who can help you in your quest for success at marketing. Not only can they become customers, but also their own circles of influence can become customers. These circles of influence are often the starting points for a viral marketing campaign. And the good news is that absolutely everyone is part of such a circle.

Market to these people just as you'd market to prospects, knowing that they know you, trust you, and like you. That's a wonderful place to start. It's also a wonderful place to learn of your marketing weaknesses, if any. And it helps you to determine your most compelling benefits. In rare cases, your circle of influence can provide you with enough business to cease marketing altogether.

It's said that everyone knows at least twelve influential people. And those people probably know twelve more. And those twelve know twelve more. That's a very healthy ripple effect for you. So be careful. Just as the good word about you spreads rapidly, the bad word may spread even more quickly.

Your circle of influence is probably much larger than you realize. It's an ideal starting point for a word-of-mouth campaign. Don't overlook your circle. It's often neglected by people who feel that they must market to the world at large and forget that their friends are the best starting point of all. Of course, you've got to have a quality offering for these people to rave about you in public. They're putting their reputations on the line. But if you have a solid offering with a galaxy of benefits — or even one serious competitive advantage — you'll find that the members of your circle will be delighted to help you spread the word. Did I tell you the cost of a circle of influence? Of course not. You already know that.

Contact Time with Customers

In some businesses, customers walk in; say, "I'll take two of these and three of those"; then plunk down their credit card, sign, and leave. Other businesses require half an hour or more to transact business. Those are the lucky ones.

Those people can use that valuable contact time with their customers as a marketing opportunity. They can use it to intensify their bond with the customer, to enlarge the size of the transaction, to prove that they sincerely care about the customer, and to gain valuable referrals. The cost of this contact time is zilch, and the payoff can be quite handsome.

If the customer buys a product, you might offer a companion product or a service. If the customer purchased a service, possibly you can offer a related service or product. Certainly, you'll ask for the customer's e-mail address. The whole idea of contact time with customers as a marketing dream come true is one of mutual gain. The customer gains because he or she learns of allied offerings that can be of help; you gain for the obvious reasons. Rather than being a pressure situation, contact time is a relaxed circumstance that will motivate the customer to help you, to buy from you, to refer you.

A myriad of opportunities are available to capitalize on during this contact time. It takes place not only when a person is buying something from you but also when people are shopping, coming in for repairs, updating, even visiting you to register a complaint. All these are superb opportunities for you to render superlative service and to market your other offerings.

A national chain of hairstyling salons increased its profits by 29 percent by marketing hair care products while providing services. My sister returned from her hairstylist sporting a new hairstyle along with a new necklace and bracelet, purchased from the guerrilla stylist. Now there's a stylist who truly understands the value of contact time.

As long as the customer benefits, you both come out as winners. Disney understands this. Most professional sports teams understand it as well. The people are in a buying mood, prove that they patronize you, and are already inclined to purchase what you offer.

Amazingly, some business owners resent the time they have to spend with customers. But not you. You cherish it.

How You Say Hello and Goodbye

The three most important things for you to know about saying hello and goodbye to customers and prospects are:

1. *Smile.*
2. *Make eye contact.*
3. *Use the person's name.*

Note, not one of these things costs you a cent, but they all pay rich dividends. As I've mentioned before, the most beautiful words in the language are the words in the name of your customer. Say them, and you'll automatically stand apart. Just ask yourself, how often have you been greeted at a business by a smile, eye contact, and the sound of your name?

It rarely happens, which is why you'll score brownie points by saying hello and goodbye the right way. If you don't know the customer's name when you say hello, learn it during your conversation with the customer, and use that name when you're saying goodbye. Just by asking the person's name, you'll be proving that you care about him or her as a person, not just as a customer.

If your customer contact is primarily by phone, let the customer hear your smile in the tone of your voice, and be sure to use that person's name. Sorry, I can't help you on the eye contact part here.

It's just human nature that people enjoy doing business with folks they like. And I guarantee that they'll like you a lot more if you smile at them, look into their eyes, and say their favorite words. It will make them feel special. It will prove to them that you will always treat them with special care.

Funny how TV and magazine advertising are so much more costly than saying hello and goodbye properly, as well as being less effective in making lifelong friends. If the person contacting your business is made to feel like the most important customer ever, that person is very likely to buy from you, to return to make more purchases, and to say good things about you behind your back.

I suppose that you already know this, but just in case you don't: Human kindness is part of the spirit of guerrilla marketing. Warmth and caring are also part of it. Personal attention is still another part. None of these cost money. And they don't even ask for a lot of time, energy, and imagination.

Stories

It's one thing to relay a fact to a person. It's a whole different thing when you tell a story. An old tale best illustrates this point: Truth went wandering into a village. She knocked on door after door, but the doors would open, then immediately close in her face. Wherever she went, she was denied admittance.

Eventually, she went to the house of Fable and asked, "Why do none of these people open their doors and invite me in?" Fable told her it was because people could not handle the nakedness of truth. She suggested that Truth don a cloak of fable. Then, when Truth knocked on doors, each one would open and she would be invited inside.

So it is for your business. People will not be interested in the facts you relay, but they'll be fascinated by the stories you tell. The children's TV show *Blues Clues* proved that when you tell a story, people pay rapt attention. When the story is over, many kids even ask you to tell it again.

The entire concept of an attention span goes up in smoke when viewed in the context of a story. Tell stories whenever you can rather than relate facts. That's the spoonful of sugar that helps the medicine go down.

Sales Training

I've worked for and with a lot of companies. Some were committed like crazy to advertising; others, to direct mail. But it's the ones that stressed sales training that earned the most profits, year after year. Engrave this in marble: Sales training is one of the most cost-effective tactics in marketing.

To be accomplished properly, sales training sessions should take place at least weekly. They should be run by the sales manager, the head of the company, the best salesperson, or an outside expert. As repetition is one of the keys to implanting a marketing message, it is also paramount to successful sales training. Don't worry about repeating yourself. Worry instead about your sales reps missing one or two crucial points when making a sales presentation. With repetition of your sales training, that's probably not going to happen.

Keep in mind that great salespeople are not born; they're trained. Even Andre Agassi, Tiger Woods, Michael Jordan, LeBron James, the Williams sisters, and Michelle Wie, though hardly salespeople, were trained to become as good as they are. The top salespeople in the United States probably weren't born that way. They may have had many inherent talents, such as enthusiasm and sincerity, but you can be sure that they were trained to sell as well as they do.

During sales training sessions, which should run from thirty minutes to an hour, try a bit of role playing, with one salesperson acting as the prospect and another playing the salesperson. The prospect should come up with all the usual objections, and the salesperson should handle them, one by one, in the proper manner. Ask the other salespeople for feedback. They may come up with a few ways to handle objections, ways you haven't yet considered. When involving your entire sales staff and requesting their input, you'll be able to share the most wisdom and avoid the most common mistakes.

Amazingly, sales training can be a lot of fun as well. Good sales trainers are able to inject just enough humor to make the session enticing beyond its promise of a loftier income. Unless you're engaging in sales training on a weekly basis, you're not really taking it seriously enough.

Networking

Networking may be the diametric opposite of what you think it is. Instead of being surrounded by peers and handing out business cards while talking about yourself, networking is your big chance to be surrounded by prospects, collect business cards, ask questions of the people you meet, and focus on their problems. *Networking success isn't determined by the number of business cards you pass out but on how many you collect.*

If you're a silver medal guerrilla, you'll contact each person who gave you a card within a week. If you're a gold medal guerrilla, you'll have taken notes during the networking function so that you can refer to what the people said when you contact them the next day. During any networking, adjust your radar to spotting problems. If you can solve them, you're more than halfway home.

When you attend a function, you must have the attitude of having a good time, not making money. Realize that you'll have only a brief moment with many of the people, so make it count. The more fascinating, the better. Have a selection of conversation starters in your mind. Get them by reading the newspaper, watching the tube, going to movies and concerts, and surfing around cyberspace. Read the newsletter, if any, of the organization sponsoring the event.

Look for people with whom you can network later. Find fusion-marketing partners. Look for leads. When you do pass out your business card, be sure it is a minibrochure that also describes the services you offer and the benefits of doing business with you. Comment on any business cards handed to you.

I hope I don't have to remind you to make eye contact and smile. Shake hands with a firm grip. Listen for all you're worth. And give total attention to the person you're talking or listening to. Don't scan the room while engaged in conversation. It's stupid and common.

Booze is served? Not a problem. If you must have a drink, nurse it slowly. But don't overdo booze or food. You already know how the surgeon general and I feel about smoking. Sprinkle your conversation with touches of humor. Be sure not to offend anyone. Don't remember a person's name? Admit it at the start. Read *Guerrilla Networking,* which I wrote with Monroe Mann, and *Networking Magic* by Jill Lublin. Reintroduce yourself to those who may have met you. Follow up in a hurry, have a good time, and realize the value of each one of your contacts.

Affiliate Programs

Affiliate marketing is one of the best innovations in the electronic world. The combined power of this tactic and the vast number of people online can prove to be an extraordinary source of profits to your business. Affiliate-marketing programs are simple partnerships between onliners who want to extend their reach beyond their own Web sites and their affiliates — other sites or individuals who agree to sell or market your offerings in return for a slice of the action.

From your standpoint, this is free marketing with the potential to attract traffic and generate sales. From the standpoint of your affiliates, you're offering a viable source of additional revenue in exchange for a small piece of advertising on its Web site. One of the most successful of all affiliate programs is run by Amazon.com. It was also the first online. Although Amazon calls it an Associates Program, it's an affiliates program nonetheless. This program offers commissions to referring Web sites when Amazon sells merchandise to referred visitors.

Affiliate programs such as Amazon's are astonishingly simple to set up and initiate. Just place a link on your site. It should contain a special code that tells the system at Amazon which visitors came from your site. If that visitor makes a purchase, you get a slice of the pie.

If you set up your own program, keep in mind that your affiliates are paid only when you make a sale or other criteria are met. You might even give a higher commission if an affiliate brings in a high volume of sales. The objective of an affiliate program is to lower your customer-acquisition costs. So it makes sense to grow your affiliate base as large as possible. If you want to keep matters simple, consider joining an existing network. You can find them in one of many affiliate directories. Find them at refer-it.com, affiliatematch.com, associate-in.com, mlmwatch.com, or cashpile.com. Affiliate-Announce.com will even submit your affiliate program for you.

Once you have affiliates, treat them with loving care. After all, they are now your business partners. Communicate with them. Keep them updated. Thank them when they are successful for you. To get a real bead on the majesty of an affiliate program, consider becoming an affiliate yourself. Many business owners would love to sign you up. You'll discover the ins and the outs. And as you learn, you will earn. Don't forget to consult your friendly search engine for more learning.

And whatever you do, don't miss out on being a guerrilla affiliate. Just click on over to gmarketing.com and sign up.

Satisfied Customers

One of the most power-packed media of all is something you already have and doesn't cost you one cent. It's satisfied customers — people you've delighted in the past. They are terrific sources of testimonials and referrals and serve as a landmark to which you may point with pride — proof that you live up to your promises.

Satisfied customers also have a wonderful way of being transformed into repeat customers. Savvy marketers invest 10 percent of their budget marketing to everyone in the universe in general, 30 percent talking to their prospects — those members of the universe who fit their customer profile — and 60 percent talking to existing customers. Keep marketing to these people. They're an exceptionally lucrative source of business.

If you consider every single satisfied customer to be an unofficial member of your sales force, you've got the right idea. Only unlike salespeople who sell only your offering, satisfied customers sell and buy your offering, a winning combination if ever there was one. Always remember that it costs only one-sixth as much to keep an old customer as to earn a new one.

So treat your satisfied customers with love, loyalty, devotion, consideration, and professionalism. That, plus their positive experience with you, will keep them satisfied. Just because they're customers doesn't automatically mean that they're satisfied. The more satisfied customers you have, the more satisfied customers you'll gain. It's an endless circle that gets bigger and bigger — along with your profits.

Among your most precious business assets are your credibility, reputation, marketing calendar, and list of satisfied customers. Stay in touch with them. Revere them. They are the springboards to marketing effectiveness that money can't buy.

I've written many guerrilla marketing books. But I would have written and been able to sell only one if I didn't have a lot of satisfied customers.

Designated Guerrilla

Here you are, learning all that you must know about guerrilla marketing, but perhaps you're too busy in other aspects of your business to devote ample time to running your marketing show. That is no reason not to proceed full steam ahead with your marketing. If you're not in charge of activating your marketing program and riding herd on it regularly, you need someone to do it for you. You need a designated guerrilla.

Perhaps that designated guerrilla will be someone from your own ranks, someone who lights up with excitement at the thought of an aggressive marketing campaign. No matter whom you select, be sure that person loves the challenge and loves marketing in the first place.

You might also select a designated guerrilla from the galaxy of brilliant marketing consultants out there who know marketing from A to Z. They can help you craft a strategy, put together a calendar, and even create a theme and a meme for your company. They can oversee the day-to-day details of your marketing foray. They are experienced and in all likelihood are talented.

But I've got to let you know that the best designated guerrilla on the planet is the one you see whenever you look in the mirror. You can delegate the marketing tasks, delegate the marketing details, and delegate the marketing assignments. But you can't delegate the passion or the vision. Those have to come from you.

If you're too busy attending to the production or financial or selling activities, you should ask yourself whether you've got your priorities straight. Even if you've got the production, financial, and sales responsibilities totally covered, remember that marketing is what will fuel your fires. Marketing will make all your other tasks worthwhile. Marketing will breathe fire into your goals.

Somebody has to oversee that function and do it with enthusiasm. And of all the people who can do it, nobody will do it with as much passion and ardor as you. Nobody will see the big picture as clearly as you. If you truly are a guerrilla, you will also be your best designated guerrilla.

An Interest in People

No matter what you think you do for a living, you're really in four businesses at once. The first is the business you think you're in — the one mentioned on your business card.

The second is the marketing business. Whatever you offer must be marketed. If you don't keep thinking that thought, chances are slim that you'll succeed. One of your most important tasks is to continually strive to improve your marketing. Guerrillas are always thinking about how they can, which is why they're guerrillas and why they're earning such impressive profits.

The third business you're in is the service business. Customers must be served and helped from the moment you meet them. If you realize that you truly are in the service business, you'll render the kind that leads to repeat and referral sales.

The fourth business you're in is the people business. Your products are made by people, marketed by people, sold by people, and offered to people. There's a close correlation between your interest in people and your ability to convince and motivate them. There's not much I can do in this book to interest you in people other than to call your attention to the monumental importance of being a people person.

An honest interest in people will be reflected in your ability to ask the kinds of questions that draw people out — that prove to them that you care about them — and to listen very carefully to what they say to you. The more interested you are in people, the better a listener you are. Guerrillas are superb listeners.

No wonder they are so skilled at developing lasting relationships. No wonder prospects are so readily converted into customers.

All — and I mean all — people are fascinating. I hope you know that already. If you do, it's going to be a lot simpler to be interested in them. Your interest will be rewarded by their continuing patronage of your business. Deep down, I'm hoping that you already have an honest interest in people.

14

Nonmedia Marketing

Some of the most crucial marketing you do will require no media whatso-ever. Yet each of the upcoming nonmedia methods is capable of making significant contributions to your profits.

Don't underestimate the potency of these weapons simply because they don't require a financial investment on your part. They do require the guerrilla investments of time, energy, imagination, and information. But you can leave your wallet at home.

Treat these nonmedia with the same care and respect you'd lavish on any maxi- or minimedia. There is no question that these are media, too — only not the kind of media that nonguerrillas focus on, often to the exclusion of these highly effective nonmedia. Chances are, your company will be known for some of these nonmedia tactics far more than for your forays into the paid media. My advice: Focus on these guerrilla media, and don't be misled by their lack of cost. Concern yourself instead with the lack of profits you'd suffer if you overlooked these puppies.

Service

Whatever you think or thought service was, let me give you a new definition — a definition for guerrillas, a definition for a time when small businesses need all the help they can get and every possible competitive advantage. *Service is anything the customer wants it to be.* Service is not what it says in your service manual, not what you've rendered in the past, and not what customers dread it will be. Instead, it's what they pray it will be. If you can live up to this definition of service, you'll be practicing one of the most powerful marketing tactics in history — and also one of the very newest.

At first, businesses strived to deliver customer satisfaction. Then they realized that they should provide customer delight. Guerrillas have long known that it is customer bliss for which they should aim. The only way to achieve that blessed state is by doing anything that the customer wants you to do. Rest assured, hardly any request will be unreasonable and insane. The vast majority of customers will be sensible, intelligent, and willing to refer your business to the skies. The best referrals always come from the most satisfied customers.

The fact that there are a lot of new books about customer service attests to the reality that customer service is a crucial part of marketing and of business. Whatever business you think you're in, you're also in the marketing business, because what you offer must be marketed, and in the service business, because what you sell must be serviced. So you're in the service business no matter what it says on your business card.

One of the keys to rendering superlative service is to be able to listen to what your customers say. Listen to their words and listen to what's between the lines, those unsaid things they want but don't dare say. By responding to their dreams and desires without making a big deal of it, you'll earn their gratitude as well as their loyalty. This means that you might have to provide services you've never provided before. So what? If it earns the gratitude of customers who will laud your business to the skies, it's worth the effort.

Of the five most important reasons that people patronize businesses, service ranks third, just behind confidence and quality, just ahead of selection and price. There may be fifty reasons why people patronize a business, so you can't afford to overlook the third most important. Okay, time for a test: Q: What's the definition of service? A: Whatever the customer wants it to be.

Public Relations

Public relations means exactly what it says. It's also accurate to say that it means publicity — free stories and news about you and/or your company in newspapers, magazines, newsletters, on radio and TV, and in any other type of media. It means *any* relationships you have with *anybody*. In fact, the purest form of public relations is *human* relations.

Here's what is good about publicity: It is free. It is very believable. It gives you and your company a lot of credibility and stature. It helps establish the identity of your business. It gives you authority. It is read by a large number of people. It is remembered.

Many entrepreneurs feel that there is no such thing as bad publicity; that as long as you get your name out there before the public, that's a fine thing. But most guerrillas know that bad publicity leads to negative word-of-mouth marketing, known to spread faster than wildfire. Bad publicity is bad. Good publicity is great.

Some bad things about publicity: You have no control over it. You have no say-so as to when it runs. You have no control over how it is presented. It is rarely repeated. You cannot buy it. On balance, however, publicity is an excellent weapon in any well-stocked marketing arsenal. And any marketing plan that fails to include some effort at public relations is a marketing plan that isn't going all out.

Public relations offers, as an unstated but ultravaluable benefit, decades of staying power. Reprints of positive publicity can be framed, made parts of brochures, included in ads, put onto flipcharts, and leaned on for precious credibility. The day the story appears is a heartwarming one, but the years afterward are when the marketing power abounds. The single most important factor in obtaining free publicity is to provide news worth publicizing. The news media need news, and if you have the news, you are exactly what the media are looking for. My book *Guerrilla Publicity*, coauthored with Rick Frishman and Jill Lublin, can fill you in on a lot of important details about PR. In it, you'll learn that you've got to knock yourself out to get the "free" publicity that helps so many companies. Instead of paying for the publicity with money, you pay with work: phone calls, writing, time, determination, and endless follow-up. But that effort will be worth your time. People who expend it say that PR really stands for profit. When the circus comes to town and you put up a sign, that's advertising. If you put that sign on the back of the elephant and march the elephant through town, that's sales promotion. If the elephant, with the sign still on its back, tramples through the mayor's flower garden and the paper reports it, that's publicity. If you can get the mayor to laugh about it and forgive the elephant and then ride in the circus with no hard feelings, you've become a master of guerrilla PR. Without publicity, a terrible thing happens: nothing.

But nothing is rarely what happens if you enlist the aid of a PR pro. It's one thing to send a press kit, complete with black-and-white glossy photo, press release, and fact sheet, to the media. It's something totally different if you call your friend, Diane, at the local newspaper. You say, "Diane, I have something that I know will interest your readers. I'd like to take you to lunch and tell you about it." Diane, being a human being who likes free things, goes to lunch with you, hears your news, and then accepts your press kit. Two days later, your story appears in her newspaper.

That's why PR pros charge so much for their services. They have a Rolodex that's bulging with the names of publicity contacts. One of your tasks as a guerrilla is to get the same kind of Rolodex. The more publicity contacts you have, the more free publicity you'll generate. It's that simple. I can't overstate the importance of your cultivating media relationships — the real secret of successful publicity campaigns.

Media relationships should be mutually beneficial. You want the media to publicize your product and service, and the media want you to provide publishable stories. Always keep in mind these four rules.

1. You are a resource for the media.
2. It's never personal.
3. The media can change the rules, but you can't.
4. All that a trout thinks about is food, and all that the media think about is what you can do for them and their audience.

Attend networking functions at which you can meet members of the media. Join the local press club. Hang out at the bars, coffeeshops, and restaurants where they hang out. Become a media resource to them. Ask what they're working on. Get their contact info so it's easy to get in touch with them.

Once you've established a media contact, stay in touch with that person. E-mail seems to be the preferred method of contact these days. Play by the media rules. They have the upper hand. They have the power. It's very important that you stay on their radar screen.

Being on a first-name basis with members of the media ranks in importance with having significant news for them to publish. Nearly 80 percent of press kits are tossed away before being read. But knowing the person to whom you send the kit will keep yours away from the dreaded wastebasket.

A final word before we leave PR behind: *buzz*. Marketing communications — in particular, advertising — is both expensive and exposed to a marketplace that is increasingly weighted down with clutter. Too many messages are being broadcast too often, with diminishing impact on the consumer. This situation grows even more acute in the case of the Gen X and Y segments. These groups are still highly susceptible to brand influence but show signs of being more cynical in their response to the marketing message and are eager to acquire brand news and information from less traditional sources.

That's why buzz marketing is one of the industry's newest buzzwords and buzzphrases. It's a combination of a number of influences, including good old word of mouth, viral marketing, and the current fixation on early trend setting and spotting. Buzz marketing works because it is both interruptive and yet subversive. It's marketing's Trojan horse, and its growing acceptance is evidenced by the fact that some of the world's most authoritative marketers have now entered the field. As online marketing newsletter *ICONOCAST* notes, "To get clients to spend on fringe ideas, agencies are creating buzz marketing units. An example is MindShare's WOW Factory, which is characterized as a group of people dedicated to surprise."

Buzz marketing and its earlier incarnation, word of mouth, have been around for some time. Record companies and fashion-related brands are notorious for some of their stunts. In the case of the liquor industry, it was not uncommon to have paid agents provocateur visit trendy bars, order the brand of choice, and strike up conversations with both barkeeps and customers in order to establish cool buzz for the brand. And in many cases, it worked. Formerly unknown brands acquired hip acceptance and generated volume growth without an outrageously expensive advertising or marketing budget.

The process continues even today. Abercrombie & Fitch, the national chain that retails primarily to the college crowd, creates and lives by what *Potentials* magazine terms fake controversies "in which the company creates a storm of controversy around the brand name, apologizes (or not) for any offense then sits back and watches as curious shoppers react."

In its introductory campaign for a T68i cellphone, Sony Ericcson hired 120 actors and actresses to play tourists at popular attractions around the country, such as New York's Empire State Building. These paid performers asked passersby to take their picture with the company's T68i cellphone, which offers an add-on digital camera. And what the unknowing consumer gets is a marketing message not from a corporate pitchman but from a much more powerful endorser: a cool, attractive, enthusiastic stranger. And so the viral marketing process begins. When it touches a topic or product of compelling interest, buzz can be an extremely effective way to spread the news without incurring much expense.

How did Hotmail gain more than 12 million subscribers in eighteen months? How did the very low budget movie *The Blair Witch Project* become such an incredibly successful phenomenon? The answer lies in the power of buzz. Buzz, or word-of-mouth, marketing influences more people to buy, or not to buy products and services, than most other forms of marketing. We tend to listen to buzz more readily than to most mass-media messages.

- Brainstorm all possible groups of people who might be interested in your products/services. Consider including the media, opinion leaders, influencers, lead users, politicians, and analysts. Don't forget chat rooms and newsgroups, although buzz still spreads primarily by personal interaction.
- Research how information spreads among your customers. Ask them how they usually learn about new products/services. Who are their major information sources? Whose information do they value? You're looking primarily for groups of people rather than individuals. However, don't discount individuals, as they may well be powerful opinion leaders.
- Develop a clear and concise message highlighting the product/service benefits you want to filter through these different groups. Zero in on your product's uniqueness and what it can do, for example, to help save time and money — two basic elements most people seek.
- Think about ways to tap into these groups to spread the word about your products or services.
- Offer prospects easy ways to try your product/service. For example, the makers of Pictionary gave demos in parks, shopping centers, and other gathering places.
- Come up with other creative ideas to enhance trade show demonstrations. What can you give people to take away to remind them of your company, products, and positive show experience? Think about something that will help create the buzz. It'll have to be more creative than a keychain or stress ball. The more product related, the better. You want people to remember and talk about you — positively!
- Try to identify special groups you might offer a product discount, a loaner, or even a freebie. You're looking for groups and individuals whose direct product experience will help spread the word. For example, when FedEx started out, it offered free shipping to show people how its program worked. America Online continuously finds ways to offer hundreds of free hours of trial usage to entice new users.
- Use press conferences for major announcements and new-product introductions, but do so only if they are truly new or improved or general industry trends — what's hot and what's not.
- Use sneak previews at trade shows to build anticipation and help create a buzz on the show floor. Give people a fun experience and a behind-the-scenes view of what's coming. TV and the movies have got this down to a fine art with their coming attractions.

The power of buzz far exceeds many conventional marketing vehicles. It is probably the oldest, most well-used, and valuable one out there. See how you might make it an integral part of your existing marketing plan.

Trade Shows

Some wildly successful entrepreneurs use one major method of marketing: They display and sell their wares at trade shows, exhibits, and fairs. These people realize that many serious prospects will attend these gatherings and therefore put all their efforts into exhibiting and selling their merchandise (they usually sell products rather than services). This is not to say that their show booths are their only marketing vehicles. But they are their primary ones. And in a few instances, this is the only way a person needs to market. I don't like telling this to you for fear it might encourage a lax attitude, but it is the truth.

The marketing plan of many a guerrilla consists of appearances at four major shows or fairs, plus circulars or brochures to be distributed at the shows. Nothing else. Nothing else is needed.

I once attended a large national furniture show with a client who owned a chain of furniture stores. He very much wanted to be one of the first people through the doors at the three-day event. When I asked him why, he told me that he would first breeze through the show, making notes and looking at all the exhibits. Then he would quickly return to the displays that had caught his attention and order a full year's worth of items, making certain to get agreements that he would be the exclusive outlet for each item.

Sure enough, it took him, with me hot on his heels, a mere thirty minutes to walk the miles of aisles. Then he spent the next two hours dickering with the manufacturers or distributors that tickled his fancy. At the end of two and a half hours, he was delighted, having signed up for a year's worth of purchases, all with exclusive arrangements. And just as happy — maybe even happier — were the entrepreneurs who had attracted his attention with their merchandise, displays, salesmanship, and readiness to grant concessions. I well recall the look on one man's face when he realized that in only ten minutes, he had sold half a million dollars' worth of goods. Fifty thou per minute is a luscious sales rate.

I suggest that you browse through a copy of *Tradeshow and Convention Guide* at your library, or order a copy from Budd Publications, P.O. Box 7, New York, NY 10004, to learn of a multitude of shows at which you can display your offerings. The shows are worth your time. If you opt for this method of marketing, I not only suggest but urge you to read *Guerrilla Trade Show Selling: New Unconventional Weapons and Tactics to Meet More People, Get More Leads, and Close More Sales,* by yours truly, Mark S. A. Smith, and Orvel Ray Wilson.

There are a couple of ways to display what you sell at trade shows. One way, the standard way, is to rent a booth for several hundred or several thousand dollars, set up a display, and give it your best. Another way, the guerrilla way — and a fine method of testing the efficacy of trade shows as a nonmedia marketing medium for you — is to visit a show, find a display booth that offers merchandise compatible with yours, and strike up a deal with the exhibitor whereby you share a portion of the next booth the exhibitor rents. That means you pay part of the rental fee, assume part of the sales responsibility, and allow your items to be displayed and sold along with those of your new compatriot.

When you visit one or two shows, you will learn of products that compete with or complement yours. You'll also discover products that knock your socks off — products with which you would love to become associated and possibly could, as a fusion-marketing partner. You'll learn the right way to display goods and the wrong way. You'll pick up some dandy ideas for brochures, signs, and demonstrations. You'll learn a heck of a lot from the mistakes of others — people who have great merchandise but don't know how to market it. And you'll meet people who may be able to help you distribute what you sell.

Let's look at a case in point. A man-and-wife team who marketed greeting cards all by themselves by calling on stationery stores were soon alerted to the existence of stationery shows at which greeting cards are displayed. There, they were told, they could display their own cards and make sales, team up with other card manufacturers, and better yet, meet distributors who could distribute their cards throughout the country. The two budding entrepreneurs went to the show, looked at others' cards and displays, and met several representatives who offered to distribute their cards. Because they were greenhorns at the business, they were delighted and signed on with several of the reps.

Their business grew in the next year. But in talking with a few fellow card sellers, they learned that there are basically two kinds of reps one meets at shows: ordinary reps and Rolls-Royce reps. Ordinary reps conduct an ordinary amount of sales activity and achieve ordinary distribution in ordinary stores. These, alas, were the kinds of reps the man and wife had signed up. Rolls-Royce reps, however, can move prodigious numbers of greeting cards by distributing only in high-volume stores and expending a great deal of selling energy.

The following year, the man and wife went to the stationery shows and signed up with only Rolls-Royce reps. By doing so, the couple increased their sales fivefold over the year before, propelling themselves into a deliriously wonderful tax bracket. If you are looking for national distribution of your goods, do look for Rolls-Royce reps at major trade shows.

While displaying your products in your own booth — something you'll most likely want to do when you begin to take large orders — you can engage in four other types of marketing at the same time.

1. *Hand out circulars.* I suggest that you hire someone, preferably a gorgeous woman (or a gorgeous man, if women are your prime prospects), to distribute your circulars while walking through the show. The cost to hire the person will be about $75, and for that, she or he will pass out as many as 5,000 circulars — all inviting people to visit your booth. If you do that, you will instantly rise above most of the other exhibitors, since they will not be practicing such a guerrilla-like tactic. You'll also attract more prospects.

2. *Give away brochures.* Because brochures are more costly than circulars, you won't want to give as many away. But by disseminating them only at your booth, you'll be able to narrow the distribution down to serious prospects only. And your brochures will do heavy-duty work for you. Many people attend shows and exhibits merely to collect brochures. Then they study the brochures and place their orders on the basis of the information.

3. *Demonstrate your goods* to real prospects who are in a buying mood. You can demonstrate your offerings to large groups of people. And since your competitors too will probably be at the show, you'll have a good opportunity to prove the advantages of your product.

4. *Offer free samples.* Rarely will you be afforded the chance to give samples to so many potential customers. If it's possible to let people sample your merchandise, a show or an exhibit is the place to do it.

Entrepreneurs avail themselves of the opportunities at shows with 100 percent effort — they concentrate their marketing energies and dollars on shows. Of all sources of purchasing information that businesspeople rate "extremely useful," trade shows are at the top of the list, mentioned by 91 percent of respondents. Also, trade shows aid and abet your other marketing efforts. A typical direct-mail campaign nets about 13 percent readership and a 2 percent response rate, which is considered good by nonguerillas. That same direct-mail campaign, if based on contacts made at a trade show, generates 45 percent readership and a 20 percent response rate, which is considered quite acceptable by guerrillas.

Why do guerrillas exhibit at trade shows? Our *Guerrilla Trade Show Selling* book lists fifteen reasons:

1. To sell what you offer to visitors
2. To sell what you offer to other exhibitors
3. To get leads for your sales force to follow up
4. To network and troubleshoot with other professionals
5. To establish your industry positioning
6. To meet with existing customers
7. To visit with people whom you otherwise wouldn't see
8. To introduce new products to the market
9. To do market research
10. To find new dealers, representatives, and distributors
11. To find new employees
12. To conduct business meetings
13. To scope out the competition
14. To get smart
15. To gain media exposure

Here are ten more reasons:

16. To generate thousands of qualified leads
17. To build rapport with customers and prospects
18. To increase your name awareness
19. To penetrate new markets in a brief time
20. To present your business in a new perspective
21. To increase contact with your suppliers
22. To find names for your mailing list
23. To make friends
24. To immerse yourself in your own industry
25. To separate yourself from the competition

Guerrillas are well aware that a trade show begins long before the doors open. Guerrillas begin trade show promotion by identifying and contacting their key prospects and then inviting them, along with good customers, to their show booth. Guerrillas send both the invitations supplied by the show organizers and personalized invitations. Guerrillas are acutely aware of the power of personalization.

They promote their attendance at trade shows with ads in trade magazines, faxes, e-mail, personal letters, and telephone calls. Because they're guerrillas, they learn of the hotels at which attendees are staying and then place fliers and invitations under the hotel room doors.

A major guerrilla secret to successful trade shows is follow-up. As interactive as trade shows are, the most crucial interactivity often takes place after the show — follow-up leads to success.

Today, 75 percent of the people who attend trade shows know exactly what they want to see, whom they want to see, and how much time they'll spend at the exhibit. I hate to tell you this, but 90 percent of the literature they collect at the shows gets tossed before the attendee goes home. And more gets tossed at home. That's why many guerrillas send their literature *after* the show.

Pay close attention to this next guerrilla secret. It frequently means the difference between astonishing success and depressing failure. Let me make it obvious right here and now: Your main purpose in having a booth at a trade show, fair, or exhibit is *to sell your product.*

Yes, it is important to display, to demonstrate, to educate, to get names for your mailing list. But you really want to *sell.* You need to take orders right there at your booth. You must have a person there who is dedicated to selling. You should aim for a large volume of sales at the show itself, in spite of the brochures you will distribute. Don't forget the furniture store entrepreneur I wrote about earlier: He visited the shows to look and then to buy. He didn't care about brochures. He wanted to place his orders at the show.

If you don't sell a lot of what you want to sell at a show, you may have failed in this marketing effort. If you have not sold a large volume, you have not taken advantage of the glorious opportunity afforded you by such shows. I recall two competitors at a national show. Both had attractive displays, both gave imaginative demonstrations, and both handed out compelling brochures. But the first company assumed that the show was a place to display — and it made no sales. The second company, a small, young partnership, figured that the show was a place to sell — so it made $4.5 million in sales in a three-day period. I've made my point.

Fusion Marketing

Back in prehistoric times, one caveman probably grunted to another, "Hey, Uru, I'll scratch your back if you scratch mine." Since that time, fusion arrangements have grown and grown until they now have several phrases to describe them: tie-ins, collaborative marketing, comarketing, partnering, and a lot more.

You see a TV spot for what you think is Coke. Later, you think it's for McDonald's. And at the end, you realize that all along it was for the latest Disney movie. The point is that there's a lot of fusion marketing going on, and most of it is among small businesses. Fusion marketing allows you to spread your marketing word while sharing the costs.

"Hey, I'll put up a sign for you in my place if you put up a sign for me." "I'll add a link to your Web site if you add a link to mine." "I'll enclose your circular in my next mailing if you enclose my circular in yours." "I'll refer my customers to you if you refer your customers to me."

This time-honored way of doing commerce without spending money is common, very effective, and extremely simple to set up. All you've got to do is ask. Most business owners will go along with the idea because it makes so much sense.

Understand that you're not going into a real legal partnership with someone, so don't think marriage. Instead, think fling. If it's fun, you'll do it again. If not, well, nobody was hurt. Many astute small-business owners have twenty or more fusion-marketing partners. Japan seems to lead the world in this regard, with huge corporations fusing with tiny one-person businesses — and everybody gains.

In many communities, lawyers, insurance agents, and CPAs have formed "leads clubs." At the end of each month, they simply trade leads, since they each have the same kinds of prospects. When you're setting up a fusion-marketing arrangement, look for businesses that have the same prospects as you and the same standards as you. Many businesses can fulfill those requirements. Your job as a guerrilla is to locate them and then suggest the tie-in. This is one of the most profitable of all tactics to help you market aggressively. Do it!

Community Involvement

As all guerrillas and even nonguerrillas know, people would much rather do business with friends than with strangers. When you become involved with the community, you separate yourself from the ranks of strangers. But becoming involved in the community isn't simply signing up to serve on a committee and then staying an arm's length from that committee.

Becoming involved means working your tail off for your community, proving with deeds what you could never prove with mere words. When people in your community see how hard you work and how conscientious you are, they'll know that you're doing it on an unpaid basis, and they'll assume that you work even harder on a paid basis, so they'll be attracted to your business.

When you serve your community, you're doing noble and necessary work along with incidentally marketing your business. Of course, you should not really act as though you're marketing. That part will take care of itself simply because of your good works.

Being involved with your community puts you into a splendid position to network. It helps you tune in to the community's problems, some of which you may be able to solve. It does take your time, even your energy, but it costs nary a cent. For some people, it's all the marketing they need.

Community involvement takes many forms. Perhaps you can develop a promotion involving a local school. You might establish tie-ins with local stores. You can offer your product or service to a local charity as part of its fund-raising effort. You might donate your offering to a local park or public place. Perhaps you can support the local media. A client of mine made lots of new contacts by sponsoring a 10K race. Others have had essay contests or painting competitions. There are abundant opportunities to get your name known while performing a good deed.

There is no question that your community needs you. It needs your hard work and your time. It needs your participation. Many people work for their community strictly for altruistic reasons. I hope your reasons are altruistic, but it's also cool if they're capitalistic. Become involved with your community, and it will become involved with you.

Memberships in Clubs

You join clubs and associations for similar reasons that you become involved with the community. It helps you prove your dedication to quality and service through your actions rather than your words. It puts you on a first-name basis with important movers and shakers. It gives you access to inside industry information.

Again, you might want to join these clubs even if they don't help you add muscle to your marketing. But the truth is that they do. They help to make you a known quantity rather than another face in the crowd. They might not be able to drum up many new customers, but those that they do attract might be very important customers. And they are the basis for a lot of referral business.

Many guerrillas secure all the business they need simply by joining social clubs, country clubs, civic clubs, service clubs, professional clubs, health clubs, trade associations, and the many other organizations that exist to serve our herd instinct. But if you join a club strictly to get business, that's a crass thing to do, and club members will be quick to sense the shallowness of your motives.

As you can turn people on by your joining, you can also turn them off. The intelligence level of people must never be underestimated. In the past, that level was thought to be on par with that of a twelve-year-old. Today, it's widely believed that it's on par with the intelligence level of your mother. And you know she's no dummy. She knows the phony from the real.

Joining a club allows you to meet a lot of prospects, referrers, suppliers, and fellow guerrillas, not to mention members of the local media. You can learn which customers are unhappy, get a line on your reputation, learn of industry advancements, and gain access to the grapevines of others. You can become close friends with some of the members. The old adage reminds us that there are three things that money can't buy: love, friends, and home-grown tomatoes.

Above all, you can make a contribution to your industry. That's a lot of good things that you can accomplish by becoming a joiner. And all along, you get to keep your wallet in your pocket or purse. More deals are closed on golf courses, card rooms, and club rooms than you might imagine. Maybe that's sad, but it's undeniably true.

Follow-Up

Why do most businesses lose customers? Poor service? Nope. Poor quality? Nope. Well, then, why? *Apathy after the sale.* Most businesses lose customers by ignoring them to death. Apathy after the sale causes a numbing 68 percent of all business lost in America.

Misguided business owners think that marketing is over once they've made the sale. *Wrong.* Marketing begins once you've made the sale. It's of momentous importance to you and your company that you understand this.

First of all, understand how guerrillas view follow-up. They make it part of their DNA because they know that it now costs six times more to sell something to a new customer than to an existing customer. When a guerrilla makes a sale, the customer receives a follow-up thank-you note within forty-eight hours. The guerrilla sends another note or perhaps makes a phone call thirty days after the sale. This contact is to see whether everything is going all right with the purchase and whether the customer has any questions. It is also to help solidify the relationship. Guerrillas know that the way to develop relationships is through assiduous customer follow-up and prospect follow-up. Guerrillas send their customers another note within ninety days, this time informing them of a new and related product or service. Possibly it's a new offering that the guerrilla business now provides. And maybe it's a product or service offered by one of the guerrilla's fusion-marketing partners.

Guerrillas are very big on forging marketing alliances. These tie-ins enable them to increase their marketing exposure while reducing their marketing costs, a noble goal. After six months, the customer hears from the guerrilla again, this time with the preview announcement of an upcoming sale. Nine months after the sale, the guerrilla sends a note asking the customer for the names of three people who might benefit from being included on the guerrilla's mailing list. Because the guerrilla has been keeping in touch with the customer — and because only three names are requested — the customer often supplies the names. After one year, the customer receives an anniversary card celebrating the one-year anniversary of the first sale.

Perhaps a coupon for a discount is in the envelope. The customer becomes a repeat buyer and refers others to the guerrilla's business. A bond is formed. The bond intensifies with time and follow-up. This same follow-up should be used with prospects. Follow-up will transform them into customers.

Follow up or fail. It's your choice.

Word of Mouth

Very frequently, you'll send five e-mails, post five signs, have a killer Web site, run a quarter-page magazine ad in a local magazine, then have a PR story placed in a local paper. People will see this marketing, then decide to patronize your business. You'll ask them, "Where did you first hear of us?" The answer you'll often get: "A friend recommended you."

One real truth is that people dislike admitting that they're affected by marketing, so they'll usually give the credit to a friend. Another real truth is that people do check with friends before patronizing a business, so it's in your best interest to work like crazy developing word-of-mouth referrals.

If you do everything right 24 hours a day, 365 days a year, you'll get a lot of powerful word-of-mouth marketing. But guerrillas know a few ways to speed up that process.

The first way is to prepare a simple document that you give only to first-time buyers. When a person buys anything from you, there's a phenomenon known as the "moment of maximum satisfaction" — the MMS. It lasts from the moment of the sale to thirty days after that. During that time, people are most likely to talk about your company, partly, because of their enthusiasm. Partly, it helps to justify their purchase in their minds. So if you hand them a brief document summarizing the best benefits you offer, you'll be putting the right words in the right mouths at the right time. No wonder you'll get a large number of word-of-mouth customers.

Another tactic is to ask yourself, "Who else do my prospects patronize?" A local restaurant asked that and came up with the answer: beauty salons. So the restaurant offered two free dinners to all the salon owners within a two-mile radius. This was not one of those "Buy one; get one free" deals or "You must dine between 5:15 and 5:35 on a Wednesday evening." This was two free meals, everything included. The salon owners sampled the fare at the restaurant, loved it, and talked it up in their salons — properly identified as the nerve center of the community.

It didn't take long for the reservations book to be bursting at the binding and for long lines to appear at the restaurant. The cost for this breakthrough marketing: two free meals. Hardly a major cost. But the results were so gratifying that I hope you'll ask the same question, do a favor for the people your prospects patronize, then sit back and marvel at the cost-effectiveness of this brilliant but little-known tactic.

Another new restaurant found a unique and imaginative way to generate quick word of mouth. The proprietor invited a dozen close friends to have dinner at the restaurant at no cost. All he asked the diners to do was to line up outside the door of the restaurant the next evening. Of course, they complied, and of course, motorists driving by the restaurant, seeing the crowd and the commotion, felt that they might be missing out on a good thing. Before too long, the restaurant was crowded and has stayed crowded because of the unspoken word of mouth communicated by all those people outside the door.

Contests

The main reason to have contests and sweepstakes is to get names for your mailing list. Now that you're clear on that, also keep in mind that a Web site is one of the best places ever to announce your contests. Just tell visitors that to enter, all they've got to do is provide their e-mail address.

If you have a retail establishment, put the entry box for your contest in the rear of your store. That way, entrants can see what else you offer, read your signs, and become more familiar with you and your employees. Familiarity leads to profitability, so you must do all you can to make people familiar with your business.

Should you award a prize to the winner of your contest or sweepstakes? The answer is a resounding no. Instead, award ten prizes to ten winners. You'll discover that many businesses will be delighted to furnish free prizes to you in exchange for your mentioning their name in your store, on your site, or in your other marketing.

When you see a local business offer a free trip to Las Vegas as a prize, you can bet — no pun intended — that a local travel agency provided it in return for the visibility someone provided to the agency. Sounds fair to me.

In addition to attracting names for your mailing list, contests and sweepstakes also attract media attention. That's one more reason that they're gaining popularity so rapidly. Once you've awarded your prizes, let the media know who won. After all, the media are interested in news, and your contest and its winners are news — especially locally.

Now that we both know how seriously you are taking the marketing process, we both know that you should contact all entrants to your contest within thirty days, while your name is fresh in their minds and their names are fresh on your mailing list.

Be certain to comply with local and national regulations on contests. You don't want to be the jail prisoner with the longest mailing list. As you already know, people would much rather make purchases from friends than from strangers. Once they enter your contest, winner or not, you'll no longer be a stranger to them.

Competitive Advantages

Many other businesses like yours offer a whale of a lot of benefits. Prospects will study them as they study your business to determine how these benefits can have a positive impact on their lives. But they'll probably end up buying from the business that offers what you don't have. Meaning: You've got to offer what they don't. You've got to not only offer but also feature benefits not available from your competition.

There were loads of delis where we lived. They all supplied about the same quality and selection, and they charged about the same prices. But we patronized only one of those delis. We did it because they delivered within an hour of our placing the order. That's a tough promise to live up to, but because they did it, we gave them all our Sunday deli business. That competitive advantage was enough for us. Some of the delis have learned that now they must also deliver within an hour of the placement of the order. But it's too late. Our business and our loyalty remained with the first that offered this benefit, though that business and loyalty are moot points now that we're in an RV a zillion miles from the deli.

There were tons of hairdressers around as well. But my wife patronized the one who came to our home to do her hair. That's a powerful competitive advantage — so powerful that even though her prices were a mite higher than those of her competitors, my wife was willing to pay more for the convenience she offered.

You should center your marketing on your competitive advantage. If you don't have one, you should create one. Invent it, then live up to it. All other things being equal, the business with the most competitive advantages will win out every time. It does not cost a lot to offer such an advantage. Time, energy, imagination, and knowledge will be your primary investments.

The richer your imagination, the easier it will be to come up with competitive advantages. Exercising your imagination in this way will be one of the most cost-effective uses of that imagination. Just take a few moments to examine your business through the eyes of your customers, and you'll soon see benefits that you can offer, benefits not offered by those who compete with you. I hope you have a long list of them, but the truth is that you don't need many. You need only one good one.

Elevator Speech

An elevator speech is created by a guerrilla just in case he or she happens to get in an elevator with his or her most promising prospect and have only that limited time to make the pitch. Today, with time and attention so difficult to come by, it's very important for you to create an elevator speech for yourself. After creating it, memorize and rehearse it to the point that it is coming direct from your heart.

The elements of a good elevator pitch are straightforward. It describes how you offer value, benefit, and quality. An elevator pitch takes no longer than ten seconds; it comes out so naturally that you can say it in your sleep. The real truth is that you are your elevator speech.

While you're delivering your brilliantly conceived pitch, here's what the person listening to you is most likely thinking: So what? Guerrillas don't let that happen to them. Talk about yourself and you'll bore the listener. Encourage the listener to speak, and you're a brilliant conversationalist.

If you think that your elevator speech will be given only in elevators, you're only partly right — because that's the time span and setting for many an elevator pitch. You'll also use it while introducing yourself to people, on the phone, leaving a voicemail message, on your outgoing voicemail message, on your business card, on your Web site, on your resume, on your bio, in your e-mail signature, in your marketing materials. It will become one of your hallmarks at networking functions.

You may be doing the most exciting work on Earth, making breakthroughs that will be featured on the cover of *Time* magazine. Still, people don't care. They care about themselves. So relate most of what you say directly to them, to their lives, to their business, to their family — to anything concerning them. It's their favorite topic.

Developing and polishing your elevator speech may be one of the most important tactics you use. It may end up being the key to your fame and fortune. But still, people aren't eager to hear it. It's not something they look forward to when they awaken in the morning. Still, you've got to have one, and the better it's honed, the more you'll appreciate the time and effort you put into creating it.

The opposite of having a well-tuned elevator pitch is not having one at all. Nonetheless, most small-business owners don't have one, haven't given it a thought, and blow many opportunities when an elevator pitch may have saved the day. Don't get me started on the foolishness of their oversight.

Guarantee

A guarantee is your way of removing any feeling of risk on the part of your prospect. How big, specific, and outrageous a guarantee can you think of? What would set your industry on its ear? What would keep your competitors up all night worrying about you? That's the kind of guarantee you want to create.

Kevin Michael Donlin, author of *Guaranteed Sales Résumés*, provides us with example guarantees to help get your creative juices flowing. See if you can find one that applies to you and your business.

Industry	Guarantee
Real estate	I'll sell your home. Or give you $1,000 cash.
Restaurant	You'll love our food. Or the next meal is free.
Sports therapist	We'll stop your pain. Or we'll visit your home and provide a free follow-up session.
Dog-walking service	We'll be there on time, every time. Or you get a $50 bag of dog food free.
Florist	Free box of chocolates if our flowers ever disappoint you.
Computer repair	We'll fix it right. Or repair it free and give you $100 cash.
Retail store	Double your money back if you find it cheaper elsewhere.

A bakery can offer money back — and a dozen cupcakes. A computer repair shop can offer money back and provide a free shareware program. A book publisher can offer money back and let readers keep a special gift just for their trouble. A courier service can refund the purchase price if it fails to deliver on time, as FedEx does. Or you can offer customers their money back — plus $5, $10, or $50 for their trouble.

A company that works fast can guarantee delivery times — by 10:00 A.M., within twenty-four hours, whatever. Do you have the widest selection in town? Guarantee it by daring customers and competitors to find more products somewhere else. Just be sure that you can back this up. Do not simply guarantee "satisfaction." That's lazy. Instead, guarantee in detail what that satisfaction will look like to your customer.

And remember: The longer the guarantee, the better. If it's a lifetime guarantee, people figure that there's no rush, but it will attract a lot of business. And hardly anyone will ever take you up on it. Just ask L. L. Bean, the legendary clothing company with the lifetime guarantees.

Branded Entertainment

This is one of the marketing vehicles that wasn't happening — except in soap operas — when I wrote the first and even the second and third editions of *Guerrilla Marketing*. But it's something we're seeing more and more as we watch the tube.

Branded entertainment is the combination of an audiovisual program (TV, radio, podcast, videocast) and a brand. It can be initiated by either the brand or the broadcaster. The purpose of a branded entertainment program is first to entertain. The other purpose is to give the opportunity for brands to echo their commercial benefits.

Branded entertainment started some fifty years ago under the name of soap operas. Now it's become a way for advertisers to let their messages come across in a "not so commercial" way. This development is one of the consequences of the fragmentation of media and the fact that the good-old thirty-second TV spot has become less and less effective to reach consumers fragmented over hundreds of channels and the Internet.

This much-publicized union of Hollywood glamour and deep-pocketed consumer brands is the talk of the town. But as high-profile brands line up to invest an estimated $2 billion in film and TV cross-promotions this year, one question remains for both sides: What is branded entertainment worth? More specifically, how do advertisers — who routinely risk tens of millions of dollars on a single promotion — measure their return on investment? And how do studios value placement in a film or TV show?

"I think it's one of the key questions," says former Walt Disney Co. TV executive Rich Frank, cofounder and managing partner of Integrated Entertainment Partners, a high-profile newcomer that independently matches consumer brands and entertainment properties. "It's a question that will evolve over the next few years because there is no right or wrong answer to it."

The advertising industry has long settled on CPM (cost per thousand) as the unit for valuing media buys — be they magazine ads, TV commercials, or banner ads. But branded entertainment has no such standard — yet. Amid rising costs of TV advertising and a steady erosion of its impact and value, advertisers are seeking alternatives that are accountable to real-dollar metrics. "Today, brands need to know exactly what they're getting in return for their spending, especially when the economy is not strong and budgets are tight."

Jeep and Toyota paid more than $10 million each to cast the Rubicon and the Tundra as "hero cars" in, respectively, Paramount's *Lara Croft Tomb Raider: The Cradle of Life* and Warner Bros. Pictures' *Terminator 3: Rise of the Machines*. Mitsubishi spent $25 million to showcase its cars in Universal's *2 Fast 2 Furious*. All three films were major summer releases. Were those good deals for both sides?

Awareness is key in valuing branded entertainment. Even if a studio sees a film as a box office dud, an integrated sponsor might think otherwise if it is receiving the level of exposure on which it was counting. Attention is the most sought-after commodity today. You're marketing these products and services with one goal in mind: You want to hear "cha-ching" at the end of the line. So any time you can get attention, it's very valuable.

Some promotions are easier than others to evaluate. The second season of Fox's *American Idol,* for example, boasted three major sponsors: Ford, Coca-Cola, and AT&T Wireless. Coke sponsored a branded Red Room and had the show's judges sipping from Coca-Cola glasses; Ford sponsored "entertainment" segments, during which the show's finalists drove a Focus. Both companies enjoyed fantastic brand exposure at a low CPM because *Idol*'s ratings were double what Fox originally expected.

But AT&T Wireless enjoyed those perks as well as numbers that made a lot of sense: The *Idol* finale was the biggest text-messaging event to date — rounding out a season during which 7.5 million were sent — and each message registered a quantifiable "cha-ching" in the company's coffers.

Hundreds of thousands of AT&T subscribers used text-messaging for the first time during the show — and they're continuing to text-message, which is creating a long-term revenue stream that will more than pay for the sponsorship dollars put against the program. The company's brand exposure alone would have made the sponsorship worthwhile. There is little doubt that the partnerships forged between studios and brands are an important part of breaking through modern-day clutter.

Apple Computer frequently places its products in films and on television, where they therefore seem much more common than in most real-world offices and homes. In a twist on traditional product placement, Hewlett-Packard computers now appear exclusively as part of photo layouts in the IKEA catalog, and plastic models of its computers are put in IKEA stores — having taken over Apple's similar position in the Swedish furniture retailer's promotional materials several years ago. Some people believe that product placement is out of control and has become too pervasive in today's society.

As you can easily see, new options are available to the guerrilla marketer, as new ones still will always be developed. The wise guerrilla is aware of all these options and experiments with many of them. "In the fool's mind, there are many choices; in the wise man's mind, there are few."

PART V

The Nature
of the Guerrilla

15

Guerrilla Company Attributes

You might be a marketing guerrilla through and through, but if your company lacks certain attributes, all your good efforts might go for naught. These attributes don't cost you any money, but without them, you may be losing out on a lot of money you'd otherwise earn.

Many companies have a few of these marketing tactics down pat; other companies are oblivious to all of them. Of course, to get them, you'll require time, energy, imagination, information, and patience. But those investments will pay off in the long run and on your bottom line.

It's pretty easy for me to rattle these off in the pages of a book, but for you to bring them alive is hardly a cinch. These attributes are not difficult to create, implement, or understand, but so many companies operate without them that you'll have several competitive advantages just by bringing them to life in your company.

Name

Guerrillas are careful not to make a major error with their first business decision: the name of their business. From the naming consultancy Lexicon, which is responsible for such names as Pentium, PowerBook, and DeskJet, we learn five guerrilla guidelines to powerful brand naming.

1. *Does your name break the rules?* In a cluttered marketing environment, names that simply fit in with the rest are lost and very easy to ignore. Your name must stand apart from the competition.

2. *Will your name cause your competitors to grimace?* A registered brand name is something that they can never take away from you, so it must be powerful enough to make them wince every time they see it. The better the name, the more they'll want to steal it from you.

3. *Does the name make a promise or tell a story?* Great names are like tiny poems; each letter, word unit, and sound should work with the others to deliver strategic messages. The right name can be the cornerstone of a lasting customer relationship. It is an ultrapowerful marketing weapon.

4. *Does the name describe or suggest a feature or benefit?* Great names suggest the most compelling benefit the prospects will need over the next decade or longer. There is no confusion about what you offer.

5. *Does the name make you feel a bit uncomfortable?* Great names provoke people, attract attention, take chances. They don't simply fit right in.

Few things are more frustrating than having to change the name of your business once it's up and running. So the idea is to start out with the right name in the first place.

Guerrillas realize that there are only two kinds of names: bad names and good names. Bad names are difficult to pronounce, exaggerative, common, suggestive of other companies, and difficult to spell. Almost all the others are good names. Your job: Select none of the bad names and one of the good names.

Don't let your name paint you into a corner. A company specializing in making copies named itself "The Copy Factory." A few years later, when it discovered that its prime source of profits was printing, it had to rename itself "The Print and Copy Factory." A showroom with a wide selection of beds called itself "Santa Rosa Bedding." Sounds good. But because it sold so much furniture that was not related to bedding, the business had to go through the process of changing its name to "Santa Rosa Bedding and Furniture."

Don't let your name prohibit your growth, expansion, or diversification. Tailor the name to how you'll use it. If people will look you up in the yellow pages or a directory, it might be a good idea to start your name with two As. Being first on any list is always a good idea. Let your name be part of your sales pitch rather than meaningless. "LightSpeed Software" tells you more than "Zednia."

Remember that the shorter your name, the larger you can make it in your marketing materials. I hate to be the one to tell you this, but size does matter. Don't dive into marketing your name until you've checked that it's available, legal, and protectable.

Lots of huge companies out there have nondescript names, such as Sherwin Williams, Westinghouse, and Honda. But they invested fortunes in helping people know the companies behind those names. You'll be investing nothing. So you must make your name part of your marketing.

It can work for you or against you. There are many facets to your business and your marketing. The first that your prospects will see is your name. The part of your business that will get the most usage: your name.

Meme

A *meme* is a new word, coined in 1976. It's the simplest possible way to communicate an idea. A caveman named Uba once stood in a chilly stream up to the middle of his thighs, attempting to catch a fish with his bare hands. Not surprisingly, Uba didn't catch one. When he returned to his cave and told his despondent family that there would be no dinner that night, he noticed three rudimentary drawings on the wall of the cave. One was of a thunderbird. Another was of a deerlike figure. The third was a stick figure of a man holding a stick with a fish impaled on the end. Uba rushed back down to the stream, broke a branch from a nearby tree, sharpened the end with a rock, and then caught enough fish to feed himself and his family.

They were all saved by a meme, an instantly recognizable transmission of an idea, simple and clear, no explanation necessary. Memes can be visual, such as an international traffic symbol; verbal, such as "Lean Cuisine"; or active, such as a hitchhiker's stuck-out thumb.

In this day of endless and ever-proliferating marketing from all sides, you need a meme to stand out in the clutter. You should use that meme in all your marketing, on your Web site, on your stationery, on your business card, wherever and whenever you can. A logo is no longer enough. It represents a company, but that stops too short. A meme represents both a company and an idea — most likely, the main benefit offered by that company. The Green Giant is a meme. So is the Michelin Man. The Marlboro cowboy is a meme. Your job: Develop a meme for your business. Do it now, and use it for the life of your business.

Memes travel from mind to mind. They're easy to spread and easy to create. Just think of the major competitive benefit that you offer; then determine how to best communicate it visually or with a phrase. Think of how the eagle is a meme for America, flashing headlights a meme telling you to dim your brights, and the flamingo a meme for Florida, and you'll realize how common memes are.

But they're not yet common in marketing, so the sooner you get one, the more quickly you can put it to work. Get your own Pillsbury Doughboy, Energizer Bunny, or Aunt Jemima, and let it spearhead your marketing. Just visualize your main benefit; then distill it, compress it, simplify it, and focus on it; and you're off to a good start in the meme-creation department. The most powerful meme in history may have been the wheel. As it carried things from place to place, it also carried the idea of a wheel from mind to mind.

Theme Line

It doesn't cost you one penny to develop a winning, lasting, and memorable theme line. A theme line is a set of words that describe the spirit of your company. "You're in good hands with Allstate." "Be all that you can be." "In the valley of the Jolly Green Giant." I think you get the point.

Your theme line should be created to last a century or longer. Instead of changing every few years, it should never be changed, for it increases in strength each year. The Green Giant started becoming jolly in the 1930s and today is as jolly as ever. Mr. Clean never looks dirty to me.

You should use your theme line wherever you can: in your advertising, on your Web site, e-mail signature, business cards, stationery, even your tattoo, if you have one. Many Harley-Davidson owners have tattoos of their emblem, the ultimate in brand loyalty. That theme line grows from your identity and makes people think lofty thoughts about you whenever they see or hear it.

Combined with your meme, your theme — an unintentional rhyme — gives you double-barreled memorability. So you should create it with the future in mind, not using words or phrases that may soon be outdated. Once you have it, hold it up to the light of uniqueness. If it reminds you of any other company's theme line, abandon it and get something you can call your own.

Ideally, your theme line will be only a few words. If you want it to fit on a business card or in the yellow pages, you've got to keep it short. Unlike Coca-Cola, which has had a series of brilliant theme lines, you won't have to change yours owing to overexposure. Deep down, I think that Coke has frequently had a theme line it could use forever, but I guess that the company gets tired of it after investing several billion bucks promoting it.

The best theme lines say something good about a company but never seem to use superlatives. "Diamonds are forever." "Just do it." "Breakfast of champions." No bragging in any of those. Your theme line must as believable as all your other marketing. If it exaggerates, it will undermine you every time you use it.

As with a meme, the sooner you begin to use your theme line, the better. Because it gains strength with time, there's no sense in putting it off. Even though it's only a few words long, don't underestimate its importance. It will carry your banner forward in all your other marketing.

Branding

The *Harvard Business Review* once warned the growing number of small-business owners that there will soon be so many small businesses, owners will have to develop their own brand name in order to succeed and then make prospects aware of that name. In case you haven't been paying attention to commerce these past ten years, you may have missed out on one of the most sparkling and talked-about concepts: *branding*. The awareness it breeds of your company is priceless. Even MasterCard would agree. If you're a true-blue guerrilla, you'll want that awareness regardless of what any publication says. Brand name awareness equals credibility. Awareness of your brand or your business usually means confidence in it, and confidence is the key to healthy sales.

Many people have purchased products or services simply because they were familiar with the name. They might have known zilch about the benefits or the price, but they bought anyhow. Simply being aware of the name was enough. Researchers asking, "Why did you buy this product or service?" very frequently get this answer: "Because I heard of it." "Because I heard of it" is synonymous with brand name awareness.

So how does a company achieve brand name awareness? By constant repetition of its name. This repetition can come from frequent marketing, continual exposure to a sign, repeated stories in the media, or a combination of all these. The repetition penetrates the unconscious minds of the prospects. That's where most purchase decisions are made. No wonder so many people buy things "because they heard of them."

People trust brand names. I do. You do. People enjoy buying from friends. Frequent exposure to your name breeds a sense of familiarity that puts you into that lofty category of friend. It results in what's called "top-of-the-mind awareness." It creates the share of mind that must first precede share of market.

Brand name awareness of the highest quality is a lasting awareness. A person can read one of your marketing messages and then remember your name for a week or two. But unless exposed to your name after that, the person will probably forget it. The key to lasting brand name awareness comes with consistency. Awareness does not automatically lead to sales. But if a person is going to buy something in your category of business, you've got a whopping advantage over any company of which he or she is not aware.

This awareness takes time, but it's always worth the wait. So is anything else that ensures the survival of your business.

Positioning

No matter what you do, your business will stand for something in the minds of your prospects. That something is your niche, also known as your positioning. What's the first thing that should enter the minds of your prospects and customers when they read or hear your name? You're in charge of the answer to that question, so give it careful thought.

Do you want to be known as least expensive, the one that imports goods from Europe, the fastest, the friendliest, the most expert, the most fastidious, the one specializing in apartment dwellers, the one that is devoted to helping home-based businesses? There are many niches from which you can choose. Your choice can determine the fate of your company.

Whatever positioning you select, be sure that it's able to be clearly communicated to your target market. Once you begin to establish that position, it will be very difficult for anyone to take it away from you. When selecting it, take into consideration your strengths, your competition, and trends in the marketplace. If your position is different enough, you won't have much, if any, competition. Winston Churchill said, "Out of intense complexities, intense simplicities arise." Your niche must sing with simplicity.

You can differentiate from your competition in at least ten ways: place, price, promotion, people, product, service, selection, quality, convenience, and speed. The area in which you decide to differentiate is your market position.

It should come shining through in all your marketing. It must be easy as pie to communicate in even a thirty-second, even a ten-second, elevator pitch. It must be simple to say, to show, to prove. It not only grows out of your marketing plan but also is an integral part of that plan.

Your name should reflect your position and vice-versa. Be careful not to choose a position based on a fad. Fads and trends are diametric opposites. Don't think that you'll give your position a try and see whether it works. Instead, give it ultracareful thought, bounce it off others who have succeeded, and then commit to it forever.

Who do you suppose cares the most about the positioning you select? It's not you. It's your prospects. They care whether it will affect them in any way. If they figure that it's a positive effect, you've got yourself a winning position.

Quality

There are two crucial things to learn about quality right from the get-go. The first is that quality is the number-two reason that people patronize a business, ranking just behind confidence in the business and just ahead of service. The second thing to know is that quality is not what you put into your product or service but what your customers get out of it.

You should also be aware that quality is now the price of admission to succeeding at business. Without it, guerrilla marketing will simply speed the demise of your operation, because more people will learn of your shabby quality faster and less expensively than ever. I hate to be the first one to tell you this, but marketing is a waste of money if you have poor quality.

These days, quality refers to both your product and the way you serve people. They're going to equate every aspect of your business to quality, so it's a good idea for you to do the same.

Deep down, I'm hoping that you can skip this part about quality because you knew it all already, but just in case, you've got to remember that people assume you already have it and are quick to recognize any lack of it. Do I really have to be telling you these things?

Your quality will help you compare what you offer to what your competitors offer. It will juice up your word-of-mouth marketing. It will nourish all your other marketing. If you have the best quality in the universe, hardly anybody will know about it unless your marketing informs them of it. If they already suspect it, your marketing will reassure them that buying from you is the way to go.

Guerrilla marketing does sell products and services. But it sells them only once. It's the high quality you offer that will bring in the repeat and referral sales. That same quality will make life easier for those who sell what you offer. It will give your customers something wholesome to talk about. If they say anything about you behind your back, just pray that it's to rave about your quality.

The lowest prices on Earth won't be able to rescue you from poor quality. The speediest service and widest selection won't be able to protect you from the ravages of poor quality. Quality: Don't go into business without it.

Location

Everybody knows the three main secrets of a guerrilla marketing location: Internet, Internet, Internet. It's not the corner building downtown anymore. It's not the high-rent spot in the mall. It's not the high-traffic place right off the freeway exit.

It's online — on the computer screens of the millions of people who use the Internet before they leave the house for any purchase. In many instances, 90 percent of them look online before they look anywhere else. Why not? The selection is so vast. The time is so short. The parking is so easy.

Suddenly, the high-rent district is replaced by the no-rent district. The world is, indeed, learning to shop and buy things a new way. That way is on the Internet. To increasing numbers, it's becoming the only way. Nearly 75 percent of Americans are online an average of almost fourteen hours a week, and those figures rise each month. These people are spending less time with books, magazines, and newspapers. And their TV consumption is 37 percent less than that of Internet nonusers. The Internet is growing at a faster rate than any other medium. Does that sound like a prime location or not?

Think of how fortunate you are to be able to afford a top-flight, extremely visible, increasingly popular location. Whether they want to search for, learn about, or buy products or services, people hasten online before they hasten anywhere else. The Internet is getting better, bigger, simpler, and more valuable by the day. If your location is not smack-dab in the middle of it, you're going to be lost. And prospects won't find you where they are looking these days.

This should come as extremely good news to you, because we all know the value of a dynamite location. And we all knew that it was very pricey. But now, it's free. What other marketing venues can you say that about?

People never expected to find you at the corner of State and Main, on Fifth Avenue, or in the Mall of America. But they do expect to find you on the Internet. If you're not there, say bye-bye to your dream of greatness and wealth. Ain't gonna happen.

Think of it this way. You now have millions of locations — right in the homes or offices of your best and hottest prospects. Is that a blessing or what? Heck, even McDonald's should be jealous of you.

Opportunities to Upgrade

If ever there was an example of free marketing, it's this one: giving customers a chance to enlarge the size of their purchase once they've decided to buy from you. They're already in a positive frame of mind, so it shouldn't be too difficult to get them to upgrade their purchase.

Perhaps they'll buy a companion product. Maybe they'll buy a deluxe model rather than the economy model. Instead of signing up for your service for a month, you can sign them up for a year. In each one of these instances, the cost to market your offerings is nil. All profits go right to your bottom line.

Car dealers are superb at upgrading the size of the transaction. A customer decides to purchase a car — the cheapest one in the showroom. But the automobile salespeople are trained in upgrading, so the chances are, that customer is going to drive out in a more expensive model with more bells and whistles.

You can apply the same technique by packaging your products in a bundle. Instead of purchasing one book, the customer sees a wicker basket with five books, the other four relating to the one he or she had planned to purchase. Suddenly, your transaction quintuples. Same for your profits.

Guerrillas know that they should offer deluxe versions of their basic product or service. They know very well the importance of upgrading and the lack of cost associated with it. And they know that very frequently, customers will purchase the highest-priced offering. Be sure you have one for them.

Do you want a five-year warranty with that product? When the customer says yes, you've upgraded the size of the transaction. Do you want a donut with that coffee? Another upgrade. Do you want a tie and shirt to go with your new suit? We've all purchased upgrades, and you know what? We've appreciated it when the salesperson made the suggestion.

Whatever business you're in, you'll find it very simple to offer ways for customers to enlarge the size of their purchase. These are free ways to market, and you'd be seriously nuts not to avail yourself of the opportunities they provide for you. A person orders my newsletter, and I offer him or her audio tapes, CDs, and a videotape or DVDs at a discount. It's very simple for the person to accept my offer. Now, it's your turn to dream up upgrades that you'll offer.

Referral Program

An overwhelming majority of successful business owners will tell you flat out that obtaining referrals is the most powerful tactic for attracting new customers. They'll add that old customers are your best source of new customers. And all you've got to do is ask them. Simply review your customer list and your list of contacts, and then ask these good people to recommend you to others. Testimonials are nearly as good as money in the bank, but referrals really *are* money in the bank.

To get the most, make it easy for people to give you referrals. One technique is to send them an e-mail asking for the names of three people who might benefit from hearing from you. By keeping the number down to three, it will not be a daunting task for them to furnish names and e-mail addresses to you. By doing it by e-mail, you'll cut out the expense and cut down on the time you need to devote to this.

Everyone who works for you should be trained in asking for referrals by saying something like, "We're able to keep our prices in line by getting customer referrals rather than relying on expensive advertising. We'd be deeply appreciative if you could give us the names of just three people who you feel should be added to our mailing list." The leads that convert to sales at the highest percentage are referrals from current customers. As a guerrilla, you treat these people right, so they'll want to help you.

A referral program is a simple system that is set up for you to send letters asking for referrals automatically and on a regular basis — about twice a year. Thank those people who supply them. No other gift is necessary. I once participated in a teleconference with three hundred chiropractors. We asked how many of them got 50 percent of their business from referrals, and one hundred of them did. We asked how many got 80 percent or more from referrals, and only three did. When we asked how they did it, they told us that all their employees asked for referrals. Even the telephone operator was involved. When a person called to make an appointment, she would ask, "Is this only for you, or do you also want to make an appointment for some members of your family?" Such an easy question! So many referrals came from it!

By having a referral plan and sticking to it, you'll begin to amass a list of new customers. And each one can give you another three referrals. Make it ultraeasy by having your referral e-mail letters written and ready to send. Then get ready for a new influx of profits.

Testimonials

If someone you know or respect recommends a product, that carries more weight than if you or a salesperson recommends it. That's only one of the reasons why guerrillas obtain, publish, and lean on testimonials. Some of the other reasons are that testimonials are free, easy to get, timeless, readily available, and flexible to empower many other weapons. They are also believed. One of the biggest business oversights is failure to get a testimonial, even though all it takes is a simple request.

Testimonials that use the words "good" or "fine" or "valuable" aren't worthless, but they're not far from it. Instead, they should say, "We increased our profits 19 percent in sixty days thanks to your remarkable service." Or, "My husband never compliments me on my cooking, but he actually hugged me after I served him your gorilla stew!" The more specific the testimonial, the harder it will work for you.

The best testimonials state the problem, use real words said by real people, and state real numbers, along with real solutions to a problem. I'm not sure about you, but I have trouble believing testimonials signed by, say, Mrs. J. T. Dallas. I have no difficulty at all believing complimentary comments made by Steve Neese, 6808 Crandon Avenue, Chicago.

You benefit even more if your testimonials are from people meaningful to your prospects. In their inner minds, prospects unconsciously ask, "Is this person like me?" "Does this person have the kind of problems that I face?" "Did he or she want the kind of results that I want?" "Is that person's situation like mine?"

You need yes answers to these questions for testimonials to work to the max. For them to work even better, include the phone number of the testimonial giver, and invite prospects to call. Be sure you check this out first.

Once you've got a battery of testimonials, use them prominently — on your Web site, as headlines, in special boxes, as parts of body copy. It's often a good idea to put them into a different typeface so that they'll stand out. To get them, simply ask customers why they bought from you and whether their purchase met their expectations. Sometimes, a person will ask you to write the testimonial and will then sign it. If so, you're one lucky guerrilla.

Credibility

The road to profitability is paved with credibility. Credibility is something you earn by how you market, where you market, how you treat people, how you act, and your overall level of professionalism. Away from the business arena, the term is *street cred*, and it's the road to respect.

Most of the tactics mentioned in these pages can obtain this credibility for you. Each one is another feather in your credibility hat. The more of it that you have, the easier you'll be to trust. I don't have to remind you that trust leads to sales and profits.

Publicity stories cost you nothing but give you loads of credibility. You can get a lot more by your Web site, even by your use of the language in your marketing. One misspelled word or improper use of grammar subtracts from your credibility.

There aren't many shortcuts to credibility, but your commitment to your marketing plan is one of the biggest contributors of all. And that doesn't cost any money. When people see that you're truly interested in them and that you continue to curry their favor, they'll believe in you. Believing in you means that you've won credibility in their minds.

You don't have to invest in expensive marketing to get the credibility you need. The biggest advertisers on Earth know that advertising doesn't necessarily equate with credibility. It helps, but it doesn't guarantee a thing. Your quality, consistency, and service — those give you credibility. Your commitment, PR, ability to give talks or write articles — those give you even more credibility.

Don't forget: You can't buy credibility, but you can earn it by your attitude and your spirit. Word of mouth is one of the best sources of credibility. Same for testimonials, which are written words of mouth. Can you give a talk at a local club? If so, score one more point in your credibility department. Can you make contributions to your community in the way of your time and energy? If so, that is also a huge leap forward in your credibility.

As much as you must concentrate on gaining credibility, you must also focus on anything that might detract from it. Credibility is enormously powerful. So do all you can to gain it and to never diminish it.

Reputation

It's darned tough to build a good reputation but pretty easy to destroy it. You can spend years gaining it but just moments losing it. If one person has a bad experience with your business, count on twenty-two more people hearing about that bad experience within a month. If that's not bad enough, consider that 13 percent of the people spread the bad word to forty others. What a sorry situation. People just love to spread bad word of mouth. That's why it spreads slightly faster than wildfire and reaps even more destruction. Alice Roosevelt was quoted as saying, "If you can't say something nice about someone . . . pull up a seat next to me and let's talk!"

Your reputation is something you get by doing the right things over a long period of time. Just like credibility, it's not something you can pay for but something you have to earn. And it takes time to earn it. Nobody has a great reputation right from the start. All the esteemed businesses that have earned your confidence didn't have it at the start. They had to do many good things over and over again just to begin earning a good reputation.

All guerrillas know that the number-one factor in determining where people do business is confidence in the business. And they know that a top-rate reputation begets a load of confidence.

You get that top-rate reputation by doing everything right — on all levels. It comes to you slowly but is always worth the wait. Being predictable adds to your reputation. Knocking yourself out rendering service adds even more. Your customers want to do business with you because they know they can count on you. That's what reputation is all about.

Everyone who works with you must know what you're learning about the importance of a good reputation. You know what they say about one bad apple. That means that your employees and associates must know how important they are in crafting your reputation and how crucial your reputation is to your success and, ultimately, to their own.

Does it take money to build an outstanding reputation? It does not. Does it take time? It does. And it takes effort. Your reputation may end up being your most important business asset. Build it. Guard it. Be proud of it. But be ready to pay your dues by hard work and customer care to earn it.

Partial-Payment Plans

If there's one thing a customer likes more than a high number, it's a low number. The moral for you is to take your price, however low it may be, and break it into even lower numbers. If the cost for what you sell is $50, you can say, "That's only five small payments of $10 each."

Many people will gladly pay the $50 because the $10 number removes some of the pressure of buying. Talk in terms of monthly payments or anything that will enable you to offer a partial-payment plan. "No down payment" has a kind of magic to it. "No payments till 2010" is also very enticing. The idea is to remove any financial pressure.

Another way to do this is to mention that you accept all credit cards. Many people are up to or over their limit on Visa or MasterCard, so be sure also to accept American Express, Discover, Diner's Club — anything that makes it simpler for the customer to make a purchase from you. Put up signs mentioning that you accept all credit cards. Other signs should mention the astonishingly low monthly payments. Be certain that your sales reps reflect this ease of paying.

Your parents and grandparents learned about partial-payment plans when purchasing a house, car, or large kitchen appliance. But now, you can subscribe to a magazine and pay with three or six easy payments. The world is not only getting used to partial-payment plans but also hoping for them. Don't let them down.

Just as you should orient your firm to being easy to do business with, so too should you orient your prices to being easy to afford. Partial payments are very easy to afford. That's why it makes such good sense to stress them. Savvy guerrillas market their availability of easy financing along with their partial-payment plans and willingness to accept a bevy of credit cards. There is no cost to you if you decide to put small instead of big numbers in front of your customers, but there is a high probability of increased profits.

Can you possibly offer partial-payment plans with zero interest? Oh, boy; I'm optimistic about your future if you can answer *yes* to this cogent question.

Spying

A mandatory weapon in a guerrilla's arsenal is a clear picture of reality. Reality? What's that? It's the difference between the way you are conducting business compared with the way your competitors are conducting their businesses. The whole idea is to do absolutely everything better than your competitors. But how the heck can you accomplish that? Answer: *by spying*.

Guerrillas spy on their competitors, their industry, and especially, themselves. Just realize that business information is more plentiful than ever and that your competitors aren't dummies. They're getting smarter every day, and the only way you're going to know how you measure up to them is by actively engaging in regular spying.

Call a competitive company and request some information. If your voice is too well known by those who would dare to compete with you, have a friend make the call. See how you are treated on the phone. See how your information request is processed and how long it takes. See whether there is any follow-up and how good it is. Then, call your own company and request the same information. Again, since your employees probably already know the sound of your voice, engage a friend to help you spy. Are you treated as well as your competitors treated you? Is your information request processed as well and as quickly? Is your follow-up better than your competitor's follow-up? If your competitors are doing anything better than you, make the changes so that you are doing everything better than they are.

Seek out competitors in your own field, in your community, in the entire nation. If you ever find one who operates his or her business better than you do, feel good about it, because you can learn from it and then make the necessary improvements.

Spying is both inexpensive and informative. It should be practiced regularly, at least twice a year and even more if you're serious about being a guerrilla. Guerrillas know in their bones that the truth is a valuable ally. Truth finding is a painful job, especially when you learn that you are falling behind, but the opportunities to make your company the best makes up for the pain. Be prepared, if you're to be a serious guerrilla spy, to face up to some awful truths about your company. There's a tiny chance that you're doing everything better than your competitors, but if you spy properly and learn from your espionage, there's a great chance that you will be.

A Cause to Support

One of the fastest-growing areas of marketing is cause-related marketing. Embracing a cause and contributing money or time to it is a way to help that particular cause, your business, your customers, and your planet.

Let the world know that you're an environmentally responsible business; then put into action environmentally safe practices and behavior, using "green" products, recycling, and conservation of resources. Market your environmental concern, and you'll see that it attracts like-minded people. Many causes deserve the help of your business and others: helping to get the homeless off the streets, curing multiple sclerosis, finding a treatment for AIDS, rescuing abused women and children. Devote a portion of your profits to one of these causes, and you'll be doing a good deed that also can be mentioned in your marketing.

Research has shown that 63 percent of Americans will pay as much as 36 percent more to patronize a business that is environmentally friendly. When they see that they can purchase what they need or want and help their fellow citizens of the world at the same time, they'll be inclined to do business with you. Cause-related marketing is more than a promotional ploy. It means practicing what you preach — putting your time and energy into supporting noble causes, contributing your efforts for the good of humankind — and contributing a portion of your income as well. When I wrote my first books on guerrilla marketing in the 1980s, I didn't write of this method of marketing, because it didn't exist. But it exists now in a big way, and it's an ideal opportunity for you to help others as you help yourself.

Recent cause-related marketing efforts that have attracted national attention for their marketers include the Avon Crusade Against Breast Cancer, Walkers/News International's Free Books for Schools, British Gas and Help the Aged Partnership, Iceland and Alder Hey Children's Hospital, and Tesco Computers for Schools. A lot of needy causes out there require any kind of help they can get. Along with helping them, you might also attract media attention. Think of the causes that you'd support regardless of your business: Then find a way to let your business embrace them.

16

Guerrilla Company Attitudes

I've been writing about all the relatively formal things relating to marketing. You should also be aware of the informal things. That means your attitude. It shows in everything you do. You already know that you are your best marketing weapon. That *you* I refer to is both you the individual and you the company — even if you have no employees.

You can activate all the good tactics we've been talking about and still fall on your keister. If you do, that indicates a problem in your company's attitude. Prospects are more wary and experienced than they used to be. Customers have high expectations and are used to your meeting and surpassing them. If you fall short in the attitude department, that's going to undo a lot of your good and well-intentioned works.

As marketing is everything you do, attitude is probably the most important of those things. It shows in every word you say, in your tone of voice, every time you communicate, every day you're in business. You may have run that yellow pages ad two years ago, but today, some people are going to see it and become aware of you for the very first time. They may call or visit you. Because they care so intensely about themselves, they're going to be very tuned in to your attitude toward them. Your company attitudes are going to be omnipresent and visible from the moment they hear about your company. These are the elements they'll unconsciously factor into their relationship with you — or the lack of a relationship.

Passion

The marketing fires are fueled by enthusiasm and passion. Enthusiasm means being honestly excited about not your product or service but what it can do for your customers. This kind of enthusiasm is highly contagious and very desirable. It shows to your customers. But it starts with you, the owner of the company and then spreads to your staff, salespeople, and customers and then to their friends and associates.

Enthusiasm at its highest form is called passion. The most successful guerrillas feel this passion every working moment of every day — and they feel it about the benefits they offer. If you don't feel true passion for your offering, perhaps you ought to look into getting into a different line of work. Without passion, there is little enthusiasm. Without enthusiasm, profits are few and far between.

How can you develop true passion for what you offer and what your company offers? By studying your offering and focusing on the main benefits it offers. The more you know about it deep in your heart, the easier it will be for you to feel passionate about what it offers the world. The more competitive advantages that you offer, the more passion you can feel growing within you.

On an unconscious level, your prospects are hoping that you'll display this passion, hoping that you believe in your product or service so much that they'll understand why they should make it a part of their lives. If they sense a lack of enthusiasm, they'll see little reason to want it.

Enthusiasm and passion originate in the brain but are conveyed by the heart. You've got to make sure that everyone knows about the benefits you offer and that they become as excited as you are. Not easy — unless you're passionate about your story. My daughter was supposed to give a commencement address from her university. She was terrified at the thought of speaking in public. I advised her to think not of herself or her audience but of the passion she felt for her topic, which was helping the homeless. That passion helped her deliver a compelling talk without a trace of nervousness.

Passion is fairly rare. You find it in romances, in love of nature, and in some cases, love of money. I hope that you feel it deeply about your business — and your life away from business. In the heart of the guerrilla, passion rules.

Generosity

You don't have to give away free things in order to be generous. You can prove your generosity by your ability to listen and see things from your customer's point of view. You can prove it by your willingness to share information, by the inside tips you give to your customers.

There's a big difference between generosity and negotiation. You can demonstrate your generosity by your willingness to cut corners in your customer's favor, but you don't have to cut prices.

As if I had to tell you, it does help if your margins allow you to give some things away — especially after you've made the sale. That's where generosity really stands out — when people don't expect it. My client who tosses in a free set of linen once a bed has been purchased, the car dealer who gives a free GPS system once a car has been purchased — those companies are known for their generosity because the customers want to talk about such a delightful and surprising thing that just happened to them. It's true. Customers *do* talk about positive happenings they've had during their purchase experience, and if your generosity is apparent, that's a very positive thing to talk about. Of course, you aim for bliss in every detail of the purchase experience. Generosity is just one of those details.

Speed

Time, though you've probably lived all your life believing the contrary, is not money. If you run out of money, there are many ways to scrounge up more. If you run out of time — well, that's all she wrote.

The Roper Poll, Gallup Poll, Harris Poll, and the universities of Maryland and Pennsylvania conduct studies each year on what Americans cherish the most. In 1988, time hit the top of the list. It has remained there ever since and will remain there for the rest of our lives. Time, rather than being money, is life itself. And everyone knows it. That's why, if your business does not focus on speed, you're in serious trouble. People do not like to wait. They want what they want when they want it. Usually, that means right now. Making them wait is showing a disrespect for their time, and time is something they cherish.

If they call with a request, grant it ASAP. If they send you an e-mail, respond within twenty-four hours, though two hours is far better, and two minutes is best. If they order something, do all you can to ensure on-time delivery. Even if they must be put on hold when they call you, be sure you fill that hold time with marketing messages that enlighten and fascinate them.

I had a client running an urgent-care center, and his research showed that people hate waiting. So his marketing message became: "If you have to wait more than twenty minutes to see the doctor, your office visit is free." He broke the bank with that claim, and he lived up to it. Although he could have mentioned a myriad of other benefits, it was the lack of waiting that hit the bulls-eye for him.

Speed will become one of the most important things you can say or do. If you don't say it or live up to it, a competitor will take that business away — simply because that competitor shows a respect for people's time. You should apply the concept of speed to all contacts with you: to how you fulfill orders, how you service whatever needs servicing, your delivery time, and especially your ability to solve problems. People don't like to wait: on the phone, on your site, in your office, in their office, and when dealing with you and any of your people. They know that time is not money. So save their time whenever you can.

Neatness

Neatness is hardly something you'd expect to learn about in a marketing book or a marketing course. And yet it's part of the Disney marketing plan and the Nordstrom marketing plan. They're well aware of the power of neatness as well as sloppiness.

If people see that your premises are neat, they assume that's the way you do business. If they see that your space is sloppy, they'll assume that you do business the same way. Why do you suppose that people visit McDonald's? First reason: clean rest rooms. Second reason: great french fries. What do women look for when selecting a service station? Right, clean rest rooms.

The Disney organization is superb at keeping its premises neat. The rest rooms are cleaned every fifteen minutes, and litter is picked up within moments of being dropped. It turns out that Disney founder Walt Disney and McDonald's owner, Ray Kroc, were neat freaks, and their awareness of it is one reason that their businesses reflect their passion for orderliness. That passion has been translated into profitability.

Neatness is not something you do on a Monday morning. Keeping everything tidy is an all-the-time job. It doesn't cost anything except for time and energy. You'd probably be appalled if you knew how many people refuse to patronize a business with, for example, dirty floors.

When I'm talking about neatness, I'm talking about your office, your store, your car, your delivery vehicles, your service people, your telephone manners, your signs, your correspondence, your windows, and the space around your workplace. They're all part of your marketing, as every guerrilla knows.

Be sure that your business associates are on the same wavelength as you when it comes to neatness. With all of them aware of its importance, it won't be difficult for you to keep everything looking spic and span. Naturally, that includes yourself and your employees. If your place of business shows that you can't keep it looking professional and orderly, people will figure that you run your business unprofessionally and disorderly. I'm sorry to sound like your mother, but I'd hate for you to lose business just because you neglect to empty the wastebaskets or have a messy desk. In a world in which mass marketing reigns, there's an important place for neatness. That place is where you work.

Telephone Demeanor

The most special minority group in the world is made up of those people who call your business. They should all be treated not as interruptions of your business — which, alas, many are — but as the reason you're in business in the first place.

I was part of a group that did a survey of Midas Muffler Shops. We learned that Midas was getting 100 percent of its initial contacts by phone. That's the good news. The bad news is that only 71 percent of those calls were being converted into appointments. The reason for this dismal conversion rate was that the phone was being answered by the person closest to the phone — often, somebody who was more interested in automotive exhaust systems than in people. Or by somebody in a bad mood. Or by a person who was too busy to speak on the phone.

We recommended a half-day telephone training system for Midas. And Midas instituted one new rule: You must attend the telephone training program before you answer the phone at Midas. As a result, Midas began converting 94 percent of callers into appointments. Everyone who answers the phone sounds as though he or she is in a good mood and delighted that you called. No wonder the company's profits soared as a result of becoming aware of the importance of incoming phone calls.

People who call your business should be able to sense the smile in the voice of the person answering the phone. They should be treated graciously and made to feel important, for indeed they are. Callers should be made to believe that they are right — even if they're wrong.

Each phone call is a golden opportunity for you to intensify your relationship with the caller. Or to blow it out of the water. Try to answer each question as clearly and sincerely as possible. Remember the immense importance of first impressions, and remember that a phone call is often the first impression the caller will have of your business.

Your phone should be answered the same way each time, giving first-time callers the unmistakable impression that you're professional through and through, and giving customers a sense of consistency and continuity. Believe me, they'll appreciate it. And you'll appreciate the growing profits that can come from proper telephone demeanor.

Value

Let's cut right to the chase. *Value is far more crucial than price. And perceived value is far more crucial than value.* People will pay higher prices for products and services that deliver more quality for the buck. And they'll pay higher prices still for products and services that they believe deliver more quality for the buck. If this were not so, Rolls-Royce would be out of business. Ferrari would be long gone.

I have a raftload of business books, many on the topic of marketing. I'm floored at how few discuss the significance of value, especially of perceived value. Hello? Am I missing something? I don't think so. I think that the others are too wrapped up in the concepts of quality and service, excellence and teamwork, statistics and technology — so wrapped up that they're taking their eye off the ball. The ball is the value that the customer thinks he or she is getting. It doesn't have much to do with price. It has a lot to do with perception. Guerrillas are cognizant that perception is reality. People have to feel that you're the kind of company that offers a great value.

Many experts believe that value is simply the difference between anticipated price and the price asked. In this definition, a good one, there is no difference between value and perceived value. That's a bright observation because it takes into account that perception reigns supreme.

The secret, then, is to control the anticipated price. You may not have much to say about the actual price — production and materials are somewhat out of your control. But anticipated price? That's up to you. You can raise the price anticipation with your reputation, the presentation of your offering, even with your marketing copy and graphics. If your offering is carried in expensive stores, people will expect your price to be higher. They'll also be influenced by your stationery, address, office decor, and attire.

A restaurant with soft candlelight and romantic music charges more for meals than does a harshly lit cafeteria with the sounds of dishes clacking. The cost of the food ingredients, cooking, and refrigeration is the same at both restaurants. But the perception of value is raised by lighting, music, and decor. The world's best marketing can enhance your reputation and build your credibility, but it can't do beans for your lighting and decor.

When you can't either, that's when to turn to the copy and visuals of brilliant marketing. It can do wonders for your perceived value.

Easy to Do Business With

I once had a client that doubled its sales the first eight years it was in business. I attended a board meeting the next year when the chairman announced that the year would be devoted to no growth. No growth? I heard the sigh and the moan from the other directors.

The chairman explained that the company had been growing so rapidly that it was no longer able to accomplish twenty-four-hour turnaround and to say yes to all customer requests. He said that the rapid growth had made the company less easy to do business with and that the coming year would be devoted to changing that inability to render perfect service to customers.

It worked. The company barely grew that year. But the next year, it again doubled its sales, and the year after that, it was purchased by a Fortune 500 company for an obscene amount of money. Very few businesses would even consider disregarding growth for a year while striving for perfection in company service. Most grow to where they're too unwieldy to act like a mom-and-pop business. Most have their minds focused on growth and money rather than on service and ease of doing business.

The cost of making it easier to do business with you? There is no cost. All that's required is heightened awareness and acute sensitivity to customer needs. The business I mention didn't come to its realization because of customer complaints. The business headed those complaints off at the pass because the chairman was so tuned in to his customers and the crucial need to be easy to do business with that he didn't need suggestions from the outside. He knew in his heart that the company sometimes had to say no to customers who were used to the company's always saying yes.

Guerrillas regularly examine their business from the standpoint of customers, often asking friends, posing as potential customers, to call the company and ask for complex favors. Only when viewing their business through customers' eyes can you get the real truth about the ease of doing business with you. If there's even one impediment, make changes. Stop problems before they arise.

Zen and the Art of Motorcycle Maintenance is all about the necessity for making repairs before repairs are needed. Robert Persig, the author, regularly maintained his motorcycle, so it never needed repairs. Moral: Your business is your motorcycle. Fix it before it breaks.

Flexibility

Every decade seems to be fueled by a different business concept. In the 1980s, that concept was quality. It became so endemic in business that the price of admission for doing business became quality. People took it for granted.

In the 1990s, the overriding concept was flexibility. Businesses learned to be flexible with their service, product availability, selection, and staffing. During the first decade of the 2000s, innovation seems to be the concept du jour.

But I'm concerned about those businesses that are still resting on their laurels of the 1980s and have not yet learned to provide flexibility. It's not too difficult for you to offer, and yet your customers pray that you do. Flexibility means being able to grant almost all customer requests. They can't come to your place of business when you want them to? Offer to come to them. They can't get the style they want? Offer to obtain it for them. You don't carry the brands they want? Do what you must to add those brands to your inventory. As you can see, flexibility relates to service, quality, selection, price, payment plans, and even days and hours of operation.

Just as quality is now taken for granted, flexibility is also now expected by more and more of your customers. If you don't offer it, somebody else will. And it will be a major uphill struggle to get those customers back. It's a sorry situation if you're hidebound in tradition or in the way you used to do business when your customers need something different.

One of the areas that most cries out for flexibility is service. Guerrilla companies knock themselves out giving their customers superb service, and that often requires flexibility. My daughter just purchased a new saltwater aquarium, a complex system, especially in the hands of amateurs like her.

She asked the pet store owners whether they could help us with the aquarium during the first few months. Their response, "We don't usually do that, but we'll come over once a week if you'd like." That's flexibility. And that's one of the things she mentions to everyone who compliments her on the beauty and vitality of her aquarium. Does she pay for this extra service? Of course she does. It's a nominal figure, but she doesn't mind paying it at all. Flexibility is why she'll be a patron of the store for the rest of her life.

If people sense that you're a flexible sort, they'll be more inclined to do business with you. If they sense just the opposite, they'll likely do just the opposite. Wouldn't you? Life tosses us curve balls, more than we expect. We need to be doing business with flexible companies and flexible people so we can duck out of the way of a painful encounter. Thomas Jefferson said that one of the secrets of life is the avoidance of pain. Your being flexible conveys an attitude to customers that it won't hurt to do business with you.

17

Guerrilla Marketing Psychology

You already know the immense importance of psychology to marketing. You know that 90 percent of purchase decisions are made in the unconscious mind and that we have a surefire way to access that unconscious mind: *repetition*. You also know that all purchase decisions are made for emotional reasons and that we use logical reasoning to justify these decisions.

You certainly know that there are left-brained people, who respond to logical, sequential reasoning, and right-brained people, who respond to emotional, esthetic appeals. Since about half of us are left-brained and half are right-brained, you know how it makes a whole lot of sense to direct your messages to *both* left- and right-brained people — or you'd be wasting half of your marketing investment.

You should know that to appeal to left-brained people, your messages should have *a lot of numbers* because brain lefties love specific references. Those messages should have *a lot of words* because those same people like copy. The messages must have *logic* because those people always want to know why. They should have *lists* — and those lists should present facts in *bullet-point form*, so you can skip the narrative. And they should have *a lot of details* because brain lefties are influenced by the tools of persuasion.

So to address left-brained people, you use numbers, words, logic, lists, and details. To address right-brained people, you use pictures, appeals to the imagination, color, rhythm, and space.

The pictures can come in the form of audiovisual aids and demonstrations. When enlisting the imagination of right-brained folks, try to engage their senses. When using color, keep in mind that they respond well to all colors. You use rhythm in the pace of your communications and follow-up, in the patterns in which you present facts, and in the beat of your Web site and sales presentation. Use space in your design — package, office, and Web site. Brain righties love open space.

But as I said, you know all those things already, and you didn't need this fourth edition to tell you what you already know. But you do need it to take you up to the next level in guerrilla marketing, a level pioneered by Guerrilla Marketing Master Trainer Paul R. J. Hanley, who coauthored with me *The Guerrilla Marketing Revolution: Precision Persuasion of the Unconscious Mind*. Not long after publishing the book in 2006, Paul was killed while piloting his own two-seater airplane in the north of England. Much of the information in this chapter is his legacy to guerrilla marketers everywhere. That legacy begins with his warning to you *not* to think of a blue elephant.

Along with that warning comes a strong suggestion that you market directly to the unconscious mind of your prospects. There are five reasons you should do this.

1. *The brain uses images to help the conscious mind understand.* All the readers of this chapter will definitely think of a blue elephant, in spite of what I said. But no two of those blue elephants will be identical. And so it is with your prospects. They conveniently fall into several demographic groups, but they remain individuals — and only by treating them as such will they relate to you the way you want. Implanting images in their minds should be part of your message, but they are not the message.
2. *The unconscious mind is much smarter than the conscious mind.* In spite of that, the unconscious mind rarely vetoes a decision made in the conscious mind. Overusing credit cards, smoking cigarettes, and eating the wrong foods are examples of the wise unconscious mind allowing the not-very-wise conscious mind to do the wrong thing. The decision was made after interaction between your conscious and unconscious — an internal dialogue. In most internal dialogues, the unconscious mind gets shortchanged.
3. *The unconscious mind controls the internal dialogue.* Your prospects will experience an internal dialogue, whether or not you have anything to say about it. But as a guerrilla, you should see your job as helping your prospects have dialogues that result in positive states of mind. That means tossing aside the notion that it's best to sell the so-

lution to a problem ("Without a security alarm, your home and family are at risk") and replace it with something that puts the prospect into a positive state ("Sleep soundly in the safe knowledge that you have protected your home and family"). Yes, it's still true that selling solutions is often just the ticket, but new findings in psychology are showing us that selling positive benefits isn't to be neglected.

Studies show that only 34 percent of people would purchase the same product or service from the same store or seller if given the choice again. Often, they're stricken with buyer's remorse. Buyer's remorse usually fades into nothingness if the customer is in a positive state. Interject it into internal dialogues if you can.

4. *The unconscious mind can understand and link multiple messages.* For precisely this reason, guerrillas market to the unconscious mind because they can simultaneously appeal to several parts of the mind, using multiple messages. This speeds up the decision-making process. Providing the unconscious mind with a set of marketing messages that it can use to produce a single, coherent marketing message usually results in a more rapid and committed decision. After all, the unconscious trusts its own judgment better than any direct instruction from someone else.

5. *The unconscious mind makes decisions before consulting the conscious.* That enables guerrillas to help a prospect make a decision before he or she is consciously aware that a decision has been made. It helps that the unconscious mind cannot work slowly but only at high speed. Instead of asking clients, "Do you have problems closing new business?" which is easily answered *no*, guerrillas ask, "When do you have problems closing new business?" which immediately builds rapport.

If your goal is prospects who make rapid yet stable purchasing decisions, you must consciously begin to market to their unconscious minds. Don't ignore the conscious mind, though ego gets in the way of it going along with all unconscious decisions, but don't forget who wears the pants in most minds.

I have something else for you to never forget: a key psychological truth. First of all, I want to be sure that you know about the visual, auditory, and kinesthetic systems. Visual people say, "I see what you mean," "I can't picture that," and "Can you show me the way?" Auditory people say, "I hear you now loud and clear," "That name rings a bell," and "To tell the truth, I'm not sure." Kinesthetic people say, "I'll lay my cards on the table," "I'll get in touch with them," and "That doesn't feel right."

Do you remember the last time you felt really cold? Remember how you first became aware of the cold, then felt it move throughout your body? There. You were just in a kinesthetic state.

What I'm about to tell you here can improve the speed and efficiency of all marketing campaigns. But don't worry. Hardly anyone knows it, though those who do are able to translate it into substantial profits and in a brief time. You bought this book for any of a number of reasons. This should have been the number-one reason. Here it is: *A prospect cannot make a purchasing decision until he or she has experienced a kinesthetic sensation that takes place after the purchase.*

Are you clear on that? Did you notice how I said that prospects must have a *kinesthetic sensation* and that *it must relate to the time after the purchase?* Those are the keys to the profit kingdom for you — if you focus on acting on it.

The simple point is that people want to feel good about themselves and about the decisions they make. Build that into your marketing, and watch your results begin to improve. Alas, although this contradicts what I had learned in the past, the reality is that making people feel bad about their problems and then showing how to ease their pain does not make them feel good about themselves.

Your body can do what your mind tells it to do, and you can control your mind. You can also help others control their minds. You can truly build positive states in others and then watch the positive changes that occur. You can even get people to think of blue elephants if you want.

According to Paul Hanley, marketing to the unconscious mind involves engaging in a lot of conscious marketing behavior.

- Contact clients only when you have something new to say.
- Make it easy for your clients to do business with you.
- Stress your unique selling proposition in everything that you do.
- Be completely and totally honest while obeying the highest code of ethics.
- Understand and address your customers' needs.
- Recognize who your customers are.
- Be consistent and predictable in your marketing.
- Use precision persuasion.

In order to market at the purest level, it is important to *act like a child.* I don't mean for you to be a behavior problem, but a behavior master.

- Children are persistent.
- Children ask a lot of questions.
- Children refuse to be restricted by the realities of others.
- Children have very active imaginations.
- Children rarely accept no as a final answer.
- Children enjoy learning.
- Children love to be the first to talk about something new.
- Children try to make everything fun.
- Children talk until they believe that they're understood.

Children also examine all new facts with wonder and curiosity. I ask you to do the same. If you are not marketing to the unconscious minds of your prospects, it may be that you are marketing to a vacuum.

As always, the roots of genius can be found in new truths. But the flower of genius must be found in the miracles that come when they bloom. Guerrilla marketing has been planted, nourished, and allowed to bloom. I have been both a farmer and a witness to what is turning out to be an endless harvest.

It looks like next year is going to be the best ever.

The 200 Weapons of Guerrilla Marketing

Minimedia

1. Marketing plan
2. Marketing calendar
3. Identity
4. Business cards
5. Stationery
6. Personal letters
7. Telephone marketing
8. Toll-free number
9. Vanity phone number
10. Yellow pages
11. Postcards
12. Postcard deck
13. Classified ads
14. Per order/inquiry advertising
15. Free ads in shoppers
16. Circulars
17. Community bulletin boards
18. Movie ads
19. Outside signs
20. Street banners
21. Window display
22. Inside signs
23. Posters
24. Canvassing
25. Door hangers
26. Elevator pitch
27. Value story
28. Back-end sales
29. Letters of recommendation
30. Attendance at trade shows

Maximedia

31. Advertising
32. Direct mail
33. Newspaper ads
34. Radio spots
35. Magazine ads
36. Billboards
37. Television commercials

E-Media

38. Computer
39. Printer/fax
40. Chat rooms
41. Forums boards

42. Internet bulletin boards
43. List building
44. Personalized e-mail
45. E-mail signature
46. Canned e-mail
47. Bulk e-mail
48. Audio-/videopostcards
49. Domain name
50. Web site
51. Landing page
52. Merchant account
53. Shopping cart
54. Autoresponders
55. Search engine ranking
56. Electronic brochures
57. RSS feeds
58. Blogs
59. Podcasting
60. Own e-zine
61. Ads in other e-zines
62. E-books
63. Content for other sites
64. Webinars
65. Joint ventures
66. Word of mouse
67. Viral marketing
68. eBay/auction sites
69. Click analyzers
70. Pay per click ads
71. Search engine keywords
72. Google adwords
73. Sponsored links
74. Reciprocal link exchanges
75. Banner exchanges
76. Web conversion rate

Info-Media

77. Knowledge of your market
78. Research studies

79. Specific customer data
80. Case studies
81. Sharing
82. Brochures
83. Catalog
84. Business directory
85. Public service announcements
86. Newsletter
87. A speech
88. Free consultations
89. Free demonstrations
90. Free seminars
91. Article
92. Column
93. Book
94. Publishing on demand
95. Speaker at clubs
96. Teleseminars
97. Infomercials
98. Constant learning

Human Media

99. Marketing insight
100. Yourself
101. Your employees and reps
102. Designated guerrilla
103. Employee attire
104. Social demeanor
105. Target audiences
106. Your own circle of influence
107. Contact time with customers
108. How you say hello and good-bye
109. Teaching ability
110. Stories
111. Sales training
112. Use of downtime
113. Networking
114. Professional title

115. Affiliate marketing
116. Media contacts
117. A-list customers
118. Core story
119. Sense of urgency
120. Offer limited items/time
121. Call to action
122. Satisfied customers

Nonmedia

123. Benefits list
124. Competitive advantages
125. Gifts
126. Service
127. Public relations
128. Fusion marketing
129. Barter
130. Word of Mouth
131. Buzz
132. Community involvement
133. Club and association memberships
134. Free directory listings
135. Trade show booth
136. Special events
137. Name tags at events
138. Luxury box at events
139. Gift certificates
140. Audiovisual aids
141. Flipcharts
142. Reprints and blowups
143. Coupons
144. Free-trial offer
145. Guarantee
146. Contests and sweepstakes
147. Baking or craft ability
148. Lead buying
149. Follow-up
150. Tracking plan

151. Marketing on hold
152. Branded entertainment
153. Product placement
154. Radio talk show guest
155. TV talk show guest
156. Subliminal marketing

Company Attributes

157. Proper view of marketing
158. Brand name awareness
159. Positioning
160. Name
161. Meme
162. Theme line
163. Writing ability
164. Copywriting ability
165. Headline copy
166. Location
167. Hours of operation
168. Days of operation
169. Credit cards accepted
170. Financing available
171. Credibility
172. Reputation
173. Efficiency
174. Quality
175. Service
176. Selection
177. Price
178. Opportunities to upgrade
179. Referral program
180. Spying
181. Testimonials
182. Extra value
183. Noble cause

Company Attitudes

184. Easy to do business with
185. Honest interest in people

186. Telephone demeanor
187. Passion and enthusiasm
188. Sensitivity
189. Patience
190. Flexibility
191. Generosity
192. Self-confidence
193. Neatness
194. Aggressiveness
195. Competitiveness
196. High energy
197. Speed
198. Focus
199. Attention to details
200. Action

Acknowledgments

You'd think that if you had authored or coauthored fifty-six books, you'd have an increasingly long list of acknowledgments. That's what I figured. But when it came time to put the deserving many into print, it turned out that there were only a deserving few.

Book after book, my literary agents, Michael Larsen and Elizabeth Pomada, have exceeded my expectations and transformed my dreams into reality. They've given superb advice, protected me from the publishing minefields, treated my wife and me to some of the most scrumptious meals of our lives, and given me someone I could literally and literarily lean on. They are as much a part of the guerrilla brand as the camouflage design of the book jackets. So too is my editor, Eamon Dolan, who has called many shots and imparted valuable — to me — and profitable — to you — suggestions. Eamon became the *enfant terrible* of the brand, allowing me to get away with things that might have made other editors blanch. I owe gratitude to Ken Carpenter, who is my new Eamon and has already shown the spunk and spirit of Eamon and editors past — Gerard van der Leun and Marnie Patterson Cochran. The whole gang at Houghton Mifflin continues to demonstrate why it was the publisher of choice by Henry David Thoreau and Mark Twain.

I want to single out Roger and Betsy Parker, who have, in the words of an Australian member, made our regular Guerrilla Marketing Association Wednesday evening phone calls "the most priceless hour of our week."

Errol Smith, our Emmy Award–winning podcaster, deserves a high five for the Guerrilla Marketing Radio Network and for helping our podcasts ring from sea to shining sea to shining sea.

There is no end of gratitude that I owe to Guerrilla Marketing Master Trainers Will Reed and his efforts at making Guerrilla Marketing a household word (however it's pronounced) in Japan; Larry Loebig, founder and director of the Guerrilla Marketing Academy; Todd Woods, director of our Franchise Training Program; and the late Paul Hanley, our man in Europe, Russia, and the Middle East, whose private plane went down in 2006 but whose spirit lives forever in his teachings, writings, and loved ones.

Orvel Ray Wilson has been a shining light for all things guerrilla, from the brand to many of the books. Bill Shear was a true source of the brand's vigor. Jeremy Rhoten, our Webmaster and behind-the-scenes guerrilla, is one key reason those scenes exist in the first place. Mitch Meyerson has done a better than magnificent job creating, then running, the Guerrilla Marketing Coaching Program, training sharp and knowledgeable guerrillas throughout the world. I bow low to Mitch and all our certified Guerrilla Marketing Coaches. The brand owes an untold debt of appreciation to Anthony Hernandez, mastermind of our Association chats and our forum board. And I'd never overlook Mary Ann Crossman, our bookkeeper, who keeps our records tidy. That may be a tougher job than all the others listed here.

I've saved the best for last. The hardest, most time-consuming, and most on-the-button research for this book was done by daughter Amy Levinson, who also happens to be our company vice-president and jill-of-all-trades. And mother of three of my twenty-six grandkids. Mother of the parents of the other twenty-five is wife Jeannie Levinson, who has kept this manuscript in one piece while traveling in an RV through thirteen states and living in six of them, editing and cheerfully tossing off marketing epiphanies and home-cooked meals as we meandered across America. I drive; she navigates. It is true that I am the father of guerrilla marketing. That truth means that Amy is the daughter of guerrilla marketing and Jeannie the mother.

Few expanded and updated books have been authored with such a stellar family and support team — and under such spectacular sunsets. Thank you, universe.

Jay Conrad Levinson
From the open road

Information Arsenal for Guerrillas

Jay's Publications, Products, and Resources

Books and Articles

Gallagher, Bill, Orvel Ray Wilson, and Jay Conrad Levinson. *Guerrilla Selling: Unconventional Weapons and Tactics for Increasing Your Sales.* Boston: Houghton Mifflin, 1992.

Lautenslager, Al, and Jay Conrad Levinson. *Guerrilla Marketing in 30 Days: A 30-Day Tactical Plan to Maximize Profits and Increase Customers.* Irvine, CA: Entrepreneur Media, 2005.

Levinson, Jay Conrad. *Bigwig Briefs: Guerrilla Marketing — The Best of Guerrilla Marketing & Marketing on a Shoestring Budget.* Boston: Aspatore Books, 2001.

——. *Earning Money Without a Job: Revised for the '90s.* New York: Holt, 1991.

——. *555 Ways to Earn Extra Money: Revised for the '90s,* rev. ed. New York: Holt, 1991.

——. *Guerrilla Advertising.* Boston: Houghton Mifflin, 1994.

——. *Guerrilla Creativity: Make Your Message Irresistible with the Power of Memes.* Boston: Houghton Mifflin, 2001.

——. *The Guerrilla Entrepreneur.* Garden City, NY: Morgan James, 2006.

——. *Guerrilla Marketing Attack for Attorneys.* San Ramon, CA: R. W. Lynch Company, 2006.

——. *Guerrilla Marketing Attack: New Strategies, Tactics, and Weapons for Winning Big Profits for Your Small Business.* Boston: Houghton Mifflin, 1989.

——. *Guerrilla Marketing During Tough Times.* Garden City, NY: Morgan James, 2005.

——. *Guerrilla Marketing Excellence: The 50 Golden Rules for Small-Business Success.* Boston: Houghton Mifflin, 1993.

——. *Guerrilla Marketing for Free: 100 No-Cost Tactics to Promote Your Business and Energize Your Profits.* Boston: Houghton Mifflin, 2003.

——. *Guerrilla Marketing for the New Millennium*. Garden City, NY: Morgan James, 2005.

——. *Guerrilla Marketing for the Nineties: The Newest Secrets for Making Big Profits from Your Small Business*. Boston: Houghton Mifflin, 1993.

——. *Guerrilla Marketing: Put Your Advertising on Steroids*. Garden City, NY: Morgan James, 2005.

——. *Guerrilla Marketing: Secrets for Making Big Profits from Your Small Business*, 3rd ed. Boston: Houghton Mifflin, 1998.

——. *Guerrilla Marketing Weapons: 100 Affordable Marketing Methods for Maximizing Profits from Your Small Business*. New York: Plume, 1990.

——. *Guerrilla Marketing with Technology: Unleashing the Full Potential of Your Small Business*. Reading, MA: Addison-Wesley, 1997.

——. *Mastering Guerrilla Marketing: 100 Profit-Producing Insights You Can Take to the Bank*. Boston: Houghton Mifflin, 1999.

——. *The Ninety-Minute Hour*. New York: Plume, 1991.

——. *Quit Your Job! Making the Decision, Making the Break, Making It Work*. New York: Dodd, Mead, 1987.

——. *The Way of the Guerrilla*. Boston: Houghton Mifflin, 1998.

Levinson, Jay Conrad, and Jay Aaron. *Guerrilla Marketing to the Masses*. Garden City, NY: Morgan James, forthcoming.

Levinson, Jay Conrad, and Bruce Blechman. *Guerrilla Financing: Alternative Techniques to Finance Any Small Business*. Boston: Houghton Mifflin, 1991.

Levinson, Jay Conrad, and Theo Brandt-Sariff. *Guerrilla Travel Tactics*. New York: American Management Association, 2004.

Levinson, Jay Conrad, Rick Frishman, and Michael Larsen. *Guerrilla Marketing for Writers*. Cincinnati, OH: Writer's Digest Books, 2001.

Levinson, Jay Conrad, Rick Frishman, and Jill Lublin. *Guerrilla Publicity: Hundreds of Sure-Fire Tactics to Get Maximum Sales for Minimum Dollars*. Avon, MA: Adams Media, 2002.

Levinson, Jay Conrad, and Seth Godin. *Get What You Deserve! How to Guerrilla Market Yourself*. New York: Avon, 1997.

——. *Guerrilla Marketing for the Home-Based Business*. Boston: Houghton Mifflin, 1995.

——. *The Guerrilla Marketing Handbook*. Boston: Houghton Mifflin, 1994.

Levinson, Jay Conrad, and David Hancock. *Guerrilla Marketing for Mortgage Brokers*. Garden City, NY: Morgan James, 2005.

Levinson, Jay Conrad, and Paul Hanley. *Guerrilla Marketing Revolution: Precision Persuasion of the Unconscious Mind*. London: Piatkus, 2006.

Levinson, Jay Conrad, and Anthony Hernandez. *Guerrilla Marketing Success Secrets*. Garden City, NY: Morgan James, 2006.

Levinson, Jay Conrad, and Loral Langemeier. *Guerrilla Wealth: T,he Tactical Secrets of the Wealthy . . . Finally Revealed*. San Rafael, CA: Live Out Loud, 2004.

Levinson, Jay Conrad, and Al Lautenslager. "Mind over Market," *Entrepreneur* magazine (March 2005).

Levinson, Jay Conrad, and Dean Lindsay. *Cracking the Networking Code*. Plano, TX: World Gumbo, 2005.

Levinson, Jay Conrad, and Monroe Mann. *Guerrilla Networking*. Garden City, NY: Morgan James, forthcoming.

Levinson, Jay Conrad, and Jane Marriott. *An Earthling's Guide to Satellite TV.* Mendocino, CA: Quantum, 1985.

Levinson, Jay Conrad, and Michael W. McLaughlin. *Guerrilla Marketing for Consultants: Breakthrough Tactics for Winning Profitable Clients.* Hoboken, NJ: Wiley, 2005.

Levinson, Jay Conrad, and Mitch Meyerson. *Guerrilla Marketing on the Front Lines.* Garden City, NY: Morgan James, forthcoming.

———. *Guerrilla Marketing on the Go.* Garden City, NY: Morgan James, 2006.

Levinson, Jay Conrad, and David Perry. *Career Guide for the High Tech Professional.* Franklin Lakes, NJ: Career Press, 2004.

———. *Guerrilla Marketing for Job-Hunters: 400 Unconventional Tips, Tricks, and Tactics to Land Your Dream Job.* Hoboken, NJ: Wiley, 2005.

Levinson, Jay Conrad, and Charles Rubin. *Guerrilla Marketing Online: The Entrepreneur's Guide to Earning Profits on the Internet,* 2nd ed. Boston: Houghton Mifflin, 1997.

———. *Guerrilla Marketing Online Weapons: 100 Low-Cost, High-Impact Weapons for Online Profits and Prosperity.* Boston: Houghton Mifflin, 1996.

Levinson, Jay Conrad, Mark S. A Smith, and Orvel Ray Wilson. *Guerrilla Teleselling: New Unconventional Weapons and Tactics to Sell When You Can't Be There in Person.* New York: Wiley, 1998.

———. *Guerrilla Trade Show Selling: New Unconventional Weapons and Tactics to Meet More People, Get More Leads, and Close More Sales.* New York: Wiley, 1997.

Levinson, Jay Conrad, and Kathryn Tyler. *Guerrilla Saving: Secrets of Keeping Profits in Your Home-Based Business.* New York: Wiley, 2000.

Levinson, Jay Conrad, Orvel Ray Wilson, and Mark S. A Smith. *Guerrilla Negotiating: Unconventional Weapons and Tactics to Get What You Want.* New York: Wiley, 1999.

Levinson, Jay Conrad, Orvel Ray Wilson, and Elly Valas. *Guerrilla Retailing.* Boulder, CO: Guerrilla Group, 2004.

Levinson, Jay Conrad, and Todd Woods. *Guerrilla Marketing for Franchisees.* Garden City, NY: Morgan James, 2006.

DVDs and Audio

Goldring, Norm, and Jay Conrad Levinson, comps. *The Career Elevator,* 4-part DVD series, 2006: thecareerelevator.com.

Holmes, Chet, and Jay Conrad Levinson, comps. *Guerrilla Marketing Meets Karate Master Home Study Course.* Complete DVD home study course: chetholmes.com/GMK_program.htm.

Levinson, Jay Conrad. "DVD/CD. Includes Workbook." *Guerrilla Marketing 101: Lessons from the Father of Guerrilla Marketing.* Garden City, NY: Morgan James, 2005.

———. *Guerrilla Marketing for the New Millennium Audio CD Set.* Garden City, NY: Morgan James, 2005.

———. *Guerrilla Marketing 101: Bootlegged! Five-Hour CD Set.* Garden City, NY: Morgan James, 2005.

———. *Guerrilla Marketing 101 Lab Workbook.* Garden City, NY: Morgan James, 2006.

Levinson, Jay Conrad, and David Garfinkel. *Guerrilla Copywriting 2-Disc CD Audio Set.* Garden City, NY: Morgan James, 2006.

Web Sites

Jay Levinson's interactive member Web site: guerrillamarketingassociation.com.
Jay Levinson's official Guerrilla Marketing homepage: gmarketing.com.

Recommended Books and Resources

Abraham, Jay. *Getting Everything You Can Out of All You've Got: 21 Ways You Can Out-Think, Out-Perform, and Out-Earn the Competition.* New York: Truman Talley Books/St. Martin Press, 2000.

———. *93 Extraordinary Referral Systems.* Nightingale Conant-Audio CD Set, 2004.

Acuff, Daniel. *What Kids Buy and Why: Psychological Secrets to Creating Products That Kids Love.* New York: Free Press, 1997.

Adams, Bob. *Streetwise Small Business Start-Up.* Holbrook, IL: Adams Media, 1996.

Albrecht, Donna G. *Promoting Your Business with FREE or Almost Free Publicity.* Englewood Cliffs, NJ: Prentice Hall, 1997.

Albrecht, Karl. *The Only Thing That Matters: Bringing the Power of the Customer into the Center of Your Business.* New York: HarperBusiness, 1992.

Allen, Robert G. *Creating Wealth,* rev. and updated. New York: Simon & Schuster, 1986.

———. *Multiple Streams of Income.* Hoboken, NJ: Wiley, 2004.

———. *Multiple Streams of Internet Income: How Ordinary People Make Extraordinary Money Online.* Hoboken, NJ: Wiley, 2006.

Ambler, Tim. *Marketing from Advertising to Zen.* London: Pitman, 1996.

Anderson, Kristin, and Ron Zemke. *Delivering Knock Your Socks Off Service,* 2nd ed. New York: AMACOM, 1997.

Anthony, Joseph. *Kiplinger's Revised and Updated Working for Yourself.* Washington, DC: Kiplinger Books, 1995.

Anthony, Robert. *The Ultimate Secrets of Total Self-Confidence.* New York: Berkley, 2006.

Anthony, Robert, and Jim Blau. *Job Surfing Freelancing: Using the Internet to Find a Job and Get Hired.* New York: Random House, 2002.

Applegate, Jane. *The Entrepreneur's Desk Reference: Authoritative Information, Ideas, and Solutions for Your Small Business.* Princeton, NJ: Bloomberg Press, 2003.

———. *Succeeding in a Small Business.* Bergenfield, NJ: Plume, 1992.

Arkebauer, James B. *The McGraw-Hill Guide to Writing a High-Impact Business Plan,* New York: McGraw-Hill, 1995.

Armstrong, Gar, and Philip Kotler. *Marketing: An Introduction,* 7th ed. Upper Saddle River, NJ: Pearson/Prentice Hall, 2005.

Assaraf, John. *The Street Kid's Guide to Having It All.* San Diego, CA: Street Kid Company, 2003.

Astle, Richard M. *The Common Sense MBA: The Seven Pursuits of Enduring Business for the Entrepreneur.* New York: St. Martin's Press, 1994.

Aurich, Barry, and Len Gill. *Event and Entertainment Marketing.* Chicago: Probus, 1994.

Bade, Nicholas. *Marketing Without Money.* Lincolnwood, IL: National Textbook, 1994.

Bangs, David H. *The Market Planning Guide: Creating a Plan to Successfully Market Your Business, Products or Service.* Dover, NH: Upstart, 1994.

Barnhart, Tod. *The Five Rituals of Wealth: Proven Strategies for Turning the Little You Have into More Than Enough.* New York: HarperBusiness, 1995.

Baron, Gerald R. *Friendship Marketing.* Grants Pass, OR: Oasis Books, 1997.

Barrett, Gavin, *Forensic Marketing: Optimizing Results from Marketing Communications.* New York: McGraw-Hill, 1995.

Barter Publishing Staff. *Barter Referral Directory: Small Business Edition.* Denver: Prosperity & Profit Unlimited, 1992.

Beatty, Jack. *The World According to Peter Drucker.* New York: Free Press, 1998.

Beckwith, Harry. *Selling the Invisible: A Field Guide to Modern Marketing.* New York: Warner, 1997.

Beemer, C. Britt, and Robert L. Shook. *Predatory Marketing.* New York: William Morrow, 1997.

Bell, Chip R. *Customers as Partners: Building Relationships That Last.* San Francisco: Berrett-Koehler, 1994.

Bendinger, Bruce. *The Copy Workshop Workbook.* Chicago: Copy Workshop, 1993.

Blackwell, Roger D. *From Mind to Market: Reinventing the Retail Supply Chain.* New York: HarperBusiness, 1997.

Bobrow, Edwin E. *The Complete Idiot's Guide to New Product Development.* New York: Alpha Books, 1997.

Bond, Jonathan, and Richard Kirschenbaum. *Under the Radar: Talking to Today's Cynical Consumer.* New York: Wiley, 1998.

Brandenburger, Adam, and Barry Nalebuff. *Co-Opetition.* New York: Doubleday, 1996.

Bredin, Alice. *The Virtual Office Survival Handbook: What Telecommuters and Entrepreneurs Need to Succeed in Today's Nontraditional Workplace.* New York: Wiley, 1996.

Bregman, Walter. *Spray the Bear: Reminiscences from the Golden Age of Advertising.* Bloomington, IN: Authorhouse, 2002.

Brooks, William T. *Niche Selling: How to Find Your Customers in a Crowded Market.* Burr Ridge, IL: Irwin, 1992.

Burg, Bob. *Endless Referrals: Networking Your Everyday Contacts into Sales.* New York: McGraw-Hill, 1994.

Burgett, Gordon. *Niche Marketing for Writers, Speakers and Entrepreneurs.* Santa Monica, CA: Communications Unlimited, 1993.

Bygrave, William D., and David Ackroyd. *The Portable MBA in Entrepreneurship,* 2nd ed. New York: Wiley, 1997 (also available on Dove Audio).

Cafferky, Michael E. *Let Your Customers Do the Talking: 301+ Word-of-Mouth Marketing Tactics Guaranteed to Boost Profits.* Chicago: Upstart Publishing, 1996.

Canfield, Jack, and Mark Victor Hansen. *The Aladdin Factor.* New York: Berkley, 1995.

Canfield, Jack, Mark Victor Hansen, and Les Hewitt. *The Power of Focus.* Deerfield Beach, FL: Health Communications, 2000.

Canfield, Jack, and Janet Switzer. *The Success Principles: How to Get from Where You Are to Where You Want to Be.* New York: HarperCollins, 2005.

Caple, John. *The Right Work: Finding It and Making It Right.* New York: Dodd, Mead, 1987.

Caples, John, and Fred E. Hahn. *Tested Advertising Methods,* 5th ed. Paramus, NJ: Prentice Hall, 1997.

Carnegie, Dale. *How to Win Friends and Influence People.* New York: Pocket Books, 1982.

Carter, Susan M. *How to Make Your Business Run Without You! Streamline Your Busi-*

ness Operations to Pave the Way for More Business, Bigger Profits, and a Business That Virtually Runs Itself. Bloomington, MN: Nasus, 1999.

Chapman, James. *Street-Smart Business Tactics.* San Mateo, CA: Human Intellect Press, 1990.

Cialdini, Robert B. *Influence: The Psychology of Persuasion.* New York: Morrow, 1993.

Clancy, Kevin, and Robert S. Schulman. *Marketing Myths That Are Killing Business: The Cure for Deathwish Marketing.* New York: McGraw-Hill, 1994.

Cohen, William A. *The Marketing Plan,* 2nd ed. New York: Wiley, 1998.

Connor, Dick, and Jeff Davidson. *Getting New Clients.* New York: Wiley, 1993.

Covey, Stephen R. *The 7 Habits of Highly Effective People: Powerful Lessons in Personal Change.* New York: Free Press, 2004.

Crandall, Rick. *Marketing Magic, Proven Pathways to Success.* Corte Madera, CA: Select Press, 1996.

———. *Marketing Your Services for People Who Hate to Sell.* Chicago: Contemporary Books, 1996.

Cyr, Donald G., and Douglas Gray. *Marketing Your Product.* Bellingham, WA: Self-Counsel Press, 1994.

Davidson, Jeff. *Marketing on a Shoestring.* New York: Wiley, 1994.

Debelak, Don. *Marketing Magic: Action Oriented Strategies That Will Help You.* Holbrook, IL: Bob Adams, 1994.

Decker, Sam. *301 Do-It-Yourself Marketing Ideas: From America's Most Innovative Small Companies.* Belmont, CA: South-Western Educational, 1997.

Dennison, Dell. *The Advertising Handbook for Small Business.* Bellingham, WA: Self-Counsel Press, 1994.

Desatnick, Robert L. *Managing to Keep the Customer Happy.* San Francisco: Jossey-Bass, 1987.

Dewitt, Paula Mergerhagen. *Targeting Transitions.* Chicago: Probus, 1994.

Dobkin, Jeffrey. *How to Market a Product for Under $500.* Merion Station, PA: Danielle Adams, 1996.

Donnelly, James H., Jr. *Close to the Customer.* Burr Ridge, IL: Irwin, 1991.

Dru, Jean-Marie. *Disruption: Overturning Conventions and Shaking Up the Marketplace.* New York: Wiley, 1996.

Dunckel, Jacqueline, and Brian Taylor. *Keeping Customers Happy.* Bellingham, WA: Self-Counsel Press, 1994.

Dunn, Declan. *Winning the Affiliate Game (Audio Cassette),* ringbound edition. Chico, CA: ADNet Intl., 1999.

Edwards, Mark, and Ann Ewen. *360 Degree Feedback.* New York: AMACOM, 1996.

Edwards, Paul, Sarah Edwards, and Laura Clampitt Douglas. *Getting Business to Come to You.* New York: Tarcher/Putnam, 1991.

Eker, T. Harv. *Secrets of the Millionaire Mind: Mastering the Inner Game of Wealth.* New York: HarperCollins, 2005.

Elton, Kim. *Net Benefits: The Internet Beyond the Technology and Down to the Bottom Line.* Victoria, BC: N. B. Publishing, 1997.

Falk, Edgar A. *1001 Ideas to Create Retail Excitement.* Englewood Cliffs, NJ: Prentice Hall, 1994.

Feig, Barry. *Marketing Straight to the Heart.* New York: American Management Assoc., 1997.

Fisher, Roger, and William Ury. *Getting to Yes: Negotiating Agreement Without Giving In*, 2nd ed. New York: Penguin Books, 1991.

Floyd, Elaine. *Marketing with Newsletters*. St. Louis: Newsletter Resources, 1996.

———. *Quick and Easy Newsletters*. St. Louis: Newsletter Resources, 1998.

Fortini-Campbell, Lisa. *Hitting the Sweet Spot: How Consumer Insights Can Inspire Better Marketing and Advertising*. New York: AMACOM, 1994.

Fournles, Ferdinand F. *Why Customers Don't Do What You Want Them to Do — and What to Do About It*. New York: McGraw-Hill, 1994.

Frause, Bob, and Julie A. Colebur. *Environmental Marketing Imperative*. Chicago: Probus, 1994.

Frishman, Rick, Jill Lublin, and Mark Steisel. *Networking Magic*. Avon, MA: Adams Media, 2004.

Garfinkel, David. *Advertising Headlines That Make You Rich*. Garden City, NY: Morgan James, 2006.

Gelb, Michael. *How to Think Like Leonardo Da Vinci: Seven Steps to Genius Every Day*. New York: Delacorte Press, 1998.

Gerber, Michael E. *E-Myth Mastery: The Seven Essential Disciplines for Building a World Class Company*. New York: HarperCollins, 2005.

Gerber, Michael E., and Patrick O'Heffernan. *The E-Myth: Why Most Businesses Don't Work and What to Do About It*. Cambridge, MA: Ballinger, 1986.

Gill, Michael, and Sheila Patterson. *Fired Up! From Corporate Kiss-Off to Entrepreneurial Kick-Off*. New York: Viking/Penguin, 1996.

Gitomer, Jeffrey H. *How to Not Suck at Sales*, DVD Video. Better Life Media, 2005.

———. *Jeffrey Gitomer's Little Red Book of Sales Answers*. New York: Prentice Hall, 2006.

Gladwell, Malcolm. *The Tipping Point: How Little Things Can Make a Big Difference*. Boston: Back Bay Books, 2002.

Godin, Seth. *The Big Red Fez: How to Make Any Web Site Better*. New York: Fireside, 2002.

———. *Free Prize Inside: The Next Big Marketing Idea*. New York: Portfolio, 2004.

———. *Permission Marketing: Turning Strangers into Friends, and Friends into Customers*. New York: Simon & Schuster, 1999.

———. *Purple Cow: Transform Your Business by Being Remarkable*. New York: Portfolio, 2003.

———. *Small Is the New Big and 183 Other Riffs, Rants, and Remarkable Business Ideas*. New York: Portfolio, 2006.

Goetsch, Hal. *Developing, Implementing and Managing an Effective Marketing Plan*. Lincolnwood, IL: NTC Business Books, 1994.

Goodman, Andrew. *Winning Results with Google AdWords*. New York: McGraw-Hill Osborne Media, 2005.

Gordon, Josh. *Tough Calls: Selling Strategies to Win Over Your Most Difficult Customers*. New York: AMACOM, 1997.

Green, Chuck. *Design It Yourself Graphic Workshop: A Step-by-Step Guide*. Gloucester, MA: Rockport, 2004.

———. *The Desktop Publisher's Idea Book*, 2nd ed. New York: Random House, 1997.

Griffin, Jack. *The Do-It-Yourself Business Promotions Kit*. Old Tappan, NJ: Prentice Hall, 1994.

———. *Customer Loyalty: How to Earn It*. San Francisco: Jossey-Bass, 1997.

Gumpert, David E. *How to Really Create a Successful Marketing Plan.* Boston: Gold-hirsh Group, 1997.

Hahn, Fred E., and Kenneth G. Mangun. *Do-It-Yourself Advertising and Promotion,* 2nd ed. New York: Wiley, 1997.

Hall, Doug. *Jump Start Your Business Brain: Win More, Lose Less, and Make More Money with Your New Products, Services, Sales, and Advertising.* Cincinnati, OH: Brain Brew Books, 2001.

Hall, Robert E. *The Streetcorner Strategy for Winning Local Markets.* Austin, TX: Bard Books, 1994.

Hamper, Robert J., and L. Sue Baugh. *Strategic Market Planning.* Lincolnwood, IL: National Textbook, 1998.

Hansen, Mark Victor, and Robert G. Allen. *The One Minute Millionaire: The Enlightened Way to Wealth.* New York: Harmony Books, 2002.

Harding, Ford. *Rain Making: The Professional's Guide to Attracting New Clients.* Holbrook, IL: Bob Adams, 1994.

Harrell, Wilson. *For Entrepreneurs Only: Success Strategies for Anyone Starting or Growing a Business.* Franklin Lakes, NJ: Career Press, 1995.

Hiam, Alexander. *Marketing for Dummies.* Foster City, CA: IDG Books, 1997.

Hiebing, Roman G. Jr., and Scott W. Cooper. *How to Write a Successful Marketing Plan.* Lincolnwood, IL: National Textbook, 1997.

Horner, Jody. *Power Marketing for Small Business.* Grants Pass, OR: Oasis Press/PSI Research, 1993.

Hughes, Arthur M. *Strategic Defense Marketing.* Chicago: Probus, 1994.

Hunter, Victor L., and David Tietyen. *Business to Business Marketing: Creating a Community of Customers.* Lincolnwood, IL: National Textbook, 1997.

Jackson, Robert R., and Paul Want. *Strategic Defense Marketing.* Lincolnwood, IL: National Textbook, 1994.

Jones, John Philip. *When Ads Work: New Proof That Advertising Triggers Sales.* New York: Lexington Books, 1995.

Joyner, Mark. *The Irresistible Offer: How to Sell Your Product or Service in 3 Seconds or Less.* Hoboken, NJ: Wiley, 2005.

Kabodian, Armer J. *The Customer Is Always Right! Thought-Provoking Insights on the Importance of Customer Satisfaction from Today's Business Leaders.* Cambridge, MA: Harvard Business School Press, 1996.

Kaden, Robert J. *Guerrilla Marketing Research: Marketing Research Techniques That Can Help Any Business Make More Money.* Philadelphia: Kogan Page, 2006.

Kawasaki, Guy. *The Art of the Start: The Time-Tested, Battle-Hardened Guide for Anyone Starting Anything.* New York: Portfolio, 2004.

——. *How to Drive Your Competition Crazy: Creating Disruption for Fun and Profit.* New York: Hyperion, 1995.

——. *Selling the Dream: How to Promote Your Product, Company, or Ideas — And Make a Difference — Using Everyday Evangelism.* New York: McGraw-Hill, 1995.

Keirsey, David. *Please Understand Me II: Temperament, Character, Intelligence.* Del Mar, CA: Prometheus Nemesis, 1998.

Kennedy, Dan S. *How to Succeed in Business by Breaking all the Rules: A Plan for Entrepreneurs.* New York: Dutton, 1997.

——. *No B.S. Business Success: The Ultimate No Holds Barred Kick Butt — Take No Prisoners Tough and Spirited Guide.* Irvine, CA: Entrepreneur Media, 2004.

———. *The Ultimate Marketing Plan: Find Your Hook, Communicate Your Message, Mark Your Mark.* Avon, MA: Adams Business, 2006.

Kiyosaki, Robert T., and Sharon L. Lechter. *Rich Dad, Poor Dad.* New York: Warner Books, 2004.

Klaus, Peggy. *Brag! The Art of Tooting Your Own Horn Without Blowing It.* New York: Warner Books, 2003.

Kotler, Philip. *Ten Deadly Marketing Sins: Signs and Solutions.* Hoboken, NJ: Wiley, 2004.

Kotler, Philip, and Gar Armstrong. *Principles of Marketing,* 10th ed. Upper Saddle River, NJ: Prentice Hall, 2004.

Kotler, Philip, and Eduardo L. Roberto. *Social Marketing: Strategies for Changing Public Behavior.* New York: Free Press, 1989.

Krass, Peter. *The Book of Business Wisdom: Classic Writings by the Legends of Commerce and Industry.* New York: Wiley, 1991.

Kremer, John. *The Complete Direct Marketing Sourcebook.* New York: Wiley, 1992.

Kremer, John, and J. Daniel McComas. *High-Impact Marketing on a Low-Impact Budget.* Rocklin, CA: Prima, 1997.

Lakhani, Dave. *Persuasion: The Art of Getting What You Want.* Hoboken, NJ: Wiley, 2005.

Lambesis, Barbara. *101 Big Ideas for Promoting a Business on a Small Budget.* Phoenix.AZ: Marketing Methods Press, 1989.

Landon, Hal. *Marketing with Video: How to Create a Winning Video for Your Small Business or Non-Profit.* Slate Hill, NY: Oak Tree Press, 1996.

Langemeier, Loral. *The Millionaire Maker: Act, Think, and Make Money the Way the Wealthy Do.* New York: McGraw-Hill, 2006.

Lant, Jeffrey. *Cash Copy.* Cambridge, MA: JLA, 1992.

———. *Money Making Marketing.* Cambridge, MA: JLA, 1993.

———. *The Unabashed Self-Promoter's Guide: What Every Man, Woman, Child & Organization in America Needs to Know About Getting Ahead by Exploiting the Media,* 2nd ed. Cambridge, MA: JLA, 1992.

Levitt, Theodore. *The Marketing Imagination.* New York: Free Press, 1986.

Lichtenberg, Ronna. *Pitch Like a Girl: How a Woman Can Be Herself and Still Succeed.* Emmaus, PA: Rodale, 2005.

Lonier, Terri. *The Frugal Entrepreneur: Creative Ways to Save Time, Energy & Money in Your Business.* New Paltz, NY: Portico Press, 1996.

———. *Working Solo: The Real Guide to Freedom & Financial Success with Your Own Business.* New York: Portico Press, 1994.

———. *Working Solo Sourcebook: Essential Resources for Independent Entrepreneurs.* New Paltz, NY: Portico Press, 1994.

Lopiano-Misdom, Janine, and Joanne De Luca. *Street Trends: How Today's Alternative Youth Cultures Are Creating Tomorrow's Mainstream Markets.* New York: HarperBusiness, 1997.

Luecke, Richard. *Managing Projects Large and Small.* Boston: Harvard Business School Press, 2004.

Mackay, Harvey. *Dig Your Well Before You're Thirsty: The Only Networking Book You'll Ever Need.* New York: Currency/Doubleday, 1997.

Maltz, Maxwell. *The New Psycho-Cybernetics: The Original Science of Self-Improvement and Success That Has Changed the Lives of 30 Million People.* Edited and updated by Dan S. Kennedy. Paramus, NJ: Prentice Hall, 2002.

Mann, Monroe. *The Theatrical Juggernaut: The Psyche of the Star.* Bloomington, IN: Authorhouse, 2001.

Marconi, Joe. *Creating the Marketing Experience: New Strategies for Building Relationships with Your Target Market.* Belmont, CA: South-Western Educational, 2005.

———. *Image Marketing Using Public Perceptions to Attain Business Objectives.* Lincolnwood, IL: National Textbook, 1996.

Marder, Eric. *The Laws of Choice: Predicting Customer Behavior.* New York: Free Press, 1997.

McCrimmon, Mitch. *Unleash the Entrepreneur Within: How to Make Everyone an Entrepreneur and Stay Efficient.* London: Pitman, 1995.

McDonald, Malcolm H. B., and Warren J. Keegan. *Marketing Plans That Work: Targeting Growth and Profitability.* Boston: Butterworth-Heinemann, 1997.

McKee, Lex. *The Accelerated Trainer: Using Accelerated Learning Techniques to Revolutionize Your Training.* Burlington, VT: Gower, 2004.

McKeever, Mike. *How to Write a Business Plan.* Berkeley: Nolo, 1992.

McKenna, Regis. *Real Time: Preparing for the Age of the Never Satisfied Customer.* Boston: Harvard Business School Press, 1997.

Meyerson, Mitch. *Success Secrets of the Online Marketing Superstars.* Chicago: Dearborn, 2005.

Misner, Ivan R. *Seven Second Marketing: How to Use Memory Hooks to Make You Instantly Stand Out in a Crowd.* Austin, TX: Bard Press, 1996.

———. *The World's Best Known Marketing Secret: Building Your Business with Word-of-Mouth Marketing.* Austin, TX: Bard & Stephan, 1994.

Moore, James F. *The Death of Competition.* New York: HarperBusiness, 1996.

Moser-Wellman, Annette. *The Five Faces of Genius: The Skills to Master Ideas at Work.* New York: Viking, 2001.

Murphy, Dallas. *The Fast Forward MBA in Marketing.* New York: Wiley, 1997.

Nelson, Carol. *How to Market to Women.* Detroit: Visible Ink, 1994.

Newberg, Jay, and Claudio Marcus. *Target $mart! Database Marketing for the Small Business.* Grants Pass, OR: Oasis Press/PSI Research, 1996.

Newell, Frederick. *The New Rules of Marketing: How to Use One-to-One Relationship Marketing to Be the Leader in Your Industry.* New York: McGraw-Hill, 1997.

Nicholas, Ted, and Sean P. Melvin. *How to Form Your Own Corporation Without a Lawyer for Under $75.00,* 26th ed. Chicago: Dearborn, 1999.

Nulman, Philip R. *Start-Up Marketing: An Entrepreneur's Guide to Advertising, Marketing and Promoting Your Business.* Grants Pass, OR: Oasis Press/PSI Research, 1996.

Ogilvy, David. *Confessions of an Advertising Man.* New York: Atheneum, 1988.

———. *Ogilvy on Advertising.* New York: Vintage Books, 1985.

Olivier, Richard. *Inspirational Leadership, Henry V and the Muse of Fire: Timeless Insights from Shakespeare's Greatest Leader.* Dover, NH: Industrial Society, 2001.

Parker, Roger C. *Design to Sell: Use Microsoft Publisher to Plan, Write and Design Great Marketing Pieces.* Redmond, WA: Microsoft Press, 2006.

———. *Web Content and Design.* New York: MIS Press, 1997.

———. *Web Design and Desktop Publishing for Dummies.* Foster City, CA: IDG Books Worldwide, 1997.

Parmerlee, David. *Developing Successful Marketing Strategies,* 2nd ed. Chicago: NTC Business Books, 1997.

Peppers, Don, and Martha Rogers. *The One-to-One Future: Building Relationships One Customer at a Time.* New York: Currency Doubleday, 1997.

Perry, David. *Career Guide for the High-Tech Professional Where the Jobs are Now and How to Land Them.* Franklin Lakes, NJ: Career Press, 2004.

Peters, Tom. *The Brand You 50: or : Fifty Ways to Transform Yourself From an "Employee" into a Brand That Shouts Distinction, Commitment, and Passion!* New York: Knopf, 1999.

Phillips, Michael, Salli Rasberry, and Diana Fitzpatrick. *Marketing Without Advertising.* Berkeley, CA: Nolo, 2005.

Pink, Daniel H. *A Whole New Mind: Moving from the Information Age to the Conceptual Age.* New York: Riverhead Books, 2005.

Pinskey, Raleigh. *101 Ways to Promote Yourself.* New York: Avon Books, 1997.

Pinson, Linda, and Jerry Jinnett. *Anatomy of a Business Plan.* Chicago: Dearborn Trade, 1993.

Port, Michael. *Book Yourself Solid: The Fastest, Easiest, and Most Reliable System for Getting More Clients Than You Can Handle Even if You Hate Marketing and Selling.* Hoboken, NJ: Wiley, 2006.

Putnam, Anthony O. *Marketing Your Services: A Step-by-Step Guide for Small Business Professionals.* New York: Wiley, 1990.

Rackham, Neil. *The Spin Selling Fieldbook: Practical Tools, Methods, Exercises, and Resources.* New York: McGraw-Hill, 1996.

Ragas, Matthew W., and B. J. Bueno. *The Power of Cult Branding: How 9 Magnetic Brands Turned Customers into Loyal Followers (and Yours Can, Too).* Roseville, CA: Prima, 2002.

Ramacitti, David. *Do-It-Yourself Advertising.* Saranac Lake, NY: AMACOM, 1992.

———. *Do-It-Yourself Marketing.* Saranac Lake, NY: Random House Value Publishing, 1994.

Rapp, Stan, and Thomas Collins. *Beyond Maximarketing.* New York: McGraw-Hill, 1993.

Reed, William. *Ki — A Road That Anyone Can Walk.* New York: Kodansha America, through Oxford University Press, 1992.

Reichheld, Frederick F., and Thomas Teal. *The Loyalty Effect: The Hidden Force Behind Growth, Profits, and Lasting Value.* Cambridge, MA: Harvard Business School Press, 1996.

Reitman, Jerry I. *Beyond 2000: The Future of Direct Marketing.* Lincolnwood, IL: National Textbook, 1994.

Restak, Richard M. *Mozart's Brain and the Fighter Pilot: Unleashing Your Brain's Potential.* New York: Harmony Books, 2001.

Reynolds, Don. *Crackerjack Positioning: Niche Marketing Strategy for the Entrepreneur.* Tulsa, OK: Atwood, 1993.

Rheingold, Howard. *The Virtual Community: Homesteading on the Electronic Frontier.* Reading, MA: Addison-Wesley, 1993.

Ries, Al. *Focus: The Future of Your Company Depends on It.* New York: HarperBusiness, 1996.

Ries, Al, and Laura Ries. *The 22 Immutable Laws of Branding: How to Build a Product or Service into a World-Class Brand.* New York: HarperBusiness, 1998.

Ries, Al, and Jack Trout. *Marketing Warfare,* 20th anniversary ed. New York: McGraw-Hill, 2006.

———. *Positioning the Battle for Your Mind,* 20th anniversary ed. New York: McGraw-Hill, 2001.

———. *The 22 Immutable Laws of Marketing: Violate Them at Your Own Risk.* New York: HarperBusiness, 1993.

Ritchie, Karen. *Marketing to Generation X.* New York: Lexington Books, 1995.

Robbins, Anthony. *Awaken the Giant Within: How to Take Immediate Control of Your Mental, Emotional, Physical and Financial Destiny.* New York: Simon & Schuster, 1992.

———. *Unlimited Power: The New Science of Personal Achievement.* New York: Simon & Schuster, 1997.

Roberts, Ralph, and John Gallagher. *Walk Like a Giant: Sell Like a Madman.* New York: HarperBusiness, 1997.

Ross, Marilyn, and Tom Ross. *Country Bound! Trade Your Business Suit Blues for Blue Jean Dreams.* Chicago: Upstart, 1997.

Rossman, Marlene L. *Multicultural Marketing: Selling to a Diverse America.* New York: AMACOM, 1994.

Sanchez, D., S. Heiman, and T. Tuleja. *The Selling Machine.* New York: Times Business, 1997.

Sanow, Arnold, and Daniel McComas. *Marketing Boot Camp.* Dubuque, IA: Kendall/Hunt, 1994.

Schmitt, Bernd, and Alex Simonson. *Marketing Aesthetics: The Strategic Marketing of Brands, Identity, and Image.* New York: Free Press, 1997.

Schultz, Don E., Stanley Tannenbaum, and Robert E. Lauterborn. *Integrated Marketing Communications: Pulling It Together & Making It Work.* Lincolnwood, IL: National Textbook, 1996.

Scoble, Robert, and Shel Israel. *Naked Conversations: How Blogs Are Changing the Way Businesses Talk with Customers.* Hoboken, NJ: Wiley, 2006.

Seda, Cathryn. *Search Engine Advertising: Buying Your Way to the Top to Increase Sales.* Berkeley, CA: New Riders Press, 2004.

Shane, Michael. *How to Think Like an Entrepreneur.* New York: Brett, 1994.

Shapiro, Stephen. *Goal-Free Living: How to Have the Life You Want Now!* Hoboken, NJ: Wiley, 2006.

Shefsky, Lloyd E. *Entrepreneurs Are Made Not Born: Secrets from 200 Successful Entrepreneurs.* New York: McGraw-Hill, 1994.

Shook, Hal, and Allen Overmeyer. *Flying Spirit: A Leader's Guide to Creating Great Organizations.* Huntington, WV: Humanomics, 1998.

Silber, Lee T. *Time Management for the Creative Person.* New York: Three Rivers Press, 1998.

Sinetar, Marsha. *To Build the Life You Want, Create the Work You Love: The Spiritual Dimension of Entrepreneuring.* New York: St. Martin's Press, 1996.

Slutsky, Jeff. *How to Get Clients.* New York: Warner, 1992.

Smith, Jeannette. *Entrepreneur Magazine: Guide to Integrated Marketing.* New York: Wiley, 1996.

———. *The New Publicity Kit: A Complete Guide for Entrepreneurs, Small Businesses and Non-Profit Organizations.* New York: Wiley, 1995.

Spoelstra, Jon. *Ice to the Eskimos: How to Market a Product Nobody Wants.* New York: HarperBusiness, 1997.

Stanley, Thomas J. *Marketing to the Affluent.* New York: McGraw-Hill, 1997.

Stansell, Kimberly. *Bootstrapper's Success Secrets: 151 Tactics for Building Your Business on a Shoestring Budget.* Franklin Lakes, NJ: Career Press, 1997.

Stephenson, James, and Courtney Thurman. *Ultimate Small Business Marketing Guide,* 2nd ed. Irvine, CA: Entrepreneur Press, 2007.

Stevenson, Doug. *Never Be Boring Again: Make Your Business Presentations Capture Attention, Inspire Action, and Produce Results.* Colorado Springs, CO: Cornelia Press, 2003.

Strauss, Judy, Adel El-Ansary, and Raymond Frost. *E-Marketing,* 4th ed., Upper Saddle River, NJ: Prentice Hall, 2005.

Sugarman, Joseph. *Advertising Secrets of the Written Word: The Ultimate Resource on How to Write Powerful Advertising Copy from One of America's Top Copywriters and Mail Order Entrepreneurs.* Las Vegas: DelStar, 1998.

———. *Triggers: 30 Sales Tools You Can Use to Control the Mind of Your Prospect to Motivate, Influence and Persuade.* Las Vegas: Delstar, 1999.

Sussman, Jeffrey. *Power Promoting: How to Market Your Business to the Top!* New York: Wiley, 1997.

Sykes, Timothy. *Self-Publishing Ebooks & Pods: One Step at a Time.* Spring, TX: Forager Publications, 2004.

Tracy, Brian. *Getting Rich Your Own Way: Achieve All Your Financial Goals Faster Than You Ever Thought Possible.* Hoboken, NJ: Wiley, 2004.

Trout, Jack. *A Genie's Wisdom: A Fable of How a CEO Learned to Be a Marketing Genius.* Hoboken, NJ: Wiley, 2003.

———. *The New Positioning: The Latest on the World's #1 Business Strategy.* New York: McGraw-Hill, 1997.

Trout, Jack, and Steve Rivkin. *Differentiate or Die: Survival in Our Era of Killer Competition.* New York: Wiley, 2000.

Truax, Pamela, and Monique Reece Myron. *Market Smarter, Not Harder.* Dubuque, IA: Kendall/Hunt, 1996.

Trump, Donald. *The Way to the Top: The Best Business Advice I Ever Received.* New York: Crown Business, 2004.

Trump, Donald, and Meredith McIver. *How to Get Rich.* New York: Random House, 2004.

Trump, Donald, and Tony Schwartz. *The Art of the Deal.* Boston, MA: G. K. Hall, 1989.

Unruh, James A. *Customers Mean Business: Six Steps to Building Relationships That Last.* Reading, MA: Addison-Wesley, 1996.

Vitale, Joe, comp. *The Power of Outrageous Marketing.* Nightingale-Conant audio course. 1998.

———. *Hypnotic Writing: How to Seduce and Persuade Customers with Only Your Words.* Hoboken, NJ: Wiley, forthcoming.

———. *There's a Customer Born Every Minute: P. T. Barnum's Secrets to Business Success.* New York: AMACOM, 1998.

Wallace, Carol Wilkie. *Great Ad!* Blue Ridge Summit, PA: TAB Books, 1990.

Wares, Bruce. *Partner$ell: Creating Lucrative and Lasting Client Relationships.* Dubuque, IA: Kendall/Hunt, 1994.

Whitely, Richard, and Diane Hessan, *Customer-Centered Growth.* Reading, MA: Addison-Wesley, 1996.

Williams, Roy H. *The Wizard of Ads: Turning Words into Magic and Dreamers into Millionaires.* Austin, TX: Bard Press, 1998.

Williams, Roy H., Janet Thomae, and Chris Maddock. *Accidental Magic: The Wizard's Techniques for Writing Words Worth 1,000 Pictures*. Austin, TX: Bard Press, 2001.

Wilson, Jerry R. *Word-of-Mouth Marketing*. New York: Wiley, 1994.

Withers, Jean, and Carol Viperman. *Marketing Your Service Business*. Bellingham, WA: Self-Counsel Press, 1992.

Woolf, Brian P. *Customer Specific Marketing*. Greenville, SC: Teal Books, 1996.

Yohalem, Kathy C. *Thinking Out of the Box: How to Market Your Company into the Future*. New York: Wiley, 1997.

Yudkin, Marcia. *Six Steps to Free Publicity and Dozens of Other Ways to Win Free Media Attention for You and Your Business*. Bergenfield, NJ: Plume, 1994.

Ziccardi, Donald. *Master Minding the Store: Advertising, Sales Promotion, and the New Marketing Reality*. New York: Wiley, 1997.

Ziglar, Zig. *Selling 101: What Every Successful Sales Professional Needs to Know*. Nashville, TN: Thomas Nelson, 2003.

Useful Web Sites

About.com's small business resource center: marketing.about.com/od/smallbusinessmarketing/.

American Marketing Association: marketingpower.com/.

Dr. Syed Tariq Anwar's massive international marketing links Web site: wtamu.edu/~sanwar.bus/otherlinks.htm#International_Business_Links.

Entrepreneur Media online: entrepreneur.com/.

Fortin, Michel, comp. *The 10 Commandments of Power Positioning*: successdoctor.com/.

International Chambers of Commerce: iccwbo.org.

Jackstreet Media's podcasting/nanocasting Web site: theann.com/.

Jupiter's business research Web site: jupiterresearch.com.

Microsoft Small Business Center: microsoft.com/smallbusiness/resources/articles.mspx?xid=OVPI233884278.

Mitch Meyerson's Guerrilla Marketing Coach Certification program Web site: gmarketingcoach.com.

United States Census Bureau: census.gov/.

United States Chambers of Commerce: uschamber.com.

United States Federal Statistics Web site: fedstats.gov/.

United States Small Business Administration: sba.gov.

Yahoo's small business resource guide: smallbusiness.yahoo.com/marketing/.

Index

Get the Complete Guerrilla Arsenal!

GUERRILLA MARKETING: EASY AND INEXPENSIVE STRATEGIES FOR MAKING BIG PROFITS FROM YOUR SMALL BUSINESS

The book that started the Guerrilla Marketing revolution, now completely updated and expanded. Full of the latest strategies, information on the hottest technologies, details about the fastest-growing markets, and management lessons for the twenty-first century. 0-618-78591-4

GUERRILLA MARKETING ATTACK: NEW STRATEGIES, TACTICS, AND WEAPONS FOR WINNING BIG PROFITS

Guerrilla Marketing Attack explains how to avoid running out of fuel by maximizing limited start-up resources and turning prospects into customers and investments into profits. 0-395-50220-9

GUERRILLA SELLING: UNCONVENTIONAL WEAPONS AND TACTICS FOR INCREASING YOUR SALES

Today's increasingly competitive business environment requires new skills and commitment from salespeople. *Guerrilla Selling* presents unconventional selling tactics that are essential for success. 0-395-57820-5

GUERRILLA MARKETING EXCELLENCE: THE 50 GOLDEN RULES FOR SMALL-BUSINESS SUCCESS

Outlining fifty basic truths that can make or break your company, *Guerrilla Marketing Excellence* takes readers beyond do-it-yourself marketing guides, explaining not just how to market but how to market with excellence. 0-395-60844-9

THE GUERRILLA MARKETING HANDBOOK
An essential companion to *Guerrilla Marketing*, this practical guide offers thousands of contacts, ideas, and examples that will help transform plans into specific actions, turning any business into a marketing powerhouse. 0-395-70013-2

GUERRILLA ADVERTISING: COST-EFFECTIVE TACTICS FOR SMALL-BUSINESS SUCCESS
Full of anecdotes about past and current advertising successes and failures, *Guerrilla Advertising* entertains as it teaches the nuts and bolts of advertising for small businesses. 0-395-68718-7

THE WAY OF THE GUERRILLA: ACHIEVING SUCCESS AND BALANCE AS AN ENTREPRENEUR IN THE 21ST CENTURY
A blueprint for future business success, *The Way of the Guerrilla* includes advice on everything from preparing a focused mission statement to sustaining one's passion for work. Entrepreneurs will discover the means to achieving emotional and financial success. 0-395-92478-2

GUERRILLA CREATIVITY
The guru of guerrilla marketing unveils his methods of optimizing originality and creativity for successful marketing. Levinson focuses on memes, simple symbols that convey complex ideas — how to generate them and how to disseminate them. 0-618-10468-2

GUERRILLA MARKETING FOR FREE: DOZENS OF NO-COST TACTICS TO PROMOTE YOUR BUSINESS AND ENERGIZE YOUR PROFITS
The guru of guerrilla marketing teaches entrepreneurs how to market aggressively without spending a cent. Levinson, the authority on big-business marketing on a small-business budget, proves that aggressive marketing doesn't have to be expensive if you use creative and unconventional means. 0-618-27679-3

These books are available in bookstores, or order from Houghton Mifflin customer service at **1-800-225-3362.**

Visit our Web sites: **houghtonmifflinbooks.com** and **gmarketing.com.**